Euripidean Drama

It is a commonly held view among historians of Greek literature that with the advent of Euripides the tragic structure, even the tragic outlook of Greek drama suffered a breakdown from which it never recovered. While there is much truth in this opinion, it has tended to put too much emphasis on "Euripides the destroyer" rather than "Euripides the creator." In this study the author's main purpose is to redress the balance and to discuss the structure and techniques of Euripidean drama in relation to its new and richly varied themes.

The consistent dramatic form evolved by Aeschylus and Sophocles had grown out of their conception of tragedy as the resultant of the tension between the individual will and the universal order suggested in myth. For Euripides, who never fully accepted myth as the real basis of tragedy, alternate ways of using the traditional material became necessary, and the playwright continually changed his dramatic structure to suit the particular tragic idea he was seeking to express. Viewed in this way, Euripides' dramatic technique may be seen in positive as well as negative terms—as something other than the breakdown of structural technique and mythological insight under the overwhelming force of his ideas. Professor Conacher offers here a new view of Euripides as the first Greek dramatist properly to understand the world of myth, and so, in a sense, to stand a bit outside it. He shows how Euripides, far from being an impatient or incompetent craftsman, used traditional myth as a basis for inventing new forms in which to cast his perceptions of the sources of human tragedy.

All the extant Euripidean drama is examined in this book; the result is an intelligent guide to the plays for all students of dramatic literature, as well as a convincing defence of Euripides the creator.

D. J. CONACHER was born and grew up in Kingston, Ontario. After receiving his B.A. and M.A. degrees from Queen's University, he went to the University of Chicago for his Ph.D. He has been the recipient of numerous postgraduate and postdoctoral fellowships and awards including the Nuffield Travelling Fellowship for Research at Oxford, Research Travel Grants from the Humanities Research Council and the Canada Council, and a Visiting Research Scholarship at Fondation Hardt, Geneva. He has taught in several Canadian universities and is now Head of the Department of Classics, Trinity College, University of Toronto.

Euripidean Drama

MYTH, THEME AND STRUCTURE

D. J. Conacher

UNIVERSITY OF TORONTO PRESS

Reprinted in paperback 2015
London: Oxford University Press, 1967
ISBN 978-1-4426-3931-7 (paper)

Preface

In the ancient division between formal criticism, on the one hand, and historical, biographical and "cultural" criticism, on the other, Euripidean studies have tended, at least until quite recent times, to choose the latter approach. Possibly because Euripides has appeared to some scholars to be more "engaged" than were the other two great tragedians in the political and philosophic issues of his time, the historical critics in particular have constantly sought in his plays clues to contemporary situations and, conversely, have sought to elucidate his plays in terms of such situations. In this and in other partially biographical approaches to Euripidean drama, the assigning of various plays to specific periods of the poet's development must necessarily play an important part. Such divisions of Euripidean plays have, of course, also been made, and are still being made, on a much broader basis than that of the alleged reflection in them of contemporary events and of contemporary Euripidean attitudes. One of the earliest of such attempts, and still one of the most useful, was the parcelling of Euripidean drama into four neat periods, determined mainly by the subject matter of the plays concerned. This criterion has, perhaps, an unfair advantage over other such instruments, in that it is applicable, to some degree, even to "lost" plays of which we know something of the content. More recent and more precise studies have concentrated more on stylistic, metrical and dramaturgic considerations as criteria for such divisions.

Useful as all these approaches have been in determining the development and the historical changes in Euripidean attitudes, technique and interests, I believe that by now this vein has been nearly worked through, and I would suggest that it is by no means the only way in which the dramatist's work can be considered. My own interest, though it does not exclude the cultural and even the political environment of certain dramatic productions, lies rather in seeking to relate the varied and often novel structures and techniques of Euripidean drama to the varied and often novel themes which the dramatist has chosen to expound. This interest has led to the discovery, or at least the description, of several different kinds of Euripidean tragedy which are largely, though not entirely, determined by the dramatist's varied approaches to the traditional material of myth or (to look at the matter in another way) by the different levels of reality which he has chosen to employ in different plays. These divisions do not correspond very precisely to any historical grouping of the poet's plays (insofar as their dates can be determined), and so it has seemed best to abandon the genetic approach to Euripides in this instance, while admitting its cogency in other kinds of study of his work.

If a distinction in material may be made between formal and historical criticism, a distinction in means and method may be made between intuitive and academic criticism. The completely intuitive critic states as directly as possible, without proof, discussion or reference to other views, the essential meaning which a given work has for him, his own aesthetic experience "in the raw," as it were. At its best (in, say, an essay like Simone Weil's, *The Iliad or Poem of Force*) such criticism is of incomparable value: written, usually, by poets rather than by scholars, it provides us with an articulate response to the work in question which is almost as intense and personal as poetic creation itself. Such a critic, like a poet writing a poem on a nightingale, need never worry what other men have said, for he knows that what he says will be different. Good criticism of this kind, which is very rare, is as uniquely valuable as good poetry and quite as independent.

Any aesthetic experience, particularly one concerning so "public" a vehicle as a play, must be in one sense unique, in another sense shared. No one and nothing should be allowed to replace the unique personal core of that experience, but unless one is completely satisfied with one's private view and of one's ability to transmit it in creative terms, the large peripheral area of shared experience may, when refined to sharper focus, turn out to be a very rich source for understanding and expounding any given work. One has only to remember one valuable discussion of a given play, seen or read, with a fellow being who has been (in the full sense of the words) similarly engaged to admit the principle behind this observation.

It is in this peripheral area of his experience that the academic critic should be prepared to expand his own awareness of a work's meaning or, it may be, to sharpen and intensify his personal view of it, by listening to its echoes in other minds. Where one finds stimulating criticism, one should be prepared to make use of it, either in alliance with, or in dialectical opposition to, one's own analysis. Indeed, in the case of plays whose interpretative and structural problems are justly celebrated, it would surely be hybristic to embark on one's own analysis as if no word had yet been spoken. In such cases, the sampling and evaluation of a fairly wide area of critical opinion (itself of some intrinsic interest) often turns out to be a useful device for formulating the relevant critical questions, for it is the shortcomings as well as the merits of "other views" that often goad one into defining one's own position.

In any study of all extant Euripidean drama (fragments excepted), the area of disagreement with or independence of the views of other critics will vary greatly in different plays. It would obviously be much easier to write a more "original" book only on those points, or on those plays, in which one finds oneself in sharp disagreement with all other views. To do so, however, would be to sacrifice too much in the interests of preserving a somewhat dainty and artificial form of "originality." In the first place, it is preferable, in fairness to the plays one believes to have been particularly "misunderstood," to study them in relation to the complete extant *corpus* of the poet. In the second place, it would surely be foolish to exclude one's own analysis of a play simply because, in certain particulars, one agrees with other critics. My own views of the theme and structure of Euripidean drama have evolved from my own analyses of the plays, not formed in isolation but expanded, tested and (I think) strengthened by consideration of other views as well. Just as, in some cases, I have attempted to sharpen an original view by rebutting competing views, so I have not hesitated, in other cases, to incorporate (with due acknowledgment) into my own analysis of a play any perceptions of other critics which I have found particularly helpful or congenial. This strikes me as a legitimate application of normal scholarly procedure to the particular problems of literary criticism.

Another feature of this book, distinct from, yet supplementary to, its literary-critical purpose, may need an additional word of explanation. Throughout the study of Euripidean drama various more or less technical problems inevitably appear: uncertainties concerning the authenticity of substantial passages of text or the evidence for dating "undated" work and, in the case of certain plays, uncertainties concerning the antecedent mythological tradition or the reconstruction of lost members of a possibly connected trilogy. Such problems will all be familiar to the specialist, but too often the general student of Greek drama must depend, even for notice of them, on scholarly editions and specialized articles not readily available to him. In my own limited treatment of such problems, where they are relevant to the understanding or the reading of any given play, my intention has been simply to make the student aware of their existence and nature, and to suggest, within the limits of a general study, the current state of critical opinion upon them. In this ancillary part of my work, I have not hesitated to make generous use of more specialized studies and to refer the reader to them for further discussion of the points concerned. Thus the occasional note or appendix on these more technical matters makes no great claim to originality, and in most cases the judgments tentatively offered are no more conclusive than the present state of scholarly opinion on them seems to warrant.

One notable omission among problems of this nature is "the *Rhesus* question." Since recent studies of this question have convinced me (though this has not always been their intention) that the authenticity of the *Rhesus* has not yet been established, I have withdrawn my own analysis of this play. Such an analysis would need to be preceded by a re-examination of evidence and arguments clearly beyond the scope and competence of this present study. On this whole matter, it must suffice to refer the reader to two or three recent publications in which the fundamental issues and differences of opinion have been clearly set forth. The first of these to be mentioned must be William Ritchie's *The Authenticity of the Rhesus* (Cambridge, 1964); while this work does not (as I have suggested in my review of it *CJ* LXI [1966], 187–89), completely establish the conclusion which its title implies, it does present, fairly and clearly, the greater part of the relevant evidence, and it includes a full bibliography and discussion of the various critical positions which have been taken with regard to the *Rhesus*' authorship. Major difficulties in the way of accepting Professor Ritchie's arguments for Euripides' authorship of the play are to be found in Professor Fraenkel's review of this work (*Gnomon*, XXXVII [June, 1965], 228–41, as well as in certain observations concerning the psychology and technique of the play in an earlier article by H. Strohm ("Beobachtungen zum *Rhesos*," *Hermes* LXXXVII [1959], 257–74) to which Fraenkel refers in his criticism of Ritchie.

Certain chapters included in this book are based on articles which I have published, as indicated below. In the first four instances, the chapters concerned are in fact the same as the articles in question, except for very minor adaptations, such as the addition of subheadings. Chapter 4 is based on my article, "Theme, Plot and Technique in the *Heracles* of Euripides," *Phoenix*, IX (1955), 139–52. Chapter 5 is based on my article, "Religious and Ethical Attitudes in Euripides' *Suppliants*," *Transactions of the American Philological Association*, LXXXVII (1956), 8–26. Chapter 8 is based on my article, "Euripides' *Hecuba*," *American Journal of Philology*, LXXXII (1961), 1–26. Chapter 15 is based on my article, "The Paradox of Euripides' *Ion*," *Transactions of the American Philological Association*, XC (1959) 20–39. The introductory chapter is based *in part only* on my article, "Freedom and Necessity in Greek Tragedy," *Queen's Quarterly*, LXVII (1961), 514–29. Chapters 2 and 3 derive a few points from my article, "Some Euripidean Techniques in the Dramatic Treatment of Myth," *University of Toronto Quarterly*, XXII (1952), 55–71. Chapter 2 at one specific point makes use of conclusions first expressed in my article, "A Problem in Euripides' *Hippolytus*," *Transactions of the American Philological Association*, XCII (1961), 37–44.

It remains only to acknowledge with gratitude the assistance, tangible and intangible, which I have received during the years in which I have been engaged in this work. For substantial assistance in my research, I should like to thank: The Nuffield Foundation for a Travelling Fellowship to Oxford in 1957–58; the Humanities Research Council, Canada Council, and the University of Toronto for short-term grants in aid of research; and *Fondation Hardt, pour l'étude de l'Antiquité Classique*, Vandœuvres-Genève, for hospitality and research facilities in the summer of 1963. This work has been published with the help of a grant from the Humanities Research Council of Canada using funds provided by the Canada Council, and with assistance from the Publications Fund of the University of Toronto Press.

I should also like to express my gratitude for the help and encouragement of various friends, colleagues and students with whom I have discussed my ideas or who have read parts of my work in manuscript. In particular, I should like to thank Mr. Emmet Robbins for invaluable assistance in checking the final typescript.

D.J.C.

Contents

PART THREE: WAR AND ITS AFTERMATH

PART FOUR: REALISTIC TRAGEDY

PART FIVE: TRAGEDIE MANQUEE

PART SIX: ROMANTIC TRAGEDY

PART SEVEN: SATYRIC (AND PRO-SATYRIC?) DRAMA

TO MY WIFE

Euripidean Drama

MYTH, THEME AND STRUCTURE

1

Introduction

Some Tragic Approaches to Myth

It is a commonly held view among the historians of Greek literature that with the advent of Euripides the tragic structure, even the tragic outlook of Greek drama suffered a breakdown from which it never recovered. While there is much truth in this opinion, it has tended to put undue emphasis on "Euripides the destroyer" with the result that, too often, insufficient justice is done to "Euripides the creator." Euripides based his tragic ideas on a very different view of reality from that of his predecessors. It is in terms of this difference that we should discuss those deviations from established tragic patterns which Euripidean drama shows. It may then appear that Euripides, far from being an impatient or incompetent craftsman, was constantly inventing, under the pressure of his complex view of reality, new forms in which to cast his varied perceptions of the sources of human tragedy.

The Greek tragic idea seems to have had its roots in the desire to find some principle by which the catastrophic suffering observable in the world might appear not as chaotic, haphazard and senseless, but as a part of an intelligible order. Whether or not this idea sprang from ritualistic attempts to coerce nature, tragedy always seeks some kind of victory or control over suffering and evil,[1] and the reduction of the realm of Chance, most abhorrent of all deities to the Greeks,[2] was

[1]Cf. Gilbert Murray, *Aeschylus*, 5–9.

[2]Among the Greek philosophers, the distrust of popular conceptions of *Tyche* is most pithily expressed by Democritus, frg. B 119 ("Men have devised an image of chance as a cloak for their own lack of good counsel. . . ."), B 197, B 210, D-K. Perhaps the most telling of the many assaults on *Tyche* by the tragedians are to be found in Sophocles' *Oedipus Tyrannus*, especially in the dramatic refutations, immediate and terrible, which follow Jocasta's and Oedipus' celebrations of the goddess at vv. 977–83 and 1080–85, respectively. The more cynical Menander, while allowing one of his characters to say that "Chance governs all" (fr. 483,

perhaps the earliest and most enduring form of this victory. However, this idea of tragedy operated as a dynamic, not as a static, principle. The attempt to oust Chance itself produced the formulation of certain necessary sequences in human as in natural events; we find these exemplified in such superstitions as familial curses, "blood guilts" affecting future generations, in such gnomic sayings as "Insatiate disaster burgeons forth from great prosperity,"[3] and in the conception of jealous gods, which is the mythological expression of the same idea. These patterns of necessity themselves provided another challenge to the Greeks, a challenge to human freedom and to the noble desire to be captain of one's fate, for good or ill. However, the idea of *human* responsibility for suffering thus engendered never developed, in tragedy, into simple presentations of crime and punishment. Aristotle wisely warns us of this aesthetic danger by pointing out that the mere downfall of a villain inspires neither of the tragic emotions of pity and fear, "for pity is aroused by unmerited misfortune, fear by the misfortune of a man like ourselves."[4] Thus most tragedy seems to involve a kind of dual motivation: it may be shown to result from something in the character and actions of the sufferer, but also from some necessity (which goes by many names) over which he has no control. Even in tragedies involving moral guilt there always seems to be one sense at least in which the hero does not deserve to suffer, or does not deserve to suffer quite so much. Thus the conflict between freedom and necessity is never quite resolved: however much the poet seeks to conquer the inexplicable, the "external," in human suffering, a certain element of it remains.[5] If this seems inconsistent, one should remember that tragedy is not philosophy. Since tragedy seeks to imitate life, it must present it *as it appears to man*; thus while it often seeks to reduce life to some intelligible order, it must preserve something of its mystery as well. It is this tension between freedom and necessity, appearing in a variety of forms according to the different conceptions of the poets, which supplies one of the chief tensions in the tragic drama of the Greeks.

Kock), certainly felt that, as far as his dramatic art was concerned, Chance must be replaced by the artist's deft manipulations of contrived coincidence. (Cf. Gilbert Norwood, *Greek Comedy*, 360.)

[3]See Aeschylus, *Ag.*, 750–62 where the Chorus dissociates itself from this ancient maxim.

[4]Aristotle, *Poetics*, xiii. 1453a5–6 (Butcher's translation).

[5]Cf. William Chase Greene, *Moira*, 95–96: "Tragedy thus arouses in us a sense of incongruity, a *malaise*, a 'qualm,' as it has been called. And many critics feel that in such cases our moral sense has been challenged, not to say outraged." Cf. also Greene's references to P. H. Frye, *Romance and Tragedy*.

The plot material of Greek tragedy was drawn, for the most part, from the traditional myths and legends of the past. There were sound historical reasons for this convention, but even apart from these the removal of tragedy from the experience of everyday living was of great advantage to its creators. It is difficult to attach ideas on the nature of the universe, and on the meaning of suffering and evil, to the particular and contingent happenings of everyday life. The myths supplied the dramatist with certain well-known and catastrophic happenings in the lives of ancient heroes. How much more universality the poet's tragic view achieves when it is demonstrated not in situations made especially for the purpose but in famous paradigms of human suffering which have already acquired a certain archetypal status! Saga, the oldest repository of these tales, was wont to dwell more on events than on explanations, or, if reasons *were* given, they were expressed in the unintellectual terms proper to myth (for example, "Such and such happened because the goddess Hera was angry"). But the real meanings, the expressions of tragic significance in these clashes between the divine and human will, were the business of the individual dramatist who chose to adapt these myths to his own purposes and to express through them his individual view of life. Thus, to observe the individual approaches taken to the traditional material of myth serves as a useful introduction to the tragic ideas and dramatic structure used by the three tragedians.

As long as the properly mythical view obtains—the view which accepts the existence of another order of reality, external and divine, above and beyond the human psyche—we find the Greek tragedian using the supernatural element in myth to embody that mysterious external necessity which we have described as one of the essential poles of his art. Aeschylus and Sophocles, for all their differences, both maintained this view; Euripides abandoned it, to a greater or lesser degree, in many of his tragedies. Thus it is not until Euripides that a really major change takes place in the structure and ethos of Greek tragedy.

Aeschylus began writing his tragedies at a time when the mythological account of the universe was being challenged on two fronts.[6] Philosophers were formulating physical principles of law and order in the universe, while on the political front the Athenian body politic, after its victorious struggles both with its own tyrants and with the Persian despot from abroad, was emerging from its crucible of suffering as the democratic city-state. In this new atmosphere, men looked for a moral as well as a physical order in the universe and in the affairs of men,

[6]For a brilliant discussion of the cultural climate in which Aeschylus wrote his tragedies, see Werner Jaeger, *Paideia*, I, 237 ff.

and this was hardly to be found in myth's somewhat primitive formulations of human suffering and in the arbitrary activities of the Homeric gods fulfilling their various spites and affections.

Aeschylus took up this challenge on behalf of the mythological view of life. In dramatic terms, he reformulated the myths which he treated in such a way as to present a picture of the universe and of the world of men as divinely ordered and essentially good. Contemporary events and institutions first informed and then became a part of Aeschylus' mythological view, as these historical particulars were given universal meaning in his drama. Thus the victorious struggle with the Persians provided the poet with great evidence both of the good which comes out of suffering and of the operation of divine justice. To Athenian eyes, the Persian King was the epitome of *hybris*, that overweening pride which must be levelled by the gods, but Aeschylus saw that Xerxes was the target not merely of the *jealous* gods, but of the justice of Zeus, since his overstepping of his alloted portion was an affront to the divine order. This theme (which is expounded at length in the speeches of Darius' ghost in the *Persae*) is vividly dramatized in the image of Xerxes' audacious yoking, with his bridge of ships, of the sacred Hellespont.

Again and again two principles are found operating in Aeschylus' treatment of human suffering: one, *drasanti pathein* (i.e., "the doer of the evil deed must suffer") concerns human responsibility; the other, *pathei mathos* ("by suffering comes knowledge") indicates the ultimate plan of Zeus. The harmony which Aeschylus envisaged was an evolutionary one, and the consecutive trilogy, the form in which most of his work was cast, was ideally suited to his mighty themes which cover generations, or even aeons of time, before the tragic lesson is fully learned.

Aeschylus' treatment of a familial curse, such as one finds in the Oresteian trilogy, provides the clearest example in tragedy both of these ideas and of the double motivation, the individual will and a certain externally imposed necessity. In the first play the murder of Agamemnon by Clytemnestra and Aegisthus appears both as the requital of Agamemnon's sacrifice of his daughter Iphigenia and as the fulfilment of a familial curse arising from father Atreus' murder of his brother's children. In the second play, Orestes, at the command of Apollo, avenges his father's death by slaying Clytemnestra; in the third, Orestes is in turn pursued by avenging furies until finally we reach the typical Aeschylean evolution of good out of suffering and evil: the establishment, by the gods, of a human court of justice which puts an end to blood feuds and to the supernatural curses which each blood-letting has released.

However, it is in the treatment of individual sufferings within such family curses that the opposition between the sweep of necessity and some idea of individual responsibility is most evident. While Aeschylus is careful to play up Agamemnon's guilt, and the divine punishment it must receive, he still preserves the idea of a familial *alastôr* (or "curse personified") dating from Atreus' crime against Thyestes, as Clytemnestra's coadjutor in her vengeance; indeed, in Cassandra's vision of the deed to come, the spectacle of Thyestes' murdered children, holding their butchered entrails in their hands, is one of the most terrible assurances of the inevitability of Agamemnon's death; and even the slaughter of Iphigenia, when, as Aeschylus puts it, he takes on himself "the yoke of necessity," is in part the result of the terrible dilemma which the gods themselves have thrust upon him.[7] It is precisely this hint of something "not quite fair," this intrusion, for all our philosophy, of the uncontrollable element in human destiny, which, as we have suggested, brings tragedy within the range of human sympathy. We find it again in the *Persae*, in the Chorus's description of the temptation of Xerxes:

Deceitful deception of god—
What mortal man shall avoid it? . . .
Benign and coaxing at first
It leads us astray into nets which
No mortal is able to slip,
Whose doom we can never flee.[8]

. . . and yet the god-tempted King is later to be punished for his *hybris*. Certainly this tension between freedom and necessity, this impression of a hero's fulfilling by his free actions a doom toward which the gods are tempting him, is invaluable as a dramatic principle. It provides the major excitement in Aeschylus' *Seven Against Thebes* in which Eteocles and Polyneices fulfil the curse of their father Oedipus by dying in fratricidal strife. As a herald describes each successive chieftain who will attack one or another of the seven gates, Eteocles, the defending King, selects a

[7]For the passages in the *Agamemnon* referred to above, see vv. 1500–1508, 1217–22, 218–20, respectively. Professor Denys Page's view of the complete *personal* innocence of Agamemnon in this play (see *Denniston and Page, Aeschylus, Agamemnon*, xx-xxix) has, I think, been sufficiently refuted in the reviews of H. D. F. Kitto (*Gnomon*, XXX [1958], 163–68, esp. p. 68), and S. M. Adams (*Phoenix*, XII [1958], 75–78), though I would make some qualifications concerning the latter's view of Agamemnon's responsibility, along the lines of the "dual motivation" argument advanced above. (Cf. also N. G. L. Hammond, "Personal Freedom and Its Limitation in the *Oresteia*," *JHS*, LXXXV, 42–55.

[8]Aeschylus, *Persae*, 93–100, in part, translated by Seth G. Benardete. (Other passages quoted below from the *Persae* are also from Benardete's version.)

warrior whose specific excellence will best oppose the darker valour of the enemy outside. We *know*, of course, what must happen at the seventh gate, even before Polyneices is announced as its attacker, but by this brilliant device of having appropriate opponents chosen in each case, the impression of Eteocles' freedom to choose his doom mounts *pari passu* with the very sense of inevitability about his final choice . . . "I'll go myself. What other has more right?" (672–73) . . . "It is the god that drives the matter on." (689)

Thus, in most of the extant drama of Aeschylus, the will of the gods, most particularly the will of Zeus, may be identified with that external necessity which (usually in correction, occasionally in fulfilment, of the will of individual heroes) guides the tragedies to their inevitable conclusion. The *Prometheus Vinctus* may seem at first to provide an exception, for there Fate itself (*Moira*, sometimes "the *Moirai*") seems to oust even Zeus from his pre-eminence. This impression is due in part to the dramatic requirements of the play, in part to the theme of the whole trilogy which we may guess to have been concerned with the evolution of a perfect Zeus. In the *Prometheus Vinctus*, we are presented with an irresistable force, the all-conquering Zeus, who has overthrown his father Kronos and the old order of the gods, and Prometheus, the unrepentant rebel who is being punished for saving the feeble race of men from the annihilation of the new and intolerant perfectionist. To the deadlock of wills there is added a kind of moral deadlock: we cannot doubt that the new order of Zeus is the only right one, for numerous passages in the play,[9] as well as the subsequent course of Aeschylean and Greek theology, affirm it; at the same time we are led to sympathize with Prometheus as the saviour of men and to detest the harsh tyranny of Zeus so brilliantly dramatized by the actions of his minions, Kratos and Hermes, and by the frantic cries of his gentle victim, Io.

In order that there may be some progress in the trilogy, some eventual resolution of this situation, a higher power even than Zeus must be invoked. It is Prometheus' knowledge of Fate which provides him with his one hold over his tormentor, and it is Zeus' futile attempt to wrest from Prometheus the secret on which his own future safety depends

[9]As well as the "error" of Prometheus imputed by the Chorus and admitted by him (*P.V.* 259–66), we should note that the Chorus honours "the harmony of Zeus" which "mortal plans will never transgress" above Prometheus' services to man. (542–51) Furthermore, Prometheus' own prophecies concerning the ultimate, gentle liberation of Io and the happy outcome prophesied for the Danaids (her descendants), culminating in the birth of Prometheus' own liberator, are surely intended (though not by Prometheus!) to suggest to us that eventual good will come out of all Zeus' tyrannies.

which leads to the climax and the catastrophe of the present play. It is on Fate that Prometheus depends for his eventual freedom, and Zeus himself, he tells us, is subject to the *Moirai*. (511–18) In what circumstances the crucial secret was eventually revealed, we cannot tell, but we do know that this was dependent on Prometheus' release from Zeus' bondage. (757–72, 989–91) Thus Fate, as well as supplying the fulcrum for the present plot, enables the poet to show us that the Zeus of this play must change his ways before he becomes the Zeus whom Aeschylus elsewhere honours without reservation.

The difficult theology of this situation has been well expressed by a well-known critic of the "fatalistic fallacy" concerning Greek tragedy:

> Not even here is there predestination; the fatality to which Zeus is subject is not mere mechanical necessity but is the moral nature which he must in time assume and which therefore defines his freedom of action.[10]

Thus the kind of tension between freedom and necessity which we find in the other plays of Aeschylus has been changed in the *Prometheia* in only this particular: because of the particular dramatic situation in which the gods themselves have become the *dramatis personae*, it is now the *Moirai*, rather than the gods or the will of Zeus, who appear as "the helmsmen of Necessity."

With Sophocles, the tragic approach to mythical material undergoes a drastic change. In Aeschylus, it is "the doom"[11] which interests us, and the tragic sufferer is often important for what he or his career represents rather than for himself, considered as a personality or "character." Sophocles was more interested in man, not in all men or in Everyman, but in certain idealized studies of heroic individuals. He developed the classic type of tragic hero, a lonely figure struggling against tremendous odds (his "fate" or "the gods" or "circumstance") but who, suffer as he must, leaves his mark by establishing his own personal vision, his unique conception of *aretê*, that particular form of excellence or nobility which he feels called upon to fulfil.

Professor Kitto has thus described the Sophoclean formula: ". . . a hero of a certain kind is placed in circumstances such that the play between character and circumstances is bound to result in disaster for the hero."[12] For Sophocles, then, the traditional material of myth served largely to provide the context of necessity, the given situations over which the heroes have no control but within which they make their free

[10]Greene, 108.
[11]Cf. Jaeger, 252.
[12]Kitto, *Greek Tragedy*, 196.

—and fatal—decisions. In his very excellence the hero carries within himself the seeds of his own destruction: the loyalty and mettle of an Electra or an Antigone must respond as they do to the terrible dilemmas in which the heroines are placed, even though in their dedications (Electra to a career of vengeance, Antigone to defiance of an impious law), these heroines destroy their own lives and all other aspects of their personalities.[13] So, too, it is the devotion of Creon, perhaps the most culpable of Sophoclean sufferers, to order and discipline which blinds him to his own ill counsel (*aboulia*) in the application of his principles. Oedipus, reader of riddles and city-defender *par excellence*, must, if he is to remain himself, complete his long voyage of discovery, once the city's riddle and its plague is again set before him. The valour of Ajax, for whom life's meaning is renown in battle, can only respond to humiliation in *that* sphere by suicide. The words of Ajax as he ponders this epitomize the absolute quality of Sophoclean *aretê*:

> What can I do? Some feat
> To make my poor old father understand
> He has no soft-bellied coward for a son.
> Long life? Who but a coward would ask for it,
> Beset by endless evil? Can he enjoy
> Counting the days that pass; now a step forward,
> Now a step backward, on the way to death?
> Who'd be that man? To huddle over the coals
> Of flickering hope. Not I. Honour in life,
> Or honour in death; there is no other thing
> A nobleman can ask for. That is all.[14]

Nowhere in Greek tragedy is the tension between freedom and necessity more tightly drawn than in Sophocles. In the first place, as we have suggested, the situation in which the hero finds himself is one in which he has been placed through no fault or choice of his own; in the second place, many of the plays end with the fulfilment or the vindication of an oracle, contrary to the expectation and sometimes even the efforts of the characters concerned. Finally, by certain ironic hints, Sophocles frequently suggests that the action, even though it proceeds naturally "in accordance with probability and necessity," is at the same time proceeding in accordance with the will of the gods, so that we may well imagine with Kitto a kind of divine volition paralleling the human action of the

[13]For a discussion of Sophoclean *aretê*—excellent, save that it tends to overshadow the other aspects of the plays discussed—see Cedric H. Whitman, *Sophocles*, Part 2, pp. 57–99.

[14]Sophocles, *Ajax*, 470–80, translated by E. F. Watling.

play.[15] Nevertheless, we should guard against viewing Sophoclean tragedy simply as a working-out of a hero's god-determined destiny. In Sophocles the gods are both everything and nothing, which is why they have been subject to such widely varying interpretations. They are everything in that nothing ever happens in a Sophoclean tragedy contrary to what they, or their human spokesmen the prophets, say will happen—and no man ever really gets the better of them; they are nothing in that the action of every Sophoclean play is, throughout, the direct result of human character and human will.

In this connection it is interesting to note the reticence of Aristotle (whose remarks on tragedy seem to fit the Sophoclean variety best) on the subject of fate in tragedy. This is in keeping with his insistence that tragic effect depends on the proper choice and proper treatment of plot and character. Plot itself, he clearly implies (though he never states it in quite such formulaic terms), should arise from the interaction of character and situation. Little or nothing is said of *external* causation, except for the significant warning that "within the action of the play there must be nothing irrational (*alogon*). If the irrational cannot be excluded, it should be outside the scope of the tragedy. Such [Aristotle adds significantly] is the irrational element in the *Oedipus* of Sophocles."[16] Sophocles' *Oedipus Tyrannus* is frequently cited, misleadingly I think, by those who emphasize the fatalism of Greek tragedy. In view of several excellent studies of the play which concern themselves with this matter, and of my own summary of the problem elsewhere, I must refrain, in the present context, from this more detailed discussion.[17]

Aeschylus and Sophocles dramatized the essential elements of freedom and necessity in tragedy by expressing a certain tension between the world of myth, with its fixed patterns of events indicative of some divine plan or order in the universe, and the individual will of the tragic hero. Thus both succeeded in presenting a single view of tragic suffering and of preserving a consistent dramatic form for its expression in a variety

[15]See Kitto, *Form and Meaning in Drama*, chap. 5, *passim* (where, in his discussion of the *Antigone*, Kitto cites several examples of this "dual plane" of operation) and chap. 8, especially pp. 238, 243–44.

[16]Aristotle, *Poetics* xv. 1454b 6 ff. (Butcher's translation).

[17]Of the many studies of the *Oedipus Tyrannus*, I have found those of Bernard Knox (*Oedipus at Thebes*, chap. 1, especially pp. 14–33) and G. M. Kirkwood (*A Study of Sophoclean Drama*, 55–56, 127–35) most useful on the relation between character and plot in the play. For a detailed discussion of the relation between Fate and the will and character of Oedipus, see Greene, 154–62. Cf. also my summary of the problem in "Freedom and Necessity in Greek Tragedy," *Queen's Quarterly*, LXVII (1961), 521–23 and n. 2.

of different circumstances. It is precisely this singleness of view and consistency of form which Euripides is most criticized for lacking.[18] This alleged inconsistency in Euripides springs, I think, from two main sources. Never fully accepting the world of myth as the real basis of his tragedies, he used this traditional material in a variety of ways and this very virtuosity has sometimes been mistaken for confusion and uncertainty on the poet's part. Secondly, particularly in those plays in which the supernatural world of myth does not play a significant role, Euripides sought in the shifting world of experience that element of necessity with which man's free choices come in conflict. The result was that Euripides wrote several different *kinds* of tragedy, depending on what aspect of human suffering he chose to examine in any given play, and (very sensibly in my opinion) he varied his structure to suit the particular tragic idea which he was seeking to express. Detailed illustration of this formal variety of Euripidean tragedy must await our examination of specific plays; nevertheless, it may be possible to indicate in general terms certain contrasts which may be expected between this new tragedy and those at which we have already glanced.

Professor Kitto has already shown us that, since Euripides' tragic conception . . . "implies no tragic interlock between character and situation," we need not expect his plays to show the same kind of organic structure as we have found in Sophocles.[19] We may, perhaps, go further than this. The "man against fate" conception of tragedy we have found to imply some kind of tension between the individual will of man and the divine order of things imposed by the gods, and this conception, as we have seen it in its various modifications in Aeschylus and Sophocles, itself determines that the tragic hero (either for his own sake, as in Sophocles, or for the kind of "doom" that he symbolizes, as in Aeschylus) must be at the centre of the action and that his catastrophe must be the climax of the play, "the moment of truth" at which the whole meaning of the tragedy becomes clear. Euripides, however, in many of his plays was not pitting man against, or fitting man into, an objective supernatural world of reality; therefore he sometimes presents us with tragic situations and tragic actions, within a human or social context, in which

[18]See, for example, Jaeger, 332 ff.; Greene, 216–18; D. W. Lucas, *The Greek Tragic Poets,* 175 ff. (Criticisms of various formal peculiarities are legion and must await treatment of individual plays for discussion.)

[19]See Kitto, *G.T.*, 196–97 and chap. 8, *passim*. (Certain detailed qualifications of Kitto's views will appear later in this study; sometimes, for example [see Kitto, 219–20; 230–31], this critic's concentration on the tragic ideas of Euripides leads him to do less than justice to the novel structural devices by which the dramatist expresses them.)

the catastrophe is no longer the dramatic centre of the play and (in a few instances) in which the individual tragic hero is no longer regarded as the only and indispensable focal point in the depiction of human suffering.

Euripides' varied approaches to myth provide, then, an initial difficulty in comparing his drama with that of the other Greek tragedians. Here we may begin with a major dualism. On the one hand, Euripides devoted a certain measure of his dramatic energy to the ridicule of, and satire on, literal belief in the traditional gods of myth and in the incredible "horrid tales made up by poets" (*Heracles* 1346) about them. Sometimes this takes the form of "between-the-lines" comment such as Helen's ambiguous remark on her mythological birth ("No woman, Greek or barbarian, ever produces her offspring in an egg as they say that Leda bore me to Zeus," *Helena*, 257–59) or Iphigenia's, on the bloodthirsty rites which she is required to perform for the Tauric Artemis ("I think that these people, being man-slaying men themselves, put their own fault upon the goddess. For in my opinion no one of the gods is evil," *I.T.*, 389–91).[20] Sometimes this satire is bound up with the whole play, as in the *Ion* where unforeseen human developments frustrate the plans of Apollo, god of prophecy. However, parody and satire are not the stuff of tragedy and it is in the tragicomedies and melodramas that this aspect of Euripides' approach to myth is most emphasized. On the other hand, in a few plays (such as the *Hippolytus* and the *Bacchae*) Euripides takes myth seriously and uses anthropomorphic gods to symbolize certain real forces which, he believed, vitally affect the lives of men. In between these two extremes there are certain plays (such as the *Heracles* and the *Troades*) which are undeniably tragic in their effect and yet which *do* involve a negative or sceptical attitude to the gods of mythology. In such plays, however, the mythical element is not, in itself, of any real significance in the tragic action; it may, as in the *Heracles*, supply some violent

[20]Criticisms of Euripidean "inconsistency" in mythological approach is a commonplace among commentators. See, for example, Greene, 217; Lucas, 176; Jaeger, 347–48, and other critics to whom reference will be made later, with regard to specific plays and passages of Euripides. Such criticism is intensified when the "inconsistency" occurs within a single play: when, as in the passages (particularly *Heracles*, 1341–46) cited above, a Euripidean character casts doubt on the nature of the gods presupposed in the very myth on which the play depends. (Much of Verrall's fantastic "shadow-writing" of Euripidean plots is due to the critic's jibbing at such dramatic mischief.) However, most examples of this device are to be found in the tragi-comedies, where no serious point of tragic meaning is involved. In the serious tragedies, the passage just cited provides the most glaring instance of the alleged fault; it will be considered later, in the discussion of the *Heracles*.

intervention from outside, but the only dramatic function of such events lies in their effect upon the human characters.

Generally speaking, the farther one gets from the truly mythical view, the more severely the classical form of tragedy (so well epitomized in Sophoclean structure) is stretched. The *Heracles* makes use of and yet abuses the "other world" of myth and in order to do so employs one of the strangest dramatic structures in the whole of Greek drama. Beyond this, the tension between the world of experience, of the individual will, and the world of supernatural reality, snaps entirely, and we find in many Euripidean plays myth being used, not re-created, for melodrama, parody and tragicomedy (in which, as Professor Kitto has shown us, the whole serious basis of reality has been cut away)[21] or else, as happens in other quite different kinds of Euripidean tragedy, abandoned altogether.

Thus a study of the themes and structures of Euripidean drama should begin with those plays which may properly be called "mythological," the *Hippolytus* and the *Bacchae* (for these are the ones which offer the clearest comparisons and contrasts with the tragic conceptions of Aeschylus and Sophocles), and then proceed through the gradual declension of Euripidean tragic form from the "near-mythical" *Heracles* to the political and social tragedies (*Supplices, Heracleidae*)[22] and the tragedies of war and its aftermath (*Troades, Hecuba, Andromache*) where the poet's eye rests squarely on the world of human experience and on man's dealings with his fellow-men. Lastly, of the properly tragic plays, our study should reach such tragedies as the *Medea* and the *Electra* and perhaps the *Orestes*: these stand at the opposite pole to the "mythological" tragedies, for though like them they deal with individual and self-destroying tragic sufferers, they do so in the realistic terms of individual psychology and environment which finds little use, except at certain isolated moments, for myth even in its symbolic uses.[23]

Only when this, the major part, of the study of Euripidean tragedy has been completed, should we turn to the other kind of Euripidean play which we may conveniently call "romantic tragedy" and, finally, to two

[21]See Kitto, *G.T.*, 316.

[22]From the critical approach here attempted, it will be obvious that considerations of date will not determine the sequence in which the extant plays of Euripides will be discussed. However, in certain cases the date of a Euripidean tragedy will turn out to be relevant to some aspects of the discussion.

[23]Cf. Max Pohlenz, *Die Griechische Tragödie*, 265: "In der *Medea* ging alles rein menschlich zu." Pohlenz contrasts this aspect of the *Medea* with the *Hippolytus*: "Im erhaltenen *Hippolytos* tritt uns gleich anfangs die Gottheit leibhaftig entgegen."

plays which as satyric or pro-satyric drama stand a bit outside the rest of the Euripidean *corpus*. Here we may accept in principle (though not, perhaps, in all its applications) Kitto's valuable distinction of Euripidean "tragicomedy and melodrama" (to use his terminology) from the serious tragedies: namely, that when the plot is "artificial," based on some impossible situation removed from human experience, we can no longer look for "tragic, that is to say universal, reality" or for characters whose experiences will seriously engage our emotions.[24] It is in plays of this kind (e.g., the *Ion*, the *Helena*, perhaps the *I.T.*: they are not as numerous as has been thought) that we find the "fantastic" treatment of myth, including even parodies of myth, as well as much of that iconoclastic and incidental satire on outdated Olympian personalities which has sometimes been mistaken for Euripides' whole attitude to the mythological tradition. Further consideration of the purpose and effect of these romantic tragedies must await detailed discussion of the plays concerned. To what degree, for example, does Kitto's account of the entertainments of "theatrical reality" do them justice? It may be that the *genre* which Kitto has so brilliantly described is not, in fact, as "pure," in Euripides, as clearly divorced from serious meanings, as the nice discriminations of critics would have it.

The groupings of Euripidean drama suggested above, though based for the most part on differences in the kind of dramatic material treated, are intended as a critical convenience rather than as rigid and mutually exclusive categories. Thus distinctions between plays clearly opposed in mythical approach (the *Hippolytus* and the *Helena* for example) or in the kind of reality which they treat (the *Bacchae* and the *Troades*, for example) are readily recognizable. But among plays which operate on the same general level of reality, no such clear distinctions can be made. Thus it becomes a matter of choice whether one groups the *Hecuba* with the *Troades* (in terms of the causes of the tragic situation) or with the *Medea* (in terms of the psychology of vengeful heroines).

This relatively relaxed attitude toward critical distinctions, however valid in theory, allows us to admit as well that there are some plays which successfully resist *any* too specific grouping. The *Phoenissae* and the *Iphigenia at Aulis*, for example, while they lack the credibility and thematic concentration of tragedy nevertheless contain certain paratragic effects and are quite different in substance and tone from romantic tragedy.

A brief illustration of Euripides' *tragic* approaches to myth, and of their structural corollaries, may help to indicate the kind of contrasts to

[24]See Kitto, *G.T.*, 315–16, and chaps. 11–12, *passim*.

be observed first, between the Euripidean and the more traditional or "classical" styles of Greek tragedy, and secondly, between the several kinds of tragedy which Euripides himself composed.

Even in those Euripidean plays which accept the world of myth and which use traditional stories of the dealings of the gods with men as the basis of serious drama, we may expect to find considerable divergence from the mythical attitudes of Aeschylus and Sophocles. The *Hippolytus* and the *Bacchae* are based on myths of divine vengeance in which a personally vindictive god punishes a human hero for failing to give that god his due. In both plays, the prologue (spoken by the god) and the epilogue state clearly this literal level of the myth, but in both plays the dramatic action in between (supplemented, particularly in the *Bacchae*, by the choral odes) expresses the real meaning of the hero's tragic fall. Aphrodite, in the *Hippolytus*, tells us that she will ruin the chaste Hippolytus by causing his step-mother Phaedra to fall in love with him and thus unjustly bring the wrath of Theseus upon his head. By several skilful devices, the poet leads us to interpret this theme in human terms while still preserving, for dramatic purposes, the framework of the myth. Aphrodite as a goddess is intentionally overdrawn and unconvincing; far more convincing is the moving picture of Phaedra struggling with a guilty passion which she can conquer only by her death. Secondly, the whole one-sided characterization of Hippolytus demonstrates his lack of self-knowledge and his fatal—and freely-chosen—limitations. Finally and most significantly the poet makes the hero himself supply, in a particularly characteristic way, the immediate cause of his own destruction, for it is Hippolytus' wilful blindness to the power of human passion which leads him to his fatal castigation of its noble and all but helpless victim.

In the *Bacchae*, Pentheus, the puritanical King of Thebes, confusing Dionysianism with debauchery, denies the god's divinity and suppresses his worship in the state; Dionysus, after testing the King's obdurate blindness by a series of miracles, finally destroys him. As in the *Hippolytus*, the action of the play transforms this crude myth of divine vengeance into a dramatization first of the real meaning of Dionysianism (that irrational, recreative but potentially dangerous urge in "social" man) and then of the ruinous career of Pentheus who would suppress this power only to have it reappear in monstrous forms to crush him.

In what happens to Hippolytus and to Pentheus we see the results, inevitable and tragic, of the whole of their one-sided personalities. Can we find in this treatment of myth any reflection of that necessity which, in the other tragedians, always appears as some divine pattern of justice, externally imposed, which both limits and defines man's freedom? I think we can. The mythological features of these two tragedies, however symbolic their presentation, still present certain necessities with which, in these instances, the hero fails to cope, but now these necessities have moved within the world of experience, even within the soul of man. Artemis, Aphrodite and Dionysus represent essential elements in life: we see them in tense isolation in the doomed figures of Hippolytus, Phaedra and Pentheus. Only when they are harmonized in the typically Greek virtue of *sôphrosynê* (so badly misunderstood by Pentheus and Hippolytus) can the soul of man be freed from their fatal constraint.

The action of the *Heracles* falls into three clearly distinguishable parts. In the first, Heracles, son of Zeus, returns from his labours just in time to save his family from the villain Lycus, who has overcome the valiant efforts of Amphitryon, Heracles' "human father," to defend them. In the second, Iris and Lyssa, agents of the jealous Hera, arrive to drive the hero mad, so that he slaughters his beloved wife and children. In the third, Theseus, once saved by Heracles from Hades, now saves him in return, recalling him from his despair to that heroic stature which can alone defeat the afflictions of the hostile gods.

The most outrageous structural feature of this play is surely the catastrophe which breaks suddenly and without cause into the centre of the action. Clearly this structural violence is intentional. Just as in our other plays the slow growth of the catastrophe from the action of the play bespeaks the inevitable operation of some divine or natural law, so the present gratuitous thunderbolt denies the very existence of such laws, and points (if such mythology be true)[25] to wilful and arbitrary gods. This is not to say that dramatic structure and tragic meaning are abandoned in this play, but the relation which exists between its parts is not a causal one and the victory over evil which it presents lies in the hero's recovery from the assaults of Chance rather than in the presentation of catastrophic sufferings as part of a coherent order of events. Like the operation of *Tyche*, the intrusion of Hera is completely external and irresponsible: the catastrophe afflicting Heracles and his family is uncaused and chaotic, as far as the hero's own character and actions are concerned.[26] Thus it is Euripides' destruction of the mythological cosmos erected by the other tragedians which

[25]Cf. *H.F.* 1341–46.

[26]The whimsical and arbitrary actions of the traditional gods are "absurd," as far as the hero is concerned, in the same way as the assaults of Chance are absurd. Whether in turn this affliction is to be thought of as a specific mental or physical disease is surely irrelevant to Euripides' tragic purpose here. It seems hardly probable that what Euripides was "about" was "an astonishing demonstration

here accounts for, and is reflected in, the violent displacement of normal tragic structure.

Thus Heracles is a victim in a much more real and helpless sense than either Hippolytus or Pentheus (or, at the other pole, Medea) are "victims." In this sense he and the whole direction of his tragedy are closer to the Trojan Women and *their* tragedy, except that in the latter case the suffering is explicable at least in terms of man's inhumanity to man.

In the *Troades* then, we find ourselves at a slightly further remove from the mythical view, and here too we find a structural dislocation at least comparable to that of the *Heracles*. Here, as in the *Heracles*, the catastrophe is no longer central to the dramatic meaning; indeed in this play we have a whole series of catastrophes in the successive woes which the Greek victors at Troy inflict upon the captive Trojan Women. Once again, as in the *Heracles*, it is not in these sufferings (which bear no relation to the characters of the sufferers) but rather *in their effects* that we find the tragic meaning of the play. Here, however, the disjuncture between this meaning and explanations such as traditional "mythological tragedy" would provide, is of a particularly subtle kind. The action of the play is explicable in the strictly human terms of cruelty of conquerors to conquered; at any rate, these catastrophes reflect no mythical pattern, no divine order of things which will give reason to such horrors. Hecuba, however, until almost the end of the play, keeps calling on the gods for justice. What sort of gods could allow such things to happen? Either none at all or the kind we are offered in the prologue where we have seen that the fates of Greece and Troy depend not on justice but on the changing humours of divine prejudice and favour. We may take our choice, for in neither case will prayers for justice avail us. But not until the play's end, when for the last time they have vainly invoked the gods and now turn to them no more, do Hecuba and her captive followers reach this tragic knowledge.

The *Troades* has been considered, for all its pathos, as somewhat flat and lacking in dramatic structure. The impression is largely due to the nature of the subject-matter. This is one of those plays in which Euripides is concerned more with the effects than with the causes of suffering, and with such helpless sufferers we cannot expect to find the kind of evolving action possible when the protagonist in some sense brings the catastrophe upon himself. Nevertheless, within these limitations, the structure of the

---

of an epileptic *furor*"! (See E. M. Blaiklock. *The Male Characters of Euripides*, 126.) Nor is there the slightest evidence in the text for Kitto's otherwise attractive suggestion that Hera represents jealous Nature levelling at last the Zeus-given genius of Heracles for taming Earth for mankind.

plot leads quietly and inevitably to the sombre conclusion of the play. It is a mistake to regard Hecuba and her fellow sufferers simply as numbed and passive victims. Between each onslaught of disaster, Hecuba rallies the flagging spirits of her followers: the rhythm of the play depends on these fluctuations between hope and despair till eventually tragic understanding, which is wiser than hope and stronger than despair, is reached.

In the *Supplices*, we find a further example of Euripides' tendency to secularize the themes of Greek tragedy, and once again the descent from the absolute situations of myth to the complex world of experience results in certain structural eccentricities. In this play, the Argive King Adrastus, accompanied by a Chorus of Suppliant Women, seeks help from Theseus of Athens to recover the bodies of the slain chieftains which the Theban victors have denied the Argives. The contrast between Euripides' approach here and the approach of Sophocles to the same situation, viewed quite differently, in the *Antigone*, provides us with a striking example of the difference between mythical and secular tragedy. From an issue fraught with religious connotations and the spiritual fate of individuals, Euripides develops a theme which is essentially political in emphasis. Not all secular tragedy need, of course, be social or political, but in the present instance this is one of the forms which the secularization takes. Theseus' decision to fight a just war in defence of Argive rights stands as a vindication of his declared belief in a world based on law and order. Now the only character remotely resembling a tragic sufferer in this play is the Argive King himself: in his case, Euripides does show that ruin has come about as the result of his own impetuous misjudgment and the hybristic ambition of his followers. However, Adrastus as a tragic sufferer is overshadowed, partly by the ideal political theme which has Theseus at its centre, partly by the sorrowing mothers of the Chorus, for in a sense they generalize (or "socialize") the tragic suffering which should belong to him.

In spite of certain moving passages and of the intrinsic interest of its political material, the *Supplices* is, formally at least, one of the least successful of Euripides' serious tragedies. In both the *Heracles* and the *Troades*, theme and structure combine to produce tragic effect; in both we experience the catharsis of pity and fear and at the same time gain an impression of human triumph over suffering and evil. In the *Supplices* the ferment of ideas, and the complexity of experience, are not successfully contained within a single form. The triumphant element represented by the just Theseus is kept too separate from the pathetic element: some of the most moving passages occur after the restoration of the bodies of the chieftains, when the dominant theme of which Theseus is the centre has been completed. Thus themes intended as complementary become competitive and the tragic hero finds himself being relegated to second place.

The *Heracleidae*, the other clearly political play of Euripides, also deals with the theme of supplication, but this time the emphasis is on the duties of the suppliant rather than of the suppliant's champion. The political aspects of *charis*, viewed as the obligations which gratitude places on the suppliant, provide a theme with some claim to universal significance; however, in the context in which it is treated, it is not given tragic or, indeed, consistently "universal" scope. In the first place, the particular circumstances of the action, especially the Spartan, Argive and Athenian relations at its close, bear too closely on specific international issues and events. In the second place, the improbable heroics of Macaria's self-sacrifice and of ancient Iolaus' contribution to the military victory are a travesty of tragic effect which verges on the melodramatic where melodrama is neither called for nor, one suspects, intended.

The *Andromache*, like the other Euripidean plays which deal with politics and the aftermath of war, also deserts the world of myth to concentrate on a particular area of human relations. The play is worth mentioning in this summary because it represents an extreme of the diminishing role of the tragic hero in the more "passive" type of Euripidean tragedy, where the suffering bears little relation to the hero's character or actions. In the first part of this play, the childless and jealous Hermione and her father Menelaus seek to destroy Andromache and her child Neoptolemus, until old Peleus, championing his grandson's more fruitful liaison, turns the tables on the wicked pair. In the second part, Hermione is in turn rescued by Orestes who arranges the murder of the absent Neoptolemus in Delphi and whisks Hermione away to Sparta to be his wife. In the epilogue, Thetis assures a continued future for Trojan and Phthian stock by arranging that the little son of Neoptolemus and Andromache shall one day found a new and glorious dynasty.

The central irony of the play concerns the basic affinity between the two heroic but once opposed elements, the conquered Trojan and the conquering Phthian (the Peleus-Achilles stock) and the basic *antipathy* between the "noble" Phthians and their "wicked" Spartan allies. The action of the play illustrates these basic affinities and antipathies and ultimately leads, by a rather drastic sorting-out process, to more congenial dynastic arrangements. Once this point has been grasped, individually brilliant scenes such as the quarrel between Hermione and Andromache, and old Peleus' defence of his grandson's spear-won mistress, will no longer strike us merely as lively episodes but as parts of a clear and consistent pattern of feelings and events.

Once again it is interesting to compare (at least by speculation) the kind of theme which Sophocles elicits from this myth. It seems probable that in his *Hermione* the death of Neoptolemus, presented as the result of his own *hybris* toward Apollo, provided a tragic climax to the action.[27] In Euripides' play, on the other hand, we can hardly regard this event as tragic since we never even meet the man who dies. As in the contrast between Sophocles' *Antigone* and Euripides' *Supplices,* we see that Euripides has intellectualized and "socialized" a situation which Sophocles developed in terms of an individual tragic hero and his fate. In this case, Euripides' secularization of his material, his switch from the "mythical" view (which concerns the individual in relation to the gods) to an interest in the shifting patterns of human experience, actually leads to the loss of the tragic hero himself.

Let us turn finally to two tragedies which, in my opinion, stand a little apart from those which we have so far considered. The *Medea* and the *Hecuba* are unlike the *Heracles* and the political and "war" tragedies in that they have tragic heroes of the dominant type whose own natures, in response to the circumstances in which they are placed, bring about the catastrophe of their respective plays. (Let us leave aside for the moment the obvious differences between the regal grandmother turned to fiendish vengeance by her suffering, and the catastrophic personality of Medea, who ends her career with Jason as she began it, in blood.) In this respect, in the relation of character to action, the *Medea* and the *Hecuba* bear some similarity to the *Hippolytus* and the *Bacchae,* and in each of the four plays some power of the emotions or the passions seems to play a central part in the catastrophe as well. Why in two of these plays does Euripides retain the "mythological approach" while in the other two he abandons it almost entirely? In the case of Hecuba and Medea the nearly complete absence of divine machinery until after the catastrophe,[28] gives an impression, at least, of greater freedom than that enjoyed by the tragic sufferers in the two mythological plays.

[27]See Nauck, *TCF,* 176 and schol. *Od.* iv. 4; cf. Wolf H. Friedrich, *Euripides und Diphilos,* 47–49. (Further discussion of Sophocles' *Hermione* will be postponed till chapter 8, on the *Andromache.*)

[28]Medea's dragon-drawn chariot of the sun-god and the prophecy concerning "hound-dog Hecuba" are, so to speak, symbolic extensions of the dramatic characterizations of these women which are not introduced until the action of the plays is over. On the former point, cf. Kitto, *G.T.,* 198–99.

In the *Hippolytus* and the *Bacchae* the gods are used to symbolize the destructive power of passion and of the emotions; in the *Medea* and the *Hecuba*, the heroines' own fury effects their own and others' ruin with no need of gods to help them. The difference is not merely one of technique; rather it is a difference of dramatic needs which dictates different techniques. In the *Medea* and the *Hecuba*, the protagonists themselves embody (in their different ways) the dangerous excess of passion. In the *Hippolytus* and the *Bacchae*, Hippolytus and Pentheus are destroyed by the emotional, the visceral elements in life for the very reason that they deny them. Thus it is when Euripides needs to objectify these elements, to project them (since his tragic heroes show no awareness of them) outside the personality, that he has recourse to mythical divinities.

Are the sufferers in both these types of Euripidean "tragedy of passion" simply the helpless victims, as some have maintained, of forces stronger than themselves?[29] If so, there is less freedom in Euripides than in Aeschylus and Sophocles for all their avenging furies, oracles and family curses. No one would deny that the destructive power of the passions is a recurrent theme in Euripidean tragedy, but surely it is through understanding the whole of life, through *phronêsis* and *sôphrosynê* that these dangers may be averted. Pentheus and Hippolytus are shown to lack the very qualities on which they pride themselves, for Pentheus' cleverness is not true wisdom[30] and Hippolytus mistakes the real meaning of *sôphrosynê*. Both Pentheus and Hippolytus are warned—and ignore the warnings. Tiresias, on the other hand, accepts Dionysus in the *Bacchae* because he understands that there is a part of life which *is* emotional and irrational. Why, if Euripidean heroes are mere helpless victims, is the moral contrast between Polyxena and the tragic Hecuba so clearly drawn? Or why is the testing of Pentheus in the *Bacchae*, and the conflict between mother-love and passion for vengeance in the *Medea* expounded with such dramatic intensity? Medea's simple admission of defeat ("I know my sin; my fury is stronger than my better counsels," 1078–79) *sounds* like fatalism, but is it? Medea loses her struggle as do all the sufferers in Euripidean plays of passion, since this is tragedy. But it would not be tragedy unless, in addition to the necessitous element (Medea's extreme nature, Hecuba's extreme cir-

[29]See E. R. Dodds, "Euripides the Irrationalist," *CR* XLIII, 98–100, 103–4 (contrast Jaeger, 338 ff., who classes the rationalist spirit of Euripides with that of Socrates and Thucydides). See also Kitto, *G.T.*, chap. 8, *passim*, e.g. 195 and 203, where Medea, Hecuba and Hippolytus are all described as tragic "victims".

[30]Cf. *Bacchae* 395–96.

cumstances) some significant operation of the human will were also possible.

In this whole question of "tragic victims" (as Professor Kitto calls them) in Euripides, it seems necessary to make some distinction between "strong" tragedies in which, as we have just seen, the catastrophe does depend, in some sense, on the character and will of the protagonist, and other tragedies like the *Heracles* and the *Troades* in which the catastrophe is imposed on the sufferer by some agency completely external to himself. It is only in the latter kind that the term "tragic victim" applies in the full "helpless" sense of the word, and in these cases, just as the dramatic interest lies not in the cause but in the *effect* of the catastrophe, our interest in the tragic sufferer will be limited to his reaction to his sufferings.

It is this distinction between the active and the helpless tragic sufferers that Kitto refuses to make. In the demonstration of his idea of Euripides' tragic conception—"that the passions and unreason to which humanity is subject are its greatest scourge"—he ranges through most of the tragic plays to show that in them the sufferers are all alike as victims of "passion and unreason," but whether it is their own or someone else's passion does not seem to affect his view of their responsibility.[31]

[31]See Kitto, 196, and, for application of the "tragic victim" idea to various plays, see Kitto, 195–96 (*Medea* and *Hecuba*), 211 (*Troades*), 223 (*Supplices*), 236 (*Heracles*).

PART ONE

MYTHOLOGICAL TRAGEDY

2

THE *Hippolytus*

The Mythological Prologue

The mythological approach which Euripides chooses in the *Hippolytus*, and certain ambiguities in which his symbolic use of myth involves him, have already been considered in the Introduction. We must now seek the clues by which that symbolism may be read: the devices by which the poet transforms a simple myth of divine vengeance (as it is represented in the prologue) by a goddess whose cult has been neglected, into a tragedy explicable in terms of human psychology.[1] Here perhaps the chief danger which besets the modern critic is that of overdoing the rationalistic interpretation which the play in many ways invites: we have already seen enough of Euripides' kaleidoscopic use of myth to beware of separating too rigorously the natural from the supernatural in his plots.[2] Phaedra's passion, for example, and her own reflections on it, are treated in terms so realistic and rational that we seem justified in viewing her part in the action in natural, as opposed to supernatural, terms. Nevertheless, if we ask why Phaedra has fallen helplessly and hopelessly in love with Hippolytus, we must accept the only answer which is given to us in the play: the mythical answer of the prologue, that Aphrodite has caused this as a means of vengeance on Hippolytus. Nor can we ignore this fact once we have finished with the prologue. The most important feature of Phaedra's characterization is her innocence (at least with regard to her passion for Hippolytus), for on this depends the injustice of Hippolytus' treatment of her: the many naturalistic devices by which the dramatist expounds that innocence are heavily supported by the impression in the back of the audience's mind that she is in some sense the pawn of Aphrodite.

[1]For other views concerning the myth and its treatment in this play, see Appendix I to this chapter.

[2]See Appendix I, section 2.

It is this comparative lack of freedom which distinguishes Phaedra from tragic heroines such as Medea who is at the centre of her play and whose passionate nature is presented as an essential part of the tragic characterization, without recourse, on the dramatist's part, to any god. Nevertheless, it may be possible to restrict the helplessness of Phaedra to the simple fact that she is incurably in love with Hippolytus. In what she elects to do about it, she seems to show her own moral personality.

It is this single aspect of the myth's function in the *Hippolytus* which renders the play's "realism" faintly ambiguous. Apart from this necessary "pegging" of Phaedra as a helpless victim, the dramatist does take pains to limit the myth to its symbolic meaning and to expound the tragedy which overtakes Hippolytus as something more intimately connected with human experience than the anger of a spiteful goddess. To this end, Euripides employs several devices to weaken our literal acceptance of such a goddess and to strengthen our expectation of some catastrophe arising from the strictly human motivations of the play.

The first device, which is contained in the prologue, is a bold one and it is one which Euripides uses over and over again in his plays. It is the simple trick of ruining an idea by overstatement—in this case of casting doubt on the less credible features of a myth by an exaggerated emphasis upon them. The Aphrodite of the prologue, while she is presented as a being of awe-inspiring majesty and power (1–6), compares her outraged vanity to human feelings (7–8). Hippolytus' affront and her reaction to it she expresses in purely personal terms which carry no suggestion of any system of divine justice. ("I ruin those who have proud disdainful thoughts [φρονοῦσιν . . . μέγα] towards me." [6; cf. 10–13, 21–22, 48–50]) She glories in her power to take swift vengeance on Hippolytus and openly admits, only to dismiss as of no account, the cruelty to Phaedra which her revenge involves: "Phaedra, though of good name she be, still must perish; for I'll not count the wrong to her of greater moment than the satisfaction to me of just vengeance on my enemies." (47–50)

Gods such as the Aphrodite of this prologue are much closer to the Homeric model than are the gods of the other Greek tragedians. If we observe the contrast between, on the one hand, this bludgeoning of the audience with the crudest form of divine motivation (simple "human" spite), and, on the other, the approaches of Aeschylus and Sophocles, surely we must see the effect which this neo-Homeric primitivism would have had on a fifth-century audience. (In their own cultural context, of course, the Homeric gods strike us as anything but primitive.) In the *Agamemnon* of Aeschylus, Zeus' effect on the action appears as part of his cosmic plan for justice, and though his will is apparent throughout the play, it is referred to only in the veiled lyrical comments of the chorus whose mythological paradigms and hymns to Zeus allow us to see its application to the dramatic theme. In Sophocles, the subtle hints of the divine will moving behind the scenes, paralleling the human actions in such plays as the *Electra* and the *Antigone*, suggest, in a manner still less intrusive on the human action, a divine order of things harsher and less easily defined but no less cosmic and impersonal than that of the Aeschylean Zeus. Surely, then, Euripides' apparent retrogression, coming at the end of a tradition which had sought to save the mythological gods from such attacks as Xenophanes had made upon them,[3] must be taken as an attempt to impugn, by a sort of *reductio ad absurdum*, the old anthropomorphism (which was by no means dead) and all its implications.[4]

There are, moreover, two additional hints in the prologue that Aphrodite as she is to function in the action of the play is more closely identifiable with human experience than the Olympian virago to whom we have been listening. One is the failure of the goddess (at v. 42) to tell us *how* Phaedra's secret will be revealed to Theseus—an omission which leaves room for the human motivation by which Hippolytus' downfall is actually to be secured. The other is the description of Hippolytus' affront to Aphrodite—no matter of prayers or votive offerings but of sex and marriage, which he totally rejects. Even in the prologue then, a hint of the real meaning of Aphrodite appears: thus offended, she *is* physical love, personified, not merely the goddess of it, and her vengeance means the disaster which ensues when man ignores this force.

Here and there throughout the action, in the asides of minor characters and in the occasional reflection of the Chorus, the poet provides several hints belying the crude anthropomorphism of the prologue. Thus, for example, the question raised in our minds by the gentle remonstrance of Hippolytus' servant ("Gods should be wiser [i.e., in the context, "more tolerant"] than men," 120) receives its answer in the Nurse's later comment, "Cypris all this time was not a god but something, if it exists, more powerful." (359–60) In the midst of the naturalistic action of the play, it is only the Chorus which sustains for the most part the mythological version of this power.

Hippolytus and Phaedra

The most fundamental technique whereby Euripides translates this myth of divine vengeance into a tragedy of human responsibility lies, of

[3]See Xenophanes, frgs. B 11–16, B 23–26, D-K.

[4]See Appendix I, section 3.

course, in the characterization of Hippolytus and Phaedra. Hippolytus is presented to us in three contexts: first on his own ground, as it were, in the company of his servant and of his fellow-devotees of Artemis (the huntsmen chorus), next, in relation to Phaedra, when he learns her secret from the Nurse, and finally in conflict with his father, Theseus, after Phaedra's death. In each passage, we find the same features of his character, emphasized by the repetition of certain thematic words. Of these three nerve-centres, the crucial one is revealed in the hero's reaction to the plight of Phaedra. It is for this reason that the dramatist takes such pains with the Queen's character and situation; while the nature and fate of Hippolytus form the central issue of the tragedy, it is only by an intimate and sympathetic understanding of Phaedra and her plight that we can see the culpable and fatal aspect of Hippolytus.

It is the parallel characterization of these two, Hippolytus and Phaedra, which informs the well-nigh perfect structure of the first half of this play,[5] and it is this too which helps us to see the tragic outcome in human rather than in mythological terms. Each is presented first in isolation, then, without actually meeting, in fatal reaction to the other. After a brief but revealing introduction to Hippolytus come two long and agonizing scenes between Phaedra and her Nurse, leading to the first crisis of the play: the revelation of Phaedra's secret to Hippolytus. The hero's reaction to that secret is both the immediate result of the preceding episode and the fulfilment of earlier hints we have had about his character. Equally in accordance with "probability and necessity" is Phaedra's incrimination of Hippolytus, which follows: it is the immediate result of Hippolytus' treatment of her, and it is consistent with her earlier concern, which now becomes exacerbated, for *eukleia*, good reputation. After such tensions and their resolutions, the Theseus episode may be felt to contain an element of anticlimax, but at any rate the necessary and probable sequence of the action is just as clearly marked. Theseus' cursing and exile of his son is the direct result of Phaedra's incriminating letter, and Hippolytus' inability to defend himself springs

[5]This aspect of the *Hippolytus* has generally been much admired; see, for example, the eloquent appreciations of critics as diverse as André Rivier, *Essai sur le Tragique d'Euripide*, 64–65; Gilbert Norwood (usually a severe critic of Euripidean structure), *Essays on Euripidean Drama*, 74; R. P. Winnington-Ingram, "*Hippolytus*: A Study in Causation," 171. This general agreement on the formal excellence of the *Hippolytus* tends to refute Kitto's view that it was when Euripides was not concerned with serious tragic ideas that his technical skill was most in evidence. (See Kitto, *G.T.*, 185–86, 312, 317.) It should be admitted, however, that Kitto appears to regard the *Hippolytus* as the closest of Euripides' tragedies to the Sophoclean dramatic style. (*ibid.*, 200; cf. 185)

from the two aspects of his character with which we are by now most familiar: his sense of honour (which prevents him from breaking his oath of secrecy to the Nurse) and his somewhat alienating quality of aloofness.

Our earliest impression of Hippolytus is in many ways a most favourable one.[6] He first appears leading a band of hunters whose invocation to Artemis provides an aptly ironic transition between Aphrodite's prologue and the hero's own prayer to the rival goddess. In this prayer (Hippolytus is offering Artemis a laurel wreath from her sacred meadow), there is a youthful freshness, a wholehearted and confident enthusiasm which reminds one of a similar dedication in a later play: the happy commitment of Apollo's temple-boy in the *Ion*, before his disillusionment. Already, however, the sequence of thoughts suggests the canker in Hippolytus' virtue, and certain words which he uses to express them are soon to reappear in grimmer context. The garland for Artemis, the hero tells us, comes from an unsullied grove (73–74), watered by Reverence (*Aidôs*, 78), sacred to those who have by nature the gift of purity (*to sôphronein*, 79–80)—and of these few it is Hippolytus' right alone to make offerings to Artemis. Thus the "virginal imagery" first applied to nature is quickly related to moral purity and then to moral superiority and exclusiveness . . . "to me alone this special honour." (84)

The peculiarly Greek concept of *sôphrosynê* includes modesty, self-control (of which Hippolytus' special virtue, chastity, is but one aspect) and in general a balanced and temperate view of life; neither the exclusiveness of Hippolytus' worship nor the smugness which attends it quite fit the virtue to which he makes such special claims. As if to underline these hints in the prayer of Hippolytus come the timid questions of his servant. The latter leads Hippolytus to agree that *to semnon*, the quality of haughtiness, makes a man hated by men and gods alike, since both use the same conventions, *nomois* (93–98); hence Hippolytus himself is running risks in his proud disregard of Aphrodite, who is herself described as *semnê* (99, accepting the reading of the MSS).

Semnos, like *sôphrosynê*, is a term which is to recur significantly later in the play. (See, for example, vv. 957, 1064, 1364.) It has two aspects. It means "revered," "august," "holy," in its good or honorific sense, but it means "pompous," "haughty," "unapproachable," when it is used to describe men who are too conscious of their own excellence or

[6]See Rivier's excellent appreciation (*Essai*, 55–56) of the charm and positive virtue of Hippolytus' devotion to Artemis. However, the description is somewhat marred, to my way of thinking, by the critic's subsequent refusal (cf., for example, p. 69), to recognize any limitation to the hero's virtue.

importance. Perhaps it is in its "good" sense that the Servant uses it of Aphrodite (v. 99, following the reading of the MSS); certainly it is in this sense that Hippolytus uses it later of himself (1364), though with dramatically ironic overtones. But he who is *semnos* in the bad sense cannot, of course, be *sôphrôn*. Hippolytus' threatening reply to the Servant's warning ("Watch out lest your tongue be your ruin!" 100) and his disdain for Aphrodite in this passage, are clear indications of this dangerous quality in him, and his statement, "As in social preferences, some cherish some gods; others, others" (104) suggests the antithesis of that balanced view of life which true *sôphrosynê* entails.

The *agôn* of Phaedra is undoubtedly one of Euripides' most successful dramatizations of the conflict between passion and intellect, between blind impulse and moral insight. So sympathetic is the characterization of the Queen, so moving and convincing the presentation of her struggle, that critics have sometimes been led to regard her dramatic significance as equal to or even greater than that of Hippolytus himself.[7] Clearly, then, any analysis of the play which treats Phaedra's role as secondary, a means to a further dramatic end, must explain what might appear to be a wanton expenditure of dramatic energy on the playwright's part.

Phaedra's situation has, in one respect at least, a greater dramatic potential than that of Hippolytus. It is she and not he who is engaged in an intense emotional struggle, for the tragedy of Hippolytus stems from the denial, the negation, of passion. We have, then, a practical reason for the prominence of Phaedra's role, and that prominence will be justified if the details of her struggle can be related to the tragic characterization of Hippolytus. In this connection, it is not Phaedra

[7]See, for example, D. Grene, "The Interpretation of the *Hippolytus* of Euripides," *CP*, XXXIV, 45–58. Grene's arguments have been effectively refuted by W. B. Stanford. "The *Hippolytus* of Euripides," *Hermathena*, LXIII, 11–17. More interesting than Grene's discussion, because more in keeping with the later development of the play, is Pohlenz' comment on Phaedra (*Griech. Trag.*, I, 269). While admitting that the play's unity depends on Hippolytus' fate and on the "*Gestalt*" of his character, Pohlenz compares the initially dominant role of Phaedra with that of Deianeira in Sophocles' *Trachiniae*, both in the break which her suicide makes in the play and in the whole new action which she introduces through the letter she leaves behind. The comparison with Deianeira is interesting in that it reminds us that here, as in certain of the so-called diptych plays of Sophocles, the fate of the tragic sufferer is inextricably bound up with the *agôn* of another character. This, however, is not quite the same thing as saying, as Lesky does, that our play is the tragedy of a double-fate (*Doppelschicksal*, A. Lesky, *Die tragische Dichtung der Hellenen*, 167), a description which Winnington-Ingram ("Hippolytus," 181–82) quotes with approval, though *his* argument, like that of Pohlenz, places the final emphasis on Hippolytus.

herself, "for her own sake," but the moral integrity of Phaedra that claims our attention, for only by dramatizing the innocence and nobility of Phaedra can the poet dramatize the terrible injustice which the hero does her through his warped view of womankind. To this end, the responsibility of Phaedra for any "discreditable" matters which the plot requires is reduced to the minimum. Aphrodite on the mythological level and the Nurse on the human level are the agents relieving her of guilt. Through the one, she is "fixed" in a hopeless passion before the action of the play begins; through the other, her secret is betrayed without (in our eyes, at least) loss of honour to herself. Even so, between these poles of responsibility we have still to be convinced dramatically of the positive calibre of Phaedra's innocence and so of the enormity of Hippolytus' unjust tirade against her. Hence the account of Phaedra's struggle—all the moral resources of a noble character pitted against the force of her affliction—is presented with the vivid emotional realism proper to the human level of the play.

Phaedra's struggles are presented in two tense episodes (198–361, 373–524) between herself and the Nurse. Passion and hysteria govern the Queen throughout the first of these scenes; reason gains control in the second, particularly in the splendid speech (373–430) with which it opens. However, while the dramatist thus indicates the almost equal balance[8] of these warring elements in Phaedra's soul, he saves his device from artificiality by a break-through of agonizing sanity in the midst of the hysterical scene at vv. 239–49, and again by a sudden (and fatal) diminuendo of self-control at the end of the second episode.

The effects of Phaedras' passion have already preceded her on-stage, like waves before a hurricane, in the excited gossip of the Chorus and (as she enters) in the grumbling flutter of the Nurse. In the second strophe the guesses of the Chorus (Could Artemis be troubling her? Or her husband's infidelity? Or bad news from Crete?) remind us, with unconscious irony, of both the human and the mythological aspects of the situation. (The Cretan motif is to recur significantly at vv. 337–41 and 752–60.) The Nurse's complaints on the other hand ("No sooner out than you want to go in again!" and so on, 181 ff.) vividly convey in contrast to the speaker's shambling gait the speed and restlessness of Phaedra's fevered pacing, indoors and out. So too the plodding literalness

[8]It is too readily assumed that Phaedra simply succumbs to her passion: e.g., by Pohlenz (in his contrast between Phaedra's mere "social morality" and Hippolytus' natural *sôphrosynê*): "She fails at the first strong temptation" (*Griech. Trag.*, I, 270); by Dodds (in "Euripides the Irrationalist," *CR*, XLIII [1929], 99 ff.), who takes Phaedra's experience as an example of the complete triumph of passion over reason.

of the Nurse's answers to her mistress ("What want you with the hunt? With fountain springs in the wilds? At home, we have a nice well-watered slope." 224–27, and the like), underline the hysterical intensity, the hidden meanings of the Queen's passionate pleadings.

What are we to make of the "mad" speeches of Phaedra in relation to the innocent and noble characterization which her function in the play requires? Insofar as Phaedra is clearly driven "out of her mind" in these speeches, they must, of course, illustrate the overwhelming power of the passion which has her in its grip. Phaedra herself, as she returns to sanity, feels it to have been a more than human force: "I was raving, overwhelmed by god-sent ruin." (241) On the other hand, the form which her hysteria has taken—mysterious pleadings for haunts and pursuits associated with Hippolytus—itself reflects some credit on the Queen. Though she cannot overcome her passion, she will not speak of it: its appearance disguised in these involuntary utterances is an index to the strength not only of her passion but of her suppression of it.

In the second half of this episode (284–361), the "virtuous characterization" of Phaedra becomes still more clearly marked, first in her explicit resolution to die (which she herself describes as "fashioning good from evil," 329–331) rather than reveal her secret, secondly (and paradoxically) in the manner and means by which the first—and fatal—breach in that secret is finally effected. It is surely a brilliant device to have Phaedra tempted from her silence only by an appeal to her virtue: the formal supplication of the Nurse. (325–35) And even after she has succumbed, her halting and indirect address, her references to her family ill-starred in love (337–43) and finally her inability to name Hippolytus (it is the Nurse who does so) all bespeak her desperate and outraged modesty. Surely no way could have been devised by which Phaedra, in saying what she should not, could have compromised her honour less.[9]

The strongly emotional introduction to Phaedra's plight reaches its

[9]Dodds ("The *Aidôs* of Phaedra, etc.," *CR*, XXXIX, 103) argues that here Phaedra is using her professed respect for the suppliant (which he equates in this context with the "bad *aidôs*" referred to at vv. 385–86) to give her an excuse for making the confession which she is in fact longing to make. This point may well be psychologically sound but it is not, if our reading of Phaedra's role in the play is correct, the one which Euripides wishes to make here. (Besides, it is difficult to see how the *aidôs* which Phaedra manifests here can *itself* be called a "pleasure," which is what Phaedra calls the "bad *aidôs*." At the most, if Dodd's interpretation of Phaedra's psychology is correct, it may be said to lead to pleasure in this specific case. This puzzling passage, vv. 383–86, will be considered more fully in Appendix II, section 2, to this chapter.

climax with the revelation of her secret and the shocked outcries of the Nurse and the Chorus. Phaedra's next speech (373–430), a reflective assessment of her situation and indeed of that of all erring mankind, stands in marked contrast to the preceding episode and to our first impressions of the Queen. Here the dramatist's presentation, hysterical cries followed by a magnificently controlled and philosophic discourse, must have reminded the audience of the way in which that more terrifying heroine, Medea, was presented a few years before. Despite the element of improbability involved, the device seems justified in the case of Phaedra: it provides us with an effective dramatization of the warring elements in Phaedra's soul and it is in this mortal struggle between reason and passion that the whole point of her characterization lies.

Phaedra's public address on human frailty may also (like Medea's address to the Corinthian women) be criticized on the score of dramatic relevance. There can be no question but that here as elsewhere Euripides is indulging his appetite, and perhaps that of his audience, for generalizations on ethics, psychology and the workings of the social organism.[10] Nevertheless, Phaedra's speech keeps the general and the particular nicely balanced, and remarkably few of its philosophic points turn out to be irrelevant to the Queen's own case.

Phaedra finds laziness and the distraction of pleasures, rather than lack of judgment, to be the main causes of human corruption. (The argument reminds us, in its terms of reference, of various contemporary and near-contemporary debates among the philosophers.[11]) Three only of the many pleasures are mentioned: long hours of gossip, idleness and *aidôs*, not in its good sense but in the sense of unhealthy interest in those matters for which we should feel shame.[12] The philosophic

[10]For a discussion of rhetorical generalizations in Euripides, based on contemporary attitudes, see J. H. Finley's interesting study, "Euripides and Thucydides," *Harvard Studies in Classical Philology*, XLIX, 30 ff.

[11]In addition to the well-known Socratic-Platonic "equation" (in some dialectical contexts) of virtue and knowledge, one thinks of the several passages in which the Platonic Socrates considers pleasure in relation to the good, e.g., at *Protagoras* 351b–360b; *Gorgias*, 468e ff. and 495a–500a. (In the *Philebus*, the whole argument is concerned with that ethical trio, pleasure, understanding and the good, with which Phaedra too is concerned.) That such discussions were current in some form in Euripides' time seems highly probable not only from the "Socratic" evidence but also from certain references in the pre-Socratic tradition. (See, for example, the relation which emerges between pleasure, understanding and the Democritean "good" [*euthumiê*] from a study of Democritus frgs. B 74, 188, 191, 211, 197, 119, 210–11, 33, cf. 172–73, 175, D-K, in that order.) See also Appendix II, section 1, to this chapter.

[12]See Appendix II, section 2, to this chapter.

basis thus established, Phaedra turns to her own case: "Since this is how I happen to view these matters, it was out of the question that I should destroy my way of thought by any drug." (388–90) Phaedra means that even in her present state she still retains her knowledge of right and wrong, and of the temptations which cause men to forget this; the lofty dismissal of drugs is, of course, a nice piece of anticipatory irony. "When love bit me . . ." Phaedra proceeds to show how she sought to cure herself by her own philosophy. Now we see the point of the "three pleasures" which, from many, Phaedra has selected as the particular corrupters of good judgment. "Leisure": of this a Queen with an absent husband has a surfeit; "Gossip": Hippolytus is later to castigate the gossip of serving-women with their mistresses, and from what we hear from the Nurse we can imagine its pernicious nature; *aidôs*: in this case the sweet shame of Phaedra's secret passion for Hippolytus. First by silence (394), then by self-control (*τῷ σωφρονεῖν*, 399) Phaedra has tried to overcome these seductions (indeed we have seen these efforts and their effects in all that has gone before). When these failed, "the best plan seemed, to die—that men may see my noble, not my baser side." (401–4, slightly paraphrased)

Here for the first time we touch the mainspring of Phaedra's conduct, *reputation* (*eukleia*) and it is this which is the subject of the next little homily on which the speaker now embarks. (407–18) Now it is true that the attack on "noble houses" (409 ff.) as first providing ill repute and bad example for women in general, has a distinctly Euripidean ring, but once more we should note that the indignation does fit Phaedra's reasoning as well. At verse 419 we are brought sharply back to the primary concern of this conscientious Queen: the good name of her family—self, husband and sons alike—which she will go to any lengths to safeguard. In this final passage of the speech, the dramatic and rhetorical elements coalesce: generalizations in Euripides' most gnomic style abound, yet the ideas are closely related to the passionate virtue which dominates Phaedra as much as does Aphrodite's visitation.

> For this, friends, is the point which seals my doom: never to be caught shaming my husband or the sons I bore him. . . . For this enslaves a man, however bold he be, to learn a father's or a mother's evil deeds. A just and upright mind: this alone, men say, is worth the price of life to him who has it. Time in its passage shows the world it's wicked, as a maid holds a mirror to her pretty face. Never with these may I be numbered. (419–30)

(The prophetic irony of this final pretty image, anticipating both Phaedra's degradation and the canker to be found in Hippolytus' maiden virtue, rivals the more explicitly savage irony of Dionysus as he leads Pentheus to his "luxurious" doom at *Bacchae*, 965–70.)

Phaedra's speech provides us with a brilliant example of the theory and practice of moral action. Professor Dodds, in his comment on 375 ff., has seized on what he regards as the Euripidean view that "the evil in human life comes not from intellectual error but from a failure of the will," and argues that it is denied in this play "that enlightenment can make men good."[13] Elsewhere, as we have seen, he uses this and similar passages in Euripides to suggest that, in stressing the uncontrollable forces of passion as the mainsprings of human activity, "Euripides the irrationalist" was setting himself against the Socratic equation of virtue and knowledge and declaring man, for all his knowledge and understanding, to be the helpless prey of forces quite beyond control of reason.[14]

Need Phaedra's views and her experience lead us to conclusions so extreme? It is true that the Queen's statements at 377 ff. place emphasis on the will rather than on the understanding in moral issues, yet the doctrine is not, perhaps, as anti-Socratic as it at first appears. In Plato's development of Socratic ethics, discrimination between pleasures is often the function of ethical judgment and, at least on the practical level with which Phaedra is concerned, error or wrong-doing is sometimes explained as due to the distraction of immediate and violent pleasures.[15] Now if one does not submit to the temptations of pleasure which Phaedra mentions, but does the good one knows, then surely right judgment is one of the causes, though (in Phaedra's view) not in itself a sufficient cause, of that right action. If this is the Euripidean

[13]Dodds, "*Aidôs*," 102 and 103, respectively. In support of the latter statement, Dodds cites, in addition to Phaedra's views at 377 ff., the words of Hippolytus and of Theseus at 79–80, 916–20. However, there is nothing in the play to suggest that either Hippolytus or Theseus is to be regarded as a good judge concerning the real meaning and source of virtue; nor indeed do they fulfil Dodds' own criterion (described in "Euripides the Irrationalist," 98) of the kind of characters who may be regarded as expressing Euripidean views, to wit, those "who are like their author, thinkers." Phaedra "passes"; Hippolytus and Theseus surely do not.

[14]See Dodds, "Euripides the Irrationalist," 97–104, and note 8, above. Dodds cites *Medea* 1078 ff., and *Hipp.* 375 ff. as the chief instances in Euripides where *thumos* overcomes reason in Euripides, but he adds many other Euripidean passages which appear to him to demonstrate the "moral impotence of the reason." Cf. Pohlenz, *Griech. Trag.*, I, 273, who suggests some qualifications of the view that the passage at *Hipp.* 377 ff. is to be taken as a Euripidean polemic against the Socratic teaching concerning virtue and knowledge.

[15]See the references to Plato above, note 11. (Plato's statements on the relation of pleasure to the good vary, of course—as do Plato's statements on any subject—in accordance with the dialectical context.)

view, then it implies an amendment to, rather than a contradiction of, the Socratic position. If it be argued against this interpretation that Phaedra does not state the possibility of overcoming such temptations, surely Phaedra's own moral struggle refutes the argument, for it is *on the basis of the views expressed* (see vv. 388 ff. and 392 ff.) that she makes her three attempts to overcome her passion. In the first two of these attempts, she fails; then, ". . . when by these means I could not conquer Cypris, I resolved to die. . . ." (400–401) It might well be argued that *at this point* Phaedra has by no means lost her struggle against "passion"; indeed, left to herself, free of the Nurse's "good offices," she would have succeeded in preserving both honour and honesty in death. The reason why she is not allowed to do so is the dramatic one: *not* that the power of her guilty passion may be demonstrated but that Hippolytus, the tragic hero of this play, may become involved in just the way the theme and plot demands.

So far, then, Phaedra has been characterized as a woman of great integrity, moral insight and moral power, and the Nurse on the human level (like Aphrodite on the mythological level) is the chief instrument by which the dramatist relieves her of guilt, at least for as long as her innocence is important to the meaning of the play. By the exploitation of her sense of *aidôs*, the Nurse has already reached her mistress' well-guarded secret. Now (433–524), in contrast to her first shocked outcry, the Nurse seeks by fair means or foul to save her mistress' life. The interpretation of this passage is fundamental to the characterization of Phaedra and, in all probability, to the essential difference between this play and Euripides' earlier treatment of the myth.[16]

At vv. 433–81, the Nurse embarks on a strenuous attempt to persuade

[16]It is almost certain that in the earlier, lost *Hippolytus* of Euripides (the so-called *Hippolytos kaluptomenos*) Phaedra did give in to her passion, and it is at least probable that she herself made a declaration to her step-son. For this, the most obvious external evidence (which receives some support from the fragments) is the slighting reference by the "Aristophanic Aeschylus," at *Frogs* 1043 and 1053 ff., to the "strumpets" Phaedra and Sthenoboea whom Euripides had put onstage, and the observation in Aristophanes of Byzantium's *Hypothesis* to our *Hippolytus* (the so-called *Hippolytos Stephanias*) that in this play "what was unseemly and worthy of censure" in the first play was corrected. The evidence, both fragmentary and external, concerning Euripides' first *Hippolytus* and Sophocles' *Phaedra* (believed to have come between the two Euripidean versions) may best be studied from the excellent presentation in Barrett, 10–11, 18 ff., and (especially) 30–31; see also Méridier, *Euripide* II, 13 ff., and now Snell, chap. 2, especially 25 ff. and further references there given. Both Méridier and Snell place rather more confidence than does Barrett in Seneca's *Phaedra* as evidence for the content of Euripides' first *Hippolytus.*

Phaedra to yield to her passion for Hippolytus rather than to save her honour by suicide. The speech, though it contains one of Euripides' most striking "symbolic" descriptions of Aphrodite (447–50), soon descends to anthropomorphic tales of her power over her fellow-gods, and then to that basest perversion of mythology (in Euripides' as in Plato's view), the use of divine example as an excuse for men's wrong-doing. "What else is this than *hybris*, to seek to better even gods in virtue? Have the courage of your love! a god has willed it!" (474–76) The speech ends with a promise, wheedlingly vague in deference to Phaedra's scruples, of some remedy (φάρμακον) for this affliction by "charms and magic words." (478–79) However, Phaedra's resistance (486 ff.) stings the nurse to express her intentions more brutally: "No fine speeches need you, but the man!" (490–91)

The vehemence with which Phaedra rejects the Nurse's "ruinous but too fair-seeming arguments" (486 ff., cf. 498 ff., 503 ff.) shows that she scorns this abdication of human responsibility as do other noble characters in Euripides to whom mythological "justifications" or exonerations are offered.[17] At the same time Phaedra's blending in three agonized replies of this rejection with the horrified fascination which she feels for the Nurse's suggestions illustrates in brilliant miniature the struggle between reason and passion which Phaedra herself, with such philosophic detachment, has previously described for us.

By the gods, no more! You speak too well these shameful things. My whole being is so constrained with passion that if you plead this shameful course so skilfully, I'll soon be mastered by the very thing I flee! (503–6)

At this point, then, the Queen, albeit with a struggle, has refused each fresh urging from her devil's advocate. But after the Nurse's speech at 507–15, she yields a grudging compliance at least to the point where the Nurse feels free to go indoors and speak with Hippolytus. What brings about the change?

My own view is that in these lines (507–15) the Nurse at least ostensibly proposes something different which Phaedra feels she can accept with less loss of honour than the blunt offer to procure Hippolytus.[18]

[17]Cf. Heracles' rejection (coupled with his own refutation of such "poets' tales" of divine misdemeanour) of Theseus' consolations, *Heracles* 1341 ff. and 1311–21 respectively. Cf. also Iphigenia's criticism, *I.T.* 389–91, of men who project their own evil impulses upon the gods.

[18]The present discussion is a summary of a more detailed discussion of *Hipp.* 505–17 and its context in my article, "A Problem in Euripides' *Hippolytus*," *TAPA*, XCII, 37–44.

In the earlier speeches, the Nurse has admitted "bed" and "pleasure" (495), however shameful (αἰσχρ', 500) in the circumstances, to be a necessary part of the rescue operation. Now however she suddenly remembers certain soothing love-charms which she has in the house (509–10), "involving nothing base" (οὔτ' ἐπ' αἰσχροῖς, 511) which will simply rid Phaedra of her love. All she needs in addition is some token from Hippolytus, either some word or some fragment of clothing. To this implied request for permission to seek out Hippolytus, Phaedra gives her hesitant and again hardly explicit consent (516–20), insisting only that the Nurse shall say nothing of her own plight to the youth.

Admittedly, a certain ambiguity hangs over this *entente* at which Phaedra and the Nurse finally arrive, and it cannot be completely explained either by the Nurse's dissimulation or by imperfectly suppressed traces of the "strumpet Phaedra" of the first edition of the play. Once a breach has been made in Phaedra's honourable silence, the fatal canker of gossip and discussion (which she herself has rightly feared) begins to work its poison on her and to eat away her self-control. Of this the poet only gives us hints, witnessing to his honest and subtle depiction of the human psyche. In all essentials he has, even to the end of this crucial scene, preserved the honour of the Queen.

The tirade of Hippolytus against women (616–68), when he hears from the Nurse of Phaedra's love, is another celebrated example of the set rhetorical discourse in Euripides. Here again the rhetoric takes its own time to reach the specific point at issue. After the shock effect of the opening rebuke to Zeus (who ought to *sell* babies and so to dispense with the need of women!) the misogynist settles down to a forensic indictment of "that monstrous growth," the female, from his particular point of view. No doubt Euripides enjoyed composing invective on such a lively theme, but, as in the case of Phaedra's dissertation (373–430), we should note that once again dramatic values are well served. Both the generalizing style and Hippolytus' fastidious postponement of reference to Phaedra herself, while they suit the poet's rhetorical purposes, also suit the character of the hero. Nor is the course of Hippolytus' rhetoric as undirected as it at first appears. Hippolytus' invective against marriage turns to invective against clever wives in particular (Phaedra is a clever woman) and against conniving servants . . . "like you, vile pimp, who come to bandy words about my father's sacred bed!" (651–52) (Even here, it is the effect on himself which seems most to affect Hippolytus: "I who feel sullied even in hearing this!" 655) Not until the final and so most emphatic part of the speech does Hippolytus mention Phaedra herself (662) and then only to turn from her in disgust in his final repudiation of all womankind: "Let someone teach them to be chaste (*sôphronein*) or let me stamp on them for ever." (667–68)

The speech is a damning piece of self-characterization, but its effect depends also on the two powerful episodes which have preceded it. It is our awareness, emotional as well as intellectual, of the truth about Phaedra that lets us feel the full impact of Hippolytus' injustice in this vilification of all womankind to which the plight of Phaedra moves him. Here where the guilty passion of the Queen finally breaks on the hero's intolerant chastity, Hippolytus shows his *semnotês* most clearly—that haughty, one-sided virtue which will never listen or sympathize where it cannot condone. It is left for Phaedra later to express the qualities implicit in Hippolytus' speech, for it corrupts even her noble resolve to die:

> . . . but in dying I will become a bane to that other one as well, that he may learn not to be so lofty about my woes; in sharing this my disease with me he will learn the true virtue of understanding [σωφρονεῖν μαθήσεται—the full implication of these words is admittedly untranslatable]. (728–31)

Thus it is the tirade of Hippolytus which leads Phaedra, partly in anger but mostly in fear for her own reputation, to write the suicide note incriminating Hippolytus as her seducer.[19] The crucial decision (in a drama which some critics think concerns mere puppets of the gods) arises naturally from the characters of both the principal figures in it, each of whom in the single-minded pursuit of his special *aretê* misreads the other and causes the other's downfall. It is chiefly Phaedra's perpetual concern with reputation, rather than the passion that afflicts her, which causes her to incriminate Hippolytus, but it is Hippolytus' righteous and intolerant "virtue" which leads her to fear him as a

[19]In emphasizing Phaedra's concern for *eukleia* (which Hans Strohm, *Euripides* [Munich 1957] 104, n. 1, has even called "das wichtigste Leitmotiv des Dramas"), one should not, of course, ignore the subtle admixture of other motives including revenge, anger and the venom of frustrated love which, as various critics have argued, influence Phaedra as well. See, for example, Winnington-Ingram, "Hippolytus," 181; Méridier, "L'*Hippolyte* d'Euripide," 238–40. Some critics (e.g., G. M. A. Grube, *Drama of Euripides*, 185; W. Zurcher, *Die Darstellung des Menschen im Drama des Euripides* [Basel], 1947, 86) appear to regard revenge as the main motive here. Norwood, *Essays*, 86, is one of the few to discount it as an influence on Phaedra's decision. Whatever her motives, it must be admitted that this decision represents a considerable fall from grace on Phaedra's part, the first and only breach in the "noble" characterization for which we have been arguing; however, as we have already noted, the main dramatic purpose of that characterization in relation to Hippolytus has already been fulfilled by this time.

potential slanderer, and which, therefore, may be said to cause his own destruction.[20]

The real tragedy, then, remains that of Hippolytus, at the end of the play as at the beginning—this much Aphrodite's prologue has indicated clearly. He who is *semnos* in the sense in which the Servant has hinted (93) that Hippolytus is *semnos*, cannot be *sôphrôn*. Hippolytus in mistaking the part of *sôphrosynê*, his special virtue, for the whole, has missed it altogether.

The working out of Hippolytus' doom through the long scene with Theseus and in the Messenger speech follows an inevitable sequence which is dramatically satisfying but which requires little in the way of comment. We should note however how neatly the scene between Theseus and Hippolytus complements the earlier impression of the hero. Granted the falsity of Hippolytus' situation and the injustice of Theseus' attack upon him, one suspects that some of the contumely which Theseus expresses represents a sort of backlog of annoyance with the irritating but till now quite unassailable virtue which Hippolytus has long manifested:

> So you are that exceptional man who associates with gods! You are "the pure one" (*σώφρων*), are you? the one untouched (*ἀκήρατος*) by any evil? . . . Go then and play the impostor with your meatless food, your bread diet. . . . But now you've been found out! I say let all beware of such as these: they hunt their prey with pompous pious (*σεμνοῖς*) speeches, devising base schemes the while. (948–57, in part)

Thesueus' specific suspicions of his son's smug and haughty religiosity are, of course, quite unjustified. But that there is something amiss in the holy dedication of Hippolytus the whole tragedy reveals, and it is no accident that the very terms which have been used in the earlier characterization of Hippolytus should reappear in this indictment.[21]

The same technique is observable in certain lines of Hippolytus' defence. However much we may admire him for keeping his oath about Phaedra's secret love, his haughty exclusiveness ("I am not skilled to speak before the mob," 986), and his fatal insistence, "No man is more chaste (*σωφρονέστερος*) than I" (995—an opinion repeated with unfavourable comparison between Phaedra and himself at 1035), both give the lie to any claim to *sôphrosynê* in the full sense of the word. Hippolytus appeals with justice to his whole character and way of life as

[20]Cf. Grube's fine description of Hippolytus as tragic hero (*Drama of Euripides*, 185), to which the present interpretation is much indebted.

[21]Cf. Norwood, *Essays*, 74–75 and Winnington-Ingram, "Hippolytus," 186, for similar comments on Theseus' indictment of his son.

a defence against Phaedra's fatal slander. The irony is, of course, that it is just this fatal limitation in Hippolytus' view of life which has from the first ensured his tragic fall. Theseus' weary conclusion, "Alas! that self-righteousness (τὸ σεμνόν) of yours will be the death of me!" (1064), might be repeated with more literal truth by the hero of himself. To the bitter end, the dramatist will not let us forget this fatal quality in Hippolytus. After the catastrophe, with the curse of Theseus all but fulfilled, he cries to Zeus:

> Zeus, do you see this? 'Tis I this holy (σεμνός) man, surpassing all in *sôphrosynê*, who now, with life destroyed, goes forth to Hades 'neath the earth. (1363–67)

More Mythology:
The Catastrophe, the Chorus and the Epilogue

An exception to the human, even naturalistic motivation of this play's action appears in the manner in which the catastrophe is effected. In cursing Hippolytus, Theseus invokes the supernatural power of one of three effective curses (v. 888) granted to him by the god Poseidon, and it is undoubtedly Poseidon's fulfilment of Theseus' curse which causes Hippolytus' fatal accident when his horses bolt before the apparition of the sea-monster.

This sudden switch from the natural to the supernatural level, or *vice versa*, is a typical feature of Euripidean drama. In the *Medea*, where the motivation and the whole meaning of the action has been expressed in the strictly human terms of Medea's passionate character, the murderess makes use of magic unguents for the actual dispatch of her royal victims and makes her escape in the fiery chariot of the Sun-god. In the *Heracles*, after the dramatist has used a miraculous event from the world of mythology (Hera's maddening of Heracles) as an essential part of the plot, he allows the hero himself (at 1341 ff.) to kick away, at least for a moment, the whole mythological scaffolding to which such events belong. It can be argued that neither of these sudden and fleeting changes in perspective (though each has its own dramatic purpose) requires us to reject for the rest of the play the particular "basis of reality" which the dramatist has led us to accept *for* that play. The same is true in the present instance. All that needs to be expressed on the human level has been expressed before the actual catastrophe; thus the actual form of the catastrophe is not essential to its meaning. Here the poet's use of the Trozenian tradition,[22] as well as providing him with one of the most exciting messenger speeches in Greek tragedy, adds perhaps a subtle extension to the meaning of the tragedy. Plunging horses and suddenly appearing bulls can be used as symbols of human passions: it is tempting to see a daring piece of symbolism in the destruction of the chaste Hippolytus by the bolting of his own bull-maddened steeds.[23]

Only by the Chorus is the mythological explanation of human sufferings kept consistently before our minds. Such imaginative treatment is well suited to the lyric portions of the play, yet even here we may note a certain progression, in successive odes, from literal and specific mention of divine visitations to a more general expression of the power in nature which such tales symbolize.

In the *parodos*, the Chorus guesses in mythological terms about the causes of Phaedra's mysterious trouble. ("Could it be Pan, or Hecate, who maddens you? . . . or Cybele? or Artemis for some forgotten sacrifice?" 141 ff.) Following the disclosure of Phaedra's passion, the Chorus sings, prettily at first, of the sweet delights of Eros . . . and then of the dangers which he brings. In the second strophic part of this ode, the Chorus turns from these generalized descriptions to specific mythological examples of *Aphrodite*'s visitations: on Iole, wooed with fire and slaughter by Heracles (545–54) and on Semele, consumed by blazing epiphany of her lover Zeus (555–62): "Dread and yet sweet the goddess comes, like the honey-bee, a flutter—and a sting!" (563–64) It will be noted that these odes tend to move from the general to the particular, or from the vaguer to the more clearly conceived mythological idea. The child Eros, for example, was by this time much closer to being a poetic conceit than was the august image of Aphrodite; the very emphasis on his lack of cult, bewailed by the Chorus in the second strophe, reinforces this distinction.

The same shift from poetic generalities to specific instances of Aphrodite's cruel power is still more marked in the two lyrics which lament, respectively, the fates of Phaedra and Hippolytus. The first begins with an escapist motif: wings for flying to some distant, happier place. In the second half of the lyric, the image is applied to more specific and

[22]According to the Trozenian, as opposed to the Athenian, version of the myth, the Trozenian god Poseidon, not the Athenian King Aegeus, was father of Theseus. See Barrett's edition, p. 2.

[23]Compare the image of the disciplined and the lawless horses as "the beloved" is approached in Plato's *Phaedrus* 254a ff. Cf. also Winnington-Ingram's suggestion that the bull which excites Hippolytus' horses is a sexual symbol appropriate to the catastrophe of this play: Winnington-Ingram, "Hippolytus," 190, 196. Cf. also Dodds, "*Aidôs*," 103, on the "submerged desires" of Hippolytus.

sinister descriptions: to the white-winged Cretan ship (752 ff.) which brought ill-omened Phaedra to Greece, there to be smitten with the dread disease of Aphrodite.

Similarly the lament for Hippolytus begins (1102 ff.) with vague ponderings, aroused by the hero's fate, about the divine direction of life but turns in its second half (1131 ff.) to lament, in a passage of singular beauty, the once "sleepless Muse" of Hippolytus, now silenced, and to declare for the first time the Chorus' anger (1146) with the gods that such things should be. There are, however, some interesting distinctions to be made between the initial ponderings about the gods in this ode, particularly if those editors are right who argue (from the genders at 1105–7–11–18–20) that the first and second strophe are sung by the Chorus of Huntsmen, the antistrophes by the regular female Chorus. The former would then appear to regard Hippolytus' death as casting some doubt on the gods' care for men; the latter, on the other hand, pray for the sort of disposition which will see them through life's vicissitudes—and which avoids the dangers of "rigid conviction" (δόξα . . . ἀτρεκής, 1115), like that of Hippolytus.[24]

The final chorus (1268–81), like the first stasimon, is concerned exclusively with the power of Love (Eros, under the queenly governance of Aphrodite). Unlike the earlier ode, however, this chorus contains no specific myths relating Aphrodite's effects to various human sufferings; indeed, unlike any of the preceding choral treatments of Aphrodite or of Eros, there is no mention at all of the suffering she causes. Here for the first time the Chorus treats Love as a positive force whose fructifying power affects man as only one among the many creatures of the universe:

> Love flies over the earth and over the deep-sounding briny sea; winged and shining like gold, he bewitches all whom he assails, maddening their hearts with his passion—wild dogs of the mountains, all the creatures of the sea and earth on which the fiery sun looks down—and men. You, Cypris, you alone rule over all these with princely power.[25] (1272–81)

So emphatically does this final chorus transcend the specifically anthropomorphic treatments by which myth usually illustrates the power of Aphrodite that the sudden return to the literal level of myth in the epilogue comes at first as something of a shock. However, the contrast

[24]For views on the divided distribution of this lyric, see Murray (OCT) and Barrett (who opposes the distribution in a lengthy discussion) in their notes *ad loc.*

[25]This symbolic view of Aphrodite and Eros has been anticipated by the Nurse at vv. 447–50—who is allowed more than one philosophic insight (cf. 359–61) in the midst of her cajoling.

between the simple anthropomorphism of Aphrodite's spite in the prologue and the real explanations of the play itself has already shown us in what spirit we are to take the mythological framework enclosing the tragic human action. Artemis, of course, tells us nothing that we do not "know" already: that Theseus was wrong in his hasty judgment of his son; that Phaedra perished "trying by reason to conquer Cypris" (1304), and that, fearful of her reputation, she incriminated Hippolytus when he learned her secret (it is interesting that Artemis blames, as we have done, the fatal breach in Phaedra's secrecy entirely upon the Nurse, v. 1305); that Hippolytus' honourable observance of his oath to the Nurse kept him from revealing the true situation to Theseus; and so on. Eventually Artemis reaches the point. Even Theseus, whom she spends so much time upbraiding, is, in a sense, not to blame at all. "For Cypris, fulfilling her own spite, willed that all this should come to pass." (1327–28)

There follows Artemis' exoneration of herself: the law (*nomos*) among the gods that no one of them may contravene the plans of another. (1328–30) Scholars have debated the theological soundness of this defence, but surely this is not the important point. Artemis' argument may or may not be acceptable on this the most literal level of myth, but Euripides has already shown us how much significance this level has for the real meanings of the play. His scornful repudiation of such shallow interpretations—the personal revenge of spiteful gods—is now repeated, briefly and ironically, in the kind of consolation he has Artemis offer to Hippolytus for the injustice which he has suffered at Aphrodite's hands: Artemis, too, will waste no time in taking vengeance on whomsoever Aphrodite holds most dear! (1420–22) A moment later, Hippolytus, showing more tolerance and justice than either one of these paper goddesses, forgives his father Theseus—a typical Euripidean comment on such divine morality and on the conception of the gods which it implies.[26]

[26]Both Spira (*Untersuchungen*, 85–93, and Knox (Yale Classical Studies, XIII, 3–31) emphasize the reconciliation of Hippolytus and Theseus as an important function of the epilogue: Spira, as a part of his thesis that the divine restoration of order and tranquillity is a characteristic function of the *deus-ex-machina* device in Euripides; Knox, with a more sensible emphasis on the "affirmation of purely human values in an inhuman universe." (p. 31)

Appendix I

The Myth and its Treatment: A Critique of Some Other Views

1. Numerous accounts of the various elements in the Hippolytus myth already exist, and since a thorough summary of the available evidence is now available in English in W. S. Barrett's edition of the *Hippolytus*, 1–15 (with an appendix on the relevant lost plays, 15–45), it would be redundant, if not impertinent, to add another. Any reconstruction of the tradition of this myth must be open to question at various points since the limited and highly elliptical evidence may often be interpreted in more than one way.

One such question should perhaps be raised here with regard to Barrett's account. Barrett puts almost exclusive emphasis on the human and secular aspects of the Hippolytus-Phaedra myth from its beginning, stressing its obvious affinity with such folk-tales as that of Bellerophon-Stheneboea and others concerning scorned adulteresses (in intention) and chaste youths. Consequently he makes very little of the role of Aphrodite in the myth in general or in Euripides' treatment of it and seems to imply that it is not until the present play (Euripides' second version of the Hippolytus theme) that she takes any part (and that a very perfunctory one, see Barrett pp. 15, 154–55) in the legend at all. This view of the background of the myth is possible, but on the whole, I think, unlikely. Here I prefer Séchans' view (*REG*, XXIV [1911], 105–51, esp. 120 ff.) that since there were shrines at Trozen for Artemis (Pausanias, II. 31–34) and for Aphrodite (three of them, Pausanias, I. 37.3, 6, 7), as well as for Hippolytus (whose development as a cult hero to whom brides sacrificed their hair is variously explained), then it seems probable that at least one pre-tragic version of the myth (whether the original one or not does not greatly matter) should have treated the origin of the Hippolytus-Phaedra conflict as due to rivalry between the god of purity and the god of sexual love. (I am aware, of course, of the affinity between Hippolytus and Aphrodite in the "brides' cult" of Hippolytus, since it is only a matter of time until these same brides are worshipping Aphrodite in real earnest: hence, perhaps, the proximity of Hippolytus' and Aphrodite's temples in Trozen [Pausanias, II. 32.1–4, cited by Barrett, 3, 5]. Nevertheless it is not unlikely that the very different phases of experience represented by Hippolytus [and Artemis] should be crystallized as opposites in myth.) Séchan suggests that the original rivalry was between Aphrodite and Hippolytus and that the congeniality between what Hippolytus and Artemis represented caused imagination in the "anthropomorphic" period to fashion a tender affection between them. From here it is an easy step (though Séchan does not express it in quite these terms) to imagine the two rival goddesses, with Hippolytus reduced to the acolyte of Artemis, scoring over and taking vengeance on one another through their human devotees.

Neither of these two views can be proved conclusively, nor, perhaps, does it greatly matter for the interpretation of the play. Whatever the historical background, it is clear that Euripides wishes to imply such a typical "traditional" myth and then (whether or not he had imagined this version for his own purposes) to rationalize it in the manner and to the degree described in the text of this chapter. There is, as we shall see, one real dramatic advantage provided by the role of Aphrodite: it helps (whether "psychologically" or otherwise) in the establishment of Phaedra's innocence in our minds, and this, as Barrett rightly remarks (14–15), is surely one of the fundamental points in Euripides' play.

With regard to these and other points, I should observe that the text of the present chapter was written before the publication of Barrett's great edition and so, with the exception of a few added notes, references to this work are sadly lacking.

2. Perhaps the sharpest distinction between the supernatural myth and the human action in this drama has been made by Dodds: "The artist has wisely made this [mythological] framework detachable, so that we may, if we please, study this drama in isolation from its traditional setting." (Dodds, *CR*, 39 [1925] 104, n. 1) For similar views of the expendability of the gods of the prologue and epilogue for the understanding of the human action of this play, cf. Wilamowitz, in the introduction to his edition (Berlin 1891), 52; Pohlenz, *Griech. Trag.*, 272; Norwood, *Essays*, 74. However, as we shall see, some of these critics do indicate in what way "the divine" in this play has real significance for them.

At the other extreme is the approach which stresses the mythological motivation of this play to the nullification, if not the exclusion, of the free and responsible operation of the human will. A subtle defence of this view is to be found in B. M. Knox, "The Hippolytus of Euripides," *Yale Classical Studies* 13, 3–31. Knox takes the statements of the Prologue and Epilogue at their face value and regards the whole complex action of the play itself as an example of the illusory quality of human freedom and the "futility of moral choice." "The alternatives before these human beings [the four major characters in the play] . . . are chosen and rejected in a complicated pattern which shows the independent operation of five separate human wills producing a result desired by none of them, the consummation of Aphrodite's purpose." (p. 15)

However, the fact that all of the characters achieve by their combined actions a result which none of them (at least with the wisdom of hindsight) would want, proves not the lack of free will nor the futility of moral choice, but rather the *limitations* imposed on both, first, by the circumstances in which these characters are placed, and secondly, by the operation of the "free will and moral choice" of the other characters. Here we have, once again, the tragic situation compounded of freedom and necessity. And if it can be shown, at least as far as the tragic hero is concerned, that his particular contribution to the total result is illustrative of his whole character, then it will still be possible to say that his downfall is due, at least in part, to the kind of man he is.

With Knox's view we may compare that of A. Spira in *Untersuchungen zum Deus ex Machina bei Sophokles und Euripides*, 85–93. Spira's treatment of the play also stresses the divine plan toward which all movements of the characters are drawn. Thus he finds that the Prologue adds to the pathetic effect of the action, for with the knowledge gained from it we realize that men are being led to their fate in ignorance and blindness. Spira's account of the play, however, strikes one as even more "god-determined" than that of Knox, in that he pays less attention to the individual human motivations within the play. Comparable similarities and differences appear in their respective views of the epilogue: see p. 46, note 26. See also L. Méridier, *L'Hyppolyte d'Euripide*, 208, and G. Soury, *REG*, 56 (1943), 40–41, both of whom also regard the apparently free human activity in the play as, ultimately, the manifestation of the divine will which controls the action.

Perhaps the most reasonable compromise between the "mythological" and the secular or "psychological" interpretations of this tragedy, and particularly of Phaedra's passion, is to be found in Pohlenz' warning against the over-simplification of regarding Euripides' psychological treatment as simply a rationalization of the divine. ". . . when unnatural desire enters so strongly into Phaedra's hitherto guiltless life . . . a modern rationalism might talk about 'elemental force'; the Greek fancied it otherwise: he perceived a divine power which was real enough, even if one could not grasp it with understanding." (*Griech. Trag.*, 273) Nevertheless, Pohlenz distinguishes the Euripidean attitude from the orthodox mythological view. He aptly compares the former with the attitude of Hippocrates, who strenuously resisted the priests in their attribution of epilepsy to a *daimon* and yet recognized epilepsy, like all other diseases, as divine in that nature itself was divine.

3. The widely differing reactions among scholars to Aphrodite's lines in the prologue should warn us of an element of subjectivity in any judgment which we may make of them. Contrast, for example, Grube, 196–97, who finds nothing in the presentation which seriously undermines "the reality" of the goddess, and Norwood, *Essays*, 103–5, whose remarks on the ultimate (and, on the poet's part, intentional) incredibility of the goddess *as she is presented in the Prologue* tend to support the estimate ventured in the text of this chapter. Now, any discussion of the treatment of the gods in Euripides must surely take into consideration the cultural climate in which that treatment is conceived. Thus when Grube (197) speaks of the details of Aphrodite's presentation in the Hippolytus as not "so inconsistent with the Greek idea of godhead as to require us to look for satirical intent," Norwood is perhaps justified in pointing out that "there was more than one Greek idea of godhead." (*Essays*, 104, n. 3) Grube's remark on the characteristics of Aphrodite in the *Hippolytus* prologue is, of course, true enough when the comparison is with Homer. That Homer *is* the comparison which Grube has constantly in mind is clear both from his defence in terms of Homeric comparisons of the "theology" of *Hipp.* 1328–34 (p. 192, n. 2), and from various remarks in his general chapter (4) on the gods in Euripides. (E.g., on pp. 41, 43, 44, especially the warning, ". . . we should never forget that Euripides and his contemporaries were brought up on Homer." p. 43)

It is not, then, Grube's comparison of the Euripidean and the Homeric gods which one finds troubling but the inference (both in the first passage quoted and throughout chapter 4 that for this reason we should not regard Euripides' picture of the gods as exceptional or suggestive of critical intent. As I have suggested earlier, it is this very exaggeration of the Homeric on the part of a fifth century intellectual, "well versed," as Grube admits (44) "in the new thought," which underlines Euripides' contempt for such personally vindictive anthropomorphic divinities.

Grube is, of course, right in insisting (46–47 and chaps. 4 and 16 throughout) on the reality and universality, to Euripides as to us, of the powers represented by Aphrodite and Dionysus, but he fails, I think, to distinguish sufficiently between this reality and the credibility of the excessively personal (and unpleasant) characterizations of so many of the Euripidean gods, including Aphrodite and Dionysus.

This objection cannot, I think, be circumvented by appealing (as Grube does) to the necessity for the dramatist to use "the mythological apparatus of his time" (44) or to represent the gods "in a manner intelligible in his day." (45) Such obligation surely does not explain Euripides' emphasis, which was greater than that of his less "advanced" colleagues, on those features of the mythological apparatus particularly uncongenial to contemporary thought. Moreover, the *kind* of criticism which I think this emphasis implies is not necessarily of the "laughing-up-one's-sleeve" variety which Grube (45) rightly declares to be inconsistent with the deep emotions proper to tragedy. It is only in the tragicomedies that the slyer sort of criticism appears—and neither here nor in the great tragedies such as the *Hippolytus* is the implicit criticism the main point of the play.

In general, though Grube mentions (42, 44) various Greek attempts (and Euripides' awareness of them) to "purify" the traditional conception of the gods, the critic actually takes little account of these circumstances when he defends the acceptability, at their face value, of the moral qualities of the Euripidean gods. Thus, to take one example, Grube reminds us that the Greek word *theos* "can be freely applied to all that is greater than man because it lasts forever" (41) and then uses this undoubted fact to suggest that to the Greeks of Euripides' day there was nothing startling about a god being "bad." However, the point surely is that Euripides and some of his contemporaries were attempting to show citizens bred on the traditional views which Grube cites so frequently that such conceptions of the gods *should* offend them. Specific passages can, I believe, be cited in support of this view, but let us first consider Grube's point about the use of the term *theos* as meaning simply "eternal." (41) Here we must surely make a distinction, at least for the mid-fifth century, between the term *theos* (or the adjective *theios*) as applied to specific authoritative Olympians and the same term as applied to anything exhibiting exceptional power, endurance or excellence, as well as to phenomena not readily explicable in terms of normal experience. That such a distinction is legitimate we see from the fact that Democritus, who must surely have paid little heed to the anthropomorphic system of gods, could still cheerfully use the word *theios* as a term of approval or awe in the secondary, almost secular sense. (See, for example, Democritus frgs. B 112, B 129, D-K, and, for the derogation of τὰ θνητά, "the mortal" in the sense of "the transient" in the choice of pleasures, B 189.) Pohlenz (*Griech. Trag.*, I, 273, in the passage discussed above, section 2 of this appendix) makes precisely the same distinction between the mythological and the non-mythological in explaining what Hippocrates regarded as "divine." From this secondary and largely secular usage, it is an easy step to the more vulgar metaphorical usages of *theos* (and *theios* "divine"), some of which appear in the examples which Grube cites (42) as indicative of the non-moral connotations of the word. Such examples do not prove a great deal about contemporary attitudes to either the traditional or the emerging idea of godhood, except in a very few cases (*Hel.* 560?) where Euripides *may* be satirizing contemporary abuse of the term.

On the other hand, with regard to the narrower, more "theological" use of the term *theos*, by Grube's own admission "the religious teachers of Greece were . . . constantly trying to free the more respectable inhabitants of Olympus, and the word *Theos*, from the amorality of natural forces, which becomes immorality once the gods are endowed with human minds and personality." (42) The idea that Euripides contributed to this attempt at least in a negative way, by insisting that "if the gods do evil they are not gods" (*TGF*², 292, 7) Grube rejects both by his whole treatment of the gods in Euripides and in his specific comment on this fragment: "This fragment tells us only that one character in Euripides gave expression to this more Platonic conception, that the poet knew of it, not that it was his own." (43) But here Grube omits from the discussion several other passages in Euripides which point to the same conception, *e.g.*, *Hippolytus* 120, *Bacchae* 1348, *I.T.* 389–91, *Heracles* 1341–46. Since the views expressed in these passages (which I discuss elsewhere in their various dramatic contexts) all contradict the mythical situation on which their plays are based but are nevertheless endorsed by the final effect which these plays have upon us, it seems reasonable to conclude that they are the poet's own.

To conclude this discussion, I should like to make it clear that I have no quarrel with Professor Grube's exposition of the *real* meaning of the gods and their influence in such plays as the *Hippolytus* and the *Bacchae*; indeed, my own reading of these plays has been greatly assisted by his penetrating and clearly expressed analyses. Rather, it is with the other side of the coin that I have been concerned in the present discussion, for, unlike Professor Grube, I believe that both in the *Hippolytus* and, by various methods, in other plays, Euripides is attacking and satirizing the conventional and traditional mythological conceptions. Indeed, the new kind of reality standing behind the stage presences of Aphrodite and Artemis itself constitutes a criticism of the traditional mythological divinities who are motivated, like the on-stage goddesses of this play, by the baser human reactions of pique, jealousy and self-conceit. The point is well summed up by Professor Dodd's comment on these same gods in the *Hippolytus*:

> From behind this transparent satire on the Olympians there emerges a deeper conception of Cypris and Artemis as eternal cosmic powers: the very point of the satire is that they must be interpreted as principles not as persons. ("Euripides the Irrationalist," 102)

Appendix II

Hippolytus 373-87

1. The general question whether or not Euripides was introducing a contemporary philosophic argument in this passage is still much debated: see, in addition to views of Dodds already cited, Barrett, 228 ff. and Bruno Snell, *Scenes from Greek Tragedy*, 48–69, especially 56 ff. (another study which, like Barrett's edition, appeared after the present chapter had been written). Barrett argues that no reference to contemporary philosophic debate is intended in the present passage, that Phaedra's account of human wrong-doing simply reflects that indecisiveness which he regards as the root of her trouble. Snell, taking issue with this view, argues on the contrary that Euripides is here answering a Socratic objection to the idea expressed in the *Medea* (1077–80) that one's *thumos* may force one to a course of action which one knows to be wrong. (Snell cites, in addition to Plato's early dialogues, the Xenophontic Socrates at *Memor.* 3. 9. 4.) However, it is not, perhaps, necessary to insist on so specific a philosophic debate to argue against Barrett that the terminology of the passage in question surely points to contemporary discussions, not necessarily restricted to the Socratic circle, about the relation of knowledge to the good. Nevertheless, Snell's argument should be read with attention, particularly that part which concerns the alleged novelty of the psychic struggles described in the *Medea* and *Hippolytus* respectively, and the distinctions between these two descriptions.

2. No one, so far as I know, has given a completely satisfactory account of *aidôs* in this passage. My own view is that "the bad *aidôs*" here regarded as a pleasure refers to the distracting enjoyment of "taboo" subjects which, when not treated with reverence, lead to shame. One such subject particularly relevant to Phaedra's situation is obviously

sex. However, I am aware that, beyond the use of τὰ αἰδοῖα in an explicit anatomical sense, parallel usages are lacking to support this view.

Various difficulties attend other explanations as well. The shortcomings in Dodds' ingenious theory have been suggested above (note 8). Méridier's simpler explanation lacks precision: "cette lâche complaisance aux entrainements du dehors qui fait oublier le devoir . . ." (*Euripide* II, *ad loc.*); this could surely refer to *any* enjoyable distraction and *aidôs* must mean more than that. Barrett seeks (not, I think, justifiably) to cut the Gordian knot by refusing to take Phaedra literally: "she adds αἰδώς to her list as an example not of ἡδονή but of something προτεθὲν ἀντὶ τοῦ καλοῦ; she has (and so have the audience) forgotten the grammatical construction of the earlier parts of the list. . . ." (p. 230) This is surely a most improbable anacoluthon and one which would interrupt the whole sense of the passage concerning the familiar triangle of judgment or understanding, virtue and pleasure. Moreover, Barrett's own explanation (in the following note) of "the bad *aidôs*" as "diffidence or indecisiveness" seems to me (however well it may fit Barrett's view of Phaedra's own character) to reverse the idea of distraction from "the good we know but pursue not" with which Phaedra's homily has been concerned.

3

THE *Bacchae*

Adaptation of the Traditional Material

In the various myths concerning Dionysus' punishments of mortals (i.e., of Lycurgus, of Pentheus, of Boutês, of the daughters of Minyas and the daughters of Proetus), two germinative elements seem to be combined. One is that of the historical persecution or suppression of the god's cult, reflected in the fact that the punishment is regularly of a king or of a royal family for some kind of rejection of Dionysus and his followers. The other is that of ritual: this is reflected in such recurrent features in Dionysian myths as the pursuit of the maenads by the oppressor (a hunt or pursuit by the priest of Dionysus was a part of the god's ritual), the maddening of three daughters of the king (corresponding to the triple *thiasoi*, or bands of Dionysian maenads, as they were known in Thebes) and the ultimate destruction of one of the children of the pursuers (which adds weight to the identification, implied above, of the persecutor in the myth and the hunting leader of the ritual).[1]

[1]The account, in this and the following paragraphs, of the traditional background of the *Bacchae* is a summary of material which has already been collected and arranged in several easily available works. It makes no pretence at originality and is presented merely as a basis for discussing Euripides' own treatment of the myth. I have depended mainly on E. R. Dodds' excellent introduction to his edition of the *Bacchae*, Part II, "Traditional Elements in the Bacchae," both for facts and opinions, to a lesser degree on W. H. Roscher, *Lexicon der Griechischen und Römischen Mythologie*, III[2] (Leipzig, 1902–1909), *s.v.* Pentheus, 1925 ff., as well as on the original sources cited by these authorities.

With regard to the "historical" and "ritual" elements, respectively, in the Dionysian revenge myths, scholars have, of course, differed in their emphasis. A. G. Bather, *JHS*, XIV, 244–63, was among the first to reconstruct a Dionysian ritual on which the story of Pentheus could be based. (It is interesting to note that long before the discovery of Dionysus' name in Linear B inscriptions, Bather had argued for the indigenous Greek or even "Pelasgian" origin of Dionysian cult.) Wilamowitz and Nilsson (see Dodds' references, xxiii) overestimated the historical

Certain elements of the myth of Pentheus in particular (the best known of the various "Dionysian" myths) suggest further features of Dionysian ritual. The most significant of these are the representation, at least at times, of Dionysus in the form of a bull, the ritual phenomenon known as *oreibasia*, a frenzied dancing and racing in the mountains, and, of course, the actual manner of Pentheus' death, which repeats the climax of the Dionysian ritual, the *sparagmos* or rending to pieces of the sacrificial animal by the worshippers of Dionysus.

In the *sparagmos*, we are brought to the core of the mystery and the meaning of Dionysianism. The original significance of Dionysus was obviously that of a male fertility god: the incarnation of the principle of vitality and growth in nature. Hence his worship always partook of the desire of the worshippers to possess within themselves the vital and life-renewing powers of the god. More than of any other Greek god it might be said of Dionysus that his *reality* resided as much in the feelings of his worshippers as in any other manifestation. Thus it was natural that the chief forms of Dionysian worship were frenzied group-dancing and the *sparagmos* and *ômophagia* of the potent sacrificial animal (bull, lion or goat) which became identified with the god. By the first of these, the worshipper felt himself take leave of his own personality and, with his fellow-worshippers, become more closely associated with the god; by the *sparagmos* and *ômophagia* he hoped to partake to the utmost of the Dionysian spirit. (Whether, in actual ritual, the divinely endowed victim was ever a human being cannot be determined on the basis of the slim evidence; such an idea is at any rate reported in the myth of Pentheus' death, for, as Dodds explains the ritualistic significance of having the king mistaken for a lion, "if Pentheus is to be the god's victim, he must also be the god's vehicle.")

All these significant features of the Dionysian cult, as they are reflected in myth, are marvellously recaptured in the *Bacchae* of Euripides. In many ways, this is the most traditional, the least novel, in its basic material, of any Euripidean play. Even in various details of the plot, it seems probable that Euripides was following a well established dramatic tradition, for there had already been several tragedies on the theme of

element, but Dodds and R. P. Winnington-Ingram, *Euripides and Dionysus*, 1–2, are surely right in not abandoning it entirely. (The discovery that Dionysus was in Greece in Mycenaean times need not, of course, upset the view that the myths concerned may represent Greek opposition to imported Thraco-Phrygian rituals. What Dionysus was like in Mycenaean times, we do not know; what is in question here is a god clearly clothed in the trappings and ritual of an eastern religion, and this indeed fits the myth of this Theban origin and eastern exile.)

Dionysian vengeance. (Of these, the most directly influential were probably Aeschylus' *Pentheus*, the third play of a lost "Theban" tetralogy, which Aristophanes of Byzantium expressly names as the source of Euripides' plot, and Aeschylus' *Lycurgeia*, another lost tetralogy among whose fragments Dodds finds several possible parallels to the imprisoning, questioning and taunting of Dionysus by Pentheus in the *Bacchae*.) Yet in spite of this dependence on traditions of various kinds, Euripides manages to give a new dimension to Dionysianism in this play. Perhaps for the first time it is seen not as the cult of a specific deity but as a universal phenomenon: man's periodic need of release from the rational and the commonplace, and of return to the elemental springs of life by means of his emotions.

Thus to the traditional material which forms the stuff of the *Bacchae*, Euripides introduces certain dramatic tensions which shed a new light on the Dionysian urge and on the dangers inherent in suppressing it. The play preserves both the original roots of the Pentheus myth: the persecution-and-vengeance theme (reflecting the historical persecution of the new religion) and the ritual-sacrifice theme in such details as I have just outlined. Yet, since this is drama, convincingly human passions and follies invade the more impersonally directed patterns of myth and ritual, and it is this which, in a large measure, provides the new insights into the realities behind the myth. In terms of the dramatic action, the motivation of the death of Pentheus appears in the characterization of a vengeful Dionysus, irked by an unbeliever, and the traditional ritual sacrifice provides the means. But in terms of dramatic analysis, the real reasons for the catastrophe appear in the characterization on the one hand of Pentheus, stubborn and incomplete of soul, and, on the other, of Dionysianism, as an irresistible human force with potential for great good or great evil.

Dramatic Analysis

In the prologue, Dionysus introduces the revenge theme in the most literal terms. Here the tone and attitude of the god remind us strongly of Aphrodite in the *Hippolytus*: there is the same emphasis on the personal affront felt by the god and the same indication of ruthless determination that it shall not go unpunished. Dionysus feels outraged with regard to his myth (his miraculous birth is rationalized by the Thebans, 26–31) and his cult (he is excluded from Theban libations, 45–46); moreover, as in the *Hippolytus*, this emphasis on personal pique declines as soon as the true significance of Dionysus begins to appear in the play itself. As in the *Hippolytus*, the vindictive god of the prologue and the epilogue shows that the innocent must suffer with the guilty, if it suits the divine plan of vengeance. (This is, perhaps, the dramatic point of Dionysus' commendation of Cadmus at v. 10, for Cadmus is to suffer with the rest.)

There is, however, one important difference between the prologues of the two plays: in the *Hippolytus*, Aphrodite has already decided on the punishment of the offender; in the present play, the plan of Dionysus is conditional on Pentheus' continued resistance (50–52).[2] This difference has important effects on the whole play: it means (as Dionysus tells us in the following lines) that the god will be present as Chief Inquisitor throughout the action. Why does the playwright so arrange matters? For one thing, this play is as much about Dionysus as it is about Pentheus, and (unlike the power of Aphrodite which works within Phaedra) various aspects of Dionysianism as it is affected by the action can be most vividly expressed with the physical presence of the god. Furthermore, there is a Dionysian element disguised and dangerously suppressed in Pentheus, and the presence of Dionysus is needed to make it manifest in properly dramatic terms.

Thus, in the *Bacchae,* the literal level of the myth is kept more constantly before us in the visible presence of the god in human form. However, thanks to the role of Teiresias, to the characterization of Pentheus, and to the splendid illuminations of the choral lyrics, the universal human theme which the myth here symbolizes is never hard to grasp.

It is this latent theme which provides the tensions and the new meanings necessary for Euripidean drama. In fact, as in most good drama, the tensions *are* the meanings. We may, perhaps, express them as follows: the tension between the beneficent and the destructive aspects of Dionysianism; the tension between the natural, instinctive wisdom of the bacchantes and the rationalistic, sophistic wisdom of Pentheus; finally, the tension within the psyche of Pentheus himself, for it is his prurience, the obverse of his puritanism, which proves the immediate cause of his undoing.

From this preliminary sketch it will be clear that the *Bacchae* is first and foremost the tragedy of King Pentheus. As such, it shows what

[2]It is surprising that several critics (e.g., Winnington-Ingram and Rivier, *Essai*, chap. 5), tend to overlook this simple but important point—to the detriment of their whole view of the play's meaning. Grube, 401 ff., and Kitto, *G.T.*, 376 ff., on the other hand, emphasize its significance for the structure of the play and for the gradual revelation of Dionysus and Pentheus.

happens, and *why* it must happen, to a king who denies Dionysus and declares that his people shall live without him. The revelation of Dionysus, first of his meaning and then of his power, is, of course, fundamental to this demonstration. But it is the tragedy of Pentheus which determines the dramatic action of the play and the significant changes in its choral themes.[3]

The dramatic movement of the *Bacchae* expresses the gradual shift from the good to the bad potentialities of Dionysianism, a change which arises from the continued suppression of the religion by King Pentheus and which results in the ruin of the oppressor.[4] The crucial conflict is presented in a series of tense scenes between the disguised god and his persecutor, which occupy the middle portions of the play. However, it is through the Chorus and through the reports of off-stage happenings that the full significance of this conflict is grasped. The Chorus is particularly well suited to the expression of the group emotionalism of the cult, and it is chiefly through this instrument that the poet indicates the declension from a state of holy equilibrium to one of violent outrage which the persecution of Pentheus brings about.

In the opening passages of the play itself, the Chorus and Teiresias express, the one in poetic terms, the other in rational, the positive and beneficent aspects of Dionysianism. The *parodos* (in content suggestive of what the dithyramb, the cult song in honour of Dionysus, may once have been)[5] expresses the vigorous happiness, the innocent, even controlled, exhaltation of the initiate. Here the bacchant is one "who purifies his life and delights his soul with worship among his fellows" (74–75); here the maenads are exhorted, for all their revelling, to be "reverent in the handling of the violent thyrsus." (113–14) The vivid description of the *oreibasia* in the epode and particularly of the leader's thirst for the blood of the slain victim (137–38) provides a moment of sinister anticipation. But the main, and certainly the overt, emphasis of

[3]This obvious point seems worth making since several otherwise excellent studies of the play have tended to regard it principally as a dramatic statement of Euripides' view on the Dionysian religion. This is true, I think, of Rivier's analysis (chap. 5) and, to some degree, of Winnington-Ingram's more detailed study in *Euripides and Dionysus.*

[4]Thus Kitto is quite justified in his comparison of this aspect of the play, the relation between plot and character, to Sophoclean drama and in finding the *Bacchae* the most organic in structure of the tragic plays of Euripides. (See Kitto, 377, 381–82, 385 and chap. 13, sec. 1, *passim.*)

[5]For an excellent discussion of the traditionally Dionysian features of the *parados,* including the "syncretic" treatment of diverse features of myth and ritual, see Dodds' detailed discussion in his commentary, especially on vv. 78–79, 120–34.

this lyric is on the joyous abandon of Dionysian worship and on the gifts ("the land flowing with milk and wine and honey," 142–43) which it brings.

To the lyric extravagances of this exotic chorus, the two aged Bacchants who now appear provide a grotesquely striking contrast. Cadmus and Teiresias, royal grandfather and aged yet ageless priest, have important functions to fulfil *vis-à-vis* Pentheus, but the purpose of the preliminary "duet" between them (178–209) is surely to indicate, not without comic overtones (Dionysus is not a solemn god), that the mysterious power of Dionysus extends to the old and wise as well as to the young and female. Such at any rate is the effect of sprightly decisions of the aged pair to dispense with chariots and to dance all night on the mountain in honour of the god. (184 ff.)

From the beginning of the scene, the wisdom of Teiresias is emphasized: three times in Cadmus' opening speech he is called *sophos* (179, 186) in himself or in his attributes. Thus even before the King can voice his suspicions, an association between Dionysianism and wisdom is established and this is rendered the more explicit by Teiresias' own warning (the context is the new religion):

> About the gods, we apply no subtle reasoning. Ancestral teachings, coeval with time itself, no argument will overthrow, whatever cleverness has been devised by lofty minds. (200–203)[6]

(Through the timeless personage Teiresias, the poet skilfully removes us from the specific historical context, for what the new religion *signifies*, which is what we are concerned with here, is (201) "coeval with time itself.")[7]

The first speech of the young King Pentheus (who now confronts the aged initiates) is a masterpiece of characterization: each disclosure with which he thinks to unveil the new religion reveals the King himself:

> . . . Our women, I hear, have abandoned our homes [ἡμῖν (217) has something of "disadvantage" in it] for feigned Bacchic revels scampering about in bushy hiding-places in the hills. . . . Full stand the wine bowls midst their revelling bands, as now one and now another girl goes slinking off to serve some master's lusts, pretending (would you believe it?) to be "inspired maenads"! Not Bacchus but Aphrodite is their leader! (217–25, in part)

---

[6]Concerning this and other passages in the play involving *sophos, to sophon, sophia, to phronein* and *nomos*, see also the appendix to this chapter.

[7]Dodds, on the other hand, regards the "glaring anachronism" of Teiresias' reference to ancestral traditions (201) as "a warning to the audience that the debate which follows will represent a fifth century controversy transposed into the mythical past."

Of the alleged god, it is his "newness" (contrast the wise Teiresias' complete disregard for this aspect) and his suspected attraction for women ("blond scented hair, fresh face and bedroom eyes!" 235–36) which particularly arouse Pentheus' ire. Throughout the speech, the telling choice of words, the vivid images reveal the heart of Pentheus and serve to anticipate the scene in which the god will lure him to his doom: the King's righteous wrath, here misapplied, assails the very deeds to which he would be privy.

The action of the whole central portion of the play, from this manifesto of Pentheus' till his dreadful "seduction" by Dionysus (810 ff.), presents a series of tests or "revelations" by which the King is given ever stronger and more compelling inducements to believe in the divinity of the god he is rejecting. The first of these is the quietest, though morally and "philosophically" the most persuasive: the favourable witness of Cadmus and more particularly of Teiresias, which carries the weight of family authority and of traditional religious wisdom.[8]

The ambiguity of Teiresias' role lies in the paradox that Teiresias the wise man (the initial emphasis on his wisdom has already been remarked) is here used as a champion of Dionysianism, the realm of irrational ecstasy. On the one hand, the prophet, in revealing that the new religion is allied with the traditional, instinctive "wisdom of the ages," indicates the proper limits of more sophisticated thought. (See specifically vv. 200–3, but the account, at vv. 274–83, of the two elements which control men's life really embodies the same belief.) On the other hand, in contrast with the more "manic" effects of the Chorus (not to mention the off-stage maenads and indeed the whole terrifying action of the play), Teiresias does represent the philosophic, the intellectual acceptance of Dionysianism. Thus, even as he deprecates the overconfident rationalism which would reject this mysterious force, he allows the King (and us) to look at Dionysianism in something like the light of reason. In so doing, it is inevitable (considering his poet and

[8]This view of Cadmus and Teiresias is, I am aware, at variance with majority opinion which tends to regard both portraits as essentially satirical. The unfavourable interpretation of the pair is expressed most strongly by Deichgräber, who likens Cadmus to a pragmatic, political sophist, a "profit-calculator" from the fifth-century scene and Teiresias to a theological sophist with a spate of fifth-century rhetoric thrown in. (See Deichgräber, *Hermes* LXX [1935], 322–49.) Admittedly there may be satirical touches in both presentations, but overemphasis on these distracts attention, I think, from the main dramatic function of Cadmus and particularly Teiresias as the first of several warnings (they are, after all, men of great authority and the sequel proves them right) to Pentheus not to continue his persecution of Dionysus.

the times) that he should blend the mythical tradition, in which "dramatically" he speaks, with the language of fifth century sophistic thought.

As one of the inducements to acceptance of the new religion, Teiresias "rationalizes"—or at least reduces the absurdity of—certain incredible stories of Dionysus' birth at which he imagines (286–87) certain hard-headed rationalists like Pentheus may laugh. True to the role we have described as his, he shows that this kind of fundamentalism is not in question; he provides instead another "myth" explaining how the first "impossible story" arose—a "pseudo-scientific" account, perhaps,[9] but one in which the details (whether we accept them or not) have no bearing on Dionysus himself. More impressive, however, is the prophet's explanation of the real meaning of Dionysus, especially in his positive and beneficent aspect, for man. He tells us, in effect, that man cannot live by bread alone; that to Demeter's "dry element" Dionysus adds the moist draught of the grapes as a complementary portion, that draught "which brings to weary men relief from pain, which brings sleep, a release from the ills of every day and which is the only cure for all our woes." (280–84) For the rest, Teiresias adds one or two of the enthusiastic "manic" effects of Dionysus, by which the god will be a boon to the state and a bane to her enemies: prophecy (a significant admission from Apollo's priest) and, in battle, panic affecting whole armies before they can even touch the spear. (298–305) The King's suspicions, too, are simply answered: self-control (τὸ σωφρονεῖν, 316) lies in the worshipper's own nature and so the chaste initiate will not be corrupted by the Bacchic revels (315–18)—an explanation to which the admonition τοῦτο σκοπεῖν χρή adds again the note of prophetic irony.

Whatever Pentheus (or we) may think of the sophistic aspects of Teiresias' defence of Dionysianism, dramatically the important point must still be that, with all his traditional authority, he *has* defended it. In these terms, it is the prophetic warning of the wise man which is most significant for Pentheus and for the action of the play:

> . . . this god you will see . . . great throughout Greece. Pentheus, mark my words: Don't boast that force has real power in mortal affairs and don't, if you have some opinion which is really sick and false, mistake that thought for wisdom. (309–12)

It is the Chorus which, in the ensuing *stasimon*, picks up the essential thematic material in Teiresias' statements about wisdom, cleverness and the Dionysian spirit. Throughout the play, the Chorus is, of course, the instrument which conveys the essential Dionysian ecstasy, first in

[9] Cf. above, note 8.

joy and then in fury, just as it is the recorder of the Dionysian reaction to the various successive stages in the King's long battle with the god. Now, therefore, the Chorus (370–433) combines its plaint against the *hybris* and impious cleverness (374 ff., 395–96) with a vivid account of the joy and peace which Dionysus can bring to the humble heart. In all this, the lyric extends and deepens Teiresias' meaning in a way which, for all his powers, is quite beyond the prophet: the joys of Dionysianism can here be expressed with an immediacy possible only in the choral song and dance. In the cries of the maenads, the praise of the traditional earthy wisdom at which the philosophic Teiresias has hinted acquires a more authentic ring.[10]

> [Dionysus] . . .
> Whose gifts are joy and union of soul in dancing,
> Joy in music of flutes,
> Joy when sparkling wine at feasts of the gods
> Soothes the sore regret,
> Banishes every grief,
> When the reveller rests, enfolded deep
> In the cool shade of ivy-shoots,
> On wine's soft pillow of sleep. (378–85)[11]

Cleverness is not wisdom, nor is it wisdom to ponder matters beyond mortal ken. Life is short: who would pursue such lofty thoughts would miss the present pleasure. Not for me the mad and foolish ways of such as these. (395–401)

As the King persists in the persecution of the god and his followers, there follows a sequence of miracles, awesome proofs, in an ascending scale, of the divinity which Pentheus questions. In a series of "cat-and-mouse" scenes between these miracles, the "captive" Dionysus, disguised as his own priest, makes trial of Pentheus and gently leads him on. Each of these miracles suggests a different aspect of the god, while the irony of the intervening dialogues reflects a potentially sinister combination of gentleness and power.

The first miracle symbolizes the liberating force of Dionysus. Even

[10]Contrast Winnington-Ingram's treatment of this choral ode (*Euripides and Dionysus*, chap. 5); he finds the Chorus's development of Teiresias' theme of sanity and wisdom so paradoxical that he doubts not its sincerity but its self-knowledge: ". . . there is an element of frenzy and cruelty in Bacchic worship that never emerges from this ode at all." (60) Here and elsewhere (cf. *Euripides and Dionysus*, chap. 7 and note 16, below) Winnington-Ingram fails to see that the dangerously destructive element in Dionysianism need not arise unless the religion, or the Dionysian impulse, is too rigorously suppressed.

[11]Philip Vellacott's translation.

as the servant leads in the captive Dionysus, "this beast gentle and submissive towards us" (436–37), he announces the miraculous escape of the Theban maenads from Pentheus' chains. This irony (which is lost on Pentheus) is sustained throughout the scene by the god's quiet confidence before the bullying threats of his tormentor. The themes of the preceding episode and chorus are sounded once again. First, there is the old quarrel about "wisdom" (here the play on the words for "wisdom," "moderation" and "right conduct" clearly indicates the ethical overtones of Dionysus' claims [see especially vv. 483–84; 489–90; 504]); then come the usual suspicions about sexual license afforded by the Dionysian rites (here the King's insistent curiosity about the *night-time* orgies [469, 471, 485, 487] is itself a little suspect); at the end of the episode, Pentheus' threat to strip Dionysus of his sacred accoutrements (the *thyrsus*, the flowing locks of hair, 493–96) anticipates the subsequent unmanning of Pentheus himself in his later attempts to strip the veil of secrecy from the Dionysian rites.

In the following *stasimon*, the Chorus continues its celebration of Dionysian myth and cult, but now the note of joy begins to give way to the plaintive fear of the oppressor as the maenads ponder the imprisonment of their leader. The description of Pentheus as a chthonic, dragon-sired monster (538–42) is suggestive both of the "gigantic" qualities of a theomachist and, perhaps, of a latent Dionysianism;[12] this "monstrous" aspect of Pentheus reappears in his own distorted image of himself (945–46, 949–50) when he has fallen completely under the sway of Dionysus. And in the prayers of the Chorus the *thyrsus* appears for the first time as a weapon against the *hybris* of the oppressor.

If the first miracle, the freeing of the Theban women, is meant to suggest the liberating power of Dionysianism, the "palace miracles" must surely symbolyze its destructive force within any individual who would suppress it. Dionysus' account of his escape, in which Pentheus is described as struggling and panting to ensnare a phantom bull, underlines, perhaps, the sexual aspect of Pentheus' private struggle.[13] The earthquake which, again according to Dionysus, "destroys the palace of King Pentheus," is a continuation, on a larger, less intimate scale, of this portent of the god's destructive power; and the springing up of the flame over Semele's tomb is yet another manifestation of his divinity.

[12]Cf. Winnington-Ingram, 79–80.

[13]Cf. *ibid.*, 84, also 8–9, and Dodds, notes to vv. 618–21. In the puritanical psyche of Pentheus, the Dionysian instinct has gone astray. As Winnington-Ingram remarks of this passage, ". . . the true, the essential Dionysus is sitting close at hand, biding his time."

That this destruction did not occur in any completely literal sense has been well established by various scholars. The *Bacchae* is not realistic drama, and here, as Winnington-Ingram has well observed, "it is essential to hold fast to the symbolic interpretation." No one has any difficulty in believing in the phantom quality of the bull which Dionysus describes Pentheus as struggling with, and whose *effect* on Pentheus, as well as on ourselves, is real enough. It is the same with the alleged destruction of the palace. The fact that Pentheus emerges from the palace with no mention of this destruction indicates, as Winnington-Ingram has shown, that "he has come less from a scene of real cataclysm than from a nightmare of terrors and phantoms and futile struggles in the dark." Now some spectacular or theatrical manifestation of these powerful effects is needed, just as, on the literal level, a messenger speech is often supported by the subsequent showing of a murdered or a dying hero. Such a need would here be satisfied by a sheet of flame from the tomb of Semele and by the Chorus's onstage observation of cracks (not necessarily visible to the audience) in the lintels of the temple columns.[14]

The Herdsman's account of the bacchantes on the mountain presents the last of the miracles by which the *amathia* of Pentheus is tested. This time the revelation is effected on a still broader and more terrifying scale, including yet transcending the partial revelations already made and anticipating the horrors still to come.

So far the Chorus has shown us something of the peaceful liberation of the Dionysian urge, and the characterization of Pentheus, together with his hopeless struggles to imprison the god, has suggested the dangers, within the individual, of suppressing it. Now we are given a first-hand account of what happens within the *thiasos* itself (that *group* manifestation of Dionysianism which is its only true fulfilment) when the impulse of the god is interfered with. The most striking feature of this account is, of course, the contrast between the *thiasoi* (or bands of maenads) before and after they are hunted by the herdsmen of the King.[15] By his description of the modest, sleeping maenads, the messen-

[14]Of the many discussions of this vexed passage (*Bacchae*, 604–41), I have found Winnington-Ingram, 82–84, Norwood, *Essays*, 52–64 and Dodds' note *ad loc.* particularly useful. My own account follows Winnington-Ingram's account the most closely of the three. I agree with Norwood's criticism (54) of Grube (410) that *δώματ' ἔρρηξεν χαμᾶζε* can hardly refer simply to the destruction of Pentheus' stables or outhouses. Dodds, however, appears to agree with Grube on this point.

[15]Other critics have, of course, remarked on this contrast and its significance. See, for example, Grube, 412–13.

ger specifically gives the lie to Pentheus' prurient suggestions. ("With limbs relaxed in slumber, they lay in random yet modest postures on the ground, just as they'd fallen; not as *you* say, drunk and seeking Cypris in the forest's solitude." 683–88) This impression continues as, through the Herdsman's eyes, we watch the maenads wake and rise up ("a spectacle of wondrous grace to see"), don their ritual garb and go about their Bacchic activities. These include (699–713) suckling the young of wild gazelles and wolves and breakfasting in the woods on milk, honey and wine secured by the mere tap of the *thyrsus*—a nice symbol of escape for women from the mundane activities of their "real" world.[16]

Not until the herdsmen attempt to capture them do the maenads go berserk. Now for the first time the dread *thyrsus* is raised in violence and, as the herdsmen flee (a vivid illustration of that "panic" effect of Dionysus which Teiresias has mentioned), there follow the rending of the cattle and the plundering of the villages at the hands of the rampaging women. In this brilliant passage we have, of course, a representation of the ritual Dionysian *sparagmos*, as well as an indication of the terrible catastrophe awaiting Pentheus. As in the case of the *sparagmos* of Pentheus, we see what happens when the Dionysian instinct surges wildly out of control in reaction to such dangerous repression.

The *Bacchae* is a drama of tensions, external and internal, and so we may expect violent changes in direction on the part of its warring elements, as one force yields suddenly to another, or as one aspect of character suddenly reappears in a different and more powerful guise. One such *volte-face* we have just encountered in the terrifying transformation of the Theban *thiasoi*. Another now occurs in the soul of Pentheus. After summoning the troops against the raging maenads and rejecting with suspicion Dionysus' last attempts to dissuade him, Pentheus suddenly finds himself agreeing to follow Dionysus to the hills, there to indulge in the guilty joy of spying on the bacchantes.

Critics have tended to attribute Pentheus' sudden yielding to Dionysus simply to the supernatural mesmerization of the god. It is true that Dionysus, when he finally decides to lure Pentheus to his destruction, radically changes his approach: instead of seeking to dissuade the King, he now appears to abet his efforts to circumvent the maenads. But in bringing the suspicious King within his power, Dionysus makes use

[16]Winnington-Ingram (92 and 97 and chap. 7 *passim.*), views this part of the description of the Theban maenads in a much more sinister light, finding even their more peaceful activities indicative of the Dionysian revolt against all civilized values.

of tendencies already present in the psyche of Pentheus. The most startling break in the King's resistance to the god comes with his sudden admission of a desire to see the maenads at their secret revels. (811–12) Even here, the policeman in Pentheus still masks the guilty puritan *voyeur* and the unconscious blend of motives is brilliantly illustrated in the assertions, wrung from him by the god, first of the pain, then of the pleasure, which the prospective sight will bring him. (813–16) Thus, in the first of these so-called mesmerizing scenes, it is the natural rather than the supernatural element which dominates. In the *last* scene between the god and the King this emphasis is reversed. In this grimly comic sequence, Pentheus, dressed as a bacchante, tittivates like a girl before a party and shows in other ways that he is beside himself, that the god has now "possessed" him. Dionysus himself has indicated the kind of difference we may expect between the two scenes we are discussing: for at the end of the first (as he leads Pentheus indoors) he cries:

> Dionysus, to your work . . . first cast him from his wits, setting a touch of madness on him: while sane, he'll never willingly don female garb, but mad, he will. (849–53)

Even so, this divine madness, this "possession" of the King by the god, is not completely contrary to his nature. We have already seen signs of the suppressed Dionysian in Pentheus, and Teiresias has told us that true *sôphrosynê* will not be corrupted by the god. (314–18) Under Pentheus' suppression, Dionysianism has turned perverse—in the King himself as in his female subjects. On stage, it takes the maddening of the King to make this manifest.

Thus the maddening of Pentheus has its *beginnings*, at least, in psychological realism. This blending of the natural and the supernatural is, on occasion, a very typical Euripidean device. The power and meaning of Dionysianism finds its best dramatic expression in mythical terms, but it is by such means as these that the poet lets us see the reality beneath the symbol.

The ironic effect of the "cat-and-mouse" scenes between Pentheus and Dionysus reaches a new height in this last encounter. Previously, that effect has depended on our awareness of the *real* contrast in power between the bullying King and the gently submissive god. Now the tragic delusion on which Pentheus' personality is based takes on a new and more terrifying dimension: the inspired King acquires a Dionysian urge for effeminate grace even as he feels the strength within himself to overthrow the mountain with his own bare hands. In both these aberrations the subtle deceptions of Dionysus (an Iago to Pentheus' noble, self-deluding Othello) encourage him, till finally the King's responses blend with the god's to bring the irony to its excruciating climax:

DIONYSUS: You will come home borne aloft . . .
PENTHEUS: What luxury you forecast for me!
DIONYSUS: . . . in your mother's arms.
PENTHEUS: You'll spoil me with such treatment!
DIONYSUS: What a spoiling *that* will be!
PENTHEUS: And yet it is my due. (968–70)

The choral odes which complement the various exchanges between Pentheus and Dionysus trace a gradual declension from the serene joy of the early odes to savage fury as the destructive power of Dionysianism is finally unleashed. We have already noted in the second stasimon (at 537 ff.) the beginnings of the Chorus's fear of the "monster" Pentheus and the first hints (550 ff.) at violence and vengeance. This destructive note recurs with more sinister emphasis in the third stasimon (862–911) which follows the gods' decision to end the trial and begin the punishment of Pentheus.

In the opening strophe (862–76), the maenad's rapture in the all-night revels is likened, in a brilliant image, to the delight of a fawn, who has finally escaped the huntsman's pack; here, too, the fawn's joy in the leafy stillness beyond the river reflects the Chorus's own relief at the coming deliverance from Pentheus.

In the antistrophe (882–96) the theme changes from escape to retribution: the slow and secret hunting down of the unholy, of those who seek to know more than what tradition has sanctified as natural for men.[17] Even here the hint of vengeance is restrained: the Chorus dwells rather on the impersonal working out of divine justice.

Only in the refrain which follows both strophes do we catch a note of triumph more personal and violent:

What, then, is "cleverness" (*τί τὸ σοφόν*)? Or, mid mortals, what prize from the gods is nobler[18] than to hold a triumphant hand over the heads of one's enemies? And what is noble is forever dear. (877–81; 897–901)

---

[17]In my understanding of this and the following passage (i.e., 895–96, 897–901 — 877–81) and, indeed, of this chorus as a whole, I have depended heavily on Dodds' admirable discussion. His notes also provide a summary of various other views of the debated passages.

[18]I read *ἤ τί κάλλιον* at 877 and 897—the reading defended by Paley and Dodds in their notes.

Thus the violent joy of vengeance replaces, for a moment, the old distinctions between true and false wisdom which the Chorus had picked up from Teiresias. It is only a flash—the concluding epode returns to the "escape theme" on an almost platitudinous level—but it shows us in what direction the Chorus, and so the Dionysiac spirit, is turning as a result of Pentheus' suppression.

In their final lyric before the catastrophe, the full destructive fury of the Chorus is at last unleashed. As Dionysus leads his victim to the mountain, these Asiatic maenads join in the coming *sparagmos* of Pentheus by summoning "the swift hounds of Lyssa" to inspire their Theban sisters. Then, in a passage reminiscent (save for its joy) of Cassandra's vision in the *Agamemnon*, and of that lyric in *Medea* (976 ff.) which anticipates the action of the poisoned robes, they picture Agave's first sighting of her spying son and the beginnings of her fell delusion. The increased fury of this lyric is emphasized by the fact that the only moderate passage in it now comes in the antistrophe, which includes yet one more glance at the old quarrel between *to sophon* and the Dionysian life.[19] But the effect of this milder passage is somewhat qualified by the savage refrain (991–96; 1011–16), a scream for bloody justice, which surrounds it.

The last song of the Chorus (1153–64) comes after the Messenger's announcement of the terrible *sparagmos* of Pentheus at the hands of his mother and the Theban maenads. It is a καλλίνικος ὕμνος—a pure song of triumph without pity for the violent destruction of Pentheus—and nothing more. The Chorus has come full cycle in its declension from innocent joy to savage delight in the destruction of the enemy.

The Messenger's account of Pentheus' destruction needs little comment.[20] Perhaps the most striking feature of this splendid passage is the skill with which the poet has adapted these traditional and symbolic features of the Bacchic *sparagmos* to the dramatic requirements of his narrative. Thus Agave's madness creeps on her gradually: at first she sees both beast and human spy, later, only the beast (1108–9; 1141–42); as for the tree, it is Pentheus himself who, ever his own worst enemy, requests this vantage-point for spying on the maenads. Through-

[19]This passage is discussed below, in the appendix to this chapter.

[20]For discussions of the possible ritual significance of various aspects of this description, see, among others, Bather, *JHS*, XIV, 249 ff.; George Thomson, *Aeschylus and Athens*, 139 ff., 166 ff.; Dodds, xiv–xviii, and notes on vv. 1058–75, 1096–98. Winnington-Ingram (24, n. 1), while admitting that Euripides here uses themes provided by ritual, questions the view that the poet actually had the ritual itself in mind.

out the speech, the poet succeeds in repeating, without loss of dramatic power, themes basic to the meaning of the play: witness the brief glimpse we are given (1051–57) of peaceful and joyous maenads, *before* they are disturbed; witness, too, the mysterious inability of Pentheus to see them in this state! (1058) And finally, when the whole dread tale is told, the Messenger himself answers the Chorus's earlier questions (877–81) about what is the wisest and what the fairest thing for man:

> Humility (τὸ σωφρονεῖν) and reverence in matters divine: this is fairest, and I think too that this is the wisest practice for men who follow it.
> (1150–52)

This is precisely the lesson which Teiresias the wise had sought to teach Pentheus.

The *exodos* of this play draws together its human and divine elements in a remarkably successful blend of realistic drama and effective "theatre." In the savage little *kommos* preceding it, the chorus has cruelly played on the delusion of Agave as she carries on-stage the head of Pentheus. In sharp contrast with this cruelty is the gentle ministering of Cadmus who now leads his daughter step by step back to reality. The psychological subtlety of this passage greatly enhances its pathos: the climax of Agave's dreadful recognition is, perhaps, the play's most poignant moment. Hard on this discovery comes the spectacular appearance of Dionysus, who states, in the pitiless terms typical of Euripidean gods, the reasons for all this suffering. (1340–43) Since the god had been present in disguised form throughout the play, this appearance in the full authority and glory of the godhood which he has so awesomely established strikes one as dramatically more appropriate than many of Euripides' theophanies.

The role of Cadmus throughout the *exodos* is interesting and important. It is through Cadmus, the least guilty member of his family, that the dramatist expresses most fully an awareness of the family's collective guilt (1249–50, 1297, 1302 ff.: it should be noted, however, that in none of these passages does Cadmus mention any specific fault of his own in connection with the stated wrong of Agave and Pentheus). Again it is the gentleness of Cadmus, both in his ministering to Agave and in his homely but effective little encomium of Pentheus (1303–22) which is set up as a contrast with the insensitive cruelty of the god and his followers, the Chorus. Thus it is fitting that it should be Cadmus who rebukes the god. Three times (1249, 1346, 1348), even as he recognizes the element of justice in the punishment, he stresses that this punishment is too extreme. Echoing the words of the servant in the *Hippolytus*

(120), he declares, "Gods should not be like men in their passions." (1348)[21]

Perhaps nowhere in Euripidean drama are theme and dramatic effect more closely allied than in the *Bacchae*: as has been noted at the beginning of this chapter, the essentially *dramatic* tensions of this play (such as the tension between Pentheus' suspicious nationalism and the earthy wisdom of the bacchantes) also provide its meanings. Clearly then, Euripides is presenting in properly dramatic form certain deep convictions of his own about the phenomenon of Dionysianism. It is important, however, to realize that it is Pentheus' quarrel with Dionysus, in all its aspects, which provides the total subject of the play. Otherwise, there is much danger that the poet's statements on this subject be misconstrued either as an irrationalistic attitude to life in general, or as a defence both of religious obscurantism and of traditional mythological beliefs. The defence by the Chorus and Teiresias of the sacred quality of "the divine," and the pious warnings that man should not seek to probe it with his reason, apply only to the divine as it is presented in this play—and even here, however successfully mythology is exploited for dramatic purposes, the psychological meaning of Dionysus shines clearly through the symbolism. For the same reason, the element of irrationalism in life on which this play insists should not be pushed beyond its context. Here, indeed, the poet's subtle treatment of such terms as *sophos*, *sophia*, *to phronein* clearly indicates that it is not reason and intelligence but the wrong use of them which he is decrying. In the case of Dionysianism, Euripides is prepared to forgo that rationalistic iconoclasm which he uses with such telling effect on various tales of the Olympian gods. The reason is not, of course, that he believes the myth of Dionysus any more than he believes that, say, of Ion and Apollo, but rather that he finds in the Dionysian religion a clear illustration of a human truth. There is an area in life where reason must give place to intuition and to feeling, where vigorous thought and action must yield to passive receptivity or simply to "rest," if such values as we have seen to be inherent in the Dionysian "release" are to come into being.

Just as Teiresias tells us that man cannot live by bread alone, so Euripides tells us that man cannot survive by reason alone. Only in his recognition of this fact, only in his saving of the intellectual life by admitting its proper limitations, can Euripides be labelled an irrationalist.

[21]Cf. A. R. Bellinger, "The *Bacchae* and the *Hippolytus*," *Yale Classical Studies*, 6 (1939), 24–27, who regards the alleged switch of sympathy from god to man as one of the chief points of comparison between the two plays: "As the first half of the play leaves us with the feeling that the mortal has been unjust to the god, so the second half leaves us with the feeling that the god has been unjust to the mortal." (24)

Appendix

A Note on *sophos, to sophon, sophia, to phronein* and *nomos* in the *Bacchae*

We have noted that in the *Hippolytus* the poet's exploitation of the terms *semnos* and *sôphrosynê*, variously used by different characters in different contexts, contributed substantially to the development of the theme. A comparable technique is to be observed in the *Bacchae* in the use of *sophos*, *sophia* and various other terms connoting intelligence, wisdom and knowledge; here, too, the tension which is dramatically developed between the right and wrong kinds of understanding is basic to the meaning of the tragedy.

This antithesis is stated most bluntly in the remark of the Chorus at v. 395: τὸ σοφὸν δ'οὐ σοφία. What are the characteristics which distinguish *to sophon* (cleverness) from true wisdom in this play, and is *to sophon* itself to be regarded as a bad or a dangerous characteristic?

Throughout the play, the adjective *sophos* is used in a markedly ambiguous fashion in contexts which imply now commendation, now condemnation and now something in between. In 179 and 186, the term is used insistently by Cadmus (three times in one speech) in praise of Teiresias; in 655, Pentheus sneers at Dionysus as a *sophos*, a "clever fellow"—in all but that at which he *needs* to be clever (a nice touch of irony, since elsewhere in the play it is Pentheus who most merits the charge of being foolishly clever), and at 266–71, Teiresias suggests that even a "clever" (*sophos*) man like Pentheus may well turn out a dangerous fool. The latter passage provides a good starting-point for a closer examination of *sophos* in this play. It is no accident that it occurs in the characteristically sophistic context of speech-making, for both the rationalizing attitude of Pentheus toward the new god (e.g., at 242–47) and indeed the poet's own verbal virtuosity in the handling of this theme remind us strongly of the cultural climate in which Euripides had spent so many years.

At verse 266, then, Teiresias begins his critique of Pentheus' attack on the new religion of Dionysus with a gnomic utterance about the clever rhetorician. The matter of this generalization is that when a clever man (a *sophos*) has a sound case to argue (see Dodds' note on καλὰς ἀφορμάς) it is easy for him to make a good speech, but that when he uses his skill and daring without real understanding (νοῦν οὐκ ἔχων) then he becomes a bad citizen. The two halves of this aphorism are separated by a specific application—Pentheus, though he sounds intelligent, shows no real understanding in his arguments—a neat device for converting an acceptable platitude into a sharp debating point. The sentiments expressed in these six lines typify the attitude to the *sophos* in this play: not the quality itself (for even Teiresias is *sophos*) but its misapplication through overconfidence (θράσει, 270) leads to trouble.

The repeated use of *sophos* in the third and crucial episode of the play indicates the poet's conscious play on the word in its good and bad senses (or should we say *contexts*?). At 641, Dionysus, referring to himself in the role of Dionysus' priest, says, "it befits a wise man (πρὸς σοφοῦ . . . ἀνδρός) to practice self-controlled good-temper." A few lines later, Pentheus sneers at what he regards as mere trickery in Dionysus with the cry σοφὸς σοφὸς σύ πλὴν ἃ δεῖ σ'εἶναι σοφόν (655), and the god accepts the term in its second application. Finally, at 824, Pentheus, himself, as he begins to succumb to Dionysus' persuasive power, praises the god for being *sophos* all along. Pentheus means this as a compliment, since he thinks that Dionysus is now protecting him, but we know that at this point the god's "wisdom" really consists in low cunning aimed at Pentheus' destruction, and the base sense of *sophos* lurks as an ironic undertone.

The contextual ambiguity attaching to the word *sophos* is echoed in various passages in which the word *phronein*, or one of its compounds or cognates, is used. Here we may note (*a*) warnings against mistaking the appearance or the sound of intelligence for the real thing (as in Teiresias' criticism of Pentheus at vv. 268–71, in Cadmus' criticism of Pentheus at v. 332 [καὶ φρονῶν οὐδὲν φρονεῖς], and, perhaps, in Cadmus' own rejection of the abuse of *phronein* in human attitudes to the gods, at v. 199); (*b*) warnings against mistaking a false opinion for a true one (as in Teiresias' admonition to Pentheus not to think he's "quite a thinker" μήδ' . . . φρονεῖν δόκει τι [311–12] on the basis of a sick opinion). Obviously, the quality implied in *phronein* is in itself good; indeed the Chorus uses it at 386–92 as a term of approbation for the

Dionysian way of life in contrast to the *aphrosunê* of the oppressor. The apparent or perhaps potential intelligence of the King is also stressed, but it is the way in which one *uses* one's intelligence, in the objects of *phronein*, that the danger lies.

Of the four passages in which *to sophon* occurs (203, 395–96, 877 ff. and 1005), the first two clearly imply a criticism of cleverness, at least in certain contexts; in the third, the Chorus scornfully dismisses questions about "cleverness" in the new and pressing context of vengeance; in the fourth, the Chorus appears (amid the obscurities of the passage) to indicate a qualified admiration of *to sophon.* Three of these passages have already been quoted as we traced the relation of "the wisdom theme" to the dramatic action of the play. Of the first two it will suffice to say that here both Teiresias' and the Chorus' criticisms of the man who would ponder things beyond mortal ken (cf. also 424–33) fits well with what we have just observed, in other contexts, about the proper objects of intelligence. In the third passage, however, the Chorus' apparent dismissal (τί τὸ σοφόν; κ.τ.λ., 877 ff. and 897 ff.) of the problem of "cleverness" is not, perhaps, as absolute as it may at first appear. In the antistrophe (882–96) which intrudes on this refrain, the pious acceptance of divine power is again contrasted with that questing rationalism which seeks "to know more than the laws allow" (890–92) and the old emphasis on the *abuse* of human understanding reappears in such contemptuous expressions as τούς τ' ἀγνωμοσύναν τιμῶντας . . . σὺν μαινομένᾳ δόξᾳ. (885–87)

In the lyric immediately preceding the catastrophe, the Chorus, at 997 ff., returns to the theme of vv. 882–96. Here death is presented as the grim corrector of the god's persecutor, with his unjust policy (997) and his lawless temper, while a painless life awaits those who know their human limitations. There follows a passage which has puzzled many editors of the play:

> τὸ σοφὸν οὐ φθονῶ.
> χαίρω θηρεύουσα τάδ' ἕτερα . . . (1005–6)

Dodds in his notes correctly defends this punctuation of the passage as follows: "Since [at vv. 395 ff.] . . . τὸ σοφὸν is clearly equated with τὸ μὴ θνητὰ φρονεῖν, it is natural to suppose that it is here contrasted with βροτείως ἔχειν. If so, the Chorus, whose constant teaching is θνητὰ φρονεῖν, cannot say here that they rejoice to pursue τὸ σοφόν." Nevertheless, though the Chorus may prefer to pursue other matters, this represents at least a qualification of their attitude to *to sophon.* (I do not think Headlam's suggestion of οὐ ζηλῶ for οὐ φθονῶ is acceptable, or even necessary, though Dodds seems to approve of it.) However, we have seen that both Teiresias and the Chorus have, in their criticism of *to sophon*, been thinking specifically of the misapplication of the intelligent and inquiring mind to matters which they regard as beyond its range. In the present passage, it seems possible that the Chorus—or the poet through the Chorus—may be suggesting the larger view, namely, that *to sophon* (like *sophos*, as its various usages throughout the play have indicated) may be good or evil, depending on its application. Nevertheless there are other great things in life which the Chorus prefers (to wit, the beauty and joy which it has throughout celebrated in the Dionysian way of life) and once again we are warned against letting cleverness which exceeds the rule of justice obstruct the piety of the initiate: "... *τὰ δ'ἔξω νόμιμα/δίκας ἐκβαλόντα τιμᾶν θεούς.*" (1009–10; cf. 387, 890–92, and especially 997) It is true that *to sophon* is not specifically mentioned here in the unjust practices which the pious man is to exclude, but, remembering vv. 201–3 and 395–96, it is easy to infer from the context that here, too, it is cleverness applied at the wrong time which leads mortals beyond what it is right for them to ponder.

We should not leave our discussion of *sophos*, *sophia* and kindred ideas in the *Bacchae* without noting the association of *nomos* and tradition with the particular kind of wisdom claimed by the bacchantes. Early in Teiresias' profession of faith, "ancestral traditions (*πατρίους παραδοχάς*) coeval with time itself" are contrasted favourably with the cleverness of subtle wits. (201–2) Dodds thinks that this "glaring anachronism (for Dionysus is a new god in the play) is a warning to the audience that the debate which follows will represent a fifth century controversy transported into the mythical past." I would prefer to think that, by this conscious inconsistency, Euripides seeks to emphasize the essential timelessness of the phenomenon which is his theme, apart from the particular myth which may serve to illustrate it; if this is so, the reference to *πατρίους παραδοχάς* merely indicates ancestral recognition, in whatever religious form might then be current, of the irrational emotional element in life which Dionysianism represents. In the speech which follows almost immediately, Pentheus sneers at the *newness* of the god. (219, 256) Now Pentheus, in contrast with Teiresias, is wrong about nearly everything else in connection with Dionysianism. Is it fanciful to suppose that Euripides means to show us that, in the sense just indicated, he is wrong in this as well?

In any case this emphasis on Dionysianism as something sanctioned by tradition and by the *nomoi* becomes more emphatic in the utterances of the chorus as the threatened punishment of Pentheus comes closer. (Thus, if Dodds is right, not merely "the debate which follows" but the whole struggle which informs the play must represent his "fifth century controversy.") Pentheus, the rationalist and persecutor of Dionysianism, is described as lawless and unjust (ἄνομον, ἄδικον, 995), and as acting with unjust judgment and unlawful passion (ἀδίκῳ γνώμᾳ, παρανόμῳ τ'ὀργᾷ, 997). In the preceding chorus, we have been told that divine justice will eventually overtake such men as Pentheus, "for it is not right to seek to know and study more than the laws allow (κρεῖσσον . . . τῶν νόμων, 891). On the other hand, the initiates of the Chorus describe their own beliefs as something traditionally accepted over a long stretch of time: here the expression τὸ τ'ἐν χρόνῳ μακρῷ νόμιμον . . . (895) reminds us strongly of Teiresias' description of such ancestral traditions (see verse 201, quoted above); later on, however, the poet, in a typical word-play, uses one of the key terms of 895 to describe the lawless practice of the unbeliever: τὰ δ'ἔξω νόμιμα δίκας. (1009)

The statement at 895–96 is particularly interesting for our study. Translated in its full context, it reads:

For it takes no great effort to realize that whatever is divine prevails (*lit.* "has strength") *and that what has been traditionally accepted in time's long ages is an eternal truth and grounded in nature.* (893–96)

The expression ἀεὶ φύσει τε πεφυκός (896) adds to the initiates' claim of traditional wisdom that quasi-timeless aspect of Dionysianism which has already been hinted at in verse 201 (παραδοχάς... ὁμήλικας χρόνῳ). Dodds (whose construing of this passage I have followed in the above translation) acutely comments: ". . . the Chorus anticipate in principle Plato's solution of the νόμος–φύσις antimony, viz., that when the two terms are properly understood, νόμος is seen to be founded on φύσις (*Laws* 890 *D*)." (See also Dodds' quotation from Anonymus Iamblichi in D-K, p. 402, 28 ff.) This statement seems basic to the whole understanding of Dionysianism as Euripides presents it, and does much to explain the insistent claim (however inconsistent with the literal interpretation of the myth) which his "Dionysians" make upon the *nomoi* and the traditional wisdom of the past.

The present essay has sought to clarify the distinctions between cleverness and wisdom, and the like, with which the treatment—and in places the defence—of Dionysianism in this play seems so intimately involved. If I have seemed to labour distinctions which οἱ σοφώτεροι will have grasped at once, I can only plead the poet's own insistence on the variations on his theme as an invitation to savour them in the various word-plays and subtle adumbrations of ideas which he provides.

4

THE *Heracles*

Some Previous Views

In the case of the *Heracles*, critics have, on the whole, tended to concentrate either on the theme—the Euripidean meaning of the play—or on the eccentricities of its plot: there may still be room, then, for a defence of the play's structural peculiarities (some have thought, faults) in terms of the peculiarly ironic relation between theme and plot. If, as we shall consider, the meaning of the play appears only with the perception of certain fantastic elements in the plot, then we should not expect that plot to conform, with Sophoclean propriety, to the laws of probability and necessity.

Before considering certain opinions as to the theme of the *Heracles*, it may be salutary to glance at a study which begins with a crucial decision concerning a point of dramatic technique. Verrall's rationalistic interpretation of the *Heracles* hardly needs further refutation today;[1] it springs, however, from an assumption concerning Euripidean technique which must be rejected before any analysis of the *Heracles* is possible. Briefly, this assumption is that Euripides observes (as literally as Verrall feels he should observe) the "laws" of dramatic consistency; the fact, whether we like it or not, is that Euripides in certain (to me, quite legitimate) circumstances, flouts them with the deliberate glee of the virtuoso.

Verrall finds the chief stumbling-block to a straightforward interpretation of the *Heracles* to be a passage (1341–46) in which Heracles rejects, as the fabrications of the poets, such tales of the gods as make

[1]For a recent and thorough refutation of Verrall on the *Heracles*, see L. H. G. Greenwood, *Aspects of Euripidean Tragedy*, 59 ff. In my opinion, the weakest point in Verrall's highly subjective interpretation is his attempt to discredit the evidence of both Theseus and Heracles that the hero has, "according to the play," actually been through his "impossible" experiences in Hades.

them manlike in their passions, sins and needs. Here, Verrall tells us, Heracles rejects his own legend as well (though, in the context of the speech, it is not specifically involved). Impelled by these six lines, Verrall finds grounds for rationalizing or disregarding any passages elsewhere in the play which appear to suggest that the supernatural elements in Heracles' legend are to be accepted as basic to the plot. Thus Verrall's interpretation of the play arises fundamentally from his refusal to accept "both the criticism [of mythological adventures] and the experience [of such adventures] as conceivable parts of the same dramatic character."[2]

This remorseless logic, this canonical righteousness, of Verrall's seems to me perverse when applied to Euripides. There are many passages in Euripides where a character is permitted to doubt the probability of happenings which elsewhere, for the purposes of the plot, he has been represented as accepting, witnessing, or actually experiencing. In the *Helen*, although the plot is based on the most fantastic version of the Helen myth, the heroine herself is allowed to offer incredulous asides on the story of her birth[3] and to suggest (261) a natural explanation of her troubles (her own beauty) as well as the supernatural one accepted by dramatic convention. In the *Iphigenia in Tauris*, Iphigenia, the unwilling priestess of human sacrifice, remarks (389–91):

I think that these people [the Taurians], being man-slaying men themselves, put their own fault upon the goddess. For, in my opinion, no one of the gods is evil.

Yet in the prologue, Artemis is represented (28–41) as having established Iphigenia in these rites. Speeches similar in tone, though not as obviously inconsistent with the dramatic experience of the speakers, occur in the *Hippolytus* and in the *Bacchae*. In the former, a servant praying to Aphrodite, reminds the goddess (120): σοφωτέρους γὰρ χρὴ βροτῶν εἶναι θεούς ("Gods should be wiser than men"). In the latter, Cadmus remarks (1348), after the revenge of Dionysus has been fulfilled, ὀργὰς πρέπει θεοὺς οὐχ ὁμοιοῦσθαι βροτοῖς ("It befits gods not to be like men in their wrath"). In both these cases, the comments suggest a view of the gods very different from that which the literal action of the play presents; yet, though the asides may voice the poet's criticism of the truth of the mythological presentation of the gods, they do not destroy the dramatic convention by which these myths are accepted as the basis of the plot.

The reason why this device, so disconcerting to the literal-minded, is

[2]A. W. Verrall, *Essays on Four Plays of Euripides*, 135.

[3]Note the tone of Helen's two references to this story at *Hel.* 17–21 and 255–59.

so common in Euripides is, of course, not hard to discover. In several of his dramas, the theme (in so far as it concerns the gods of myth) is expressed by a sort of *reductio ad absurdum* of the given material of the plot. For this technique to be successful, the fantastic elements in the plot material itself must, of course, be accepted for the duration of the play, though hints as to the real meaning may be allowed to appear here and there throughout it. Verrall's rationalizations of Euripidean plots, coming in too soon, as it were, destroy the game entirely.

A more profitable approach than Verrall's to the interpretation of Euripides appears at the end of L. H. G. Greenwood's refutation of Verrall on the *Heracles*. Accepting the rationalistic speech of Heracles (1341–46) as reflecting the opinions of the playwright rather than those of the hero, Greenwood obviates the necessity of seeking a correspondingly rationalistic interpretation of the whole by invoking his own thesis concerning Euripidean plots in general: "Euripides says to us in effect: 'What you see in my play could not have occurred; but if the received story were true, what *would* have occurred is just what you see in my play.' "[4]

While agreeing with the general truth of Greenwood's thesis, I should suggest that it does not apply to the same degree or even in the same way to various kinds of Euripidean drama. In some plays (in the *Helen*, for example) Euripides implies disbelief in the whole of the myth concerned: here, where no real, tragic theme is offered, we have parody—and only a negative kind of meaning, satirical and salutary but not tragic. In other plays (in the *Hippolytus* and the *Bacchae*, for example) Euripides takes the myth seriously, but implies that the significance of the tragic action presented lies not in the divine motivation (which, by convention, the plot of the play accepts from the myth) but in an underlying "natural" motivation: the operation of certain fatal factors in the drama of the human psyche. In the latter cases, Greenwood's "could not have occurred" in the passage quoted above can be predicated only of the divine motivation; the plot itself—and the myth, insofar as it informs the plot—is used to express a serious tragic meaning. The *Heracles* lies between these two extremes: unlike the *Bacchae* and the *Hippolytus*, it implies no motivation other than the external, arbitrary, divine one, but, unlike the *Helen*, it provides a serious, tragic action.[5]

[4]Greenwood, 67.

[5]The *Iphigenia in Tauris* also occupies a median position in this scheme, but exhibits yet another Euripidean variation in the treatment of myth. As we have seen, Iphigenia herself suggests a natural motivation, in place of the divine one, for the rite of human sacrifice which threatens Orestes and Pylades. But here the

Both the value and the limitation of Greenwood's thesis show in his analysis of the *Heracles*. As a corrective to Verrall, this analysis is valuable: it shows us that, while the "supernatural elements" have to be accepted as "true for the play," Euripides consistently works to discredit such gods, as the mythical material implies. But this much is common ground for many of Euripides' plays. Greenwood's analysis does not show how, in terms of this particular "fantasy" (as Greenwood terms it, "the inseparable complex of the credible and the incredible"), the gods of myth appear as impossible while the moving and edifying human elements in the action succeed in transcending the mythological nonsense.

Two other critics have, perhaps, made a more positive contribution to the analysis of the *Heracles*. Sir John Sheppard and D. W. Lucas have both insisted that the treatment of friendship, gratitude and ingratitude in this play is fundamental to its theme.[6] Both, however, have failed to see this treatment in relation to the antithesis between the human and divine elements in the play: Sheppard, because he is distracted by the antithesis which (gratuitously in my opinion) he finds in the play between the real values of love and the false values of riches and strength; Lucas, because he seeks to impose on Hera's persecution of Heracles a symbolic meaning which the text of the play does not support. (For Lucas, Hera represents "that factor [in the predominately wise governance of the universe by Zeus] which delays and obstructs the fulfilment of the good"; it is difficult to see, however, how the Zeus of this play can be regarded as the force of good which Hera obstructs.) Hence neither critic gives a satisfactory explanation of the incoherence, clearly intentional on the poet's part, caused by the unmotivated divine intervention *in medias res* and the apparent discreteness of the three separate panels of the play. Even Kitto, an expert at explaining structural

underlying "natural" motivation has (unlike that of the *Bacchae* and the *Hippolytus*) no relation to tragic effect. Except for this passage of rationalization by Iphigenia, the play, though grimmer in tone, is closer to the melodramatic parody of myth which we find in the *Helena*.

[6]See J. T. Sheppard, *CQ* X, 72–79 and Lucas, 214 ff. Since the appearance of the present study in article form (*Phoenix*, IX, 139 ff.) another study of the play has given some support to Sheppard's arguments concerning the recurring themes of *philia*, strength and wealth: see H. O. O. Chalk, *JHS*, LXXXII, 7–18. Chalk reinforces Sheppard's thesis by subordinating all these themes to the concept of *aretê*. He argues, in terms not uncongenial with the present discussion, that the *aretê* of Heracles the Deliverer and the more enduring and heroic *aretê* of the stricken Heracles is the tragic contrast which relates the two main parts of the play. For some interesting criticisms of Chalk's view, see also A. W. H. Adkins, "Basic Values in Euripides' *Hecuba* and *Heracles Furens*," *CQ*, N.S. XVI, 193–219. This study appeared too late for detailed consideration here.

peculiarities in terms of the special meanings of the play concerned, takes refuge in an allegorical account of this play's embarrassing catastrophe: ". . . when the Labours are finished, his [Heracles'] 'destiny' ceases to protect him, and Nature destroys what she has produced and used. . . ."[7] Much of what Kitto has to say elsewhere about the triumph of human heroism in this play is true, but his attempt to explain the lack of causal connection between its parts is not helped by imposing an allegorical interpretation on Heracles' fate. We need, rather, an explanation which will account for the play's peculiar dramaturgy by showing what significant relation *replaces* and renders irrelevant the causal relation between the play's events. And since we are given no invitation (as we are in the *Hippolytus* and the *Bacchae*) to treat the gods of this play symbolically, we must look for an explanation which works within the literal terms of the divine-human antithesis here provided.

A strong indication that we are on the right track in noting certain "humanistic" features of the present theme and the contrast which they provide with the divine action in the play is provided by the particular changes which the poet himself seems to have made in his mythical material.[8] The new motivation of Heracles' labours (now described [17–20] as an atonement to Eurystheus to secure the outlawed Amphitryon's return to Mycenae); the invention of Lycus' persecution whereby Heracles may again appear as a family defender; Theseus' promise of honours and burial for his friend at Athens (as opposed to the traditional burning of Heracles' body on Mt. Oeta): all these apparent innovations contribute to the humanization of the Heracles' myth in general and to the glorification of the human principle of *philia* in particular. On the other hand, the argument between the divine underlings, Iris and Lyssa (also, in all probability, a Euripidean insertion), serves to emphasize the gratuitous nature of the gods' ill-treatment of the kindly Heracles.

Theme and Structure

The foregoing sampling of previous analyses of the *Heracles* provides us with a fairly representative cross-section of opinion as to the meaning and, in some cases, the structure of the play. It would be possible to extend this sampling but we have already seen, in one or another of these excellent studies, not only the apparent dramatic difficulties in the

[7]Kitto, *G.T.*, 248.

[8]On the first of the two Euripidean adaptations suggested below, see Lucas, 214–15; on the third, cf. Norwood, *Essays*, 16–17; on the fourth, cf. Greenwood, 86-87.

structure and inner consistency of the play, but also most of the elements in the play which may be considered important to its theme. However, certain disagreements between these studies, as well as the criticisms we have ventured to make concerning one or another of them, would rather suggest that each has considered only a part or, at most, some parts, of the theme of the *Heracles*. Furthermore, none of the studies we have considered quite explains the difficulties which have been raised with regard to the plot of the play; in my opinion, these structural peculiarities can be understood only in terms of the theme, and of the function which each of the apparently separate parts fulfils in the gradual expression of that theme.

Any defence of the structure of the *Heracles* must rest on the assumption that there is more than one kind of dramatic integration. We shall not find in the *Heracles* the peculiarly satisfying organic perfection exhibited in Sophocles' *Oedipus Tyrannus*, where every happening and revelation proceeds, by a peculiarly ironic exploitation of the laws of probability and necessity, from some previous happening or revelation. Almost the opposite is true of Euripides' procedure in the *Heracles*, and adverse criticism of its structure springs mainly from a preference for the Sophoclean type of unity or else from an irritation with what is essentially an "actual" (in places, even a spectacular), rather than a logical, demonstration of its theme. In the *Heracles*, the action of the play is arrested and redirected by a series of three reversals, none of which is *caused* by something which has gone before, but each of which, when seen in relation to the others, expresses a part of a single theme. Admittedly, that relation *starts* from mere juxtaposition, but it is saved from being that alone in that the thematic significance of each reversal is illuminated only by the complementary significance of the other two.

As we have already suggested, Euripides devoted a considerable portion of his energies as a dramatist to showing that Greek myth, literally understood, presented a conception of the gods which was unworthy of belief by a civilized people. In the *Heracles*, he shows the inferiority of the gods of myth to human heroes with regard to the related qualities of *philia*, friendship and family affection, and of *charis*, gratitude. Even the triumph, over the unfriendly gods, of the essentially human qualities in Heracles' heroism contributes to this larger theme: it is the culmination to which the several parts of the play have, in different but related ways, been leading.

In the first part of the play, the chief dramatic excitement lies in the question, skilfully prolonged, "Will Heracles return in time to save his family?" This part of the play has been criticized as dreary by some commentators. The delaying tactics used by Amphitryon are, however, a necessary part of the plot and of the theme, and to this somewhat slim dramatic potential Euripides at least brings several supporting elements. Chief of these is the contrasting characterization of Amphitryon and Megara: Amphitryon is a lover of life and an optimist, possibly (Euripides did not mind "debunking" famous heroes) something of a poltroon; Megara is a spirited heroine willing to hope only as long as hope seems reasonable, and unwilling to postpone death at the expense of grovelling before an unworthy enemy. This characterization of Megara provides us with some fine passages, such as the splendid speech (275–311) describing the kinds of enemy with whom a woman of breeding may, and may not, bandy terms. Prominent, too, in this part of the play are the bitter remarks of both Amphitryon and Megara, and later of Heracles, about friendship (see, for example, vv. 55–59, 305–6, 551–82, *passim*); here commentators have stressed particularly the abandonment of Heracles' family by the Thebans he once defended, but more bitterly emphasized, to judge by Amphitryon's utterances, is the abandonment by Zeus in whom, as father of Heracles, the family has most cause to hope. Amphitryon scornfully expresses *his* view of the contrast between his own dutiful protection of his grandchildren and the shocking disregard of Zeus (339–42):

> O Zeus, in vain have I shared my wife with you (*ὁμόγαμόν σ' ἐκτησάμην*). In vain used we to call you sharer of our son (reading *παιδὸς κοινεῶν'* . . .). For you were less of a friend than you seemed to be. I, a mere mortal, surpass you, great god, in virtue.

The climax to this part of the play, however—the miraculous return of Heracles from Hades and his triumph over Lycus—seems to vindicate the divine father. The Chorus, which until this point has suspended judgment, underlines this "fact": in a rousing paean, rich in anticipatory irony, it celebrates the hero's triumphant return as clear proof of divine justice and of the divine origins of Heracles, so gloriously protected by his father, Zeus. (Note especially vv. 739, 757–59, 772–73, 798–814.)

In the second part of the play, Heracles, maddened by the gods themselves, inflicts on his children the violent death (now rendered most tragic by the slayer's relationship, discovered after the deed)[9] from

[9]In both these features, the "tragic deed" (*τὸ πάθος*) of the *Heracles* would appear to rank high among the kinds of *πάθη* favoured by Aristotle (*Poetics* 1453b 19 ff. and 1454a 2 ff.). Moreover, the close relation, in this play, between the Peripety and the Discovery which follows it should also have found favour in Aristotle's eyes, for he says (1452a 32–33): *καλλίστη δὲ ἀναγνώρισις ὅταν ἅμα*

which he has just saved them. With this second reversal, the ironic significance of the first is realized: now Amphitryon's sneers at Zeus (apparently silenced by the "rescue") turn out to be justified in a grimmer sense than even he suspected, and the doubts about Zeus' sense of *philia* are fulfilled all the more dramatically for having been falsely lulled. Once again the Chorus changes with the action and cries indignantly (1086–87):

O Zeus, why have you hated your son with such excessive wrath? Why have you led him to this sea of woes?

The second part of the play, then, fulfils that part of the theme which has been hinted at in the first: in allowing the catastrophe which befalls Heracles, Zeus shows himself lacking in the family love and sense of duty which Amphitryon and, to a greater degree, Heracles[10] have shown. But coincidentally with this fulfilment a new aspect of the theme emerges. With the spectacular intrusion of the goddesses Iris and Lyssa, we are forcefully reminded that it is Hera who is directly responsible for the maddening of Heracles. Now, if our view of the theme is correct, we might reasonably expect that the claims of Heracles on divine *philia* should extend beyond his filial claims on Zeus. The speech of Lyssa, as she seeks to dissuade Iris (and Hera, *in absentia*) from forcing her to madden Heracles, seems designed to meet this expectation. "I have this distinction," declares Lyssa proudly, "not to feel envy towards friends . . ." (845); she describes Heracles as not undistinguished either on earth or among the gods, and clearly states his claims to the gratitude of men and gods alike (851–53):

For he, the tamer of trackless lands and wild sea, he alone restored the honours of the gods, when they were falling at the hands of impious men.

In Lyssa's reminder concerning the debt of the gods to Heracles, we find a considerable extension of the theme, and this extension looks forward to the final movement of the play. Now we are to see the

περιπέτειαι γίγνωνται, οἷαν ἔχει ἡ ἐν τῷ Οἰδίποδι. In the *Heracles*, of course, the Discovery *follows* the Peripety, but the association is still close. Since the *Heracles* has suffered so much adverse criticism in terms of "structural principles" derived from Aristotle, it seems proper to indicate that it does possess certain dramatic features of which Aristotle approved.

[10]Family and, particularly, paternal affection is, from first to last, one of the most prominent characteristics of the Heracles of this play. In the hero's first scene, we may note particularly lines 574–82 and 631–36; the latter passage concludes with a fine gnome on the universal quality of parental love.

contrast between the ungrateful gods (Hera actively; the others by default) and a grateful Theseus.

In the final movement, Heracles, restored to sanity and to a full awareness of his awful deeds, moves from dazed despair to a heroic acceptance of his fate. The triumph of this "third reversal"—the decision to return to life—belongs to Heracles, but the friendship of Theseus plays an essential part in the regeneration of the hero. The opportune arrival of Theseus has been criticized as one of the non-consecutive, inorganic features of the play. However, as we shall see, the whole theme of this play requires a departure from the normal, "consequential" order in the plot. Thus, the integration of the play depends, not on its inner relations of cause and effect, but on the thematic relation between three otherwise isolated interventions: that of Heracles as rescuer, of Iris and Lyssa as destroyers, of Theseus as reviver. Each of these interventions is spectacular and dramatically "improbable," but, considered in relation to one another, each contributes in the same dramatic manner to the theme of *philia* as applied to gods and men.

However contrived the arrival of Theseus may appear,[11] the salutary effect of his friendship is presented in a most natural and moving fashion. Elsewhere, perhaps, Euripides has exploited pathos, but here the dramatic power of the scene resides in the candid yet dignified simplicity with which Theseus offers, and Heracles accepts, that grateful love which helps the hero triumph over the base ingratitude of the gods:

THESEUS: I hate in friends an ageing gratitude . . . (1223)
HERACLES: Unhappy man, I beg you, flee the taint of my corruption.
THESEUS: No avenging power can come to friends from friends.
HERACLES: I thank you for your kindness; my service to you I do not regret.
THESEUS: Having suffered well of you, I suffer with you now. (1233–36)

From here till the end of the play, the hero's grateful dependence on Theseus' friendship is constantly and pathetically apparent.

[11]The manner of Theseus' advent and the "external" relation which he bears to the plot remind one strongly of the significant intrusion of Aegeus (at *Med.* 663 ff.) into a plot in which, strictly speaking, he does not belong. Like Theseus in the *Heracles*, Aegeus provides a refuge—though for a very different kind of protagonist! Like Theseus again, he has an important bearing on the theme of the drama he "visits": Aegeus and his problem of childlessness have, in themselves, no importance in the play, but are used to keep the all-important "children-theme," as it affects Jason and Medea, to the fore.

But more significant even than the effect of Theseus' friendship is the approach which Theseus employs to reach his friend: in the particular way by which Heracles is won back to life there lies a meaning which transcends the more superficial demonstrations of the theme and which celebrates, in a manner peculiarly appropriate to Heracles, the essentially human aspects of his heroism.

At the end of his first speech to Heracles, Theseus states his single, but sufficient, argument: ὅστις εὐγενὴς βροτῶν/φέρει τά γ'ἐκ θεῶν πτώματ' οὐδ' ἀναίνεται. ("Whoever is truly noble bears misfortunes from the gods and does not flinch from them.") (1227–28) This gnome on "nobility and endurance" is easily expressed, but to bring it home to the dazed and despairing hero is the urgent and formidable task. Theseus effects it by awaking in Heracles an awareness of the lasting glory of his Labours and by appealing almost to the *duty* of heroism incumbent on such a famous hero. Thus, to Heracles' expression of suicidal despair, Theseus objects (1248): εἴρηκας ἐπιτυχόντος ἀνθρώπου λόγους ("These are the words of an *ordinary* man"), and again (at 1250): ὁ πολλὰ δὴ τλὰς Ἡρακλῆς λέγει τάδε; ("Is it *Heracles*, the much-enduring, who speaks thus?"). Heracles is aroused to a speech of magnificent bitterness on his life of futile labour (1255–1310), but at its end, even in his sardonic admission of Hera's triumph, he now describes himself as "the first man of Greece." (1306) It is to this theme that Theseus returns; his own reasons for seeking to establish Heracles as a hero at Athens go beyond his personal gratitude: καλὸς γὰρ ἀστοῖς στέφανος Ἑλλήνων ὕπο/ἄνδρ' ἐσθλὸν ὠφελοῦντας εὐκλείας τυχεῖν. ("For fair it is for us to gain renown from fellow Greeks by helping such a noble man.") (1334–35) Heracles accepts the honours Theseus would heap upon him; his reasons for rejecting suicide spring from those qualities of human heroism which Theseus has recalled in him . . . "lest I incur the charge of cowardice in quitting life." (1348) The lines which follow the decision show that it is the memory of the Labours which causes the hero's nobler second thoughts: . . . πόνων δὴ μυρίων ἐγευσάμην/ὧν οὔτ' ἀπεῖπον οὐδέν' . . . ("Full many labours have I tasted and never shrank from one.") (1353–54)

Throughout the play, the hero's references to his Labours have all been bitter.[12] Now, in the midst of the farewell speech to the slaughtered family, thoughts of the Labours keep recurring, but mingled with the

[12]Cf., for example, 575–76 and 1270–80. In the first passage, Heracles regards the Labours as contributing to the children's danger by enforcing his absence; in the second, he regards the slaughter of his children as the tragic climax to the bitter sequence of his Labours.

earlier bitterness about their tragic outcome is a remembrance of the noble purpose and the noble quality of the Labours themselves. (1368–1370) Furthermore, it is the memory of the Labours which prevents Heracles from discarding his weapons, grim reminders though they are of the slaughter just accomplished. In this decision, we see again a flash of the old, heroic spirit:

> . . . but, stripped of the arms with which I wrought the noblest deeds in Greece, am I to die, shamefully casting myself before my enemies? No! They must not be abandoned! At whatever cost in misery they must be saved! (1382–85)

Finally, when Heracles' resolution shows signs of breaking down, it is by almost taunting reminders of his former heroism that Theseus goads his friend to steel himself. (1410 ff.)

It is not difficult to see why, in view of the theme of the play, the Labours of Heracles and the heroic character acquired in their performance should appear as an essential part of Heracles' final victory. We have already seen how the true *philia* of Heracles and of Theseus (the family love of the one and the grateful friendship of the other) contrasts with the neglect of this virtue by the gods of this play. This domestic aspect of Heracles' virtue is not abandoned in the final movement of the play; it is, indeed, one of the many thematic links in which the play abounds.[13] But the significance of Heracles as a "champion" operates far beyond the domestic sphere and it is in the Labours that this wider significance appears. Filial duty provided the original motivation of the Labours (17–20) but in their execution, Heracles appears as (in Kitto's phrase) "the mighty friend of man."[14]

Mythological Implications

Underlying the whole theme of the *Heracles* is the dramatist's implication that the nature of the gods cannot be as it appears in myth and in this play. This ironic relation between plot and theme helps to account both for the play's unusual structure (the peculiarly disconnected,

[13]In his farewell to his slaughtered family, Heracles expresses in tragic retrospection, his former hopes for his children and his loving admiration for his wife (1367–77). This passage complements the tender scene (624–36) in which Heracles first appears as the protector of his family.

[14]See especially the long ode on the Labours. (348 ff.) As Kitto observes (248, n. 1): "The Labours are held up not as feats of strength . . . but as a purification of the earth from noxious monsters. . . . There is no word spared for . . . the miraculous nature of the achievements." The other passages which, according to Kitto, characterize Heracles as "the mighty friend of man" are 698, 849, 1221 ff.

external, and, in places, "fantastic" motivations of the plot) and for certain paradoxical, if not contradictory, elements in its treatment of the divine and the mythological. A plot which must emphasize the arbitrary intrusion of "the gods of myth" into the lives of men can hardly proceed in accordance with dramatic probability. The suffering of Heracles is not predictable: since it proceeds not from some fault in himself but from the personal prejudice of Hera, it is most aptly heralded by the violent intrusion of Iris and Lyssa upon the action of the play.[15] Once we have accepted this central rupture, we need not expect the structure of the play to depend on the normal causal relations between its parts. Instead, as we have seen, Euripides attempts a thematic integration, depending on the human and "divine" responses to the principle of *philia*, which relates the three parts of the play in a totally different way.

Thus Euripides uses the incredible myth as an essential part of his plot, the dramatic means to his *reductio ad absurdum*: yet he allows his own view to show through in hints, double meanings and, eventually, "inconsistencies," as, in the closing scenes, the need for preserving the fiction grows less. Most readers must have noticed, for example, the consistently ambiguous language in which Euripides wraps "the father of Heracles,"[16] and the remark of the orthodox chorus (696–700) that, by his services to men, Heracles has *surpassed* his divine birth, underlines, with unconscious irony, this divine-human ambiguity. In the same contrapuntal vein, the speech of Lyssa, about halfway through the play, implies a conception of the gods very different from that which is suggested by their actual activities—and abstentions—in the play. But the most outright of these contradictions Euripides saves till the final scene. At the end of his mighty lament on his troubled life, Heracles exclaims of Hera, *τοιαύτῃ θεῷ/τίς ἂν προσεύχοιθ'*; ("Who would pray to

[15]Grube (p. 255) has already remarked that this scene clearly expresses the external causation of Heracles' madness; his interpretation, however, takes the gods of this play more seriously—as ruthless governors of the world who will not brook superhuman greatness in a mortal hero.

[16]Cf., for example, 1–3, 148–49, 170–71, 339 ff., 353–54, 798–806, 1258–65. All these passages do, of course, imply "acceptance" of Zeus' fathership of Heracles. But the constant references to the human paternity as well, the ambiguous ways in which the two stories are combined, the admission by the orthodox chorus of previous doubt on the matter (801 ff.), are all indications of an intentional, rationalistic undertone on the part of Euripides, and stay as such in the ear of the audience. The alternative to the rationalistic position presents a sorry picture of Zeus, which Euripides has Amphitryon express in most emphatic terms (344–47): "You knew how to make your stealthy entries into bed, taking the wives of others, when no one gave you leave, but how to save your friends you do not know. An ignorant sort of god you are—or else not just!"

such a goddess?") (1307–8) While scholars are still pondering whether the Heracles of this play could agree with the Euripidean implication here, the hero himself utters the celebrated denial (1341 ff.) that gods ever commit adultery, ever suffer, ever inflict or submit to mastery among their kind: *δεῖται γὰρ ὁ θεός, εἴπερ ἔστ' ὀρθῶς θεός,/οὐδενός· ἀοιδῶν οἵδε δύστηνοι λόγοι.* ("For God, if he is truly God, needs nothing; these are the wretched tales of minstrels.") (1345–46)

In the mouth of Heracles these sentiments are, of course, outrageously inconsistent with the hero's own dramatic experiences of the gods; since the play is not quite finished (though what remains is essentially of the natural order), Heracles soon steps back into his proper role with references, at the end of his speech, to Hera's blows. But in terms of the theme, this arresting passage (1341–46) provides the culmination of those other passages which have sniped obliquely at the myth on which the plot depends. Once he has established his theme, the dramatist can, as a momentary *tour de force*, dispense with his dramatic scaffolding. It is an impudent and typically Euripidean device to have the hero himself, if but for a moment, destroy it.

PART TWO

POLITICAL TRAGEDY

5

THE *Suppliants*

Some Previous Views

In the many studies written on the *Suppliants* of Euripides, by far the greatest attention has been paid to the political aspects of the play. Among scholars who have approached the play from this point of view, some seek in it merely the reflection of contemporary events and contemporary political attitudes;[1] others, more concerned with literary values, have found that topical references do interfere, in places, with

[1]Among studies of this nature, the following may be mentioned as representative: G. Lugge, *Quomodo Euripides in Supplicibus Tempora Sua Respexerit* (Diss. Westphalia, 1887); P. Giles, "Political Allusions in the *Supplices* of Euripides," *CR*, 4 (1890), 95–98; C. Kuiper, "De Euripidis Supplicibus," translated and published by J. J. Hartman, *Mnemosyne*, n.s. 51 (1923), 102–28; R. Goossens, "Périclès et Thésée," *Bull. de l'Assoc. Guill. Budé* (Avril 1932), 9–40; E. Delebecque, *Euripide et la Guerre du Péloponnèse* (Paris 1951), chap. 9; J. W. Fitton, "The *Suppliant Women* and the *Herakleidai* of Euripides," *Hermes* 89 (1961), 430–61. The last of these, which is easily the most reasonable of the "historical" political interpretations of the play, appeared after the present chapter was written and published in article form, *TAPA*, 87, 8–26; for a few points of agreement and of difference in opinion see below, note 10.

The similarities between the burial issue in the *Suppliants* and the aftermath of Delium in 424, and between the Argive-Athenian pact at the end of this play and the historical pact between Athens, Argos, Elis and Mantinea in 420, serve as starting points for the arguments concerning the dating of this play and the reflection in it of contemporary affairs and attitudes in the period immediately preceding 420. In this context, the studies mentioned above discuss in detail the attitudes allegedly expressed toward the Thebans, the Spartans and the Argives, and toward the character and policies of Alcibiades, Nicias and (in retrospect) Pericles, in various attempts to assess both the political ideals of the dramatist and the specific political advice of this play. Useful as such historical studies may be, particularly in the matter of dating a play, they tend to examine each element in the play for its alleged contemporary significance only and to ignore the possible dramatic reasons for its presence.

the characterization and the "epic framework" of the play;[2] finally, a few (mostly among recent critics) have argued that the political theme of the *Suppliants* is expressed in the universal terms proper to serious drama.[3] Thus, even in the more literary discussions, it is the political and ethical aspects of Theseus' and, in some studies, Adrastus' actions, and their effect on the suffering women who give the play its name, which have been most fully considered. As a result of this understandable emphasis, relatively little attention has been paid to certain puzzling features concerning the treatment of the gods in this play. This is, admittedly, a minor theme in the *Suppliants*, but it is one which, in its peculiar relation to the major, ethical theme, may help to account for certain unusual and perhaps faulty features in the play's construction. It is, moreover, a theme of great interest in Euripidean studies generally, and particularly in this instance, as here Euripides' attitude to the gods may seem to run counter to various attitudes expressed in other plays of his. Several commentators have observed this apparent peculiarity in passing, but very few have sought to go beneath the appearance, or to explain what they have accepted as a major inconsistency in Euripides' treatment of this subject.

Most commentators regard the Theseus of the *Suppliants* as a model of conventional piety and, either expressly or by implication, suggest that in this play Euripides presents an orthodox picture of the gods as champions of justice and the authors of a certain order in the world.[4] This alleged emphasis on pious orthodoxy in the *Suppliants* has led, inevitably, to various explanations of the contrast between the poet's attitude here and that expressed elsewhere in his work. Koster and Masqueray, for example, suggest a conflict between tradition and originality, between imagination and reason and even between a poet's love of myth and a rationalist's love of truth![5] Such explanations, however, surely argue a greater degree of ingenuousness and even confusion on the part of Euripides than his actual handling of traditional themes would

[2]E.g., Grube, 239–40; W. J. W. Koster, *Mnemosyne* (1942), 161–203, especially 168–71, 200–1; Rivier, 173–74.

[3]See Kitto, 221–29; Greenwood, chap. 4; Gunther Zuntz, *The Political Plays of Euripides*, chap. 1. Grube's study, mentioned in the preceding note, might also be included with this group except that this critic is more ready to admit that certain passages of contemporary reference in the *Suppliants* have been but imperfectly woven into the dramatic pattern.

[4]E.g., Goossens, Koster and Zuntz, as cited in the preceding notes; Feugère, *De Socraticae Doctrinae Vestigiis apud Euripidem*, 60–61; Grégoire in *Euripide*, 3 (Budé), 87 ff.; Masqueray, *Euripide et ses Idées*, 117–24.

[5]See Koster, 161–64, 185–87, 201–2; Masqueray, 117 ff., esp. 121, 123–24.

suggest. Euripides was quite ready to express the truths which he perceived in life through myth; sometimes, perhaps, he was helped in finding those truths by examining myths in accordance with his own lights. The difficulty springs rather from the fact that, as we have seen, Euripides treated myth in more than one way and with more than one purpose. In predominantly "political" plays (using the term in its highest sense) like the *Suppliants*, the treatment of traditional material will need, for reasons soon to be considered, to be more conventional, but even here one need not expect the poet's quick and constant sense of the ludicrous or of the over-literal in conventional attitudes to myth and legend to desert him completely. In the *Suppliants* the imprint of this sense appears, perhaps, only in the minor themes, but one cannot help feeling that those critics who complain of the unexpected orthodoxy of this play have missed some of the asides by which the poet has saved his integrity.

Like the other critics just considered, Gunther Zuntz also finds a contrast between the optimistic rational view of the *Suppliants* and the "boundless and impenetrable world" and inexorable gods which he finds more typical of Euripides. In explaining the contrast, however, this critic does not find it necessary to accuse the poet of naïveté or confusion in the use of myth:

> His compassion for the absurd and ruinous sufferings brought upon mankind prompted Euripides, for once, to narrow his all-embracing and ironical view. Identifying himself with a definite set of contemporary ideals, he offered his fellows, in the time-honoured form of Tragedy, some definite and salutary teaching.[6]

We may readily agree with Zuntz that the play is mainly concerned with the preservation of those laws without which the well ordered world described by Theseus (at 195 ff. and elsewhere) would be impossible. Nevertheless, it is possible that the brilliant analysis by which this theme is proved presents a rather too idealized picture of that world and its gods. This tendency toward idealization leads the critic to overlook certain ironies and disturbing flashes of realism and iconoclasm which Euripides allows to play around his central theme. The most marked of these provide, in counterpoint to the general serenity, touches of ambiguity concerning the gods and religion. Some such hints occur in the earlier portions of the play but we shall find, as we look more closely, that when the political action is over and the main theme all but expressed these hints are given a more marked and sinister development.

[6]Zuntz, 22.

In sharp contrast with Professor Zuntz's "optimistic" interpretation of the *Suppliants* is that of Mr. L. H. G. Greenwood. Like Professor Kitto, Mr. Greenwood stresses the pacifist passages in the play and regards it as a serious moral tragedy; Mr. Greenwood, however, goes further in this direction and suggests that not only the war waged by Adrastus but even the apparently just war of Theseus is included in the condemnation of war implied by the pacifist tone which underlies the whole. Thus, neither in technique nor in attitude, according to Mr. Greenwood's view, is the *Suppliants* to be contrasted with other Euripidean plays; here as elsewhere, "Euripides wishes some of his readers . . . to perceive that he says one thing and means another."[7] Mr. Greenwood applies this view of the dramatist's satirical intent to the apparently glorious action of Theseus and, since he believes that Theseus is to be accepted as a thoroughly pious man, to the gods whom Theseus serves. "The piety of Theseus . . . is less attractive when the divine objects of it are shown to be unworthy of reverence and obedience."[8] Mr. Greenwood's perception that, even in the *Suppliants*, there are underlying ironies and that these attach particularly to the apparently pious and orthodox tones in the play is very valuable. But the thesis in which this perception is expressed, namely that the war of Theseus is wrong and leads only to further suffering, finds little support in the text of the play.[9] The present chapter will seek to argue that, even within a more

[7]Greenwood, 92; for the general view of the play cited above, see *ibid.*, chap. 4 *passim*, esp. 92–93, 99–103. Compare and contrast Kitto, 223, who would limit the "moral theme" to the Argive follies and their results.

[8]*Ibid.*, 113. Here and elsewhere in his analysis Greenwood's arguments concerning Euripides' implicit criticism of the gods in this play are similar to suggestions raised later in the present paper; of particularly his interpretations of *Supp.* 594–97, 731–32, 778–85, 1213–26 (Greenwood, 113–14, 117, 114, 104–5, respectively). There are, however, two important points in Greenwood's thesis with which the writer disagrees: these concern the alleged orthodox piety of Theseus (*ibid.*, 113 and 116) and the alleged Euripidean criticism of Theseus' war against Thebes (see below, note 9). Difference of opinion on these matters entails a rather different treatment of the passages concerning the gods and of the place of such passages in the structure of the play.

[9]If (as Greenwood argues, 102–3) Euripides meant us to regard Theseus' armed intervention as wrong, surely he would dwell on the suffering that it brought to Theseus and his city. But on the contrary, Theseus' triumph, his moderation in victory and his subsequent serene demeanour are contrasted sharply with the sufferings of Adrastus and of Creon for their hybristic actions in military matters. Nor can Theseus be regarded as the cause, except in a very superficial sense, of the anguished laments of the Argive Mothers, or of the immolation of Evadne, after he has won back the bodies. Greenwood's further argument that this war is "wasteful folly," because bones are not worth it, seems to

conventional, straightforward theme (such as that described by Professor Zuntz), Euripides preserves something of his own critical attitude toward conventional piety and the current modifications of myth on which it depended.

Religious and Ethical Attitudes

Enough has now been said to indicate that most critics regard the religious attitude expressed in the *Suppliants* as "orthodox" or even pious, and that many have felt that the play differs sharply, in this respect, from other plays of Euripides. From the few serious explanations which have been considered, it is clear that either one must accept this difference of approach as intentional, a part of some special purpose of Euripides in this play, or else one must re-examine the text to see whether Euripides' "orthodoxy" is not more apparent than real.

What, then, are the main bases of this general impression of a conforming traditionalism in the *Suppliants*? All but a few critics agree in accepting a straightforward interpretation of the main action of the play, that the decision of Theseus and Athens is to be regarded as the right one, and that Athens performs a noble deed in aiding the Suppliants. Professor Zuntz has given perhaps the best expression to the theme of the play as it appears from this interpretation of the central action: Theseus (in his speech at 195 ff.) has declared his belief in an optimistic view of the world, based on law and order, and the Athenian democracy (as it has appeared in Theseus' account of it to the Herald, particularly at 429 ff.) is the best embodiment of that law and order within the state; therefore Theseus and Athens go to war with tyrannical Thebes to preserve, in the international sphere, those laws without which civilization, the rational ordering of society, is impossible.[10]

To what extent are the gods involved in Euripides' expression of this

find some support in the speech of Iphis at 1104–7, which he quotes. But while line 1107 *may* represent Euripides' own view of the unimportance of the bones themselves, there is no doubt that the Suppliant Mothers want them (and find a grievous satisfaction in the obsequies) nor that Euripides, like Theseus, is defending their time-honoured rights. There is no need to quote Voltaire to suggest that these two aspects of Euripides' attitude are not incompatible.

[10]See Zuntz 7–9. Fitton's article (above, note 1) is largely concerned with an interesting but ultimately unconvincing rebuttal of Zuntz's view. He argues that, despite his lofty views on world order, Theseus' motives are actually a baser compound of national pride and personal egoism, that in real life his policies and his guilt would not be very different from those of Adrastus (see p. 437) and that Euripides expected his audience, cynical from their own experience of Athenian *polypragmosynê*, to be just as critical of his involvement of the city in

theme? First of all, the idea of recovering the bodies of the slain warriors is itself related to the religious rites which the Suppliants wish to perform for them. Secondly, Theseus himself refers to his undertaking as a championship of the νόμος παλαιὸς δαιμόνων ("the ancient law of the gods"). (563) Thus on the literal level of interpretation Theseus, in honouring the suppliants, who are protected by Zeus, and in assisting the sacred rights of the dead, may be said to be fulfilling the will of the gods—and it is mainly on this basis that one first gets the impression that Euripides is adhering to a pious orthodoxy in this play. But it is quite possible to view the accepted convention of returning the bodies of slain warriors as a test case, almost a symbol, of international law, quite apart from its technical religious associations. It is worth noting, in this connection, that Theseus, in his address to the Herald concerning the return of the bodies, uses rigorously rational arguments (524 ff.) and does not even mention the religious aspects of the convention. So also, the reported appeal of Theseus' herald to the Thebans, just before the battle, is based only on the grounds of panhellenic law. (669–72) Is it necessary, then, to believe that the gods are involved in that defence of order and justice among men with which the real theme of the play is concerned? There are several passages in the play in which a conception of the gods quite incompatible with this view appears.

It should be admitted at the outset that Aethra views the supplication in a religious light. Her statements in the Prologue, the whole significance of the Eleusinian setting,[11] and the emphasis on the suppliant bonds, which continues to the end of Theseus' initial refusal of the

---

bloody battles, however "just." The argument does provide certain healthy qualifications to Zuntz's perhaps overidealized argument; nevertheless, the Athenians themselves would never object to a mixture of political idealism and national self-interest in their leaders. Ultimately, Zuntz's (and Kitto's) distinction between Adrastus and Theseus is sound; indeed the contrast between them sketched earlier in the play is dramatically underlined by the success and self-control of Theseus in battle.

In other respects, Fitton's article has much in common with the present study, particularly with regard to the Euripidean attitude to the gods in this play and (442–43) to the ambiguous attitude toward "providence" and Chance.

[11]Euripides adopted the Eleusinian setting from Aeschylus' play, the *Eleusinians* (based on the same legend), but he used it for his own purposes. Aethra's mention of her interrupted prayer to Kore and Demeter for the Athenian crops (a prayer which she now extends to include also the happiness of her own native Argive town) permits us, for a moment, to see the whole of the subsequent action as a kind of fertility ritual ensuring Athenian and Argive prosperity: the familiar elements of carrying out the dead and pacifying the nether powers are both present and surely it is no coincidence that the Chorus cries, "Honour the chorus

suppliants, clearly start the play off on this religious basis. But Theseus himself is somewhat slow to take up this issue: his first reaction is to avoid the dangers which involvement with Adrastus seems to entail. As far as the main theme of the play is concerned, the significance of Theseus' interrogation of Adrastus, and of his consequent refusal to accept his plea, has been clearly stated by several scholars: in this episode, the dramatist first of all dissociates Theseus and Athens from the earlier guilt of Adrastus in attacking Thebes, and clarifies the motives from which Theseus later *does* decide to help the Argives: neither the original rashness of Adrastus, nor indeed Adrastus' own personal character, however hybristic, has anything to do with the principle on which Theseus ultimately acts.[12] (Various commentators have also suggested contemporary political meanings for this passage [232–45],[13] but these suggestions, whether true or not, are not needed for the understanding of its dramatic function.) However, it is in this first exchange between Theseus and Adrastus, that the dramatist also suggests, incidentally and tentatively, a hint of Theseus' view of the gods.

Our first intimation of Theseus' "theological position" occurs in connection with his attitude to augury, which is both interesting and rather perplexing. Theseus questions Adrastus closely on his initial involvement in Theban affairs and discovers that it was on the basis of a

of Hades" (75) at precisely the same line in its song as Aethra has mentioned Kore and Demeter (34) in her account of the supplication which interrupted her sacrifice.

[12]This is substantially the view of Zuntz. (7–9) Cf. also the similar interpretations of this passage by Grube (230–33) and Kitto (224–25). Grube, however, distinguishes more acutely between the religious and emotional appeal of the chorus and Aethra and the more political (and bungling) appeal of Adrastus. Kitto places more emphasis on the wrong-doing of Adrastus in relation to the major theme as he sees it: "the communal suffering that comes from communal wrong-doing and folly." (223)

[13]This is, of course, one of the key passages for those whose main interest in the play is its alleged inspiration (either in anticipation or in retrospect) by the Argive pact of 420 and by the political ferment which preceded it. For various interpretations, in these contemporary terms, of the anti-Argive sentiments inferred from this passage, cf. Lugge 23; Grégoire (above, note 4), 83 ff.; Delebecque 213–14. J. Berlage (*Commentatio*, 185), arguing in a similar vein, suggests that Theseus' criticisms at 232 ff. may be directed against Alcibiades, whereas Greenwood (112) believes that the criticism of Argos in the whole of this passage (232–45) is meant to apply to contemporary Athenian democracy. Goossens (17 ff.) pushes the historical reference of this belaboured passage some years further back: he suggests that Theseus' criticisms of Adrastus' rash attack on Thebes echo Pericles' cautious disapproval of Tolmides' subsequently disastrous expedition in 447 (see Plut. *Per.* 18.2–3).

Delphic oracle that the Argive King came to marry his daughter to Polyneices. (133–46) Next, Theseus criticizes Adrastus sharply for his neglect of his own augur, Amphiaraus, when making war on Thebes in the interest of the dispossessed Polyneices. (155, 157, 159, 161) Furthermore, in his speech on the foundations of civilization (195 ff.), Theseus praises the prophet's art, based on fire, sacrificial entrails and the flight of birds (211–13), among those gifts to man vaguely ascribed to some unknown god. (201–2) There follows (214–18) a sneer at those who do not regard such divine gifts as sufficient, who think themselves wiser than the gods, and this sneer leads directly to Theseus' main criticism of Adrastus: "yoked to the oracles of Phoebus" (220), he connected his house with a troubled, unhealthy house, and, influenced by ambitious youths, he plunged into war despite his augurs' warnings. (219–37)

It is interesting that, in branding Adrastus as one of those who are "too clever" to be content with the normal gifts of augury, Theseus should include a sneer at the Delphic Oracle. Some commentators, however, take this reference to Delphi in a concessive sense, i.e., "though you paid attention to the gods in the first instance, and so married off your children at the Oracle's behest, you failed to heed your augurs' objections to your proposed attack on Thebes."[14] It seems easier, however, to regard Theseus' criticism of Adrastus as *including* his allegiance to Delphi: Adrastus' marriage of his daughter to Polyneices, which is what this particular oracle led to, can hardly be taken as an example of following the will of the gods, for it was precisely this action which led to war with Thebes, which Theseus clearly shows to have been done in rash disregard of the gods. Though it is impossible to be certain about this passage (the point is not perhaps of fundamental importance), the implication seems to be that Delphi does not speak for the gods.[15]

In general, then, Theseus' view of Adrastus' trouble seems to be this:

[14]Cf., for example, Hermann's note to *Suppliants* 221: "'Tu,' inquit, 'filias hospitibus dedisti, oraculo monitus, ideoque sic, ut qui esse deos crederes: mox autem expeditionem suscepisti, neglectis vatum monitis, ut si nulli essent dii.' Refertur hoc ζώντων θεῶν ad ἀτιμάσας θεοὺς v. 230 [*sic*]." So also Grégoire in his note on 219–21: ". . . tu croyais bien qu'il existait des Dieux!" Grube (231, note 1) and T. Nicklin (in his edition, *ad loc.*) also find the point of this passage to lie in the contrast between Adrastus' acting first as if the gods existed and later as if they did not. Grube, however, stresses that even in the first instance only "pretended piety" is suggested.

[15]Helpful to this interpretation, but by no means essential to it, is Markland's preference (in his notes *ad loc.*) for δόντων in place of ζώντων at v. 221. He explains: "Tu putabas oraculi Apollonis jussum, idem esse quod deorum jussum."

the family of Polyneices was accursed of the gods, unhealthy, and so dangerous, and Adrastus ought to have kept his "healthy" household away from it. The reference to the gods here, far from suggesting political intervention, "side-taking," on their part, supports the common-sense judgment, not to mix the prosperous with the unprosperous:

> *κοινὰς γὰρ ὁ θεὸς τὰς τύχας ἡγούμενος*
> *τοῖς τοῦ νοσοῦντος πήμασιν διώλεσε*
> *τὸν οὐ νοσοῦντα κοὐδὲν ἠδικηκότα.*

For the god, reckoning the fortunes of both as common, is wont to destroy the one who is not unhealthy and who has done no wrong by the woes of the one who *is* unhealthy.[16] (226–28)

Certainly Theseus is "god-fearing," in the sense that he wants to keep on the right side of these dangerous powers. His attitude here reminds one of that peculiarly Homeric mixture of common-sense and superstition; indeed, many particular superstitions are merely common-sense judgments translated into supernatural terms. One gets little impression, however, that Theseus relies on any particular gods, or that he has any real assurance that the gods, generally, are on the side of justice. The passage just quoted does not suggest any scrupulous regard for justice on their part, and another passage in which Theseus indulges in general reflections on the vicissitudes of human experience even conveys an impression of rather wanton gods:

Some men fare well soon, others late. The god, then, fares sumptuously[17] for he is held in high honour by the unfortunate man, that he may become fortunate, while the prosperous man also gives him the highest praise, for fear that the favouring gale may leave him. (550–55)

---

[16]It seems preferable to take *διώλεσε* (227) as a gnomic aorist, in which case we would read *χρή*, with Hartung, instead of *χρῆν*, in 223. But if *χρῆν* is correct, then *διώλεσε* is historic and Theseus is considering what actually *did* happen in the case of Adrastus who ought not, if he were a wise man, to have so involved his household. Cf. also Paley's note *ad loc.* In 228, *τὸν οὐ νοσοῦντα* (Lambinus), which Nauck accepts, is certainly the easier reading, but if *τὸν συννοσοῦντα* is correct, the total meaning of our translation is but little affected, for either expression could be used to refer to the comparatively innocent party, i.e., the one who either is *not* (morally) sick (*τὸν οὐ νοσοῦντα*) or is so only by association (*τὸν συννοσοῦντα*).

[17]*Τρυφᾷ δ'ὁ δαίμων* (552): this interesting phrase has been variously rendered, e.g.: "Fortuna vero ludit" (Barnes); "Fortuna autem petulans est" (Markland); "illudente nobis Fortuna" (I. A. Hartung's paraphrase in *Euripides' Restitutus*, 2, 94); "Und die Gottheit schaltet mit uns nach Laune" (Wilamowitz); "Les Dieux seuls sont choyés à l'excès" (Grégoire). It is noteworthy that the later translations avoid the term *Fortuna* or its equivalents; if we do so translate

On the other hand, Theseus' wariness with regard to the gods and to those who are not favoured by them, does appear again in that passage (591 ff.) in which he insists that Adrastus shall not accompany him to battle, even in a just cause.

It is Aethra, the exponent throughout of conventional piety, who reminds Theseus of his duty to the suppliants, quite apart from the rights and wrongs of Adrastus' initial entanglement in Theban affairs. The motherly rebuke with which she begins her plea tends to substantiate the contrast which we have suggested between her piety and Theseus' attitude to the gods: "I bid you, my son, look first to what concerns the gods (τὰ τῶν θεῶν), lest in dishonouring them you go astray: for in this one matter you are lacking (σφάλλει γὰρ ἐν τούτῳ μόνῳ)[18] though in all else most wise." (301–3) Moreover, after this one reference to the gods, Aethra couches her speech in terms which will appeal particularly to Theseus. It is a speech which combines, with subtle and skilful rhetoric, political arguments on both the ideal and the practical level: intervention on behalf of the suppliants will bring Theseus and Athens honour, while abstention will look like cowardice, but the goal of this intervention spells the very meaning of civilized relations between states: . . . τὸ γάρ τοι συνέχον ἀνθρώπων πόλεις τοῦτ' ἔσθ', ὅταν τις τοὺς νόμους σῴζῃ καλῶς. (312–13)

This view of Theseus' general conception of the gods and of divine power which we have been seeking to adduce may seem to contradict his role as defender of "the ancient laws of the gods." (563) Yet neither in the arguments by which Theseus is persuaded to aid the suppliants, nor in the reasons which he himself gives for his decision, nor even in the arguments which he presents to the Theban Herald, is there any emphasis on the religious aspect of his mission. The emphasis is rather on the preservation of panhellenic law and on the punishment

---

daimôn, we should take care not to regard the expression as a mere figure of speech. In all the passages in which this word occurs in the singular in this play (463, 552, 592, 1008), there is some reference to the anonymous, divine power on whom one's fortunes, good or ill, so often seem to depend. As Nilsson has well observed, this is one of the words which, in some of their fifth century usages, preserve something of the old, pre-anthropomorphic conception of the supernatural as undifferentiated "power." (See M. P. Nilsson, *A History of Greek Religion*, 105 ff., 227, 282–85.) This suits Theseus' cautious attitude to the gods to whom he rarely refers by name and from whom he rarely seems to expect much in the way of personal favour or meticulous justice.

[18]So Nauck and Paley (following Elmsley's emendation) though both think that line 303 may be spurious. However, the sense of this passage fits well with Theseus' attitude to the gods as we find it expressed elsewhere in this play.

of hybristic tyrants who would deny the rights of other Greek states. (526–27, 538 ff., 561 ff., 575) Not until the last line of his long speech to the Herald does the expression νόμος παλαιὸς δαιμόνων (563) occur: though Theseus does not (with the exception of one conventional phrase at line 348) use the gods in his specific arguments about the law, he naturally follows tradition in speaking of them as the originators of human customs in general. A similar explanation can be given for Theseus' reference to the gods in his speech at line 195 ff., in which he states his optimistic view of the world as men know it, where the good exceeds the bad and where intelligence and order can operate if only man makes use of them. Here, too, Theseus attributes the original dispensation to the gods or, rather, to some god unknown and unnamed. (201–2) Euripides could hardly have such a legendary figure as King Theseus do otherwise.

From the difficulties just suggested, it will be apparent that one cannot be dogmatic or categorical about Euripides' attitude to the gods in the *Suppliants*. Even Theseus, the least orthodox element in the play, accepts the traditional explanations as a sort of mythical background to his world-view, but these have little influence on his actual decisions, which are based on ethical rather than on religious considerations. Moreover, as we have seen from various asides, Theseus' confidence in the gods' justice toward men is by no means absolute. Indeed, his parting words (592–97) as he leaves to wage a just war could serve as the text for another theme which receives ambiguous treatment in the *Suppliants*: the idea of the gods as moral avengers, punishing the *hybris* of men.

> For with my own *daimôn* I'll take the field, illustrious in a glorious war. One thing only do I need, to have the gods who honour justice; justice and the gods: these two together bring the victory. Valour alone brings naught, unless it has the gods' good will. (592–97)

With these words, Theseus bids the ill-starred Adrastus stay out of the battle. By the word *daimôn*, the King appears to mean his personal fate which depends on his own relationship with the gods.[19] Theseus has confidence in this, as well as in the valour and righteousness of his cause. Nevertheless, there is at least a hint in this passage that not all the gods *do* honour justice[20] and that only with the fortunate coinci-

[19]Cf. above, note 17; cf. also *LSJ* s.v. *daimôn* 1.2.

[20]Some translators (e.g., Markland, Grégoire) take ὅσοι (594) as referring to *all* the gods; Matthiae, on the other hand, translates it *quotquot*, against Markland's ill-substantiated argument that this cannot here be the meaning of the word. Although there may be a touch of ambiguity on the part of the poet here, surely it is right to take the clause as restrictive and partitive.

dence of the gods and justice will *aretê* win the day. (The passage reminds one of *Hecuba* 1029–30; there too, whichever reading we accept, we find the same idea that justice and the gods do not always coincide in issues of revenge.)

The question about the gods and justice, which is hardly made explicit in Theseus' ambiguous phrasing, is developed in the exchange which now follows between the two halves of the Chorus (598–633: Matthiae's hemi-choric distribution, which is followed by Nauck, seems preferable, in view of the disputatious content of the passage, to Murray's attributions to individual *choreutae*). The more pessimistic half of the Chorus, alarmed by the fresh outbreak of war, wonders what the causes of these things can be. When their confident companions assure them that some happy fate attends Theseus, the doubters dissociate themselves from this confidence in just gods (610) and mutter darkly that the gods differ greatly from men in many matters. (612)[21] The optimists again assure them: "though vengeance has called forth vengeance, and slaughter, slaughter, the gods eventually grant respite and set a term to all these ills." (614–16) The arrival of the Messenger with the news of Theseus' victory seems to vindicate this hope, and now the whole Chorus joins in affirming their belief in the gods as avengers of justice. (731–33) But the play is not over yet, and we are reminded of similar triumphant cries in the *Heracles* (738, 757 ff., 772–73) when gods *seem* to have wrought justice for the hero's family, only to cap their protection, in the sequel, with worse woes. No such horrendous reversal occurs in the *Suppliants*, but we are soon to see the clouds of war reforming, despite the Mothers' prayers.

The triumph of Theseus appears to conclude one of the minor themes of the *Suppliants*, the punishment of *hybris* at the hands of the just gods. This theme has been first introduced by the Theban Herald, when he warns Theseus (494 ff.) against rescuing the bodies of men whom *hybris* has overthrown. It is interesting, in view of the sequel, that it is the *hybris* of Capaneus on which the Herald particularly dwells. The Chorus accepts this guilt, but declares that punishment belongs to Zeus, who has already exacted it. When Theseus' victory is announced, with special emphasis upon the restraint of Theseus in not seeking to capture Thebes, Adrastus affirms Zeus' control of human affairs and gives moral testimony of the just sequence of *hybris* and punishment which has been suffered by the Argives and the Thebans in turn. This seems

[21]Line 612 is admittedly obscure; there may be a hint in it that the gods (in the speakers' opinion) act differently from the way which men think right. See Paley's note *ad loc.*

a neat conclusion to the moral theme, but once again, as in the apparently happy fulfilment of the Chorus' prayers, there is a sequel.

Aftermath

Whatever we may regard as the leading theme of the *Suppliants*, the play seems to undergo a curious distintegration after the triumph of Theseus over the Thebans. If we regard the theme as the vindication, by an idealized Athenian state, of those ancient laws of the Greeks on which their civilization depends, then that theme has now passed through all its phases: its first expression in the absolute and simple terms of the Prologue and the first *stasimon*, its *agôn* (rejection, reformulation and acceptance) in the "political complication," and its eventual fulfilment in the victory of the law-respecting Theseus over the hybristic Thebans. Now Euripides turns to the sorrowing mothers receiving their dead, and expresses, in pathetic counterpoint with the cries of victory and the false heroics of the funeral speech, the true picture of war's aftermath. This is a subject on which Euripides is always most eloquent, and which the Athenians of that day must have found deeply moving; in the severe terms of formal criticism, however, it must be censured as bearing little relation to the main theme as we have seen it so far.

Nevertheless, this final portion of the play (778–1234) does, when considered by itself, manifest a most satisfying form and meaning and does develop, sometimes with ironic comment, one or two of the minor themes which we have just been discussing.

The oppositions which inform this passage may be described as follows: the Chorus sets the dominant theme of lamentation, of pure grief, which wants nothing but to be left alone, with no false joy or fresh sorrow to disturb it; twice these lamentations are interrupted, once by the intrustive and banal consolations of the funeral speech and again by the promise of vengeance (reinforced by Athena's pronouncements) from the sons of the slain chieftains. It is in these interruptions that an ironic twist is given to the minor themes of the play, the punishment of *hybris* and the justice of the gods.

We have omitted the Evadne episode (990–1113) from this brief analysis: it may be regarded as an extreme, and rather intrusive, dramatization of the grief which the Chorus expresses for the dead chieftains. The fact that it is a young woman who immolates herself upon her husband's pyre permits a further dramatic parallel: the lament of Evadne's father Iphis (1080 ff.) echoes with a more immediate poignancy the grief which the Chorus has just expressed for its own children.

The dominant tone of the whole final movement of the drama is well expressed in the lyric which marks the transition from Theseus' triumph to the grief of the Argive mothers as they view their dead:

Some things are well but others are grievous; for the city there is renown, but for me it is bitter to see the spent limbs of my children . . . to gaze upon the greatest sorrow of all. (778 ff.)

The antistrophe takes up the theme which is to haunt the rest of the lamentations in this play: the grief and futility of this child-rearing, the wish for death before bearing sons for such a fate. (786 ff.; compare 918 ff., 955 ff., 1087 ff., 1135 ff.)

In sharp contrast to this grieving lyric and the first *kommos* which completes it, comes the funeral speech of Adrastus. (857 ff.) Many conjectures have been made concerning the possible fifth-century reference of the *encomia* here expressed.[22] Theseus' request that Adrastus tell the *younger* Athenian citizens whence these heroes came by their surpassing courage does perhaps suggest that Euripides is giving a lesson in contemporary virtue and the emphasis first on civic virtue and secondly on certain features of contemporary fifth-century society (e.g., at 888–95) tends to support this view. Even so, one should note that the passage is not without its ironic overtones. In the earlier parts of the play, we have seen the Argive leaders (not merely Adrastus) branded as hybristic; now, once the tumult and the shouting have died, they become, as heroes slain in battle, the exemplars of the conventional virtues. (There may be something in the view of Lucas, and of Wecklein before him, that Euripides is here satirizing dishonest exaggerations in the annual *encomia* of the city's dead.[23]) This irony is particularly marked in the case of Capaneus, now praised for a life of moderation, for the punishment of Capaneus was earlier marked by the Theban Herald, and accepted by the Chorus, as the most obvious case of Zeus' punishment of *hybris*. (496 ff., and 512) Finally, the deaths of all these heroes, previously treated as the work of an avenging Zeus, are now regarded as

[22]For a summary, as well as a rebuttal, of a representative group of such conjectures, see Gilbert Norwood, *Essays*, 126–29. (Norwood's own view of the funeral speech is considered below, note 24.) The most extreme of the "fifth-century identifications" of the chieftains celebrated in the funeral speech are to be found in Giles' article (above, note 1) which has been sharply criticized even by the "historical interpreters" of this play, most of whom are content with finding less specific contemporary significance in this passage. Delebecque (216), for example, cites the funeral speech as one of the "pro-Argive" passages, in his interpretation of the play in terms of contemporary politics.

[23]D. W. Lucas, 168; cf. also note 18 (*ad loc.*), for Lucas' reference to Wecklein.

proof that good training provides the sense of honour requisite for a noble death. In this context, the concluding aphorism on the teachability of virtue—"Courage is teachable . . . if, indeed, the child is taught to see and hear what he does not understand" (911–13)—must surely have a mocking ring to it. What have the Mothers to say of all this glory? Ἰὼ τέκνον, δυστυχῆ σ' ἔτρεφον. (918 ff.) It was not for this they raised their sons.[24]

The chorus (955 ff.) which follows soon after this restores the pure note of mourning and here the quality of grief expressed clearly gives the lie to any consolations which seek to interrupt it. The grief of an old age bereaved of children is aimless and insatiable, "wandering like some cloud" (961), belonging to neither the living nor the dead, feeding on the relics left about the empty house, waking only to fresh tears in the early morning. (968–79)

The second *kommos* is changed by the Chorus and the sons of the chieftains, who enter bearing their fathers' corpses. The Mothers continue their familiar theme, lamenting the fruitless labours of their motherhood, but again they are interrupted, this time by the cries of vengeance from the Sons. This cry brings fear rather than hope to the Chorus: "This evil sleeps not yet. . . . Enough of woe. . . ." (1147, 1149) As the Sons develop the image of themselves clad in the armour of vengeance and strive to hear an order to battle voiced by their fathers' shades, the Chorus seeks to replace these thoughts with gentler images of love.[25] The hint of vengeance seems to pass; no mention of it

[24]Norwood's attack on the inappropriateness of the funereal tributes, particularly the tribute to Capaneus, is just, but our tentative account of the whole speech as Euripidean irony seems easier than the purely hypothetical explanation which Norwood advances: that this passage (together with many others which, for various reasons, he finds exceptionable) belonged to a fourth-century closet-play whose author (later identified as Moschion) might permit himself "esoteric references and outrageous whimsies" in the company of his indulgent friends. (Norwood, 167–69; cf. chap. 4, *passim*, esp. 152 ff., for his general argument concerning the composition of the *Suppliants*.) In this as in other parts of Norwood's argument on the *Suppliants*, the thesis proposed seems more difficult to accept, failing any direct evidence to support it, than the difficulties which it seeks to remove.

[25]Lines 1140–52 have been variously assigned between the Chorus and the Sons; Kirchhoff's attribution of 1143–45 and 1150–52 to the Chorus has been responsible for much subsequent confusion: although it enables one to retain τέκνον at 1145 (the reading of both L and P, which must be changed if these lines belong to the Sons), it completely destroys the sense of the exchange between the Mothers and the Sons, and also requires further changes in the text at 1143, 1144, and 1150 (see critical notes in Murray's and Grégoire's texts). The summary of this passage given above follows Murray's text and attributions, in which

is made in the mild exchange between Theseus and Adrastus, as the human action of the play closes with Theseus' reminder and Adrastus' acceptance of the debt of gratitude which Argos owes to Athens.

This peaceful, if sombre, close to the play is abruptly rent by the harsh commands of Athena in the epilogue. Much has already been written on the possible contemporary significance both of her instructions and of the manner in which they are to be fulfilled. We may content ourselves here with suggesting the relation between these divine commands and the thought and action, on the human level, which has preceded them. Theseus, guided by Aethra, has obeyed the *nomos palaios* in helping the Argives; he asks for no specific payment, but he looks to Adrastus for the same ethical grasp of the *nomos palaios* which he has shown himself, and Adrastus gratefully accepts this bond. (1178–79) The goddess Athena is content with no such lofty covenant: she insists (1185–1210) that the Argives be bound by a unilateral military pact, ensured by the use of most sacred and enduring objects in the treaty rites.

Athena's second command (1213–26) is to the Argive Sons: let their beards not be grown before they seek murderous vengeance on the Thebans for their fathers' deaths! Certainly this idea of vengeance runs counter to the thought, so prominent in the earlier parts of the play, that the Argives have suffered just punishment from the gods for their own *hybris*. Even the Suppliant Mothers have refused the consolations of revenge: they must now remember bitterly their earlier hope that the gods grant men respite from their ills and even bring them to an end at last. (615–16) Now comes the prophecy of Athena that an Argive army will march "with god" (1226) to avenge the slaughtered chieftains. In this, as in the goddess's strictures on Theseus' merely "moral" pact, Athena's pronouncements cap the latent irony in this play's treatment of the just and kindly gods.

---

it is clear that the martial notes belong to the Sons and the peaceful dissuasions to the Mothers. It is in this context that we must understand the exchange at 1153–54; Paley's impression here of war-like Mothers seems quite gratuitous and out of keeping with their cry "Enough of woes!" at 1149. The Sons, on the other hand, reflect what Theseus has said earlier (232 ff.) about young men and war—a typical stroke of Euripidean realism and pessimism at the end of an apparently optimistic play.

6

THE *Heracleidae*

The Theme

The *Heracleidae* and the *Suppliants* have much in common. In both plays an ancient legend is adapted to emphasize the piety of Athens in her response to supplication and, more particularly, the tendency of Athens to defend a weaker state against a stronger one in what she believes to be a just cause. In both plays, this theme has a general relevance, at least, to the sort of image which patriotic Athenians would like their city to have both in their own eyes and in those of allied and of uncommitted Hellenic states in the days to which the plays belonged; and in both plays there is at least some ground for finding the theme relevant in the light of particular international circumstances.[1] Finally (and this is surely the most important of the points in common), both plays champion in their major theme political and ethical principles which, it is clear, transcend the particular circumstances of the plot and of the political actuality to which it is sometimes said to refer. These features and their effects, both good and bad, on the dramatic texture of plays in which they occur have been considered at some length in the case of Euripides' *Suppliants*. In the case of the *Heracleidae*, a less striking and less successful example of Euripides' "political drama," it will suffice to indicate the nature of its universal theme and the ways in which this theme determines the dramatic structure of the play.[2]

[1]For discussion of possible contemporary allusions in Euripides' *Suppliants*, see references in chapter 5, notes 1, 13, 22. The possible contemporary reference of the *Heracleidae* will be discussed later in the present chapter. These considerations have, of course, affected opinion on the dates of the plays concerned, neither of which can be determined precisely by external means. The fact that the *Heracleidae* *may* be as early as 430, and the *Suppliants* as late as 420, need not, in this avowedly unchronological treatment of Euripidean drama, affect the priority which we have chosen to give the latter.

[2]Considerable doubt has been expressed concerning the integrity of the central

The situation of the *Heracleidae* is that the children of the departed Heracles, led by Heracles' old henchman, Iolaus, and Heracles' widow, Alcmene, are seeking protection at Athens (or more precisely at Marathon: the state is one with Athens, but the exact locale is to have some significance later on) from the Argive King Eurystheus; the latter, for self-protection, would exterminate the offspring of the hero whom he had so long persecuted. Iolaus introduces this situation with one of those antithetical *sententiae* which, in a Euripidean prologue, may well lead us toward the essence of our play:

Long since has this been my opinion: one man is by nature just toward his neighbours;[3] another, his spirit bent entirely toward self-interest, is useless to the State and a trouble to deal with, but to himself the best of friends. By experience I know these things. (1–5)

The first type of man Iolaus exemplifies in himself, whose self-sacrificing policy in defending the children of his departed lord is dictated by a sense of honour (αἰδοῖ) and duty to his kin. (6 ff.) Clearly epitomizing the opposite type (at least in the mind of Iolaus) is Eurystheus, who, piling outrage on outrage (ὕβρισμ' . . . ὑβρίσαι, 18), now hounds Heracles' exiled children from state to state, seeking to destroy them. The contrast of individuals is followed by a contrast of states: by implication, those states who "cowering before the stronger" (25) have rejected the helpless Heracleidae, serve self-interest before honour; any state, on the other hand, which *does* heed this desperate supplication will be acting with honour on a political level, as Iolaus has acted on a personal one. The bond, similar to that constraining Iolaus, between the Athenians and Heracles is to be made more specific later, but even here one common point, the kinship which Iolaus and Theseus' sons both share (6 and 37) with the Heracleidae is mentioned in anticipation of the plea to King Demophon.

Some men recognize their obligations, some do not: it is in the development of this simple perception of Iolaus that the theme of the *Heracleidae* resides. Now awareness of the claims of *charis*, that reciprocal concept of the favour bestowed and the obligation thereby incurred,

---

and final parts of our text of the *Heracleidae*; see especially Wilamowitz, *Hermes* XVII, 337–64, who believes our text to be a cut and re-worked version of a fourth-century producer. Save for a few points (see below, notes 11, 16, 17), the question is too technical for detailed consideration here. Zuntz, *CQ*, XLI, 46–52, provides the best defence of our text available but, as we shall see, doubt must still remain concerning the weak and somewhat inconsistent finale of the play as we have it.

[3]Taking δίκαιος, "just," as predicate, with Pearson.

is but one of several sensitivities which the just man of Iolaus' opening lines must carry with him. There are, even in this play, other examples of justice and piety which fit Iolaus' opening strictures, but as the play progresses we will find that only *charis*—or its precise negation—is common to all of its parts, and that the play depends for its articulation on a series of varied applications of the *charis* theme.[4]

The Theme and the Play

The inevitable arrival of the Argive Herald from King Eurystheus, and the equally inevitable debate before King Demophon on the rights and wrongs of Eurystheus' pursuit of the Heracleidae, restate the issue which Iolaus has introduced in the rhetorical terms of political debate. Several of the Argive Herald's sophistic arguments present a kind of perversion of the *charis* theme. The speech begins with a false plea to justice and the laws of Argos (δίκαια, 138, νόμοισι, 141), on the grounds that Argives may deal with their own subjects according to their own decrees. Here the emphasis on Argive independence, αὐτοὶ καθ' αὑτῶν, of any laws except their own, reminds us, as in the case of Theseus and *his* adversary in the *Suppliants*, of the role of Athens as champion of certain rights which transcend state boundaries. However, the Herald soon abandons even this pretence of justice (it is to be easily refuted by Iolaus [184 ff.], on the grounds that the Heracleidae had already been exiled and so are no longer subject to Theban law), and bases his argument bluntly on the respective gains (τί κερδανεῖς; 154) which Athens may expect from favours rendered to the powerful Argives and to the helpless Heracleidae. Think, he says in effect, how much more powerful allies *we* would be. (153 ff.) With sarcasm rich in prophetic irony, the Herald drives his point home: at best, you've merely distant hope of recompense from these; but even full-grown and armed, they'd be no match for Argive warriors. (169 ff.) The whole argument based on *kerdos*, the counterfeit of true *charis*, is summed up in Copreus' *clausula*:

[4]I am particularly indebted to Professor Zuntz for his clear recognition of the politico-ethical principles, as opposed to specific political situations, dramatized in the *Heracleidae*. Zuntz has observed that this play, unlike the *Suppliants*, considers the obligations incumbent on *both* parties, protected as well as protector, in the "suppliant situation": "the moral law (*nomos*) to safeguard the common life, calls for the effort and devotion of everyone, and to the very limit of his ability." (Zuntz, *The Political Plays of Euripides*, 27; see also chap. 2, throughout.) Both here and later (pp. 82 ff.) in his account of *nomos*, Zuntz recognizes the importance of *charis*; he does not, however, recognize it as a major theme dominating and determining the whole structure of the play.

"Don't make that error you are prone to make: to choose weaker when you could choose stronger friends." (176–78)

The contemporary overtone of this line[5] echoes a similar hint at v. 147, where Copreus suggests that the fugitives have sought out the Athenian leader, knowing him to be an easy mark, and the whole cast of the Theban's argument has been that Demophon will have a sorry case to put before his citizens (note vv. 162 and 165–66) if he ignores Copreus' arguments and chooses war with Argos. And yet Demaphon, unlike Theseus in the *Suppliants*, does not even consult the people.

The contemporary overtone is maintained in the speech of Iolaus (181–231), first in his confidence in the opportunity of free debate at Athens (181–84), and again in his appeal to Athens as defender of freedom and honour at any price (197–201). But the main burden of Iolaus' speech lies in his statement of the true claims which the Heracleidae have on Athens' favour, in answer to Copreus' perversion of the *charis*-theme. Kinship (207–13), the requital of family favours done by Heracles (214–20, note *χάριν*, 220), and the claims of the god-protected suppliant (221 ff.): Iolaus makes his points briefly and confidently, for little rhetoric is needed in so strong a case. The three points are neatly summarized in the contrasting terms of Iolaus' peroration: "Be kin, friend . . . or even master to these children—better all that than under Argos' sway to fall." (229–31)

Each of these claims is repeated in the same order (238 ff.) by Demophon in his formal acceptance of the Heracleidae's supplication. Here the obligations of kinship and of past favours are closely linked as a single reason for accepting the Heracleidae (240–41), thus suggesting (as Iolaus has already implied in earlier speeches) that the relationships involved in *charis* bind as closely as kinship;[6] moreover the

[5]Roger Goossens, *Euripide et Athènes*, 199–200, compares the language of Copreus here with that which the Thucydidean Nicias was to use, some years later, in advising the Athenians against helping Egesta in 415. (Demophon's decision, on the other hand, is compared with Alcibiades' policy on Egesta.) Goossens' views on this play will be considered in more detail later in this chapter.

[6]Demophon announces at the beginning of his speech (236) that *three* considerations constrain him to help the suppliants. The first and greatest of these is Zeus, and the third is a sense of shame, of public reputation (*τό τ' αἰσχρόν*, 242); therefore, kinship and gratitude for Heracles' good offices to Theseus must, jointly, form the second consideration. The relevant passages in Iolaus' speeches are vv. 6–11, 207–20.

It is tempting (in view of the various passages cited) though not, perhaps, quite justifiable, to extend the bonds of *charis* to include the claims of kinship. Iolaus' own bonds with the Heracleidae have been expressed, by that worthy, in terms very similar to those we have just seen employed by King Demophon: in accor-

expression πατρῴαν χάριν (241), an accusative in apposition to the whole sentence of vv. 240–41, strengthens this association and succinctly expresses in its context the dual "favour-for-favour" aspect of *charis*.

Finally, Iophon's noble speech of gratitude (297–328) caps this initial treatment of the *charis* theme in such a way as to mark it as the distinctive feature of Demophon's decision and, more particularly, of its future implications. The speech begins with an aphorism on the boon of noble parentage and ends with praise of Demophon for proving to be that exceptional phenomenon, a son who is worthy of his noble birth.[7] Thus, once again, the poet succeeds in widening the range of *charis*, this time to relate it to *eugeneia*. In between the two passages, the *continuing* claims of *charis* are sharply underlined in Iolaus' admonitions to the Heracleidae to reverence their beloved benefactors and never to raise the spear against them—a reference to the future which, as we shall see, is fundamental to the coming action of the play and to the ironic reversal of our expectations with which it will conclude.

The first movement of the play ends with a lyric in which the citizen Chorus, returning to the latent political aspect of the theme, celebrates the city as peace-loving but well equipped and ready to defend the weak suppliant at its doors against the impious tyrant from abroad. In view of the theme whose development we have already remarked in the opening portions of the play, it seems more than mere verbal coincidence that the Chorus should conclude its praise of Athens with the poetically vague description, τὰν εὖ χαρίτων ἔχουσαν/πόλιν. (379–80)[8]

The central complication, which is now introduced bluntly "from outside," with no attempt at dramatic justification, provides an immediate opportunity to test the principle of reciprocal obligations which Iolaus

---

dance with honour (αἰδοῖ, 6) and kinship, he has shared Heracles' labours, and it is these past bonds with Heracles (among which the bond of labours shared is very like the bond of *charis*) which explain his championship of the children. Again, Iolaus expresses the particular claims on Demophon, kinship and favours owed through Theseus (207–20), in close sequence, though he does separate the second from the first by the expression ἐκτὸς . . . τοῦ προσήκοντος: "even *apart* from the kinship. . . ." (214)

[7]With this aphorism on the relative scarcity of sons worthy of their fathers, compare the questions raised about the genetic aspect of noble natures in the reflections of Orestes at *El.* 369–70, and of Hecuba (in dramatically ironic connection with her own daughter) at *Hec.* 599–601.

[8]For the use of χάριτες here, Pearson compares *I.T.* 1147, *Tro.* 835 and *Bacch.* 236; it is possible, however, to take the present passage as making a more specific reference to the blessing of the Graces than is the case in the other passages cited (so, A. S. Way in the Loeb edition).

has just enunciated. Oracles, according to King Demophon, require that a maiden of noble birth shall be sacrificed to Demeter's daughter, if the Argives are to be defeated. Now this is one prerequisite of victory which the hitherto helpless suppliants are able to provide as well as their champions. Hence Demophon, not unnaturally, leaves the matter up to Iolaus and his charges.

Iolaus' reply (427–60) is important for two reasons. First, he distinguishes clearly between that *charis* (438) which is the gratitude and obligation owed to the Athenians for their good intentions, and the actual fulfilment of the promised favour (*charis* again, 434) which, as now appears, may lie beyond their benefactors' scope.[9] Second, it is essential to our belief in the sincerity of Iolaus' own reflections on the *charis* theme (which, as we have seen, involve the suppliant as well as the champion invoked in the name of *charis*), that he should now show his own readiness to do what he can to meet the dilemma with which Demophon and his oracles confront him. Thus honour is satisfied by Iolaus' quite sincere offer to sacrifice his own life, but since the gods require the life of a well-born maiden, not of a tottering old warrior, the intervention of Macaria is needed to supply a more practical solution to the problem.

Thus Macaria's self-sacrifice, her moral response to the needs of her fellow-fugitives and of their defenders, provides the dramatic climax to the *charis* theme. In accepting her role (which the Chorus, while praising her nobility, are quite ready to call her fate or *moira* once she *has* accepted it), Macaria spells out quite explicitly the doctrine implied in Iolaus' earlier admonition to the Heracleidae:

> What can we say for ourselves if Athens elects to run grave risks for us and we, while ready to pile our troubles on others, flee dying when by dying we could save our cause? (503–6)

and again:

> And will I not feel the shame, if someone says, "Why do you come to us with your suppliant branches, when you're afraid to risk your own lives? Depart this land: we'll not help cowards!"? (516–19)

The sense of shame to which Macaria refers (αἰσχυνοῦμαι, 516) is significant, for it was to Demophon's sense of honour that Iolaus' had appealed (note αἰσχύνῃ and its context in v. 200) and Demophon him-

[9]Note Iolaus' pitiful reproach to "Hope" (*Elpis*), almost as a supernatural power, which has held out a favour (*charis*) only, it seems, to withdraw it. The "theological" implications of such passages, both in the *Heracleidae* and in the *Suppliants*, will be considered later.

self has mentioned disgrace (τό τ' αἰσχρόν, 242) as the third of the three considerations leading him to accept the suppliants. And this is the theme which Iolaus himself picks up from Macaria's speech: "At your words I feel no shame (οὐδ' αἰσχύνομαι); it is your bitter fortune pains me." (541–42)

An essential aspect of Macaria's sense of honour is her insistence that she choose her fate herself, and in this she reminds us strongly of Euripides' other self-sacrificing maidens, Iphigenia and Polyxena who, though they appear to have considerably less choice in the matter than Macaria, nevertheless succeed in, quite literally, making a virtue of necessity.[10] It is on these grounds that Macaria refuses Iolaus' suggestion that she should cast lots with her sisters. The terms in which she states her refusal shed still further light on our theme: "I would not choose to die by fortune's lot; no grace (χάρις) resides in that." (547–48) It is difficult not to imagine that the poet intends the overtone: "Not in that way is *charis* [my grateful duty to our champions] satisfied."

It would be idle, of course, to look for any significant Euripidean attitude toward the gods in his introduction, at this point in the play, of a divine demand for human sacrifice. This, like the similar oracular message in the *Phoenissae*, is included simply for the sake of the heroic response which it is to elicit, and for the significant part which this response plays in the theme as a whole.[11] There is, however, a supernatural dimension to the *Heracleidae*, just as there is to the *Suppliants*, that other dramatization of ethical principle in international politics, and the supernatural overtones in both have much in common.

In both plays there is a clear suggestion that wise policy and virtuous and valorous action do not in themselves assure success. We have already noted Theseus' somewhat superstitious attitude to the gods and to fickle fortune, his awareness of their readiness, at times, to punish the innocent

[10]See *I.A.* 1374–1401 and 1552–60; *Hec.* 547–52. (The last reference is to Polyxena's final speech, reported by Talthybius; this is Polyxena's most explicit insistence on her free acceptance of her sacrifice, though the same attitude is implicit in her noble utterances on stage as well.)

[11]Wilamowitz (*Hermes*, XVII, 338 ff.) develops the suggestion in Kirchhoff's edition (Berlin, 1867) that a lost portion of the play contained a messenger's report and a lament about the death of Macaria. However, once the maiden's free and heroic decision has provided us with an example of *charis* which will contrast with Alcmene's selfish refusal of *charis* later on, the dramatist has no further use for her; cf. Fitton's comment (*Hermes*, LXXXIX, 452), ". . . since she is a community-surrogate, she need have no character." Moreover as Zuntz (*CQ*, XLI, 52) and Grube (171) have pointed out, the self-sacrificing Menoeceus in the *Phoenissae* fares no better.

with the guilty and of the necessity, however just one's cause, of having the gods on one's side. Nevertheless, there is at the same time a kind of buoyant optimism in the Theseus of the *Suppliants*, a conviction, vindicated by the action of the play, that the world *is* ordered for the best, and that a combination of high-principled action and the necessary pious safeguards will bring victory.[12]

A similar ambiguity is to be noted in the *Heracleidae*, though the extremes of naïve superstition, on the one hand, and of expectation of moral reward from the gods, on the other, are perhaps more clearly marked. Iolaus' pitiful remonstrance to Hope (*Elpis*) at *Heracl.* 433–34 anticipates Theseus' comments on fickle fortune at, e.g., *Suppl.* 549–55, but, though Theseus insists on the necessity of having divine support as well as valour and a just cause (*Suppl.* 595–98), there is nothing in the *Suppliants* quite like Iolaus' suggestion that Athens will beat Argos because her gods are stronger! (*Heracl.* 347–52)

However, it is mainly in the choral lyrics of the *Heracleidae* that the ambiguous attitude to the gods and "fate" is, quite properly, developed. (In the *Suppliants*, it is Theseus who considers such matters, because the Chorus, themselves the suppliants in the play of that name, are busy with other matters.)

The two odes which come between the decision of Macaria and the servant's report of the battle epitomize this ambiguity. In the *stasimon* (608–29) following Macaria's decision, the Chorus prefaces its praise of Macaria's *aretê* (625–28) with a lyric statement of man's dependence on the whim of the gods and on the dictates of fate which no mortal wisdom can overcome. (608–17; cf. *Suppliants* 549–55) On the other hand, the following stasimon (748–83), sung just before the battle, emphasizes the justice of the suppliants' champions and their consequent expectation of divine protection. The first antistrophe gives particularly dramatic expression to the shift from fear (δεινὸν μὲν πόλιν . . . "Dreadful it is that spear-renowned Mycenae assails our land . . ." 759 ff.) to confidence ("Zeus is my ally, I shall not fear" 766). That this confidence stems from awareness of the justice of the Athenians' cause is made explicit in the manner in which they involve Zeus himself in the *charis* theme ("Zeus favours us, in just requital of our deeds" Ζεύς μοι χάριν ἐνδίκως/ἔχει, 767–68) and in the similar appeal to Athena, in the following strophe, to reward the virtuous and punish the impious. (773–76)

[12]See the second and third sections of my discussion of the *Suppliants*. The most relevant passages in the play itself are *Suppl.* 195 ff., 226–28, 550–55, 592–97.

The magnificent, if absurd, insistence on battle service by the ancient Iolaus, and his miraculous rejuvenation once the battle is joined, adds little, in my opinion, to the *charis* theme with which we are here concerned. True, Iolaus' will to fight is another indication, if one were needed, of the duties of the befriended to do all that they can to help their allies and themselves. Professor Zuntz would extend this interpretation to include the rejuvenation of Iolaus, seeing in this miracle a sign of the gods' approval of the old man's heroic devotion to duty which persists even in the face of physical infirmity.[13] This may be so, but one suspects that Euripides developed the traditional "rejuvenation" story as much for its own sake, for the stirring entertainment which it imparts to the account of the battle, as for any other reason. It also has the practical advantage of enabling Iolaus, rather than Hyllus, to deal with Eurystheus. This is useful on two counts: first, it is dramatically more economical to have only one real champion on the side of the Heracleidae; second, in the tradition, Hyllus slew Eurystheus, and this, of course, would not do in view of the *dénouement* of the play, and of the *charis* theme which Euripides has in mind.

Our emphasis on the *charis* theme throughout this analysis seems well vindicated by the closing scene. Alcmene, widow of Heracles, confronts the captured Eurystheus and, despite the information that Athens, in accordance with her principles, does not wish her captive slain, insists on the execution of her vengeance. Thus Alcmene ignores the wishes of her defenders who, in contrast, would preserve *nomos* as faithfully in regard to their enemy as they have in regard to their suppliants. In so doing, of course, she breaks the bonds of *charis*, neatly reversing the position of her heroic daughter Macaria, who, like Iolaus, has recognized the reciprocal aspect of the suppliant-champion relationship. (The contrast here between Alcmene and Macaria is somewhat similar to that between another Euripidean mother and daughter, Hecuba and Polyxena

[13]See Zuntz, *Political Plays*, 30 31. If Zuntz is right in this interpretation, the passage is still open to the charge of being a somewhat cheap and melodramatic exploitation of "the supernatural dimension" which is available to a dramatist writing in the mythological tradition but which should surely be sparingly used in a relatively "unmythological" play. (Here, for once, one is tempted to apply a warning of Aristotle's ["Within the action, there must be nothing irrational," *Poetics* 1454b 6] to Euripides). However, to my mind, the almost comic impression which the ancient Iolaus makes just before he totters off to battle rather belies the solemn interpretation which Zuntz places on the ensuing rejuvenation. Very different is the view of J. W. Fitton (454) who finds in the supernatural refutation of the earlier scene of ridicule an intentional contrast between the worlds of common sense and of fantasy. But if this is so, there is still an incongruity, for there is little of the world of fantasy elsewhere in the play.

in the *Hecuba*,[14] save that Hecuba, being a tragic heroine whereas Alcmene is not, reaches her moral nadir after being subjected to considerably greater external pressures.)

Alcmene's explicit awareness of how her action must strike the Chorus and, perhaps, the messenger from Hyllus attending Eurystheus, underlines the vehemence of her insistence on vengeance at whatever moral cost:

I love this city . . . *but*, once this man has fallen in my hands, no man alive will take him from me. So let who will rail at my boldness, my large demands, as unfitting for a woman. This deed by me *will* come to pass. (975–80)

Alcmene's furious spirit is, as we shall see, made all the more striking by contrast with the curious crumbling of Athenian opposition to her will.

But if Alcmene's intransigent attitude reverses the hitherto irreproachable selflessness of the suppliants, still greater upsets are in store. Eurystheus, in his two devastating speeches (983–1017, 1026–44), makes one positive and one negative contribution to the *charis* theme. Athens, because of its respect for Hellenic laws (1010) in sparing its captured enemy, will find in the spirit of Eurystheus "an avenger and a gracious friend." (1015)[15] The Heracleidae, on the other hand, will (according to an ancient oracle which Eurystheus employs as his moribund prerogative) betray in a later generation the favour they have received (χάριν προδόντες, 1036), by marching against their benefactors. It is now that we see in what a tangible way Eurystheus will show Athens the *charis* he has promised in his earlier speech. Buried by the Athenians near the shrine of Athena *Pallenis*, he will ward off the hostile Heracleidae of later years (1030–36): "In death I'll injure them and profit you, and so you'll have from me a double gain (κέρδος)." (1043–44) Significantly, Eurystheus uses the same term (κέρδος) which the Athenians have already heard (τί κερδανεῖς; 154) from Eurystheus' violent Herald when, at the beginning of the trouble, he had sought to buy Athens' betrayal of the suppliant Heracleidae.

The sorry figure cut by Athens, as represented by the Chorus, at the end of the play, must remain one of the puzzling features of the *Heracleidae*. Until the last minute, Athens has been represented as the

[14]The same comparison appears to have occurred to M. Méridier: See *Euripide* I, 194, "Macarie annonce Polyxène, comme Alcmène fait pressentir Hécube." (The passage is also quoted by Zuntz, *CQ*, XLI [1947], 51.)

[15]For the first term in this puzzling line (1015) see Paley's note *ad loc.*; for a discussion of both terms see Pearson's note *ad loc.* and, especially, his Appendix B, 4, on v. 1015.

most scrupulous observer of *nomos*, of the accepted norm of proper conduct between civilized states and individuals, both in her defence of the suppliant children of Theseus' friend and saviour, and in her initial defence of the life of the captive Eurystheus against the would-be avenger Alcmene. Now, at the very end, the Chorus, after urging Alcmene to abandon her vengeance in respect for Athens' wishes (1018–19), weakly submits (1053–55, cf. 1021) to the sophistic solution ("I'll take his life and you can tend his corpse," 1022–25) by which Alcmene pretends to salve Athenian consciences.

The inconsistency, which has led some editors to suspect at least a *lacuna* in our text,[16] is considerably greater if we follow the MSS (as I think we should) in making the Chorus and not the servant of Hyllus the reporter of the Athenian position with regard to Eurystheus and all other enemy captives at vv. 961–72.[17] But however much or little we manipulate the text and the MSS ascriptions of the lines concerned, we are left with a certain element, at least, of Athens' inconsistency and, indeed, lack of integrity, in her defence of a principle which she has championed hitherto. Unless (as is quite possible) the ending of our play has been seriously mutilated, only two explanations seem possible.

One is that Euripides, without much conscience in the matter, is simply suiting his dramatic convenience: either for "political reasons" or simply for the sake of the ironies involved, he wishes, at whatever cost, to provide an unexpected reversal of the *charis* theme with regard

[16]Murray, following Hermann, suspects a *lacuna* after 1052. See his note *ad loc.*, where it is suggested that (in the original text), half the Chorus rejected Alcmene's proposal and that the other hemi-chorus then replied, ταὐτὰ (for ταῦτα LP) δοκεῖ μοι. Murray also suspects a *lacuna* after 1017, mainly on the ground that 1020–25 do not agree with 961–72, where the Chorus has emphatically declared that, according to Athenian law, no one is to take the life of Eurystheus. But see also Pearson's rebuttal in his note to v. 1019, and my further discussion below, note 16.

[17]Editors and critics (including Tyrwhitt, Pearson and Zuntz) have denied the Chorus the lines attributed to it by the MSS, at least partly on the grounds that it could not know what orders have actually been given for the treatment of Eurystheus. But surely the Chorus is simply applying regular Athenian principles and policy to this particular case; if (as those who regard the lines as a messenger's report from Hyllus must admit) *actual orders*, based on Athenian wishes, are being reported, then the Chorus could not acquiesce, as it does, in Alcmene's suggestion at the end, without committing treason. It seems preferable to accept the MSS ascriptions, at least as far as the Chorus's lines are concerned, and to accept also the fact that the Chorus allows Alcmene to weaken its position. After all, the Chorus is the only spokesman for the Athenian position present; it is reasonable to expect it to fulfil this role here as it does later (e.g. at vv. 1018–19) in the scene.

both to the suppliants and to their persecutor. The first of these reversals (the lack of *charis* shown by Alcmene to Athens which anticipates the prophesied betrayal of *charis* by future Heracleidae) can be shown *only* if Athens seeks, initially at least, to spare Eurystheus' life. The second reversal (the unexpected gratitude shown by Eurystheus' promise to Athens) can take place only on the understanding that Eurystheus is, after all, to die on Athenian soil. (As Alcmene herself points out in her cynical clinching argument, 1045–49, only a dead Eurystheus can perform the good offices which he promises!) And so, for the sake of this double irony, this double reversal involving both the protected ones and the assailant, Athens must be made first to seek Eurystheus' safety and then to let him die, and the playwright, like the Athenian Chorus, must be satisfied, owing to the exigencies of the drama, with the poor sop to Athenian honour which Alcmene offers. (At least, if we accept this explanation, we should remember that it is only the Chorus, and not the Athenian King himself, who is put in this position.)

The other explanation, which is not really in contradiction to the one just offered and can perhaps be reconciled with it, is that suggested by Professor Zuntz. It is that Euripides intends this sudden falling-off of Athenian nobility as a dramatization of the contrast between the ideal position hitherto presented and the very real temptations and circumstances which threaten to, and sometimes do, destroy it. Thus, Professor Zuntz finds that there is in this play "a challenge . . . rather than flattery": "Instead of the fanfares of national triumph, (the Athenian audience) witnessed the spectacle of inhuman slaughter and a moral failure. . . ."[18] And again:

> The violent contrast between the Exodos as a whole and the rest of the play . . . must have left a sting in the minds of those who witnessed it. Their pride in their city, in the ideal Athens, has been stirred and they have been powerfully reminded of the short-comings which can threaten this ideal. How are they to maintain it?[19]

The Date

The general theme of the *Heracleidae* and, more particularly, the obviously contemporary relevance of Eurystheus' prophecy at the end, have led inevitably to much discussion concerning the precise historical circumstances which best fit the play and its finale, and which, therefore, may serve as an indication of its date. The various arguments have been

[18] Zuntz, *Political Plays*, 41.
[19] *Ibid.*, 42.

so thoroughly reviewed and documented by critics particularly interested in the historical approach to Euripides[20] that it will suffice here to indicate the main lines of the discussion and the most probable of the many opinions which have been offered.

In the matter both of dating and (so far as this is possible) "contemporary interpretation," the sounder arguments have tended to centre about the one part of the play, the prophecy of Eurystheus, which has a clear contemporary reference. The most difficult and tendentious arguments, on the other hand, are those which have sought to expound the whole theme and action of the play in terms of political rivalries and *rapprochements* at specific moments (variously chosen by various critics) in the history of Athenian, Spartan and Argive relations.

According to a passage in Diodorus, the Spartans, in their second invasion of Attica in 430, spared the Marathonian tetrapolis in gratitude for the favour done their ancestors, the Heracleidae, when they were allowed to advance against Eurystheus from this place.[21] Thus, in having Eurystheus foretell both the Spartan invasion of Attica *and* the saving power which the bones of the grateful Eurystheus will have, Euripides seems to be indulging in a safe prophecy based on his own knowledge of the events of 430, while, with wicked irony, switching the credit for this sparing of Marathon from the enemy Spartans to the uncommitted Argives. Mainly on these grounds, the approximate date of the *Heracleidae* was set by Wilamowitz as between 430 (after the invasion which spared the tetrapolis) and the summer of 427 (during which the Spartan devastation of Attica was pretty well universal);[22] majority opinion among critics and editors continues to accept these conclusions.

Exception has been taken on several grounds to this inference from the dramatic prophecy of Eurystheus and its apparent historical fulfilment. Zuntz argues that the dramatic prophecy could not have been made *after* 430, since "it presages the failure of the coming Spartan

[20]For bibliography of views prior to 1905 on the date of the *Heracleidae*, see G. H. Macurdy, *The Chronology of the Extant Plays of Euripides* (Columbia University diss., 1905), 12–14. In more recent times, there is an excellent summary of the major political interpretations of the play in Delebecque, 74–77. Cf. also Zuntz, *Political Plays*, 81–88 and Pearson's edition, xxx–xxxiii, both of which have been most useful in the present discussion.

[21]Diod. xii. 45.1. As Pearson notes, Thucydides (iii. 26), in his account of the invasion of 427, gives support of a negative kind to this statement by indicating that not all the land was ravaged in 430. For other references on this point, see Zuntz, *Political Plays*, 83–84.

[22]Wilamowitz, *Analecta Euripidea*, 152; see also the references to Diodorus and Thucydides in the preceding note.

invasion"; Goossens objects that Wilamowitz's view ignores Eurystheus' prophetic threat of a troublesome journey home (1042) for the invaders; Spranger argues, somewhat perversely, that since Euripides was not prone to championing oracles, it is quite conceivable that he provided Eurystheus with this one *after* it had been historically discredited in 427![23] (These objections, it should be noted, have led none of their authors to the same date for our play; Zuntz argues that the spring of 430 is the date when the prophecy would be most relevant;[24] Goossens somewhat arbitrarily selects 426 as the date when, in his opinion, Euripides ushered in his new policy of aggressive patriotism with the production of the *Heracleidae*;[25] Spranger, once he has disposed of the difficulty provided by the prophecy, finds the attitude to Argos the deciding factor in dating the play to *ca.* 420, shortly before or not long after the Athens-Argos alliance.)[26]

None of these objections, however, affects the fundamental probability of Wilamowitz's argument. Even if Eurystheus' prophecy cannot be applied successfully to the invasion of 430 as a whole, the fact that an important part of the prophecy perfectly fits the period concerned (i.e., the period between the invasions of 430 and 427) *and no other*, surely suggests that this was the period in which Euripides wrote and produced his play. An excessive confidence either in coincidence or in Eurystheus' (and Euripides') own power of prophecy must surely be needed to shake that likelihood.

Nor is this position seriously threatened by those critics who seek to base it on one or another phase of Athenian-Argive relations. Here the very plurality of views suggest the weakness of the approach. The

[23]See Zuntz, *Political Plays*, 85; Roger Goossens, *Euripide et Athènes* (Brussels 1962), 207; J. A. Spranger, *CQ* 19 (1925), 126.

[24]Zuntz, *Political Plays*, 86.

[25]See Goossens, 190, 196, as well as 207, already cited; this critic appears to regard the prophecy regarding the punishment of the Spartans (made, in his view, *after* the devastations of 427) as wishful thinking, just as the legendary victory of Demophon serves "comme la préfiguration d'une révanche, comme un moyen magique d'en hâter la venue." (196) (It should be noted that Goossens bases much of his argument about the actual dating of the play on a study by Marie Delcourt [in *Serta Leodiensia*, Liège 1930, 117–19], which I have been unable to see.) On the other hand, Goossens compares the impressions of the martial undertakings of Demophon with the optimistic attitudes prevalent at the *beginning* of the Peloponnesian War: "C'est la guerre vue par un patriote optimiste qui a oublié tous les malheurs." (208) Given a more reasonable dating of the play than that suggested by Goossens, this unusual feat of memory would not have been necessary.

[26]Spranger, 126.

weightiest of these regards the play as fundamentally "anti-Argos" (since Athens joins the Heracleidae against Eurystheus and his hybristic envoy), and refers that hostility to the Athenian attitude at the time of the Argive-Spartan alliance of 418/17. Their arguments have been well summarized by Delebecque who, despite his sympathy with the position, admits that on a variety of counts (metrical and stylistic as well as those asserted above) the play cannot be dated as late as these critics would require.[27] The same argument applies against the rather more maverick position adopted by Spranger who, regarding the whole play as mildly sympathetic toward Argos, relates it to the somewhat cautious acceptance of Argos by Athenians generally at the time of the alliance of 420. The most extraordinary feature of Spranger's argument is his attempt to identify not only Eurystheus but the descendants of the Heracleidae as "Argive"; however defensible such genealogy through Hyllus may be outside the immediate context, dramatic and mythological, it would surely be impossible to expect the Athenian audience to accept the Heracleidae as anything but the ancestors of the Spartans, and to expect them to regard both Eurystheus *and* his fugitives as Argives, in different senses!

In most of these attempts at fitting the action of the *Heracleidae* to some particular moment of fifth-century inter-state politics, a major difficulty (in addition to difficulties of date already indicated) has been the dramatic fact that Eurystheus begins villainously (through his herald Copreus) but ends nobly, by providing a surprisingly generous fillip to the *charis* theme. We have already suggested explanations of this switch in terms both of dramatic irony and of the *charis* theme with which the play is concerned, but there is no doubt that it provides a very awkward element in historical interpretations of the play. One of the more desperate "solutions" of this problem has been the suggestion that a political event, Athens' illegal execution of the captured Peloponnesian envoys in the winter of 430/29, affected the poet's sympathies in the midst of his creative labours, and caused him to sacrifice consistency to immediate political censure. Hence the transformation of Eurystheus (the only potential captive of note available) from villain to martyr; the theory does not tell us why, in this abortion of his work, the poet troubles to make Eurystheus grateful for his transformation as well.

[27] Delebecque, 75–6. Delebecque himself straddles the two major positions. He recognizes the cogency of the arguments dating the play to 430–27, but, insisting that "la note anti-argienne retentit dans la pièce entière" (76), attempts rather unconvincingly (77 ff.) to sketch a historical basis for such sentiments at Athens between 430 and 427.

There is, of course, no doubt that the *charis* theme as expressed in the *Heracleidae* has a general application to the political realities of Euripides' own day, and it is quite possible that the poet's own observation of international politics may have prompted him to treat this theme. Nevertheless, the specific details of the play, and more particularly the presentation of Eurystheus, quite properly defy the practice of the more extreme exponents of the historical method. Méridier, himself an historical critic in other contexts, is surely right to insist[28] that "la donnée légendaire" suffices to explain the hostile treatment accorded the Argives throughout much of the play. Only in the case of Alcmene and the Heracleidae, ancestors of those Spartans clearly referred to in the closing passages of the play, are we justified in finding a reference, albeit limited, to contemporary situations, and a reflection of the feelings which they must necessarily have aroused.

[28]Méridier, 195.

PART THREE

WAR AND ITS AFTERMATH

7

THE *Trojan Women*

The Trilogy

We know from Aelian (*V.H.* 2. 8) that the *Troades* was the third play in the trilogy *Alexander, Palamedes, Troades,* with the *Sisyphus* as satyr-play; that it was produced in 415 B.C. and that Euripides came second in this competition, being defeated by Xenocles (a fact which Aelian finds "laughable").

The *Troades* is one of the two extant plays which can lay some claim to membership in a connected trilogy. (The other, for which a much less definite claim can be urged, is the *Phoenissae.*) Any indication of a thematic connection between the plays of a Euripidean trilogy is itself a matter of some interest and may, in addition, affect our evaluation of the surviving play. Let us see from a summary of the evidence what sort of connection, if any, can be established for the plays of this trilogy.

The *general* subject matter of the two lost plays of the trilogy may be gleaned from Hyginus' accounts of the myths of Alexander (Paris) and Palamedes (*Fabulae* 91 and 105).

Hyginus' account of the myth of Alexander may be summarized as follows: Hecuba, while pregnant with Paris, dreamt that she had given birth to a flaming fire-brand; on the advice of interpreters, who feared evil for the country, the child which was subsequently born was given up for slaughter, but servants in pity exposed it instead. The child was brought up by shepherds who named him Paris. When he was a young man, he had a bull for a pet which Priam's servants took away from him to be a prize at the funeral games which were habitually held in honour of the "deceased" royal child. The youth, for love of his bull (*amore incensus tauri sui*), participated in his own funeral games and defeated his royal brothers, whereupon Deiphobus assailed him so that he took refuge for his life in the temple of Zeus *Herkeios.* However, when the prophetess-princess Cassandra divined that he was her brother, King Priam recognized him and restored him to his royal position.

Hyginus' account certainly provides us with the background and the general subject-matter of the *Alexander*, though, as we shall see, there are some points at which he may have departed from the Euripidean version. With this knowledge of the story, several possible reconstructions of the play have been made from the actual fragments available and from fragments of Ennius' *Alexander* which was apparently based (at least in large part) upon it.[1] I summarize this material, as briefly as possible, as it has been arranged by Bruno Snell, although, as we shall see, his brilliant and well argued reconstruction is still open to some question at one rather crucial point.

A prologue probably spoken by Cassandra provides the mythological background: the story of Hecuba's dream and the consequent exposure of the child long ago. Hecuba enters; after a brief conversation with her mother, Cassandra enters the temple of Apollo. Following the *parodos* a dialogue takes place in which Hecuba, her grief revived by the imminent memorial games, mourns for her infant son while the Chorus attempts to console her. Cassandra returns from the temple with the prophetic warning that the fiery torch so long hidden is now at hand. Further prophecies follow concerning the arrival of Helen at Troy (as a result of a judgment between three goddesses), the attack of a death-dealing fleet, the laceration of Hector's body and the "Trojan Horse" conquest of Troy. Rather later, perhaps in the second episode, an old shepherd enters announcing that a young herdsman (Paris) has come to compete in the royal memorial games, for the reason which we have already seen in Hyginus' account; he tells us, too, how Paris was brought

[1]To the fragments of the *Alexander* collected in Nauck, *Euripides* III[3]. 10 ff. (frgs. 43–65) should be added the papyrus fragments published by W. Crönert, in "Griechische literarische Papyri aus Strassburg, Freiburg und Berlin," *Nachrichten der Gesellschaft der Wissenschaften zu Göttingen* (1922) 1–17; the relevant fragments of Ennius may be most conveniently consulted in the well annotated edition of E. H. Warmington in *Remains of Old Latin* I (Loeb edition, London, 1935), Ennius, *Fabulae*, pp. 234–44, vv. 38–82. This primary material has been collected and rearranged by Bruno Snell, according to his own reconstruction of the play, in "Euripides' *Alexandros* und andere Strassburger Papyri," *Hermes, Einzelschriften* V (1937) 1–68. The papyrus fragments are also collected (with a translation and a summary of Snell's reconstruction) in D. L. Page, *Greek Literary Papyri* I (Loeb edition, London, 1942), 54–60, no. 9. (In this chapter, the references to Nauck, *Euripides*, III are to the *third* edition [1895] to conform with the references given by Snell. In other chapters, the second edition [1869] has been used.)

up by the shepherds and why they named him Alexander: because he had been an "averter" keeping robbers from the herds. In the next episode, a messenger announces Alexander's victory at the games and assures the Chorus, in answer to its questions, that despite his low birth the winner has been deemed worthy of the prize by King Priam. Hector and his brother Deiphobus enter; Deiphobus is indignant at being beaten by a slave and upbraids Hector, who tries to calm him, for slackness in accepting the situation. Probably in the next episode, Deiphobus and Alexander debate before King Priam Alexander's eligibility, as a slave, to win the games. This seems to have been a typical Euripidean debate: Deiphobus generalizes on the impossibility of improving base stock by training, and on the dangers of having slaves with thoughts above their station; Alexander replies with Euripidean aphorisms about "clever speakers," with antithetical *sententiae* about wealth and poverty in the training of the young, and with dramatic ironies about those who are slaves not by name but by fortune. Priam decides in favour of Alexander. A choral ode ponders, sympathetically with Alexander, the sources of true nobility: intelligence and understanding, the gift of god not of wealth. In the *exodos*, Hecuba, who regards the slave's victory over her sons as a slur on the royal house of Priam, conspires with Deiphobus to slay Alexander. The latter takes refuge at the altar of Zeus *Herkeios*. A despairing cry that the excellence of mind, a source of safety to other men, is the cause of his imminent death, triggers the recognition scene. This is probably completed by means of revelations and recognition tokens provided by the old shepherd and foster father, possibly the same man who had previously announced Alexander's entry into the lists. (This is Snell's reconstruction of the recognition scene which must, however, remain in doubt. It *may* be, as many believe, that Hyginus' account, which makes Cassandra the instrument of recognition, preserves the Euripidean version.) Aphrodite appears, announcing to Alexander that he is to win Helen in Greece, "for father Zeus has planned this, wishing to bring evil on the Trojans and trouble on the Greeks" (1067, Nauck: Cassandra may, on the other hand, be the speaker of the directly quoted part of this sentence).

The belief that Aphrodite appeared at the end of the play, and the consequent attribution to her of the prophecy concerning Paris and Helen, is based on scenes in reliefs on several Etruscan urns in which a goddess thought to be Aphrodite is shown protecting Paris against the assault of Deiphobus, while Hector and Priam (and in *one* representation another female, either Hecuba or Cassandra, wielding an axe), are placed on the other side of Paris in what could be either defensive or offensive positions.[2] If Snell's reconstruction of the recognition scene is correct, it is hard to see why, apart from artistic liberty, Deiphobus should be presented as threatening, and Hector either defending or threatening Paris, *with Aphrodite present*: at this point the recognition should have been completed and the threat to Paris withdrawn—unless, in the circumstances, we are to regard the recognition scene as increasing, rather than reversing as it usually does, the hostile action against the hero.

This reconstruction depends for most of the passages involving prophecy and Cassandra on the fragments of Ennius already referred to. However, Ennius' dependence on Euripides' version seems well substantiated,[3] and it appears to have been the custom of the Roman poet to imitate his Greek tragic models rather closely.[4] But even accepting Ennius as a guide in those places where the Euripidean fragments are lacking, we cannot be sure at what point in the play to place Cassandra's prophecy about the presence of the fiery torch (Paris) and the troubles it will bring on Troy. It is here that Snell departs from majority opinion which would place these prophecies at the end or near the end of both plays. There is some evidence (frg. I, Crönert) that Hecuba and Cassandra meet in the first episode of the play, probably as Cassandra comes out of the temple of Apollo. Snell argues[5] (against Crönert, Wilamowitz

[2]See H. Brunn, *I Relievi delle urne etrusche*, plates I, III, VIII and XII, reproduced in A. W. Pickard-Cambridge's article, "The *Alexandros* of Euripides," facing pp. 140–41. It is possible, as Pickard-Cambridge remarks, p. 140, n. 1, that the goddess represented in these reliefs *may* be *Nikê*, since in one instance, plate VIII, she is winged. However, this seems unlikely, unless the artist himself has added the divine figure, for Aphrodite would be by far the more appropriate divinity to appear at the end of the Euripidean play.

[3]Note, for example, the overlap between (papyrus) frg. VIII (Crönert) and Ennius vv. 57–61 (Warmington = vv. 54–58 Vahlen, the edition quoted by Snell). Moreover, Varro tells us (*L.L.* 7. 82 = 64 Nauck) of Ennius' wish to imitate Euripides in connection with another detail in Ennius' play. Snell (pp. 23–24) compares Eur. *Tro.* 919–22 with the prologue in Ennius' play to indicate in what way Ennius probably imitated and adapted the prologue of Euripides' *Alexander*.

[4]Cf. for example Ennius' *Medea* (which Cicero, *De fin.* 1. 24, with some exaggeration, includes among plays literally translated from the Greek) and the parallel passages of Euripides' *Medea* which are quoted in Warmington's edition, pp. 310 ff.

[5]Snell, 24–30, esp. 24–25, for the points to be discussed. Wilamowitz (*Troerinnen, Einleitung*, 260–61) thinks that Cassandra made her prophecies after the recognition of Paris had been effected by means of the old servant, and that the prophetess sought to check her parents' joy at the recognition with her prophetic

and others) that it must be in this meeting that Cassandra is wild in her manner and makes her prophecies (frg. VIII, Crönert; Ennius vv. 54–77 Vahlen = 57–81 Warmington); thus Hecuba's complaints (Ennius vv. 54–58, Vahlen = 57–61 Warmington) that she is not the sane and modest maiden she was a little while ago must look back for its comparison to Cassandra as she was before she entered Apollo's temple directly after the prologue.

Snell's suggestion that Cassandra's prophecies were made early in the play is well worth considering. Such a direct, prophetic anticipation of the *dénouement* of the play, the actual reappearance, after all these years, of the bloody fire-brand Paris, is dramatically sound and quite typical of Euripidean technique; moreover, Hecuba's rejection of Cassandra's warning gives an added significance to her role and to its connection with the troubles to come later in the trilogy. This is not to say that Hecuba is morally culpable for refusing to heed Cassandra: as the prophetess reminds us (frg. *adesp.* 414, Nauck, which Snell and others wisely attribute to the *Alexander*), it is her lot to be judged mad before the event and wise only when people are actually suffering from the ills which she has forecast.

Snell regards the whole treatment of Hecuba in the *Alexander* as representing one of Euripides' most important innovations in his material.[6] In addition to her scene with Cassandra, he mentions her remorse over Paris, whom she thinks to have been slain long ago,[7] and, later in the play, her plot with Deiphobus to murder the slave who has bested her sons in the games. Since Hecuba is the central character in the *Troades*, such emphasis in the *Alexander* would further support the idea of some thematic link between the first and third plays in the trilogy. In this connection, Snell notes the contrast between the stormy, sometimes too impulsive, figure whom we may dimly discern in the *Alexander* and

warnings. Wilamowitz also makes more of Aphrodite's promise to Paris as an influence on his parents' decision: the goddess' support and the glorious rewards to come continue (thinks Wilamowitz) to outweigh in the parents' mind the warnings of Cassandra that these glories will end in woe. Kuiper ("De Alexandro Euripideo") also makes much of the influence of Aphrodite: his view that through Paris she controls the whole action of the play is interesting, but receives little support from the fragments or from the tradition as a whole.

[6]See Snell, 59–66, especially 64–66, for the arguments here summarized.

[7]Here Snell suggests, in a skilful and complex argument, that according to Euripides' version Hecuba, long before the play opens, had given up her doom-laden infant for *slaughter* (later to be changed to exposure by compassionate servants) and that this version, preserved in Hyginus, may have been original with Euripides (see Snell, 60–63).

the suffering figure of the *Troades*, though he wisely repudiates the "crime and punishment" sequence by which some critics have sought to relate the doings and sufferings of Hecuba and the Trojans in this trilogy. Once again (as Snell indicates), the role of Cassandra complements this aspect of the role of Hecuba: witness both her function of forecasting the whole trilogy at the beginning and the counterpart ("*Gegenbild*") which this frenzied scene of prophecy provides with the "mad" scene in the *Troades* (308 ff.), in which she celebrates, with prophetic irony, her coming, doom-laden marriage with Agamemnon.

Regrettably little is known of the second play in the trilogy, the *Palamedes*, beyond the accounts of the relevant legend in Hyginus (*Fab.* 105) and in other ancient sources.[8] The plot concerned the dastardly vengeance in Troyland of Odysseus on Palamedes, who had detected the ruse whereby Odysseus sought to avoid service at Troy. (According to another version, Odysseus was envious of Palamedes "the wise," the inventor of the art of writing.) By a ruse of Odysseus', the innocent Palamedes is made to appear guilty in Agamemnon's eyes of betraying the Greek camp to the Trojan King Priam and, despite his protestations of innocence, is slain by the Greek army. However, Palamedes' son Oiax managed to send word of his father's unjust execution to Nauplius, Palamedes' father, by inscribing the account of it on many ships and many oars which went travelling over the seas. (Thus Palamedes' discovery of the art of writing did him some good after all, for Nauplius was later able to take vengeance on the storm-battered Greek fleet by luring it to further destruction with misleading flares.)[9]

The longest fragment which we have of the play (582, Nauck) deals with Palamedes' invention of the art of writing which is now being used to send a true account of what has happened across the sea. Others deal with such typical Euripidean antithesis as clever words and shameful deeds (587, Nauck: the reference is doubtless to Odysseus), with the more pointed contrast between the plethora of available generals and the scarcity of wise men (585, Nauck), and with a choral reproach to the Danaans for slaying "this song-bird of the Muses" who had done no harm. (591, Nauck)

The *Troades*, the third play in the trilogy, deals with events after Troy has fallen: the dread woes inflicted on the mothers, widows and children of the fallen Trojan heroes. The distance in time and subject-matter separating the three plays precludes any question of a closely related trilogy, but most critics regard the bond between them as some-

[8]See Nauck, *Euripides*, III, pp. 154 ff.
[9]See Parmentier, *Euripide*, IV, 9.

thing stronger than mere Trojan War connection. ". . . wie ein hellroter Morgen Stürme für den Abend befürchten lässt.": Welcker's fine simile[10] for the anticipatory effect of the *Alexander* may strike a modern reader as somewhat vague and impressionistic, but even a link of the kind suggested in this image would make "the Trojan plays" unique among extant works of Euripides. Others seek to give a more specific moral theme to the whole. Parmentier, for example,[11] finds a vein of human guilt (the Trojan error with regard to Paris, the Greek injustice first toward their fellow countryman, then toward the defeated enemy) which in each case is requited by suffering. The main difficulty in this view (apart from the fact that tragedy rarely deals with such simple themes of crime and punishment) is that two of the three sequences described, those concerning the Greeks, are not actually fulfilled in the trilogy at all. Even the sufferings of the Trojans, which are certainly prominent enough, are hardly presented (except by the prejudiced witness Helen) as the result of their own folly: indeed, only a few lines (597–98, 919–22—enough to mark an ironic contrast between the active and the passive phases of the Trojan experience),[12] draw any attention at all to the ancient error in letting Paris live.

Gilbert Murray also attempts, though in less moralistic style, to relate the *specific* subject matter of the three plays to a common theme. This he finds in a three-fold demonstration of *paracharaxis*, Diogenes the Cynic's expression for that reversal by which things called good by the world are shown to be evil, or at least to lead to misfortune.[13] Thus, the apparently happy ending of the *Alexander* is actually a calamity, though only Cassandra sees it; Palamedes, the inventor of writing, is undone by the art of writing (which is essential to Odysseus' trap), and the wicked Odysseus is trusted while the good Palamedes is condemned and killed; finally, what men would call victory, the Greek conquest of Troy, turns to destruction for the victors as well as for the victims. However, Murray remains true to his fundamental belief in the optimism, the element of triumph over suffering, in Tragedy.[14] The last play, though it shows "the

[10]Welcker II, 476, quoted with approval by Schmid in Schmid-Stählin, 475, n.4.

[11]See Parmentier, 4 ff. and 9.

[12]"the active phase": i.e., when Hecuba and the Trojans at least *appear* to be captains of their fate. Cf. Snell's description of Hecuba as, for all her efforts to stave off trouble and dishonour, she is eventually shown to be in this trilogy: "Sie gehört eher zu den hilflos irrenden Menschen, wie sie Euripides besonders seit der Mitte des peloponnesischen Krieges häufig dargestellt hat." (Snell, 66)

[13]See Murray, "The Trojan Trilogy," 645, 649–50, 652–56.

[14]Murray, *Aeschylus* (Oxford, 1940), 5–9.

fulfilment of both curses" and "the vanity . . . of all received values," nevertheless carries a suggestion of new values, however undefined, "stirring in the heart of darkness."[15]

This is an extremely neat and ingenious thesis (a little too ingenious, perhaps), and it has, I think, a good deal of the matter in it. But once again it must be pointed out that the third play of the trilogy does *not* deal with the destruction of the Greek fleet: only its prologue is concerned with that. Moreover (as I implied in considering Parmentier's argument), while there are hints of a mythological connection between the first and third plays, the theme of curse fulfilment, of chickens coming home to roost, is (in contrast, say, to what we find in an Aeschylean trilogy) curiously muted.

Less specific but suggestive of another aspect of this trilogy is Wilamowitz's statement about what he believes to be its total teaching, that there is no glimmer of light, of trust, of hope, no glimmer of justice even, in heaven or earth, and that the gods act only from personal motives.[16] This idea may be relieved of its complete pessimism, and brought somewhat closer to the possibility at which Murray has hinted, if we note as we read the *Troades* a curious secularization of the theme. The final darkness is, perhaps, nearly as black as Wilamowitz paints it but what advance we do find between the three plays is to be expressed as an advance in knowledge. Divine causation, the "mythological level," appears to have been more prominent in the first than in the third play and, in the third play, it is increasingly *less* prominent in the action than in the prologue. But only in an analysis of the play can this point be more fully demonstrated.

The Prologue

Euripidean prologues are seldom as straightforward as they seem. Far from giving simply a programme, a summary of events to come, they are often misleading if taken at their face value. In the present instance, the problem is somewhat different from the usual one, for this prologue, in its second part at any rate, deals with happenings which are to occur after the events of the play are over.

In his opening monologue, Poseidon tells us of known Trojan woes—the sack of their city, the desecration of their temples, the slaughter of King Priam on the altar of Zeus *Herkeios*; and of woes not yet known

[15]Murray, "The Trojan Trilogy," 656.
[16]Wilamowitz, *Troerinnen*, *Einleitung*, 263.

to the captives—the sacrifice of Polyxena on Achilles' tomb, the sacrilegious marriage which Agamemnon is to force on Apollo's virgin, Cassandra. Helen, too, is briefly mentioned as "justly numbered among the captive women" (35)—a nice irony in view of how unjustly well she is to fare in the play. Immediately after the reference to Helen, the god points to the prostrate figure of Hecuba who lies mourning her dead before the gates of the city. This juxtaposition tells us in advance how much in the way of divine justice we are to expect in the present play.

Quite as important as this statement of events are the divine attitudes expressed by Poseidon and later by Athena. Poseidon expresses his constant good-will toward the city which he has helped to build. The cause of Troy's fall is expressed (as is proper in a "divine" prologue) entirely in mythological terms: Poseidon was defeated by Argive Hera and by Pallas Athena (23–24); were it not for Pallas, Zeus' child, Troy would be standing yet. (46–47) As for his own position now, Poseidon takes it as self-evident that once a city is defeated, its divine champions will leave it: for divine service is not wont to flourish in desolated territory. (25–27) This traditionally accepted attitude on the part of the gods might perhaps seem unworthy of comment, were it not that divine attitudes in general are to come under further scrutiny later in the prologue and in the subsequent action of the play.

With this monologue to prepare us, what are we to make of the dialogue which now ensues between Poseidon and Athena? The gist of it is that Athena, claiming Poseidon's alliance "for Troy's sake" (57–58), requests his aid in destroying the Achaean fleet on their homeward voyage. The exchange between the two gods (see particularly vv. 57–74) emphasizes the personal, vindictive nature of Athena's *volte-face*. "Is it pity for the Trojans that moves you?" asks Poseidon incredulously. (59–60) He gets no direct answer but it becomes clear that Athena (whose fickleness is stressed again at vv. 67–68) pretends friendship for the Trojans (who are to get little out of it) only to spite the Greeks, since they have failed to punish Ajax for the violation of Athena's temple. (69–71)

The plan of Athena, in which Poseidon readily concurs, to wreck the Greek fleet on their homeward journey has, of course, nothing to do with the dramatic action which this prologue professes to introduce. Commentators (as we have noticed in our discussion of the trilogy) tend to explain this interest in the Greek fleet in terms of general morality rather than in terms of the theme or action (moral or otherwise) of this particular play. Not only, it is argued, will the Trojans suffer but so will the Greeks, the perpetrators of the outrageous Trojan sufferings, and that is a *good* thing and makes us feel less uncomfortable about the Trojans:

> Fool is he [thunders Poseidon, referring now to mortal rather than divine city-sackers] who sacks towns and devastates the tombs, temples and sanctuaries of the slain: he too will perish later! (95–97)

However, as far as the future suffering of the Greeks is concerned, it should be remembered that it is their personal offence against Athena, not their heinous atrocities against the Trojans, which is to bring divine punishment. Closely viewed, there is little justice in this play or in its prologue.

Nevertheless, it is hard to deny that, insofar as this play deals with man's inhumanity to man, the audience must have had some thoughts concerning the villains of the piece (though they are, for the most part, kept off-stage throughout the play) and some ethical satisfaction in the knowledge that they too will suffer. Such thoughts are all the more reasonable in view of the probability (considering the play's date, 415 B.C.) that the poet's compassionate theme was suggested by indignation and sorrow at the treatment of the Melian captives by his fellow citizens.[17] Nevertheless, the Greeks, and more particularly their fate, are ἔξω τοῦ δράματος, as Aristotle, a purist in these matters, would put it. Therefore some explanation of this divine prologue in terms of the theme and action of the play should also be forthcoming.

[17]Many critics have, of course, commented on this and similar overtones to the theme of the *Troades*. See in particular Parmentier, 14 ff., who perhaps rightly broadens the original inspiration of the play to include Euripides' concern over "le caractère de barbarie et d'inhumanité" which kept increasing in the internecine struggles of the Greeks. In support of his view, Parmentier lists (p. 15) the historical examples of the increase in domination by terror on the part of Athens after the death of Pericles, especially in the period between 427 (reduction of Mytilene) and 416 (the mass slaughter and enslavement at Melos). With regard to the Sicilian campaign (for which the Athenian Assembly voted in March, 415) and its outcome, Parmentier comments that Euripides' "moral lesson" (in the *Troades*) was made to appear later as a "prophetic warning." On this point compare H. Steiger, "Warum schrieb Euripides seine *Troerinnen*?" *Philol.*, LIX (N.F. XIII) (1900), 363–66, 388 ff. Steiger goes considerably further than Parmentier and argues that the *Troades*, composed in the period preceding the "Sicilian" decision, was a plea for peace and that its specific propagandist purpose in the immediate circumstances outweighed all other considerations, including those of formal and artistic excellence. Granted the poet's strong feelings about the horrors of the war in his own time, I think that Steiger overemphasizes the *immediate* circumstances and propagandist purposes of the play and, more particularly, their alleged detrimental effect on its dramatic qualities.

The most striking feature of the prologue is its picture of the gods as cruel and selfish in their awful decisions and fickle in their allegiances. For the time being Euripides seems to accept the mythological apparatus more completely even than Homer ever did: Greek successes and Trojan reverses in the war are simply the result of Hera's and Athena's prejudice (based, it is clear, on personal affront), and the future career of the conquerors is to be determined in precisely the same way. This emphasis is in sharp contrast to the action of the play itself, where human sufferings appear simply as the result of human cruelty.

Athena is presented as vindictive and spiteful, but the picture of Poseidon is hardly more attractive. Ostensibly bland and benevolent, this god shows first an unabashed willingness to abandon his people and later a startling readiness to join in any plan (either for or against the Trojans) which Athena may propose. (See vv. 61–64.) It may well be argued that there is little new in this presentation of the gods, that, if anything, Euripides is simply outdoing Homer in "Homeric" gods. But when we remember that the poet frequently demands, through his characters, a higher ethical standard from his gods than the tradition allows them, we may suspect that the exaggerations of this prologue, like that of the prologue to the *Hippolytus*, are really aimed at the repudiation of the mythological tradition.

Hecuba too (in the coming action) is to share with other Euripidean characters the habit of expecting more of the mythological gods than the "tradition" has given her any right to expect. Thus, if we are right in our view of the prologue's emphasis, we shall find that it bears a definite relation to the theme of the play. It is Hecuba's discovery of what these gods *are* (or, more depressing, what they are *not*) that is to form an important part of the tragic understanding (πάθει μάθος) which she achieves.

Theme and Structure

It has commonly been argued that the *Troades* is a play signally lacking in dramatic structure.[18] Some critics have condemned, or at least severely censured the work on these grounds, others have found it intensely moving, even as drama, despite this alleged defect, but however judgments have varied, the general impression of the play conveyed

[18]See, for example, Steiger, 362–63, and the comments there cited. Cf. also Wilamowitz, *Troerinnen*, *Einleitung*, 263, "Die *Troerinnen* geben keine fortlaufende Handlung, sondern eine Reihe von Scenen konvergieren auf dasselbe Ziel . . ." and Murray, 645, ". . . the only movement . . . a gradual extinguishing of all the familiar lights of human life . . ."

by the critics is that it presents a succession of unrelieved and ever deepening woe. Few will question the varied and striking successes of individual passages: the brilliant Cassandra episode, with its effective contrasts of frenzied lyric and strong dramatic exposition; the vivid choral description of the Trojan Horse *débâcle*; the final *kommos*, as the Queen and her women beat upon the soil in their last farewell to the Trojan dead. More contrived, but intensely interesting for its own sake, is the set debate between Hecuba and Helen on the question of the latter's guilt. However we may regard the incident in relation to the rest of the play, the rhetorical verve of this confrontation, in a life-and-death struggle, of the mythical and the rationalistic interpretations of Helen's story provides one of Euripides' most arresting scenes.

With all these riches, is the *Troades* still a play which fails to combine its effects within an organic dramatic structure? This seems improbable when we notice that those who like the play praise it for its final and total impact. The power of this play increases steadily until it is finished; its closing lines leave us with a sense of completeness which no mere series of episodes, however striking in themselves, could possibly evoke.

In considering the dramatic structure of the *Troades*, we should remember that it completed a trilogy which was at least loosely connected in theme: thus the whole of the present play may be regarded as in some sense a conclusion. This does not mean that it need not have a structure of its own, with its own beginning, middle and end, but it is quite reasonable to suppose that this fact may have a certain limiting effect on the play as a whole. Consider the *Eumenides* in relation to the *Agamemnon*: no elaborate analysis of either play is needed to observe that the structure of the last play of the trilogy is far less complex, just as its tensions are far less tightly drawn. There are certain obvious reasons why this should be the case generally in connected trilogies. Psychological considerations aside (a series of three plays of the power and complex tensions of an *Agamemnon* would surely reach a point of diminishing returns), the sheer density of material, both actual and potential, must be far greater in the early part of the trilogy. Every critic knows that even within any single play, the structural complexities will be greater in the earlier half or two thirds of it, as the poet seeks to make his revelations gradually in the particular dramatic form required. In the proportions of a closely connected trilogy we may expect to find not the same but an analogous situation. Each play has its own end to reach, its particular material to realize. But in the first play, *all* of the material must be present either actually or potentially, and elaborate structural devices may be needed to effect the anticipatory ironies so essential to

Greek drama. (In the case of the *Agamemnon*, anticipatory irony often gives place to veiled prophecy; consider how much the role of Cassandra is influenced by the subsequent development of the trilogy.) The total amount of unrevealed material gradually decreases as the trilogy proceeds, so that progressively less elaborate structures are required. In the case of the *Troades* something of the same process is at work, though to a lesser degree.

In most tragedies which we know, cause and effect, with sometimes an ironic perversion of purposive action, determine structure. (This is as true of *Macbeth* and *King Lear* as it is of *Oedipus Tyrannus* and *Hippolytus*.) In the *Troades*, on the other hand, the time for action has passed; Troy and her leaders have fallen and all that remains to be shown is the long passion of the Queen and her women who have survived the cataclysm. A mere sequence of disaster, however, does not make a drama, and in default of real action on the part of Hecuba there appears a faint outline of policy and even of a curious intermittent hope which punctuates the sufferings. Again and again, this hope is stamped out and gives away to desolation, only to flicker forth in some new place until its final quenching at the end of the play. Thus a certain rhythm is introduced into what would otherwise be a mere chain of woeful experiences, and it is this rhythm which informs the structure of the play.

In all this, the anticipatory "preparations" of the prologue do not come amiss. Fluctuations in the Trojans' attitudes toward the gods reflect, to some degree, the alternations just described. Viewed in this light, the play's progression might be regarded as the gradual recognition, on the part of Hecuba and her women, of the truth about the gods which the prologue has already expressed, by satiric implication, to the audience.

We may best appreciate this rhythm of hope and desolation if we read through the play rapidly, pausing only to note the dominant tone of each part, the major effect of each incident. The Chorus too, as one would expect in a play so dominated by pathos, will be seen to play an important part in reflecting the changing moods of the dramatic passages.

Both the *Hecuba* and the *Troades* begin, when the prologue is over, with a lyric passage from the Queen, but two passages show very different reactions on her part to the sufferings which surround her. In the former play, Hecuba begs her fellow-slaves (as they now are) to lift her, a tottering old woman, into the open air. (59–63) In the opening lyric of the *Troades*, Hecuba shows a full awareness of her woes, but here her first words give *herself* the command to raise her head (98), and soon she is expressing a kind of "policy in desolation" which she is to follow, and bid others to follow, throughout the play. "Sail with the flood; steer with your destiny (κατὰ δαίμονα); sail with the winds of chance; set not your prow against the flux of life." (102–4)

The repetition of the word *daimon*, which occurs four times in the opening lyric, is interesting and effective. It is one of Euripides' favourite words for that indefinite divine power, a shade more definite than *tychê*, which affects the destinies of men. Here the poet's insistence on the term, and his emphasis on the changing winds of fate (μεταβαλλομένου δαίμονος, 101) keeps fresh and immediate the impression already made on us by the fickle gods of the prologue. Hecuba is well aware that the gods have, at least for the present, turned away from her, but she does not as yet rail against them or explicitly despair of their return. Yet there is already a hint of bitterness in the nostalgic reference at the end of her monologue to the triumphal strains with which she used to lead the chorus in praise of the gods of Troy:

> . . . how strange my clamour now, like to a mother-bird's over her nestlings, not like the song I used to sing in Trojan choruses, leaning on Priam's sceptre, honouring the gods. (146–52)

Here the Chorus of Trojan women enters. Their fluttering terror, their anxious cries ("What is the news? What will happen to us all? Already the ships are moving. . . . What chieftain will take me as his slave?") Hecuba answers with the same resolute acceptance of their desperate plight which she has already shown: "I know not, but I guess the worst." (163)

In the *stasimon* which follows, the captive women develop their speculations about their future home. Vignettes of many states and colonies of Greece are included in these lyric wanderings; in the fears and preferences which the Chorus shows, the poet allows (in addition, no doubt, to some contemporary references)[19] a few gleams of hope to lighten the gloom. Thus, while one singer shudders at drudgery in Corinth, another prays that she may reach that "illustrious happy land of Theseus." Sparta, home of Helen and Menelaus, is of course the most dreaded of all, but good reports are heard of Thessaly which, for its wealth and beauty, is chosen next to Athens itself as the favourite place for slavery!

The entry of Talthybius announcing the bitter facts of the Greek choices seems timed to quench these optimistic flashes. Agamemnon is to wed Cassandra, the sacred virgin of Apollo; Andromache is to go to the son of her husband's slayer and Queen Hecuba to Odysseus, the

[19]See H. D. Westlake, *Mnem.* (1953), 181–91.

Greek whom she most despises; Polyxena, the youngest and fairest, the Greeks will sacrifice upon Achilles' tomb. These dooms could hardly be worse; a new access of woe finds expression in Hecuba's passionate outburst against "that hateful tricky monster" (282 ff.) who is to be her master.

Suddenly the gloom is rent asunder by the triumphant entry of Cassandra, shrieking ecstatically of her coming nuptials:

> Raise high the marriage torch. . . . Hymen, Lord Hymen! Blessed is the bride-groom and blessed too the bride—I who am to serve the royal bed of Agamemnon at Argos! Hail, Lord Hymen, hail! (308–14)

As Cassandra links her mother's bereavements with her celebrations, and the name of Hecate with that of Hymen, we soon catch the baleful irony, the sardonic exaltation, beneath this girlish carolling, and soon the inevitable cry to Phoebus Apollo confirms our guess that Cassandra's mockery is buoyed up by some real secret joy. (This is the twist which gives a special brilliance to the Cassandra scene: the joy with which she greets her coming marriage, and which so shocks her mother and the Chorus, is a real joy, though its reasons are the reverse of those which might be inferred from a literal reading of her lyric.) All these hints are soon fulfilled in the "sane" speech with which Cassandra (like her Aeschylean counterpart) explains her lyric. Her "marriage" will bring death on Agamemnon and the hated house of Atreus in turn will perish in matricidal murder. (354–64)

To these sardonic satisfactions, Cassandra adds further consolations to the Trojans. The war has profited them more than their conquerors: for the sake of one woman, Greeks have died far from home, without family, without burial, while the Trojans have gained the greatest glory in dying for their native land. Even Paris has gained a kind of fame in marrying Zeus' daughter! (365–99)

It is Cassandra's fate never to be heeded by her people. Her speeches here, which should provide the one great relief to Trojan gloom, have no effect. We know and Cassandra knows that the Greeks in turn will suffer, but by Apollo's trick the knowledge must still be hidden from those who need this satisfaction most. The Queen who has earlier raised her head in the midst of her miseries (98 ff.) now bids the women let her lie, and a new cynicism breaks into her habitual prayers.

"Let me lie where I have fallen. . . ." This indeed seems the final despair of Hecuba. Yet when Andromache mutters her envy of the dead Polyxena, the Queen rounds on her: "Life can never be as bad as death! Death is a nothingness, but in life is hope." (632–33)

In the rhythm of the play, the main significance of this debate between Hecuba and Andromache is the resurrection of hope which Hecuba again provides. Andromache's speech is disappointing: a set rhetorical exercise on two unrelated themes: "Death *versus* unhappy living" and "The proper deportment of wives and widows." The speech abounds in the bitter ironies and classic dilemmas of pathetic rhetoric; only the peroration addressed to Hector's shade saves it from banality. Yet once again, Hecuba finds solace. The sight of the young mother Andromache reminds her of the one remaining hope; Andromache must live to raise her son and Hector's son: ". . . Troy's mainstay now, for children sired by him may build again; our city may exist again." (703–5) Hardly has this hope been uttered when Talthybius enters with the dread announcement that Astyanax is to be cast from the battlements.

Now for the first time even the Chorus turns against the gods. Hecuba has already blamed them, though briefly. (696) Andromache has blamed everyone: the Greeks, of course (764–65), Helen in the most savage terms (766–69), even Priam and Hecuba, by implication, for letting Paris grow up (597 ff.); but most emphatically she blames the gods. (597, 599, 775–76) And now the Chorus, remembering Ganymede and Tithonus, Troy's fairest offerings, murmur "Vain indeed for Troy were these love-charms of the gods!" (858–59)

φίλτρα φροῦδα Τροίᾳ: with unconscious irony, the Chorus' words provide the cue for Menelaus, another cast-off of love, who summons Helen, the love-charm which has caused the Trojans' woe. Structurally too the entry of Helen is excellently placed, for only such a challenge could revive the flagging powers of Hecuba. At the sound of Menelaus' threats on Helen's life, Hecuba utters a new prayer of hope in the justice of the gods:

> You who contain the Earth, yet dwell upon it, Whoever you are, Zeus, hard-guessing for the wise, whether the necessary laws of nature or the mind of man, I pray to you: for walking silent ways you guide in accord with justice the affairs of man. (884–88)

This "new prayer," as Menelaus calls it in surprise (889), has occasioned much learned comment from the critics. Wilamowitz,[20] for example, observes (with certain qualifications) that Hecuba is actually invoking a power like the divine air (*ἀήρ*) of Diogenes or the world mind (*νοῦς*) of Anaxagoras, which according to the philosophers controlled the world and all its motions and thought. More significant, perhaps, is this

[20]Wilamowitz, *Troerinnen*, *Einleitung*, 283 and n. 1.

critic's observation that at this point Hecuba dares believe, now that Helen is apparently to be brought to justice, that this law of nature works, in some incomprehensible way, in accordance with justice. In any case, we may agree that this prayer recalls to the audience daring contemporary views on the gods; it serves too as prologue to Hecuba's coming refutation of Helen's "traditional" defence of her sin ("It was the gods. . . ."). For, in the debate for her life which now ensues (919 ff.), Helen follows and even improves upon the orthodox interpretation: first Hecuba and then Priam are guilty, the one for bearing, the other for not destroying, the fatal fire-brand Paris; next Aphrodite was the cause, for when Paris came to abduct her the god was with him and not even Zeus himself can resist Aphrodite. How insistent, in contrast to Hecuba's prayer, is the anthropomorphism now! The passage is, moreover, enriched by several Euripidean "improvements." To the traditional "Homeric" defence of Helen that the fault was Aphrodite's, Helen adds the boast that thanks to the lure of her beauty Greece was saved, for had Paris accepted either Hera's or Pallas' bribes, instead of Aphrodite's, Greece would have been enslaved. Again, in having Helen ask herself the crucial question: "What indeed was I thinking of, to abandon home and country for that foreigner?" (946–47), the poet makes this alleged pawn of the gods undergo a moment of uncertainty before letting her accept "the divine excuse" again.

Hecuba's attack on Helen's arguments begins with a defence of Pallas Athena and Hera against the charges of folly implied in Helen's story. This questioning of myths disparaging the gods is, of course, common in Euripidean drama; usually however, such passages abandon the anthropomorphic level of mythology on which such discreditable stories of the gods are based. Consider, for example, Heracles' argument at *Heracles* 1341–46 which ends, ". . . the god, if he be really god, needs nothing," and comparable passages in the *Hippolytus* (120), the *I.T.* (389–91) and the *Bacchae* (1348), where we find the same implication that by nature the gods should be above human passions. In the present passage, Euripides with more attention to dramatic relevance keeps Hecuba's argument on the anthropomorphic level: why should *these* goddesses, Hera who has already got Zeus, and Athena, who has chosen a virgin's life, barter their favourite states to win a prize for beauty? (976–81) Not till she deals with Aphrodite does the more typical Euripidean rationalism begin to intrude into Hecuba's argument:

> My son was peerless in his beauty; on seeing him your mind *became* the god of love. For folly is men's "Aphrodite"; hence is the name derived from foolishness (ἀφροσύνης). (987–90)

Hecuba wins the debate; she persuades Menelaus that Helen has willingly abandoned him. But it is Helen, or rather Helen's beauty, which finally carries the day. Before Helen's entry, Hecuba has begged Menelaus not to look upon her, lest desire sap his resolution. (891) Now despite more blustering from Menelaus, she hears him postponing Helen's death till they reach Argos. She persuades him not to allow Helen on the same ship as himself, but one feels that she is now fighting a losing battle. The gloomy ode which follows substantiates this sense of defeat. It begins (1060–80) with more direct reproaches to Zeus than the Chorus has yet permitted itself ("So, Zeus, you have betrayed your Trojan temple, your Trojan altar . . ." [1060 ff.] and "In vain our sacrifices, in vain the reverent music of our choirs" [1071 ff.]); it ends with a prayer for Helen's death at sea (even as she holds her "golden mirrors, delight of virgins"—a nice touch) in terms which clearly indicate fear of Helen's re-establishment in Sparta.

After the scene with Helen, there are no further resurrections, however slight, of Trojan hope. Two brusque entries of Talthybius, once with the body of Astyanax, once to announce the final burning of Troy and the order for departure, evoke two moving laments from Hecuba. (Talthybius is a harsh, sinister figure in the *Troades*, very different from the sympathetic Talthybius of the *Hecuba*; here he is used to represent the impersonal cruelty of the Achaeans; though personally guiltless of the deeds and instructions he relates, we cannot but sympathize with Cassandra's scornful comment on the type he represents. [424–426]) Hecuba's lament for Astyanax opens with a castigation of Achaean cowardice and closes with a pathetic reminiscence of Hector, suggested by the imprints left on Hector's shield on which the body of the child is to be buried. But it is Hecuba's account of the tender relations between herself and her little grandson which leads to the heart of this ultimate desolation:

It is not you who bury me, but I you, the younger one; an old woman, without city, without child, buries this pitiful corpse. Vain were my nursings, my many kisses, and vain too my dreams for you, of old. (1185–88)

In these final passages, both Queen and Chorus seem to turn completely from the gods: "From the gods, naught but trouble . . . in vain our sacrifices!" (1240, 1242) "Why call upon the gods? They heard us not, when called upon before."(1280–81) When Hecuba does call upon them, it is more in indignation than in prayer: "Son of Cronos, Lord of Troy, begetting father, have you seen what things unworthy of the Trojan race we suffer?" and the Chorus, which has earned its own share of tragic knowledge, replies, "He *has* seen—and the great city has become nothing. Troy is no longer." (1288–93) In this last *kommos* between the Queen and her women, as the smoke from the burning city rises in the background, we have reached the end of that rhythm which false and intermittent hope has lent to this theme of suffering. Yet even here there is something more than the mere desolation. It appears first in Hecuba's echo of that consolation suggested earlier by Cassandra: the recognition that, in a sense, Trojan greatness and future fame depend on this utter ruin which the gods have sent. The stature which the ruined Hecuba acquires in these final scenes reminds us of the special kind of nobility which the ruined Oedipus (in Sophocles' *O.C.*) possesses. This feeling for the nobility of an Oedipus, or a Hecuba, derives in part from the aura of almost superstitious awe with which the Greeks surrounded those necessarily great personnages who had suffered the ultimate in woe and yet endured. It derives in part, also, from the awareness which such strangely privileged beings have finally acquired of their real position in relation to the gods, or (in non-mythological terms) to the outside forces, merciless, because impersonal, which frame their destiny, and which can no longer hurt them more.

In the final lament, Hecuba has abandoned hope and vain cries to the gods, but she is still not passive. Still she leads her women in the one invocation which has any meaning left: the Trojan soil, the earth, and beneath it, the vast familial crowding of the dead.

8

THE *Hecuba*

The Myth and Its Adaptation

The plot material of Euripides' *Hecuba* falls into two clearly distinguished parts: the Greeks' sacrifice of Hecuba's daughter, Polyxena, to the shade of Achilles, and the vengeance of Hecuba on the Thracian king, Polymestor, for the murder of her son, Polydorus. This division has caused much controversy over the play's construction; indeed, so drastic has the alleged disjunction between the two parts seemed to some critics that theories of "separate composition" (explained sometimes by the political, sometimes by the cultural circumstances of the time) have been advanced to account for it.[1]

Decision concerning this structural problem can be reached only by

[1]Several summaries of critical comments on the "two parts" of the *Hecuba* have already appeared in other studies: see, *inter alia*, J. A. Spranger, *CQ*, XXI (1927), 155–58, and Ernst L. Abrahamson, *TAPA*, LXXXIII (1952), 120–29.

Among the more extreme critics of the alleged disjunction between the parts of the *Hecuba*, Spranger and E. Delebecque (*Euripide et la Guerre du Péloponnèse*, Paris 1951, chap. 6) both seek to prove that the Polymestor episode had no part in the original dramatic conception, which was a tragedy on the Polyxena theme. Spranger's explanation of what happened follows the theory, familiar to readers of Verrall and his followers, that Euripides sometimes composed shorter plays for private production and then expanded them to festival length by adding material, with (to judge from Spranger's own strictures on the Polymestor "addition") scant concern for its suitability to the original theme. Cf. the similar approach of A. W. Verrall in *Essays on Four Plays of Euripides*, 43 ff., 125–30, and of Norwood in *Essays*, 32–36, who quotes Spranger's argument on the Hecuba with approval. Delebecque's conclusion is reached by quite a different route, *viz.*, his tortuous political argument that half-way through the composition of this play, the fall of Amphipolis, in December, 424, turned Euripides' energies (at what cost to his artistic integrity!) to a concentrated attack on the King of Thrace. The analysis to be put forth in the present chapter will, it is hoped, suffice to refute these more extreme views about the two parts of the *Hecuba*.

an analysis of the play itself; however, a review of Euripides' adaptation of the legendary material (insofar as it can be ascertained) may provide some preliminary indication of the dramatist's intent.

In Euripides' version of the sacrifice of Polyxena, Achilles himself (as described by the ghost of Polydorus in the Prologue, 37 ff., and later by the Chorus, 109 ff.) appears as a shade over his tomb and demands the sacrifice as the Greek host is about to sail homewards after the sack of Troy.[2] The army assembly is divided in its opinion on the matter until Odysseus persuades it not to reject the best of the Danaans for the sake of a slave (116–40). In each of these passages, Achilles' ghost is represented as restraining the ships (38–39, 111–12), though in the subsequent plot development, little is made of the idea of obtaining favourable winds by the sacrifice;[3] indeed, Odysseus, both in the reported assembly scene (138 ff.) and in his later defence of the decision to *Hecuba*, argues only in terms of *charis*, the gratitude due to great warriors such as Achilles.

The sacrifice itself, in Euripides' play, is carried out by Neoptolemus, since he is Achilles' son. However, this scene, in Talthybius' moving account of it (518 ff.), belongs almost wholly to Polyxena, who succeeds in reducing her captors to the role of mere executors of a fate which she herself has willingly accepted.

References both to the apparition of Achilles to the departing Achaeans, and to the sacrifice of Polyxena at the tomb of Achilles, occur in the epic and lyric tradition prior to Greek tragedy. The two events are referred to separately in two passages from Proclus, one, in his account of the *Nostoi*, to the effect that Achilles' shade tried to prevent the departure of the Greeks by prophesying dire events in store for them, the other, in his epitome of the *Iliu Persis* of Arctinus, to the effect that the sacrifice of Polyxena at Achilles' tomb was narrated therein.[4]

Of Ibycus' treatment of the Polyxena theme, all we know is that here, as in Euripides, Neoptolemus is given as the slayer of Polyxena; the scholion providing this information also gives us this interesting variant cited from the Cyprian lays: that Polyxena was mortally wounded in the

[2]On the difficulty involved in the setting of the play on the shores of the Thracian Chersonese, see below, note 15.

[3]See vv. 900 and 1289–90 for the two fairly casual references to these winds.

[4]See *EGP*, 53 and 50, respectively. References to most of the sources cited in the present discussion are to be found, in one form or another, in Méridier, 165 ff., Preller-Robert, *Griech. Mythol.*[4], II, 1275 ff., and Schmid, 465 ff.; however, since it is not always clear from their discussions how much or how little information is to be gleaned from each source, it seems preferable to scan them again individually.

sack of Troy by Diomedes and Odysseus, and was *buried* by Neoptolemus.[5]

There seems, then, to be some uncertainty or, at least, inconsistency in the accounts, with regard to the responsibility of Achilles' ghost in the death of Polyxena. One authority has even suggested that this element first appeared in Simonides' treatment of the myth; however, all that we actually know of Simonides in this connection is that, according to "Longinus," he most vividly described the appearance of Achilles, over his tomb, to the departing Greeks: there is no mention of Polyxena in Longinus' reference to this description.[6] Nor does our sparse knowledge of Sophocles' *Polyxena* help us much in this matter. It is true that a scholion on *Hecuba* 1 tells us that "the part about Polyxena is also to be found in Sophocles," but this rather vague account need not be taken to include Achilles' request for her sacrifice, particularly as the fragments themselves suggest a possible indication in the other direction. None of these deals with the sacrifice itself, but we do learn (fragments 523 and 526) that the ghost of Achilles appeared in the play, gave prophetic warning of the murder of Agamemnon and, possibly (fragment 526), of the storm which was to plague the Greeks on their homeward journey.[7] There is nothing in the fragments to suggest that Achilles' ghost demanded the sacrifice of Polyxena; indeed, H. Weil has suggested[8] that the most probable place for the ghost's prophetic warnings is at the end of Sophocles' play, *after* the sacrifice of Polyxena, for

[5]Schol. *Hec.* 41 (Ibycus frg. 36). This scholiast also quotes "others" to the effect that Achilles was slain in the grove of the Thymbraean Apollo, after coming to an agreement with Priam concerning the marriage of Polyxena. Cf. also Seneca, *Tro.* 195 and 942–44, from which it is clear that the sacrifice demanded by Achilles is regarded as a kind of nuptial. Certainly the idea of an earlier betrothal of Polyxena to Achilles would help to explain the sacrifice, but all extant allusions to it are late (for a full list of such references, see Roscher, *Lexicon der Griechischen und Römischen Mythologie*, III, 2, 2720 ff.) and many, such as those in Hyginus, Philostratus and "Dictys," and in the scholion quoted above, contain details which conflict, both in tone and in fact, with epic accounts of the Trojan Wars. It is on such grounds that H. Weil, *Sept Tragédies d'Euripide*, 204–5, insists on the post-tragic origin of erotic legends linking Polyxena and Achilles. There is, at any rate, no definite evidence for the view (expressed by Méridier, 166, and others) that they may go back to the Cyprian lays.

[6]See Simonides, frg. 209 (*PLG*, p. 526).

[7]See Sophocles, *Fragments*, ed. A. C. Pearson, 2, 161 ff.

[8]Weil, 204. Pearson (*op. cit.*, 162) appears to believe that the connection between the appearance of Achilles' ghost and the death of Polyxena was made at some time later than the composition of the cyclic epics. He cites the view of F. Noack, *Ilioupersis* (Giessen, 1890) 11 ff., that Sophocles was the first to bring the appearance of the ghost into causal relation with the sacrifice, but concludes,

these warnings, coming early in a play not concerned with their fulfilment, could only serve to distract the audience (not to mention Agamemnon!) from the business on hand.

That Odysseus played some part in early versions of the Polyxena legend seems highly probable. We have already noted his "alternative" role in the euphemistic Cyprian version, and both Odysseus and Calchas (who is not mentioned by Euripides) appear as witnesses in a scene, possibly inspired by Stesichorus, on the *tabula iliaca*,[9] which shows the sacrifice of Polyxena at the tomb of Achilles. In Euripides' play, Odysseus' role in the sacrifice is quite fully developed (possibly at the expense of Calchas); here too, we should note an interesting, if minor, invention of the dramatist: the passage (239–50) in which Hecuba is represented as having once saved the life of Odysseus during the siege of Troy. This incident, together with the whole treatment of Odysseus' role, contributes to a kind of dialectic on the subject of *charis* which runs through the play.

Thus, despite the meagre evidence concerning early treatment of the details of the Polyxena legend, we can, perhaps, detect certain tendencies in Euripides' adaptation of it. By various means, he presents the sacrifice theme in such a way as to place the Greeks in the least favourable light. Achilles' ghost specifically demands the sacrifice of the maiden (whether this was the case in previous versions, we cannot be certain; at any rate, it was not the case in all versions); then Odysseus' defence of it in terms of political expediency ("Otherwise, who hereafter will fight and die for Greece?") distracts attention from the idea of religious necessity, or of supernatural blackmail ("no sacrifice, no winds") which would surely have provided the best excuse (though hardly a Euripidean one) for fulfilling Achilles' appalling command. Furthermore, Euripides' suppression of the role of Calchas, the priest, in favour of Odysseus, the politician, in the sacrifice of Polyxena, is in keeping with this tendency of his to secularize such themes, or at least to provide motives of a political, as well as those of a supernatural order.[10]

This treatment, in turn, gives occasion for other typical Euripidean ingredients: the vivid assembly debate (reported by the Chorus at 116–40), rich in contemporary overtones, and the sophistic plays on the

"... the gaps in the evidence are too wide to permit us to entertain these speculations." (Cf. also above, note 5.)

[9]On the much debated origin of this tablet, found near Bovilla, and on the sources of its scenes, see Max Paulke, *De Tabula Iliaca Quaestiones Stesichorae*, diss. inaug. (Koenigsberg, 1897).

[10]As we have noted in chapter 5, there is at least a hint of this duality in the motives, however noble, ascribed to Theseus in Euripides' *Suppliants*.

charis theme, which, as we have seen, he has taken some trouble to introduce.

Finally, the Polyxena of this play, converted from a passive victim to a heroic character in her own right, surely bears the typical Euripidean stamp, for, provided that we do not press the comparisons too closely, she shows affinities with various noble ladies who face similar deaths in other Euripidean plays.[11]

While it has been argued that there is little mythical innovation in the first part of the Hecuba, the dearth of references (in sources independent of Euripides) to Polymestor's murder and Hecubas' revenge has led some scholars to regard these incidents as the poet's own invention.[12] Neither of these extremes, however, strikes one as typical of Euripides' creative adaptation of myth. Pohlenz' view of the Polymestor-Polydorus development seems the most probable: that this particularly barbarous murder belonged to a legend arising from the hatred of Greek settlers for their Thracian neighbours in the Chersonese. As for Hecuba, Polymestor's prophecy at the end of Euripides' play, that she will turn into a hound, and that her tomb will be named accordingly, no doubt relates to an already established legend which need, of course, have no previous connection with her vengeance on Polydorus. Pohlenz, with some mythical imagination, accounts for "the baying of the hound-dog Hecuba," after her bereavements at Troy, in metaphorical terms comparable to the plaints of Philomela for her child which became changed in myth to the cry of the nightingale. This unconscious mythical metaphor became, in time, linked with one of several "Hound's Grave" (κυνὸς σῆμα) promontories in the Thracian Chersonese and so with the legend of Thracian barbarism mentioned above.[13] It is possible that

[11]E.g., Macaria in the *Heracleidae*, Evadne in the *Suppliants*, and Iphigenia in the *Iphigenia at Aulis*: granted the differences in motive and context, there is a similarity in the noble acceptance of an early and violent death.

[12]It is generally agreed that the Polyxena episode is by far the more traditional part of the plot and that Euripides' most original stroke is his joining of this myth with the story about Polymestor. See, for example, *RE*, VII, 2, 2657; Preller-Robert, 1280–81; Schmid, 465–66 and Méridier, 169–74, who remarks (172–73) on the complete silence, except for Euripides, until the *Iliona* of Pacuvius (second century B.C.) on the subject of the murder of Polydorus by the Thracian King. Some critics, e.g., Schmid and Wolf H. Friedrich (*Euripides und Diphilos*, 38–39, 52), argue that Euripides uses the traditional Polyxena material mainly to prepare for, or to support, in one way or another, the (allegedly) unknown, original material concerning Polymestor and Polydorus. However, as we shall see, opinions differ on the degree of originality involved.

[13]Pohlenz, 277–78; cf. the similar view of Méridier (173), who also ascribes Vergil's veiled reference (*Aen.* iii. 15–16) to the fate of Polydorus to a local

Euripides himself invented both the relationship between Polydorus and Hecuba[14] and the tale of her vengeance on Polymestor for his murder. At any rate, as far as we can tell, no other version of the woes of Hecuba, or of the sacrifice of Polyxena, includes this curious sequel in which the Trojan queen turns to the slayers of her daughter for aid in vengeance on the murderer of her son.

If the most distinctive feature in the plot-material of this play consists in the blending of the traditional "sacrifice myth" with an obscure Thracian legend and its Euripidean sequel, surely it is reasonable to suppose that we shall find the central meaning of the play in the dramatic exploitation of this new juxtaposition, and of its distinctly Euripidean climax. The patent dissimilarities between the two subjects, and the technical difficulties (particularly in the matter of the play's *setting*),[15] would surely seem to indicate that Euripides must have had some specific purpose in attempting such a combination. Only if we fail to find any real thematic or structural links between the two parts of the play should we seek that purpose in explanations extraneous to its dramatic meaning. Perhaps, however, it can be shown that the distinctly Euripidean adaptations noted in the first part of this play's material give rise to certain themes, and certain dramatic expectations, which find their tragic fulfilment only in the play's concluding passages.

Thracian legend. Most authorities are agreed on the pre-Euripidean origin of the "hound-dog Hecuba" myth: see Schmid, 466, Preller-Robert, 1280, Méridier, 173, note 6, and the references there given.

[14]In the *Iliad*, Polydorus is the youngest son of Priam (xx. 409–10) and of Laothoë. (xxi. 85 ff., xxii. 46 ff.) He is slain by Achilles during battle. (xx. 407 ff.)

[15]The fact that the scene of the play is laid on the shores of the Thracian Chersonese, across the straits from the traditional site of the tomb of Achilles at Sigeum, must be admitted as a Euripidean inconsistency. Euripides obviously needed the Thracian setting to make the discovery of Polydorus' body and the prompt arrival of Polymestor more probable; the geographical vagueness, or inaccuracy, does not appear to have bothered him as much as it does certain modern critics, some of whom have used this difficulty to further unlikely theories about the composition of the play as a whole. (See, for example, Spranger, 155 ff., Delebecque, 161 ff.) Apart from the intrinsic unlikelihood of these explanations, the evidence is all against attempts to place a "Polyxena play" in the Troad and a "Polymestor play" in Thrace: all the local references (30–41, 70–72, 1142) explicitly indicate the Thracian setting and none that of the Troad. Nor will it do to argue that the references to Achilles' appearance over his tomb in themselves imply the setting of the play (or a part of the play) in the Troad, for Polydorus' ghost twice emphasizes the present Thracian setting in the very passage in which he first mentions Achilles' appearance over his tomb and his staying of the ships. (30–41)

Some Critical Views

The *Hecuba* has suffered almost as badly from its defenders as from its detractors, for several critics have sought to minimize, or to explain, the play's duality in ways which tend to obscure certain essential dramatic contrasts in it. There have been two main lines of defence. According to the first, the real unity of the play lies in the person of Hecuba. Thus, Hecuba is said to "experience" both actions, the sacrifice of Polyxena being regarded, sometimes as a dramatic means of gaining sympathy for the bereaved mother, sometimes as a factor contributing to her moral break-down in the second part of the play.[16] According to the second, the structural key to the play is to be found in some form of ideological contrast between the two actions. In its simplest form, this approach has produced such analyses as that of Miss Matthaei, which presents the sacrifice of Polyxena as an example of community justice and the revenge of Hecuba as an example of individual, somehow identified with "primitive," justice.[17] Neither of these approaches has been completely successful, for neither pays sufficient attention, in considering the meaning of the play as a whole, either to the early characterization of Hecuba or to the considerable dramatic impact which the attitude of Polyxena makes on us in the first half. Two of the most perceptive examinations of the *Hecuba* (those of Pohlenz and of Kirkwood) combine both of the approaches just described; a brief examination of them may, perhaps, indicate the shortcomings of the "ideological approach" as a means of expounding the tragic change alleged to take place in the character of the Queen.

Pohlenz, agreeing with the first critics cited above about the joint and subsidiary function of Polyxena and Polydorus, finds the play's originality in the contrasting effects of their fates upon Hecuba, "the first figure of tragedy who experiences an inner change."[18] Thus the "soft and womanly" creature who accepts the sacrifice of her daughter with resig-

[16]See, for example, Méridier, 175–78; H. Vandaele, *Xenia* (1912) 10–24. The main fault with these descriptions, true enough in themselves, of Hecuba's sufferings, followed by Hecuba's vengeance, is that they fail to bring out the essential dramatic, and thematic, relations between the two parts of the play. Méridier, for example, describes the various stages in "la progression psychologique" of Hecuba, but such progression, in itself, constitutes neither tragic, nor even dramatic, form.

[17]Matthiae 118–57, especially 128 ff. Even if true, such descriptions will help us little in problems of structure and dramatic effect, for a successful drama does not deal directly with such generalized ideas.

[18]". . . die erste Gestalt der Tragödie, die eine innere Wandlung durchmacht . . . ," Pohlenz, 281. The present summary is based on Pohlenz, 277–84.

nation is transformed into a Medea-like fiend of vengeance at the death of Polydorus. In explaining these different effects, Pohlenz makes much of the idea of *nomos*. "Historically," in terms of the legend (Pohlenz argues) the ghost of Achilles *could* stop the ships; the dead had rights, in men's opinion, and so Odysseus truly argues from a position of "*Staatsraison*," while no kind of *nomos* can justify the self-interested atrocity of Polymestor. Both Hecuba and Agamemnon, however, have a share in *nomos*: Hecuba's savage vengeance is an expression of her inner conception of justice and, as such, Agamemnon acquiesces in it, while his own *nomos*, his concern for the will of his followers, forbids his lending active support to it. Thus Pohlenz concludes: "No longer does the tragic conflict spring from the struggle against superhuman fate, but rather from the coercive force of *nomos*."[19]

The suggestion that in this play the Greek's sacrifice of Polyxena is to be accepted as in accordance with *nomos* has already been ably refuted;[20] here it should suffice to add two general considerations which render such a view unlikely.

In the first place, Pohlenz's "historical" argument, in terms of the age to which the myth belongs, simply does not apply to Euripidean drama. As we have seen from such passages as *Heracles* 1340 ff., and *I.T.* 389–91, "mythical considerations" were never allowed to excuse attitudes or actions which, judged by the poet's own ethical views, could not be condoned. Whether this Euripidean trait is dramatically legitimate or not is another question, but certainly it is a part of his iconoclastic attitude to certain aspects of myth.

In the second place, the whole tone of Euripides' treatment of the sacrifice of Polyxena contradicts that in which the "*nomos*-argument" would have us take it. Listen, for example, to the terms in which Hecuba describes Odysseus' motives:

> Ungrateful is the tribe of demagogues, you who seek the plaudits of the mob! May you ever be beyond my ken, you who think naught of injuring friends, if only you may say something to win the public favour! (254–57)

This is surely an odd preparation for that "acceptance of social necessity" which some critics would have us believe to be Hecuba's ultimate reaction to the sacrifice. And what of Hecuba's sneer (260–61) at the kind of "duty" which can justify human, in place of the normal animal,

[19]"Nicht mehr aus dem Kampfe gegen übermenschliche Schicksalsmächte, sondern aus dem Zwang des menschlichen Nomos entspringt jetzt der tragische Konflikt." *Ibid.*, 283.

[20]Abrahamson, 123–24, and note 10.

sacrifice at tombs. (Here, indeed, is where the *nomos*-argument might legitimately be invoked—against Odysseus!) Finally, any attempt to justify the Odysseus of this play must surely fall before the savage paradox of his own peroration in which, without mentioning the blood of the matter, he suavely contrasts civilized Greek practice with that of "you Trojan barbarians" in the requital of national heroes.

A similar objection applies to Kirkwood's use of "the *nomos*-argument"[21] in assessing the relation of the first to the second part of the play. The *nomos-peithô* antithesis neatly distinguishes Hecuba's first and second appeals in her speech to Agamemnon at 787 ff. but there is no real ground for Kirkwood's further suggestion that Hecuba's own disillusionment with *nomos* springs from "helpless bewilderment" at its earlier evil use by Odysseus. Rather, she simply dismisses Odysseus' sophistries with the indignant contempt which they deserve. Thus, by concentrating exclusively on one aspect of the sacrifice of Polyxena (Odysseus' manner of justifying it), both Kirkwood and Pohlenz, in their different ways, miss the really significant contrast between the two parts of the play.

The dramatic centre of the first part is surely Polyxena herself. Neither the later deterioration of the character of Hecuba, nor the change in dramatic tone which this occasions, need be denied, but the essential contrast between the two actions—and the one which best illuminates this change—is to be found in the characters of Polyxena and Hecuba, as, each in turn, they face their final crisis. One aspect of this contrast has been excellently described as follows:

> On pourrait même dire qu'Euripide a dessiné comme une courbe ascendante avec le caractère de Polyxène, alors qu'il traçait une courbe descendante avec celui d'Hécube. Polyxène conduit aux sommets les plus sublimes de l'humanité, l'evolution d'Hécube la conduit fatalement à l'animalité.[22]

To this description, we should add the important reservation that (*pace* Professor Kitto) the final meaning of the tragedy concerns Hecuba;[23]

[21]Kirkwood 64–68.

[22]G. Méautis, *Mythes Inconnus de la Grèce Antique* (Paris, 1944), 109.

[23]Kitto, *G.T.*, 219, in his attack on this view, argues that "the separate actions [of the play] are meant to point to one overriding idea, the suffering which the human race inflicts upon itself through its own follies and wickedness." One could wish that this author observed in his writings on Euripides that principle which he expresses so eloquently and so consistently with regard to Aeschylus (*ibid.*, chap. 4, *passim*, especially p. 96), that tragedies are concerned not merely with ideas but with ideas conceived and expressed in dramatic terms. Surely, as Kirkwood argues (p. 63), it is Hecuba who is the dramatic focus of the more general ideas

thus the two dramatic centres are not of equal importance, since the first exists for the sake of the second. In the terms of plot, the very loss of Polyxena has an important bearing on what Hecuba becomes in the later episodes; it is for this reason, as we shall see, that the dramatist dwells so much on the pathetically dependent aspect of Hecuba, *before* she becomes the most active figure on the stage. The thematic relation is, however, the more important one, and here we are concerned not merely with the contrast between "sublimity" and "animality" (as Méautis expresses it) in the actions of the two women. Rather, the particular kind of heroism which Polyxena manifests in the face of the national enemy serves to throw into relief, almost to define, the essential nature of Hecuba's fall from queenly *aretê.*

Dramatic Analysis

Critical emphasis on the contrast between the two parts of the *Hecuba* has perhaps tended to obscure certain skilful devices by which the dramatist prepares us, quite early in the play, for the dénouement. Apart from the merely mechanical "hooks" by which the two actions are joined,[24] we may note various "dramatic expectations" which the poet arouses with regard to the later development of the theme and of the characterization of Hecuba. Prominent among these early thematic indications are the uses of rhetoric, particularly in the passage between Odysseus and Hecuba (at 218–31), Odysseus' cynical instruction of Hecuba in the political aspect of *charis* (i.e., in how to recompense one's friends) and, most important and most pervasive, the preliminary characterization of Hecuba, both by herself, as the chief sufferer among the captive Trojan women, and in relation to her children, Polydorus and Polyxena.

From the very beginning of this play, great emphasis is placed upon the helpless dependence of Hecuba, the misery of her enslaved state and (in contrast to her daughter's attitude) her own apparent acceptance of it.

Slaves, lead me out of doors, old woman that I am, set me upright, my Trojan ladies, and lead me forth who was once your Queen and who am now your fellow-slave. Take and carry me, raise me and set me on my way, with firm grasp upon my withered hand. (59–64)

---

underlying this play. Besides, though the *Hecuba* may not be a "character study," we are shown considerably more of Hecuba than Professor Kitto admits; as the subsequent analysis will seek to prove, the play expresses just those aspects of Hecuba which are essential to her tragedy.

[24]See Kirkwood, 63, note 7, for a list of these links; cf. Grube, 83.

Stylistically, the effect of the Queen's opening words lies in the alternation of *παῖδες* and *ὁμόδουλον* with the proud *Τρῳάδες* and *πρόσθε δ'ἄνασσαν* followed by the four pathetically dependent imperatives *λάβετε, φέρετε, πέμπετ', ἀείρετέ μου.* This sense of the helpless dependence of Hecuba's fallen state has already been suggested by the tender solicitude of the ghostly Polydorus in the prologue, as he retreats before his mother's entry on the stage (54–57) and it is immediately echoed by Hecuba's own prayer about her dreadful dreams, "O ghostly powers, save me my son, the sole remaining anchor of my home." (79–80)

The Chorus's announcement of the Greek decision to sacrifice Polyxena evokes another cry of helpless desolation from Hecuba (*οἲ ἐγὼ μελέα* . . . , 154; *τίς ἀμύνει μοι;* 159). Polyxena's anguish, on the other hand, is mostly for her mother: "No longer will your child be here to serve you, as fellow-slave, in your declining years." (202–4)

The brusque entry of Odysseus, come to drag Polyxena off to the sacrifice, interrupts the lament between mother and daughter, and a scene of quite another kind ensues. However, toward the end of the Queen's supplication of Odysseus, we hear again the pathetic anguish of her dependence on her child:

> I beg you, don't tear this child from her mother's arms, . . . In her I take my joy, forgetting all my woes, for she, in place of many others, is now my consolation, my city, my nurse, my staff, my guide along the way. (276–81)

To the end, Hecuba still clings to her daughter "as ivy to an oak" (398), declaring her own misery to be the greatest, and lamenting above all the bitter fate of an old age bereft of children. As Polyxena is led off-stage, Hecuba still pursues her with her cries: "My child, clasp your mother, stretch forth your hand, don't leave me childless . . . . I am lost, my friends!" (439–40)

Some modification in this depiction of the forlorn and helpless Queen must be made with regard to her scene with Odysseus. Here Hecuba shows for the first time that rhetorical power which, for good or ill, is to prove her chief strength throughout the play. After a brief exchange (238–50) in which she reminds Odysseus that once he owed his life to her, the Queen launches into a powerfully persuasive speech (251–95), a very model of the rhetorician's art.[25] It proceeds, in the approved

[25]The *Hecuba* abounds in opportunities for Euripides to indulge in several kinds of set debate. See Schmid, 465; this critic, while praising the many passages of skilful rhetoric and dialectic, suggests that, for modern tastes, this emphasis somewhat detracts from the play's impact. We may find, however, that this very emphasis plays an important part in the delineation of Hecuba's tragedy.

The rhetorical quality of many of Euripides' plays has, of course, long been

fashion, from the general to the particular, with reason dominating until its point is made, and then being swept aside in a flood of personal emotion.

The proëmium provides a general indictment of the ingratitude of demagogues, who neglect their friends but will say anything to curry favour with the mob.[26] Soon the indictment becomes more specific: what excuse, however sophistic (*τί δὴ σόφισμα* . . . , 258), can be found for human sacrifice, where cattle-slaughter is the customary rite? And how, in justice, can Achilles demand *this* girl, and not rather Helen, as an offering at his tomb? (251–70)

To "the argument from justice" (*τῷ μὲν δικαίῳ*, 271) Hecuba adds further the just plea for *charis*: her daughter's life in return for the favour owed her by Odysseus (272–78). Here the emotional succeeds the moral appeal, as Hecuba describes her desperate need of Polyxena . . . "my city, my nurse, my staff, my guide along the way." (281) After an impassioned peroration, imploring Odysseus' intervention, Hecuba ends her speech with a quiet, dignified reminder: Greek law (*nomos*) concerning bloodshed is the same for slave and free alike, but argument (*logos*), to prevail, needs power behind it. (291–95)

To this splendid appeal, Odysseus replies with a lawyer's masterpiece. The genius of the speech lies in the air of sweet reasonableness with which Odysseus surrounds his cruel argument. Each of Hecuba's claims is considered with ironic courtesy—and answered in terms which frustrate the very purpose of her plea. Gratitudes? Returns for favours once received? Odysseus is ready to save Hecuba's life, as once she saved his. Justice? Odysseus replies with a brilliant essay on the justice—and good policy—of rewarding mighty heroes, and thus ensuring loyal service from other heroes still to come: "And for this reason many states grow weak, whenever a noble, zealous warrior receives no more than baser men." (306–8) The justice of honouring the tombs of mighty heroes

---

noted, e.g., in U. von Wilamowitz, *Herakles, Einleitung*, 27: "Wohl aber hat er die Kunst des ἀντιλέγειν so sehr ausgebildet wie nicht einmal ein Rhetor, und seine ganze Technik ist davon durchdrungen." There are several good technical studies of this aspect of Euripidean drama; see, for example, J. T. Lees, Δικανικὸς Λόγος *in Euripides*; D. Thomson, *Euripides and the Attic Orators*. John H. Finley, Jr., in *Harvard Studies in Classical Philology*, XLIX, 23–68, provides some excellent parallels in form and content between the speeches in Euripides and those in Thucydides; see especially pp. 26 and 31 ff.

[26]Here we should note the play on χάρις: ἀχάριστον . . . σπέρμ' (254) scornfully echoing the ἀχάριστοι of Odysseus' original argument (138) and πρὸς χάριν (257) ironically anticipating Hecuba's own ultimate abuse of χάρις in the second part of her plea to Agamemnon, 824–30.

Odysseus describes as an enduring form of *charis* (διὰ μακροῦ γὰρ ἡ χάρις, 320), and one which pays dividends in ensuring the future greatness of the state. Thus, by a sophistic twist, Odysseus negates the arguments for justice and gratitude, for, as he defines them, all manner of barbarous deeds are countenanced in their fulfilment.

Hecuba's intervention then, changes nothing, but the scene raises various themes to be developed later in the tragedy. *Nomos* and *charis*, the basis of Hecuba's twofold appeal, have been twisted by the sophistic use of rhetoric, and *logos* not backed by power has come to naught. Hecuba is to use the same double approach in her appeal to Agamemnon, but next time it is to be the Queen herself who accepts and proves the greater power of the baser argument.

Where Hecuba has failed, Polyxena, in a sense, succeeds. In a single speech to Odysseus, she transforms the whole situation.

> I see you, Odysseus, hiding your right hand beneath your cloak and turning your face away for fear as suppliant I'll touch your beard. Take heart! you have escaped my suppliant prayer, for I will follow, both since I must and since I wish to die. (342–347)

With this scornful opening, Polyxena eschews both supplication and, with it, rhetoric and argument, batteries which the sophist Odysseus is only too well equipped to frustrate. Simply but effectively, she converts the impending slaughter of a chattel into the heroic deed of a free woman. In a few striking phrases, she paints the glory of her past, as a Trojan princess, "like to the gods, save only in mortality," and then concludes:

> And now I am a slave. The very strangeness of the name brings on the love of death . . . (357–58)
> From eyes still free, I now shut out this light. . . . Odysseus, complete your office, lead me hence! (367–69)

Thus is Odysseus dismissed from his command of the affair. It is this invincible sense of freedom, of aristocratic integrity, which enables Polyxena to transform even her enforced death into, not suicide, but an expression of her own free will.[27] In her peroration, she expresses an almost Sophoclean *aretê*:

[27]In this ability, Polyxena is, perhaps, a better exemplar of "existentialist heroism" than even Antigone or Orestes, who have been particularly chosen for that role by contemporary "mythographers": see J.-P. Sartre, "Forgers of Myth—The Young Playwrights of France," *Theatre Arts*, XXX, 324 ff., and Sartre's own play, *Les Mouches*.

Whoever is not wont to taste of ills, bears them, but shudders as he sets his neck beneath the yoke. For him, far happier death than such a life; a painful burden, life not nobly lived! (375–78)

In her scorn for "life not nobly lived," Polyxena is like the Ajax of Sophocles' play, but more fortunate: for her a fate stands ready which she may make her own.

A little later (518–82), Talthybius' moving report to Hecuba complements this impression that Polyxena has taken charge of her own sacrifice. Again she insists on her freedom: no enemy hand, but only the sacrificial blade is to touch her, since she wills her death herself. Indeed, Polyxena's personal pre-eminence in this scene, with the Greek soldiers crowding about bringing reverent adornments for her body, calls to mind those mystic sacrifices in which, to the minds of the initiated, the roles of victim and divinity are centred in a single being.[28]

The strange tranquillity with which Hecuba receives the news of Polyxena's death has often been taken at its face value, as if her daughter's nobility, or even Odysseus' arguments about national policy, had somehow reconciled her to her sorrow. However, the Queen's most violent expressions of grief have already been uttered as Polyxena was dragged off-stage to the sacrifice: the report of its consummation she receives in a state of numbed passivity, her faint protest the more poignant for its vague uncertainty:

I know not where to look amid my ills, so many, all around; if I grasp one of them, another stops me, and then a third summons me thence, bringing some fresh exchange of woes. (585–88)

Her daughter's nobility, Hecuba tells us, inhibits any excessive outcry of grief from her; this thought leads her to a queer detached little passage on the sources of such nobility. This passage should not be interpreted either as an irrelevant Euripidean aside, or as an indication of Hecuba's philosophic resignation. Hecuba is, for the moment, emotionally exhausted, and we know from the prologue that another blow is soon to fall upon her: thus, both psychological probability and a necessary dramatic economy dictate how she must be presented in this *entr'acte*. Hecuba is kept paralysed by grief; in her struggle to "blot out" (ἐξαλεῖψασθαι, 590) her daughter's agony, she seizes on the one saving aspect of it—the nobility with which her daughter died. Hecuba's mind, in spasm like protective muscles around an injured limb, quickly depersonalizes even this subject, and soon she is pondering the familiar question, "Is it parents or training that makes the difference between the

[28]See E. R. Dodds, introduction to Euripides' *Bacchae*, xvi–xvii.

noble and the base?" Thus, by the most "natural" of devices, the dramatist alerts us for the coming contrast between Hecuba's and her daughter's *aretê*.[29]

After the emotional lull of this skilful *entr'acte* comes the shocking discovery of the body of Polydorus, murdered and cast into the sea by his protector, the barbarous Polymestor. The effect of this second blow on Hecuba may be gauged from what we have seen of her so far and the moral collapse which now takes place must be regarded as the effect, inevitable and tragic, of this twofold loss on such a character as hers. Thus, the very terms in which her present plight is described by the serving woman remind us, though they are more extreme, of those used to express her earlier desolation.

Mistress, you are lost. Though your eyes still see the light, you live no longer (οὐκέτ 'εἶ), of child, of lord, of city, all bereaved. (668–69)

This emphasis on the completeness (ἄπαις, ἄνανδρος, ἄπολις) of Hecuba's bereavement, and on the idea of non-existence which accompanies it, is surely most significant. "ἄπολις," in the servant's speech, refers to the loss of Troy, but for Hecuba her city still lived in her children, for she has called Polyxena her "city" at line 281. Now, with all her family as well as Troy destroyed, Hecuba loses, as it were, all sense of moral identity; nothing has meaning for her any longer save vengeance on Polymestor, the *xenos* who has betrayed his trust. "ἀπωλόμην δύστηνος, οὐκέτ' εἰμὶ δή," cries Hecuba (683), echoing the servant's words. Only thus can her moral degradation be understood; no longer a proud queen, jealous of her city's honour, no longer even a human being in the full sense of the word, she grovels before Agamemnon, king of her city's enemies and of her daughter's murderers, because in him she sees the only means to her revenge.[30]

[29]Cf. Grube, 95–96, 220. It is true, of course, that the subject of Hecuba's little homily is rather a favourite one in "gnomic" passages of Euripides (see, for example: *El.* 367–90, *Hec.* 379–80, *I.A.* 558–67, *Suppl.* 911–17); however, this fact does not preclude the possibility of such passages having their own dramatic relevance within their specific contexts.

[30]Too much has surely been made of the alleged community of feeling between the Greeks and the Trojans of this play: see, for example, Grube 220–21, Delebecque 151–53 (where the point is urged to serve a part of Delebecque's interpretation in terms of contemporary politics). Certainly this impression is not supported by Hecuba's address to Odysseus (251 ff.) nor by the proud words of Polyxena, first to Odysseus (342 ff.) and later to those "Argive sackers of my city" who had almost presumed to lay their hands upon her. (547 ff.) Odysseus, for his part, has explicitly included the Trojans in his scornful description of barbarian races, unlike the Greeks in policy and in success. Furthermore, the

This sense of moral death, or moral abdication,[31] is dramatically conveyed by an eerie little passage of self-interrogation by Hecuba, as soon as Agamemnon arrives on stage. (736–51) However, her hesitation is pitifully brief, and the manner of her supplication heightens the contrast between her abasement and the fierce and noble freedom of Polyxena:

Agamemnon! by your knees, I beseech you, and by your beard, and by the prosperous power of your right hand . . . (752–53)
Let me take vengeance on my enemies and willingly I'll be your slave for life. (756–57)

In the long, formal speech of supplication which follows, Hecuba once again bases her argument on the claims, first of *nomos*, and then of *charis*. It is for their twofold rupture of social obligation (duty to a guest and duty to the dead) that the crimes of Polymestor, who has slaughtered a guest-friend and left his body unburied, particularly cry out for vengeance—and Hecuba again reminds us that in these matters, as in the case of Polyxena's rights, justice is the same for slave and free alike. This part of Hecuba's appeal leads to a brilliant rhetorical disquisition on *nomos* as the source not only of all man's distinctions between justice and injustice but even of our belief in the gods,[32] and ends with the statement that, if Agamemnon will not support her claims, there can no longer be justice in men's affairs. (787–805)

---

limited *entente* eventually reached between Hecuba and Agamemnon is dictated by self-interest on each side, and to reach this agreement, Hecuba has to use the basest means of persuasion on Agamemnon. There remains the Greeks' admiration, reported by Talthybius (571–82), of Polyxena's noble bearing *in extremis*, but this hardly suffices to indicate friendly and congenial sentiments between the races. The most that can be granted to Delebecque's view of the gentle treatment of the conquerors in this play is that there is not as strong an anti-Spartan bias as in the *Andromache* and, perhaps, the *Troades*. (Cf. also H. Steiger, "Warum schrieb Euripides seine *Troerinnen*?" *Philologus*, LIX (*N.F.* XIII), 389 ff. who also contrasts the *Hecuba* with the *Troades* in this respect.)

[31]Vandaele, 20, expresses a similar view of Hecuba's state at this point in the play: "Dès ce moment, le désespoir d'Hécube l'a mise *hors d'elle* . . . elle n'est pas elle-même: l'infortune l'égare."

[32]. . . νόμῳ γὰρ τοὺς θεοὺς ἡγούμεθα (800): the ambiguity of this very Euripidean (and, perhaps, Anaxagorean) remark of Hecuba's has been much discussed. Does it mean "It is by reason of the existence of the law that we believe in the existence of the gods" (Hadley), or (in a more "sophistic" vein), "By convention we believe in the gods" (and so give some authority to our distinctions between right and wrong [801] by which we live)? As T. T. Jeffrey has suggested *ad loc.* in his edition of the *Hecuba* (London, n.d.), "there may also be some political irony implied against the Athenian laws, under which a man could be prosecuted, as Socrates was, for not believing in the recognized deities."

From this appeal Agamemnon turns aside (812) and in the second part of her speech Hecuba, abandoning the "ethical argument," stoops to a base device by which to move the king. Her daughter Cassandra, she reminds him, is now his spear-won mistress; some payment (*χάριν*, 830) is surely due for the favours of love, both to Cassandra and to the mother who supplied her. And in avenging Polymestor, Agamemnon will be avenging his own brother by Cassandra. (824–35)

This passage provides a grimly ironic parallel to Hecuba's earlier appeal to *charis* in the speech to Odysseus (271–78), for now there is no question of the just payment of a favour generously given, but of bought favours and the calculated returns of whores and pimps. It may be said, perhaps, that Hecuba has learned too well Odysseus' lesson in the political uses of *charis* and of rhetoric, for even her "master" might now be shocked at the length to which she goes.

It is often assumed that in the first part of her appeal to Agamemnon, Hecuba's honour has not been compromised, that only when the argument from *nomos* fails does she undergo her fatal change.[33] It is true that Hecuba's arguments for Polymestor's punishment are irreproachable in themselves, and are rendered the more impressive by her near apotheosis of the concepts of law and justice. But Hecuba herself has already offended against another kind of *nomos*. In grovelling before her city's enemies she has already shown a considerable decline in queenly *aretê*; then, in pandering to them with her daughter's honour, she takes the final step in degradation.

This second "descent" is, like the first, marked by a moment of hesitation, of self-colloquy, in which the Queen again reminds herself that, her city and her children gone, she exists no longer: *οἴχομαι·/καπνὸν δὲ πόλεως τόνδ' ὑπερθρῴσκονθ' ὁρῶ.* (822–23) However, the most striking feature of this passage is the Queen's sudden reference to *Peithô* the only goddess, or the only power, for which she now has any use:

Alas! Why do we mortals labour at all other kinds of knowledge, and take what pains we must to track them down, while Persuasion (*Peithô*), man's only ruler (whereby t'were possible to win any argument and so gain one's end), we take no special pains—nor pay our fees!—to learn? (813–19)

Thus *Peithô*, in its various aspects, has now become the guiding genius of the Queen.[34] Persuasion, is, of course, the end of rhetoric, but

[33]Thus Sheppard finds that the refusal of Hecuba's appeal for justice, "marks the crisis in her moral catastrophe." (J. T. Sheppard, *Euripides' Hecuba*, 11.) Cf. also Matthiae 149, Kirkwood 61–62, 64–67.

[34]Kirkwood (67) remarks of the second half of Hecuba's appeal to Agamemnon, "[It] is only the beginning of Hecuba's degeneration, but by its tone it sets the

it is only rhetoric in its most ungoverned use which dispenses with all other considerations. From the first, Hecuba has shown her greatest strength in rhetoric; now, as her *aretê* declines, she openly worships it in its most vicious form. Previously, she has used it honestly and has savagely attacked the crowd-pandering of demogogues; now she, too, exploits rhetoric, using the basest of inducements to win the favour of the King. *Peithô*, as well as being the guiding genius of the rhetorician, suggested to the Greek mind what "temptation"—particularly such "passionate" temptations as lust, avarice, ambition, vengeance—does to the Christian mind.[35] Hecuba, herself in the grip of her passion for revenge, uses the temptations of lust and avarice respectively to persuade first Agamemnon and then her victim Polymestor to her will. In all of this, she depends increasingly on her power of rhetoric which becomes (in sad contrast with her honest and unsuccessful plea to Odysseus) the more effective the more unscrupulously she employs it. Finally, when the ruined Polymestor seeks to arraign her before the bar of Agamemnon's justice, it is Hecuba's power of rhetoric which once again prevails.

This general picture will, perhaps, suffice to indicate the pattern of the *dénouement*. Most commentators agree on the moral degradation of Hecuba in these final passages, though here the emphasis has been on the savagery of her vengeance on the innocent children of Polymestor—a dramatic anticipation (or interpretation?) of that "hound-dog Hecuba" myth to which the poet alludes at the end of the play. It is true that action, even melodramatic action, now takes precedence: the luring of Polymestor and his children to their destruction, the bloody slaughter of the children and the blinding of their father, the "epic exchange" of taunts and dire prophecy (1254 ff.) between the victorious Hecuba and the vanquished barbarian king. Nevertheless, even in this tumultuous close, certain ironic reminders of the earlier thematic development reappear. So might we interpret the Chorus's puzzled comment on the "*nomoi*," as Hecuba has represented them in her plea to Agamemnon ("Strange, how they've defined anew the bonds of loyalty, making

---

pattern for the rest." Méridier (212, note 1) writes of Hecuba's praise of *Peithô*, "Allusion claire aux sophistes, dont Euripide recommende ici l'enseignement." Doubtless there is a reference to the sophists here, but it is difficult to see how, in the context, anyone could regard the passage as implying the poet's recommendation of their art.

[35]Perhaps the most vivid example of this use of *Peithô* in tragedy occurs in Aeschylus, *Ag.* 385 ff., where the Chorus is describing the temptation of Paris:

βιᾶται δ' ἁ τάλαινα πειθώ
προβούλου παῖς ἄφερτος ἄτας.

friends of one's worst enemies . . . ," (846–48), and Hecuba's request that the burial of Polyxena be delayed to coincide with that of Polydorus. Agamemnon agrees, and immediately the Chorus bursts into a sombre ode on the sack of Troy, as if to underline these grim reminders of Hecuba's defection to her daughter's and her city's enemies.

In like manner, the themes of *Peithô* and *charis* reappear in ironic guise in the "trial scene" following the vengeance of Hecuba. Here Polymestor lays claim to Agamemnon's gratitude on the grounds that he has slaughtered Polydorus to make sure that Troy shall never rise again. Hecuba, in her reply, expresses the pious wish that good speeches might accompany only noble actions and that cunning words should never have the power to veil base deeds:

> Sharp men there are, all too well versed in this, but not until the end their skill prevails. Foully they perish: no one has yet escaped. (1192–94)

Of the Queen's many comments on the art of rhetoric, this must surely strike us as the most cynical—an ironic comment on her own case, and on the fate which lies in store for her. Furthermore, though Hecuba's rebuttal of Polymestor's argument is doubtless "just," the terms she uses ("How could *thy* barbarian race expect friendship with the Greeks?") are, to say the least, unfortunate, for they provide yet another reminder of that base alliance which the "barbarian" Hecuba (for so Odysseus in *his* account of *charis* has described the Trojans, 328–31) has made with her enemies, the Greeks.

Thus Hecuba, in making *Peithô* serve her ends, is herself dominated by it. Once the passion of revenge has seized her, it assumes the obsessive character so marked in the tragic *pathê* of Euripidean drama, and Hecuba is led to stoop to any base persuasion to gain her ends. She does not, however, undergo the complete and sudden transformation which some critics would have us believe to be the case. This is a strange tragedy, in that at no point does the tragic sufferer achieve heroic stature: tragic decline, rather than tragic peripety, informs the action. Once the Queen's sufferings have been foretold to us in the prologue, the tragic probabilities are not long in making their appearance: we may infer them from the weak dependence of the Queen's early utterances and from the contrast between her character and that of the heroic Polyxena. Hecuba's chief strength throughout lies in her power of rhetoric and the course of her moral disintegration may best be followed in her uses and abuses of the persuasive art. Her final violence then appears as a spectacular but not improbable fulfilment.

The sacrifice of Polyxena, far from being an action separate from the tragedy of Hecuba, helps both to cause and to define it, for Hecuba, overwhelmed by the loss of both son and daughter, avenges one child by betraying the other. Moreover, the characterization of Polyxena herself has a most important function in the play. As she meets her death, Polyxena preserves her dignity, her impregnable sense of freedom, and avoids, above all, subjection to the enemy. It is this paradigm of tragic *aretê* which shows up the essential nature of the fall of Hecuba: her self-abasement before the knees of one enemy in her passion for vengeance against another. Finally, it is at the death of Polyxena that the Queen first begins "to abdicate," to forget her essential quality as Queen of Troy. Eventually, without family, without city, she reaches that desperate state of *anomia* which spells her ruin. Only in characters such as Polyxena can *aretê* survive in splendid isolation.

9

THE *Andromache*

Myth and Theme

In the *Hecuba*, the *Andromache* and the *Trojan Women*—three plays spanning, in their production, perhaps a dozen years of the Peloponnesian War—Euripides exploits a variety of motifs drawn from the aftermath of the legendary Trojan War: the tragic lot of captive women, and the contrasting effects, ennobling and corrupting, of their sufferings upon them; the woes and the glories of both conquered and conquering, and the curious weave of conflicting sentiments—hate, pity, admiration—between them; the awful pageant of grief and cruelty, with occasional glimmers of hope, or of future retribution. Each of these Trojan plays develops its own theme from this general material, and it is interesting to observe the different lights in which similar motifs appear according to the different themes and, perhaps, the different moods of the dramatist.[1]

The *Andromache* provides a fruitful matrix for a theme which is at least hinted at in the other Trojan plays I have mentioned: the relations, both personal and dynastic, between the victors and the vanquished. I believe the critics have done something less than justice to both the theme and the structure of this play; since the present study will involve some analysis in detail, I will begin by reviewing the bare outlines of the plot.

[1]The last of these plays, the *Trojan Women* (produced in 415 B.C.), is in a sense the least self-contained in its theme; being the third play in a trilogy, it views present sufferings from farther back, as it were, from a perspective, both ethical and dramatic, which is different from that of the *Andromache* and of the *Hecuba*.

On the date of the *Andromache* (probably between 427 and 425), see below, note 7. On the date of the *Hecuba*, see Méridier's *Notice* for a review of the arguments for 424 B.C. as a probable date (L. Méridier, *Euripide*, II, 178–79).

Andromache, widow of Hector, is now settled in Phthia as the captive mistress of Neoptolemus, to whom she has borne a son. When the play opens, she has fled for her life to the sanctuary of the goddess Thetis, whither Hermione, the childless Spartan wife of Neoptolemus, pursues her. In an altercation between the two (a scene so spirited that it has distracted many critics from seeking further meanings in the play) Hermione accuses her rival of seeking, by secret drugs, to render her both childless and hateful to her husband. When Hermione is bested, verbally and otherwise, by the noble Trojan captive, Menelaus, Hermione's father, finally tricks Andromache into giving herself up for slaughter, by bartering the life of her son, whom he holds captive. Just as he is about to slay them both, they are saved by a second intervention, this time of Neoptolemus' grandfather, old Peleus, the King of Phthia. In a speech bristling with scorn for Menelaus and his childless daughter, he routs the Spartan King with the threat that he will bring up Andromache's child, scion of defeated Troy and conquering Phthia, as an enemy to the one-time ally, Sparta. Hermione, now abandoned and despairing, is rescued by Orestes to whom Menelaus, before the exploits of Neoptolemus at Troy, had once promised his daughter. Orestes tells of a plan to have Neoptolemus murdered at Delphi, where he is presently making atonement to the god Apollo. With Hermione's agreement, Orestes whisks her off to Sparta, there to seek her hand in marriage. The off-stage murder of Neoptolemus is subsequently reported by a messenger. The tottering fortunes of the house of Peleus are restored by the *deus-ex-machina* appearance of Thetis who directs that her husband Peleus shall join her as a god in Nereus' palace, and that Andromache shall marry Helenus, Hector's brother, in Molossia where her son by Neoptolemus will sire a long and prosperous line of kings. "For," she declares, " 'twere most unfitting that *our* stock and Troy's (which still is pleasing to the gods) be brought to naught." (1249–51)

The material of the *Andromache* is ingeniously contrived and adapted to the playwright's purpose from several different strands of legend. As is usual with Euripidean manipulations of this kind, the dramatist reduces to the minimum any actual changes of "fact" (in the legendary sense) in the received tradition. Rather, he changes emphases and sympathies, invents connections between relatively independent legends, and exploits gaps in the story to suit the new uses to which he puts it. Let me suggest the main tendency and purpose of Euripides' adaptations in the present instance.

Most important is the change which makes Andromache, Neoptolemus and Hermione (two women and one man) the triangle which receives dramatic emphasis. This emphasis does not appear in other versions. It has been reasonably argued that the main conflict in these legends, and perhaps in Sophocles' treatment of them in his lost *Hermione*, was between Neoptolemus and Orestes over Hermione.[2] Euripides, however, joins the Trojan War legends concerning Neoptolemus and Andromache[3] to this triangle, and invents, as far as we can tell, the conflict between Hermione and Andromache. Delphi, where Neoptolemus was slaughtered, was probably the scene of Sophocles' play; Euripides places *his* play at the storm-centre of his new domestic conflict, at Neoptolemus' home in Phthia, while Neoptolemus himself is conveniently kept off-stage at Delphi. Finally, Euripides chooses, among various versions differing on this point, that version which emphasizes the failure of Hermione (in contrast to Andromache) to provide Neoptolemus with offspring; nor, in Euripides' situation, is the biological advantage of the spear-won mistress mitigated, as in other versions, by any issue from a former union of Hermione and Orestes.[4] All this gives scope for a typically Euripidean development: the jealousy motif between the barren legitimate wife and the fruitful concubine. As a result, Andromache, from being a relatively

[2]See the arguments in Wolf H. Friedrich, *Euripides und Diphilos*, 47–49. Cf. also Vergil, *Aen.* iii. 325–32. As Paley (II, 237) suggests, Vergil is probably following accounts given in the Cyclic poets. For a partial account of Sophocles' *Hermione*, see Eustathius *Od.* 1479. 10 (Nauck, *TGF*, 176) and Schol. *Od.* iv. 4. There is no reference to Andromache, while both Orestes and Neoptolemus *vis-à-vis* Hermione are prominent in the accounts; nevertheless, there is perhaps insufficient detail in Eustathius' account to warrant Friedrich's conjecture of a direct conflict between the two heroes in Sophocles' play.

[3]The *Iliu Persis* of Arctinus was apparently the original source of various ancient references to the Andromache-Neoptolemus union and its sequence. See Méridier, 90 ff., for a good account both of these legends and of the others referred to above.

[4]See Schol. *Andr.* 32 for references to a son of Hermione by Neoptolemus. From the same scholium we learn that according to Philocles, the tragedian, and Theognis, Hermione was already pregnant by her former fiancé, Orestes, when Menelaus gave her to Neoptolemus. On the other hand, according to Pherecydes (see Schol. *Or.* 1655), Neoptolemus was slain at Delphi when he went there to inquire about the childlessness of his marriage to Hermione. Thus Euripides clearly selects only those features of any given myth which suit his immediate purpose: here he does want the childlessness of Hermione-Neoptolemus but (for reasons soon to appear) he invents a nobler motive than this for Neoptolemus' visit to the Delphic Oracle. In the *Orestes*, on the other hand, he rejects all accounts of a Neoptolemus-Hermione union when (*Or.* 1655) he has Apollo declare that such a union will never take place.

minor figure in the network, becomes a prominent and decidedly sympathetic character.[5]

Secondly, in this play our sympathies are purposefully coerced in directions by no means warranted by the tradition. No opportunity is missed to blacken the characters of the Spartans Menelaus and Hermione, and of the latter's cousin-suitor, Orestes. Indeed, in the case of Orestes and Neoptolemus, rights and wrongs are skilfully switched in Euripides' version. In other versions of the legend, many different accounts are given of Neoptolemus' death at Delphi, and several of these suggest that his death was deserved. To judge from Eustathius' account, Sophocles was perhaps the first to ascribe it to the prince's own *hybris* in demanding satisfaction of the god Apollo for causing the death of his father, Achilles; Euripides himself, in his *Orestes* (1656–57), allows this version to stand without qualification. In the present play, however, Euripides makes apology to Apollo the motive of Neoptolemus' visit to Delphi. Now, what of Orestes? Friedrich argues reasonably that in Sophocles' *Hermione*, just as Neoptolemus' death is presented as the just punishment of *hybris* against the god, so Orestes, in his marriage to Hermione as in all else, is presumably regarded as piously following the will of the gods. In Euripides' *Andromache*, on the other hand, Orestes is a self-seeking dastard, waiting about in the wings, so to speak, for the psychological moment to make his nefarious proposals to Hermione, and committing even his murder by proxy, through his Delphian allies. Apollo plays a vital part in this murder, but, in planning

[5]Friedrich (50) suggests that Euripides eschewed the on-stage conflict between Neoptolemus and Orestes over Hermione mainly for the sake of the novel dramatic potentialities in a conflict between two women over one man. He argues further (*ibid.*, 47 ff. and 51–52) that in both the *Hecuba* and the *Andromache*, we have a curious double action involving the same Euripidean technique of presenting original material under the wing of the traditional: just as the Polyxena episode serves the purpose of introducing the novel "Polydorus action," so, too, the startling newness of the "Andromache action" is tied to the known story of the Neoptolemus-Orestes conflict. What both plays have in common, Friedrich claims, is that the newly created material forms the main action, the "received" material, the secondary action. Acute and interesting as these comments are, they seem to me to involve the same half-truth. There is no doubt that the scenes of the "Andromache action" are both the most original and the most effective in the play, but to regard the "Hermione-Orestes action" and its sequel as simply tacked on to bolster up the unfamiliar material of the first half is to misunderstand the structure of the whole (as I seek to show in my own analysis). *A fortiori*, in the *Hecuba* the familiar Polyxena material is essential to the significance, in Hecuba's tragedy, of the more novel "Polydorus action."

it, Orestes is following his own self-interest, not the will of the god.[6]

Considering these new sympathies and antipathies which Euripides' adaptations evoke—with the Trojans and the house of Peleus as the good elements, the Spartans and their kin, Orestes, as the bad elements—we begin to suspect that in this play we shall find situations involving nationalities and dynasties quite as much as they do the personal affairs of young wives, husbands and concubines. Now it is the anti-Spartan bias (considered almost in isolation) of this play which has been most stressed by commentators. This emphasis is easy to understand when we listen to passages such as Andromache's diatribe when she finds that Menelaus has tricked her:

O race most hateful to all men, inhabitants of Sparta, tricky of counsel, masters of deceit, cunning devisers of evil, with no healthy thoughts, but ever pondering devious ways, it's no justice that you prosper throughout Greece. What crime is missing among you? Are you not the most murderous of men? The most eager for shameful gain? The most ready to say one thing with your tongue while plotting another in your secret heart? May you rot, the lot of you! (445–53)

The terms of this and similar speeches have led critics from the Scholiast onwards to seek the precise moment in the Peloponnesian War at which these feelings would be most appropriate at Athens.[7] Such speculations are not our concern at the moment, but even critics of mainly literary

[6]For Sophocles' treatment of Neoptolemus' death, see Eustathius, *Od.* 1479. 10 (*TGF*, 176) and comments thereon by Méridier, 93–94; cf. also Friedrich's reasonable guesses (49) about the divine and human motivation of Sophocles' *Hermione*. On *Or.* 1655 ff., and scholiastic comment thereon, cf. *supra*, note 4.

Concerning the contrasting treatment of Delphi in Sophocles' *Hermione* and in Euripides' *Andromache*, cf. also Zielinski, *Tragodumenon Libri Tres*, 114 ff., who believes that Euripides is intentionally impugning the piety of Sophocles' play. Indeed, Zielinski (*REG*, XXXVI, 467 ff.) regards all "anti-Delphi plays" of Euripides (*Electra*, *Andromache*, *Melanippe*, in his view) as specific corrections of Sophocles' "pro-Delphi plays" (*O.T.*, *Electra*, *Hermione*, *Creusa*). Zielinski's arguments are, however, guilty of some oversimplification and, perhaps, naïveté with regard to both poets on these matters.

[7]See, for example, Schol. *Andr.* 445, which on these grounds places the play near the beginning of the Peloponnesian War; Méridier, 100–6, who amends this suggestion to "between 427–425," before the victory at Sphacteria had, supposedly, sweetened Athenian dispositions; Delebecque, 182 ff., who suggests 422 as the date of the play, when a fresh outbreak of anti-Spartan feeling may have been caused by the northern machinations of Brasidas during the one-year truce. However, the presence of anti-Spartan bitterness in the play seems to offer too wide and subjective a choice when considered as sole evidence for its date. A more precise

bent tend to regard its anti-Spartan vehemence as the play's most (if not its *only*) significant element. Professor Kitto tells us, for example, "This hard and brilliant tragedy is, not incidentally but fundamentally, a violent attack on the Spartan mind, on *Machtpolitik* . . ." and again, "Nowhere is it more evident that the unity of the play lies in its idea [as just expressed] and not in its story."[8] But a diatribe is not a play, and this play, if ever a play did, progresses to a solution by its oppositions; Kitto's attempt to reduce every single effect of the play to the service of highlighting Sparta's cardinal sins does considerably less than justice to its positive, non-Spartan elements. Besides, even in Euripides' most political plays, such as the *Suppliants*, his animosities are usually related to larger, more positive, themes. It is only by careful examination of the *structure* of the *Andromache* that we can decide what that theme is.

It is precisely this aspect of the play, its structure, that has been most severely attacked. Norwood[9] clearly sums up the general feeling about its lack of unity as follows:

> In the *Andromache*, the division into two brief dramas is clear: the plight and rescue of Andromache, the plight and rescue of Hermione . . . though Andromache gives her name to the whole, she disappears early from the action and from our minds, until at the final moment Thetis tells us what is to become of her. Hermione, no doubt, has great importance in both sections but sections they remain.

---

hint is, perhaps, given by Menelaus' allusion at 733 ff. to "a certain city, not far from Sparta, which was once friendly to us but is now hostile." Hermann (vii–viii of his edition) and Page, "The Elegiacs in Euripides' *Andromache*" (223 ff.) have argued that the reference must here be to Argos about the time of the Argive pact of 420. Page believes further that the play, which we know (Schol. 445) was not produced at Athens, may have been produced at Argos. To the political argument he adds an ingenious literary argument with his suggestion that the elegiac lament, unique in Greek tragedy, at *Andr.* 103–16, may have been influenced by Dorian elegiac threnodies which, as he shows (see references *ad loc.*), were being composed from the beginning of the sixth century. Other scholars, e.g., Macurdy and Jardé, have, it is true, taken the city referred to by Menelaus at v. 433 ff. to be Mantinea and have moved the date of the play to as late as 418–17; for discussion of this somewhat improbable view, see Page and Méridier as cited above and references there given.

8Kitto, 229.

9Norwood, *Essays*, 46. Cf. Hermann, viii. In his school edition of the *Andromache*, lx–lxi, Norwood had previously expressed the rather surprising view that the character of Hermione was the foundation of the play which was to serve as an object lesson to the Athenians on the kind of wife-training that ruined homes!

Kitto cheerfully accepts the alleged "lack of unity" in the *Andromache*; he defends the play by his general thesis (surely a perverse one in so subtle a critic) that the possession of an overmastering tragic idea freed the dramatist from structural considerations. Even critics who defend the play's structure do so with distinct reservations. Professor Grube indicates the links which do exist both between the parts of the plot and between the two themes of the play, but finds that in both cases these links remain external, insufficiently worked into the stuff of the drama. His distinction between the domestic and the dynastic elements in the material is valuable but he limits its application to Neoptolemus' household and he regards it as providing two themes rather than two aspects of a single theme.[10] Méridier seeks to defend the two separate parts of the play by arguing for a certain equilibrium between them: "Vaincue et humiliée dans la première [partie], Hermione prend sa revanche dans la seconde. . . ."[11] But even apart from the inexactitude of this account, by the time that Orestes has Neoptolemus murdered, Hermione has left the scene for good and Andromache is no longer functioning as an active character.

To answer these alleged structural difficulties, it is necessary first of all to recognize that the *Andromache* is not primarily concerned with the fates of any individual character or characters. The few critics who have been willing to go thus far have still insisted on treating the play either as a conventional tragedy, or at least as a play in which failure to follow up *individual* conflicts is an annoyance. Obviously, the play is not "tragic" with regard to any individual: we never even meet the man who dies; thus we are not required to follow an action involving one noble character whose suffering will reveal the meanings of the play. If we examine the play free of these usual tragic assumptions, I think we shall see that its plot does exhibit relations and correspondences between its parts which are indicative of a most carefully contrived design. This design is independant of any individual character but the single, somewhat impersonal theme which it serves is what gives the play its unity.

In this dramatic epilogue to the Trojan Wars, we have three elements, the Phthian (i.e., relating to the house of Peleus), the Trojan and the Spartan: the two conquering Greek strains and in between them the captive Trojan one. The irony of the situation soon becomes apparent: Phthia has stronger ties with the conquered Trojans than with her Spartan allies. It is first a bond between the *real* warriors of the War (only by the valour of Achilles and, after him, of Neoptolemus, could

[10]See Grube, 81.
[11]Méridier, 98.

the Spartan Menelaus have taken Troy), and then it is a bond between their dynasties (only through the fertile Andromache can the house of Peleus survive). Andromache's bitter speech on *doxa* (319 ff.) contrasts the false reputation of the cowardly Menelaus with the true valour of Achilles and his son; Peleus, after a scathing attack on Spartan women, rejects his grandson's barren Spartan wife and champions the captive Trojan's son.

Hartung has well remarked that the point of this play is to be found not in the misfortunes of Andromache but in those of the house of Peleus owing to its association, in war and in marriage, with the evil house of Menelaus.[12] His comment serves as a useful corrective to those who can see nothing "thematic" in the play beyond the personal fortunes of Andromache, or of Andromache and Hermione. But it may well be argued that the dramatic demonstration of this "point" which Hartung has noted hardly supplies the action we look for in a tragedy, for Hartung's discussion pays surprisingly little attention to the resolution of the situation which he describes. In this resolution, the coming-together of the evil elements, Hermione and Orestes, is an essential complement to the ultimate fate of the "good" elements. Once our sympathies have been properly aroused (this is rehearsed in the Prologue and soon confirmed in the opening episodes) it becomes clear that the end toward which the action is leading is the separation of the evil Spartan elements from the noble Phthian and Trojan elements. This action is worked out on the personal and on the dynastic level and, in the lack of any individual role sufficiently sustained for the purpose, it is through this duality that one glimpses the broader meanings of the play: that behind the personal spites, antipathies and congenialities of individuals lie the larger and (politically at any rate) more significant affinities and antipathies of nations which can be ignored only at those nations' peril and which, if heeded, can transform their future destinies.

Thus the *Andromache*, a tragedy without a tragic hero, presents, at the expense of properly tragic elements, an intellectual theme in an almost artificially formal design. Each of the play's three elements (Trojan, Spartan and Phthian) is brought to life in a series of encounters lively and diverting enough in themselves though the characters which provide this vitality do not themselves survive their transient function. The tensions which inform the whole, and which supply the dynamics of the dramatic action, come from a series of struggles in which, as one victory is reversed by another, the arrangements of the three elements,

[12]Hartung, 111 and 119.

and of the issues between them, is constantly shifted in an intricate design. A brief analysis of the action will reveal this formal pattern.

Structural Analysis

When the play opens, the Phthian and Spartan elements are joined by marriage, while the Phthian and Trojan elements are joined by a less formal, but more productive, liaison. In the first scene, the jealous Hermione seeks the life of the woman she thinks has bewitched her marriage, but since Andromache is actually quite safe in the sanctuary of the altar, *this* contest resolves itself simply into a duel of wits, personality and rhetorical skill in which Andromache is easily the victor. This victory is reversed by the arrival of Menelaus, who tricks Andromache into surrender. In the third contest, just as mother and son prepare to die, the situation is again reversed, and Trojan-Phthian solidarity is emphasized by King Peleus' intervention for his great-grandson's sake. (Here, incidentally, the dynastic note sounds for the first time.) Hermione is now left despairing, but she too is soon saved by the next new arrival, Orestes. With the off-stage murder of Neoptolemus (managed by Orestes, assisted by Apollo) the Spartans seem to have won the last round, but fortunes at home are restored by the *deus-ex-machina* pronouncements of Thetis; the Trojan-Phthian stock, now freed from Spartan evil, is finally sanctioned and its future glory in the Molossian dynasty assured.

Thus we have a series of conflicts which all lead to this one conclusion, and in each instance the outcome is decided in the same manner: defeat is changed to victory by the addition, now to one side, now to the other, of a powerful new ally.[13] With the entry of Orestes, there is, to be sure, an apparent break in the action, if we are still looking only for a resolution of the clash between the two women of the play. The off-stage death

[13]For a comparable analysis of the structure of the play prior to the reported death of Neoptolemus, see Paul Friedländer, "Die griechische Tragödie und das Tragische," *Die Antike*, II (1926), 99–102. He, too, remarks on the symmetrical yet antithetical relation between the first two parts of the play in which first the innocent victim and then her guilty persecutor are rescued, Hermione's fearful expectation of punishment from Neoptolemus being reversed by the intrusion of Orestes. To explain the function of the third part of the play, involving the death of Neoptolemus, in this scheme, he suggests the novel idea that the unity of the play (though strengthened by the structural relations of the first two parts) depends fundamentally on the Absent Hero. Not only is Neoptolemus the cause of strife between Hermione and Andromache; by his continued absence he gives occasion for the actual quarrel between the two women and for the interventions

of Neoptolemus merely secures Hermione for Orestes, and Andromache seems to be forgotten. Even when Thetis re-establishes the Trojan-Phthian fortunes, we are no longer conscious of a personal triumph for Andromache, and her personal clash with Hermione, which gave the play its first dramatic spark, seems very far away. It is quite true that this play lacks the kind of unity essential to tragedy proper, in which the suffering of a certain kind of hero, in a given situation, reveals some universal truth or value in life. In the *Andromache*, both theme and structure are of quite a different kind. As we have suggested, the theme concerns the separation, through a series of struggles, of good and evil elements which at the beginning were so disastrously involved. In the working out of this theme, the poet preserves a certain structural pattern throughout, both in the consistent alternation of victory between good and evil, and in the manner in which (as I have indicated) each victory is achieved. The switch from the personal to the dynastic level comes at the end of what we might call the "Andromache-action," at the defeat of Hermione and her father, and before the entry of Orestes. The subsequent victories are still determined by the ubiquitous "newcomer," but in the final phases, it is a divine rather than a human addition which effects the dynastic changes. The unpopular god of Delphi assures the union of the wicked elements, when Neoptolemus is murdered at Apollo's Oracle, and it is Thetis who, at the close of the play, determines the future destiny of the Trojan-Phthian line.

Thus stated, I am aware that the structural development, the articulation, of the *Andromache* sounds as formal as a ballet and as dry as a theorem. Structure alone—and particularly a pattern of this kind, which is not tragic structure—does not make a play. However, the *Andromache*, most notably in its earlier episodes, is by no means lacking in the stuff of drama. Before we leave the play, let us look more closely at one or two of the scenes for which people must remember it. Possibly much of their power lies in their immediate and particular effects; nevertheless, there are clear signs that Euripides keeps the total development in mind as well, that he rarely sacrifices the final meaning to the momentary dramatic thrill.

The first episode presents the celebrated debate (if we can call it that)

---

of Menelaus, Peleus and Orestes, and that absence is, in a sense, dramatically underlined by his final appearance as a corpse. Friedländer does not, however, convince in his assertion that Neoptolemus' "role" in addition to being structurally useful is also tragic and in default of any other suggestion of a larger theme behind the particularities of the action, his analysis tends to show structural pattern unrelated to any real dramatic purpose.

between the injured wife and the captive mistress. The handling of this scene, both as an individual *agôn* and as a part of the larger, less personal theme, is surely one of Euripides' triumphs. Hermione trips on-stage gloriously arrayed in the latest Spartan styles. This finery, these flashing jewels, she informs us, assure her Spartan independence, for they are gifts from her father's, not her husband's, house. The crimes she imputes to Andromache—casting spells on respectable married women and bearing children to the house which slew her husband, Hector—she links with a general castigation of Asiatic ways:

So acts the whole barbarian race: fathers mate with daughters, sons with mothers, sisters with brothers—all these lovers wade to their wicked ends through bloodshed, and no law prevents them! Bring not these ways to us: for 'tis not right that one man drive a pair of women. Rather, the man who wants to live a proper life looks to one well-wedded wife, and loves her only! (173–80)

There is much irony in this situation in which a blooming bride with a rich dower assails a dowdy, aging slave for alienation of her husband's love. This irony is underlined by the unconscious self-characterization of the spoiled Hermione. None of these points escapes the sharp Andromache. Her opening words reveal how little chance this pouting child will have against her: "What a trial are youngsters, particularly when they're bad!" (184–85) The rivalry charges she treats with withering sarcasm: "My vanquished city, I suppose, is stronger than mighty Sparta? . . . Or is it my youth, my full young body [σφριγῶντι σώματι] that I rely on?" (194 ff.) Then unerringly she goes to the root of Hermione's trouble: the bride has not yet learned to be a wife; everything at her father's house is better than here in homely Phthia.

Your husband hates you, not from drugs of mine, but since you lack the wifely attributes (ἀλλ' εἰ ξυνεῖναι μὴ 'πιτηδεία κυρεῖς). This is the love-philtre, woman! Not beauty but the proper qualities [ἀρεταί] delight one's mate. (205–8)

Hermione's harshest words have hit at the licentious amorality of Asiatics such as Andromache. Even in the argument on chastity, Andromache skilfully turns the tables: Hermione's possessiveness toward Neoptolemus, she converts into the charge of ἀπληστία λέχους (218) and φιλανδρία (229) "man-hunger," the word which will most remind the audience of Helen, and Andromache does not fail to draw the comparison, "like mother, like daughter." Indeed, it is Andromache's reticence, her implication that she is more modest (σώφρων, 235) than the wedded wife, which most infuriates Hermione. The latter is unwise enough to revert to the subject in the brisk exchange which follows the two long speeches. Andromache replies:

ANDROMACHE: You are young—and yet you talk about immodest matters.
HERMIONE: You may not talk them, but you do them and in my despite, too.
ANDROMACHE: Can you not suffer about Love in silence?
HERMIONE: Why? Is this not first with women everywhere?
ANDROMACHE: Yes—for women who are happy in it; if not, 'tis no fit subject. (238–42)

Andromache has scored again.

The verve of this scene and its novelty in Greek tragedy show clearly how much Euripides relished the opportunity of presenting two female rivals on-stage. This is certainly the kind of passage which, allowing for the distortions of comedy, gave the Aristophanic "Aeschylus" fodder for his attack on the "passionate women" themes of Euripides. Nevertheless, marking what is left out as well as what is put in, watch how skilfully the dramatist has selected and tempered the ingredients of the quarrel so that the larger purpose of his theme can still be served. Certain aspects of this age-old altercation between wife and mistress have been wisely modified. In the first place, there must be nothing either flagrant or smug in Andromache's exploitation of Neoptolemus' preference for her: in this play, Andromache must be on the side of virtue in contrast with Hermione whose character is to fit Peleus' later castigation of all Spartan women. Hence Euripides' insistence on the modesty of the successful mistress and on the brazenness of the frustrated wife, and this restriction he even turns into a telling ingredient of the quarrel. This switch in the conventional characterizations of mistress and lawful wife is no mean achievement; it takes all of the almost sophistic skill with which the dramatist endows Andromache to bring it off. Secondly, Andromache must not be regarded as passionately attached to her spear-lord. It is as the widow of Hector that she acquires heroic stature and it is as the link with Troy that she fulfils her role in the larger issues of the play. In the prologue, Andromache has stressed the forced nature of her relations with Neoptolemus. However, in the present female altercation, we want a passage where the successful rival tells the wife just how she has succeeded where the other failed. Here once again, Euripides manages most adroitly to have his cake and eat it. Andromache does give Hermione her lesson in how to be a good wife to Neoptolemus

—but the chapter and verse by which such advice must be accompanied she draws from memories of the old days, with her husband Hector.

The succeeding episodes continue this demonstration of the respective *worths* of the play's three elements. The Spartan Menelaus is pitted first against a female slave and then against an aged king. What interests us in the former conflict is the ironic contrast between the values of the Trojan captive and of the famed conqueror of Troy. Andromache is here employing her powerful rhetoric in defence of her life. After a magnificent proëmium on the falsity of *doxa*—and of Spartan reputation in particular—she argues that this "woman's quarrel" should be beneath a great commander's dignity.

> You are not worthy of Troy nor Troy of you! . . . (328–29)
> Why suffer mighty ills for pretty causes? Surely, if we women are all a monstrous blight, 'twere better that you *men* become not like us! (352–54)

And finally: "This one thing in your mind I fear, for through that womanizing strife of yours, you ruined Troy." (361–63) What is Menelaus' answer to this challenge? "To each man his particular need is greater than the sack of Troy." (368–69) . . . ὅτου τις τυγχάνει χρείαν ἔχων . . .: the words stress the relative, the contingent, quality in this sophistic ethic, the very antithesis of heroic values. For the cuckold Menelaus, Hermione's need has a particularly piquant appeal: "For I consider this a major matter, to be deprived of one's conjugal rights!" (370–71) For such as Menelaus, Andromache's lesson in heroic issues is as unavailing as her earlier lesson to Hermione in the art of being a wife.

With the entry of King Peleus, we come to the first and only direct confrontation of the Phthian and the Spartan elements, "good Greeks" versus "bad Greeks." We have already suggested the dynastic significance of Peleus' choice of Troy over Sparta, of former foe over former ally. But this scene also complements the preceding ones in more immediate dramatic terms. Andromache has suggested the Helen-like "man-hunger" of Hermione; in the scene with Menelaus, she has pricked the bubble of Spartan repute for valour and branded the Spartan King as a dastard, good for only petty female quarrels. Now Peleus brings the triple indictment to one head in his personal grievance against Menelaus. First comes the famous tirade against Helen whose loose morals caused the Trojan War; then the sneer at uxorious Menelaus, who brought them all to bloodshed "for that creature's sake," finally the taunt at the milksop cowardice of the Spartan King who alone returns unscathed from war:

> You, the real slayer of my son Achilles, I have come to see as some obnoxious blight, you who alone have come from Troy unwounded, with your beautiful arms in their beautiful cases, just as when you went away! (614–18)

Eventually, before this furious onslaught, Menelaus backs off-stage; a dramatic example of Spartan cowardice opposed by Phthian valour.

The concluding passages of this play need little detailed analysis. It may be objected that its peripety, the murder of Neoptolemus, is effected by a complete newcomer, Orestes.[14] However, we have already seen that the persons in this play are not in themselves of primary importance, though the dramatic expression of the essential conflicts has required that they be excitingly presented. Orestes may be a new person in the play, but he is not a new *element*. All that he need be is cruel, crooked and dastardly, like his Spartan uncle, Menelaus, and this he is, most successfully. When he gets Hermione, we are able to feel that like has successfully called to like, and that both have got what they deserve. Of the off-stage murder itself, Kitto rightly remarks,[15] "No element of the sinister and hateful is wanting; it is a fine climax to a deadly play." However, this murder is the play's climax only insofar as it cuts its Gordian knot and renders possible the ultimate alignment of its good or evil elements. It means nothing to us otherwise. Why does Euripides adopt this unusual procedure of never introducing the major "sufferer" of his play alive? We have already seen that the integrity of Andromache's "Trojan aspect" is more easily preserved, if Neoptolemus, her Phthian link, is kept in the background. We now see another reason for the non-appearance of the sufferer; it is important that this necessary death should not be mistaken for a tragic event, for the intrusion of tragic emotions into this situation would seriously confuse the issue. The death of Neoptolemus was part of the legendary material, but Euripides handles the prince and his doom in such a way as to suit all aspects (both personal and dynastic) of his highly individual treatment.

In the same way, the traditional Molossian future of Andromache and her son, and the role of Helenus in this, is neatly worked into the playwright's theme. Helenus, as a brother of Hector who already has his

[14]Hermann (*Andr.* xii), says that Euripides sought to cover up the element of chance in Orestes' intrusion at this point by making Hermione his former fiancée —surely an odd suggestion in view of the fact that this relation was, as we have seen (above, notes 2 and 4) already a feature of the legend.

[15]Kitto, 234.

links with the house of Peleus, shares in both the good elements of the play. In marrying Andromache, as Thetis directs, he will in no way compromise her "Hector-and-Trojan" loyalty, as she awaits the day when the young scion of Troy and Phthia is ready to head the new line of prosperous Molossian Kings.[16]

[16]This conclusion, together with indication (see Schol. *Andr.* 445) that the play was not produced at Athens, has led a few scholars to believe that Euripides intended the *Andromache* as a compliment to Molossia for production at the royal court there. (See W. Schmid in W. von Christ's *Geschichte der Gr. Litt.*,[5] I, 343 and note 3, and D. S. Robertson, *CR*, XXXVII [1923], 58–60.) Robertson does succeed in showing the pro-Athenian tendency of Molossia at some time during the Peloponnesian War subsequent to 429 (the date at which Athens successfully supported Acarnania against Molossia); it is quite possible that Euripides intended some incidental honour to Molossia, but Robertson's insistence on the point as of major importance in the dramatist's purpose would be more impressive had Euripides invented the Molossian ending in his treatment of the Andomache legend. The rule of Neoptolemus and later of his family in Molossia is mentioned by Pindar (*Nem.* vii. 38–40; Robertson mentions this passage also), and the rule of Andromache and Helenus in Molossia (or Epirus) is mentioned by both Pausanias (I. 11. 1) and Vergil (*Aen.* iii. 295–96; cf. also 325 ff.); both accounts differ sufficiently in other matters to show that they spring from sources other than Euripides. The only change which Euripides appears to have made in *this* part of his legendary material is one required by an earlier event in his own plot: Andomache is to go to Molossia not with Neoptolemus, but after his death. Thus, with this adjustment, the dramatist is able to return, after his original treatment, to the sound basis of familiar legend to find precisely the glorious future, necessarily independent of depleted Phthia and hostile Sparta, which he wished to provide for the joint offspring of Trojan and Phthian stock.

PART FOUR

REALISTIC TRAGEDY

10

THE *Medea*

From Folk Tale to Tragedy

There is a directness and intensity about the *Medea* which elicits, even from critics, a different sort of response from that accorded to the other plays of Euripides. No gods determine, either in reality or by dramatic convention, Medea's passion. Of her adversaries, none has sufficient stature, in comparison with Medea, to modify significantly the structure of the plot. She is, to some degree, the victim of circumstance, but not in the extreme sense in which this is true of a Hecuba or an Andromache; what happens in her case we feel to be more the result of her own nature than of anything else. As Kitto has said of Medea, ". . . she was never really different from what we see her to be; [she was not] . . . a good but passionate woman who plunges into horrors only when stung by deadly insult and injury." But is Medea tragic, as this critic also avers, as "a purely passive figure," as helpless a victim of her passion as are her own victims? It is this view which categorizes Medea as "the impersonation of one of the blind and irrational forces in human nature" and which enables the critic to include her, "depersonalized" with many another Euripidean hero, in that group image of which he can say, "In the last analysis, Euripides' tragic hero is mankind."[1]

[1]For these four quotations, see Kitto, *G.T.*, 189, 195, 199 and 195, respectively. Several of the points raised in this paragraph have already been discussed in general terms in the Introduction; see above, pp. 21–23 and nn. 29 and 31. Similar questions concerning freedom and necessity in Euripidean tragedy have been raised in connection with Phaedra in the *Hippolytus*, though in her case the questions must be somewhat differently expressed due to the mythological context of the play. See above, chapter 2, pp. 37–38 ff. and nn. 13 and 14, Appendix I, and the references to various critics given in the notes. In the present chapter, I have taken Kitto as a most eloquent spokesman of the "tragic victim" view of Medea (and of various other Euripidean heroes) which is shared, at least to some degree, by many critics.

Kitto's account of the structure of this play in terms of its single-minded concentration on Medea's temperament is a valuable correction of misjudgments of that structure by Sophoclean comparisons.[2] Nevertheless, I believe it is possible to see in this Medea a more individually tragic heroine, engaged in a real *agôn* and a real choice, than the catastrophic figure, doomed by her nature to suffer and to cause disaster, which Kitto describes. Even the adaptations here made in the traditional *persona* and circumstances of Medea may serve as a preliminary indication of the poet's purpose.

The story of the Argonauts[3] goes back at least to the time of the composition of the *Odyssey* in which we find references to Jason's father, Aeson, and to Pelias (*Od.* XI. 254 ff.) as well as a reference to the ship Argo (*Od.* XII. 70) which suggests wide-spread circulation of its story at this time. Indeed, the overlapping and, in some cases, identity (e.g., Circe, the Harpies, the Sirens) of various creatures and adventures with which Odysseus and Jason are respectively involved, remind us that here, as in the "Wanderings" portion of the *Odyssey*, the traditional basis of epic has been invaded and overlaid by folk tale. Medea herself, though not mentioned by name in the *Odyssey* (the first extant occurrence of her name is in Hesiod, *Theogony*, 961) has close affinities, in blood and in profession, with Circe, the sorceress of Aeaea, whose brother Aietes

[2]See Kitto, 188–93. Cf. also Pohlenz's view of this shift of emphasis from plot to the individual nature of the tragic hero as characteristic of the difference between Euripides and his predecessors (Pohlenz, 258); cf. also John Jones, *On Aristotle and Greek Tragedy*, Part IV, who, since he minimizes the Aeschylean and Sophoclean concern with "character," expresses this contrast in rather more extreme terms.

[3]The following summary of the ancient evidence about Jason and Medea is drawn mainly from the excellent accounts in D. L. Page's edition of *Medea*, xxi–xxx and in L. Méridier, *Euripide* I, 105–10, and from the ancient authorities there cited. The most sustained of the ancient accounts of Jason's quest for the golden fleece, of the aid afforded him by Medea at Colchis, and of their subsequent adventures there and at Iolkos and Corinth, is to be found in Apollodorus, I. 9. 16–28. In that part of the legend which coincides with the action of our play, Apollodorus' account (sec. 28) is the same as that of Euripides, but Apollodorus' additional reference to a different version of the murder of the children, as well as one or two differences in detail (e.g., in the circumstances of Medea's murders of Apsyrtus and Pelias), show us that he was familiar with other ancient traditions on Jason and Medea besides the one which Euripides was following. The earliest continuous account of these exploits up to Medea's slaying of Pelias at Iolkos is to be found in Pindar, *Pythian* IV. (For other, fragmentary references to the legend in the lyric poets, see Méridier, 106, nn. 4–5.) Reference to various other versions (some going back to cyclic epic) of the doings of Jason and Medea at Corinth will be made in subsequent notes.

is Medea's father. Certainly the services which Medea, the witch (*pharmakis*), as Apollodorus calls her, renders Jason in Colchis, aiding him to subdue the brazen-footed, fire-breathing bulls, to sow the dragon's teeth and to defeat the dread guardian of the golden fleece, all fulfil the regular folk-tale characteristic of suspending the natural order of things by magical means.

This character of a folk-tale witch still attaches to Medea in the exploits recounted of her in Greece: witness the fiendish and magical manner in which she disposes of Pelias of Iolkos, her husband's enemy, and of Glauke and Creon, at Corinth. However, as we approach the Greek part of Medea's exploits, we notice certain interesting variations in the accounts given. Several traditions, for example, link Medea with Corinth but in a way rather different from that suggested by Euripides and Apollodorus.

According to an account originating in the eighth century with Eumelos, Helios, Medea's grandfather, gave Corinth to Medea's father Aietes; when his heir Bounos died, the Corinthians summoned Medea to be their queen, and through her Jason became king.[4] These circumstances do not readily provide the motive for the sort of *crime passionel* which we find in Euripides. According to Pausanias II. 3.11 (following Eumelos), Jason abandoned Medea because she had concealed her children in a temple of Hera, believing that they would be made immortal. As Page has observed, the explanation of this truncated narrative appears in a scholium to Pindar (Schol. g, *Ol.* XIII. 74) in which we learn that though Hera had promised immortality to Medea's children (because Medea had refused the embrace of Zeus), the children died; thus Jason, it would appear, abandoned Medea not merely for concealing her children in the temple of Hera, but for exposing them to some treatment which caused their death.

Two other ancient accounts (summarized in Schol. *Med.* 264) agree in blaming the Corinthians themselves for the murder of Medea's children, though they differ greatly in their statements of the circumstances and the sequel of the deed. According to Parmeniskos, the Corinthians acted simply from resentment of the rule of a foreigner and a witch, and later were forced to expiate their deed. According to Creophilos, Creon's relatives murdered them in vengeance for Medea's murder of Creon, and then blamed all the murders on Medea, who had fled to Athens.

The interesting feature about all these accounts is that none of them

[4]See Schol. f, Pindar *Ol.* XIII. 74 (which includes a quotation from Eumelos), Schol. *Med.* 9, and the complementary account in Pausanias II. 3. 10–11.

makes Medea responsible for the intentional slaughter of her children, though two of them (considered jointly) suggest that she was accidentally responsible for it, while another one claims that she was unjustly accused of it.

From this summary, two points relevant to our study of Euripides' treatment of Medea[5] may be stated. One is that, by a blend of two conflicting versions, together with some necessary adaptation of his own, Euripides himself made Medea responsible for the murder of her children. It is tempting to infer as well that the whole element of the *crime passionel* at Corinth is also a Euripidean innovation, but of this we cannot be sure: Medea must have had *some* motive for the murder of Creon which is reported in Creophilos' account, and there are one or two other hints in the non-Euripidean part of the tradition that the story of Glauke's agonizing death may have existed independently of our poet.[6]

The second point concerns the change which Euripides makes in the general image which the pre-Euripidean Medea presents. In the tradition, Medea shows little affinity with the tragic, or even with the heroic type. She is a creature of folk tale, an outlandish barbarian, a witch who has helped Jason by a mixture of black magic and inhuman savagery. Even those versions in which it is Medea and not Jason who establishes the family at Corinth smack of the folk-tale tradition: in Olympian mythology the sun god does not go about giving Greek cities to individuals, least of all to barbarians. In these same versions, Medea's search for everlasting life for her children, like the black magic by which, elsewhere, she claims to be able to restore youth from age, is also a folk-tale motif: in the more proper world of myth and tragedy, it is only the gods who are immortal. To this witch of the folk tale, Euripides adds a new dimension; while denying her neither her fury nor her magic, he yet makes her a woman of stature, of potentially tragic power.[7] And the plot, while it

[5]In speaking of "Euripides' treatment," I leave out of account the opinion, quoted in an anonymous *Hypothesis* of Euripides' *Medea*, that this play was based on a plot of Neophron's. The improbability of this opinion has already been well established by Page, xxxv–vi, whose position on the matter has not, I think, been overthrown by E. A. Thompson (*CQ*, XXXVIII [1944], 10–14), one of the relatively few recent critics to maintain the anteriority and influence of Neophron's *Medea*. A thorough summary of the whole "Neophron problem" is also to be found in L. Séchan, *Etudes sur la Tragédie Grecque*, Appendix VII, 592–94, together with references to the main authorities arguing for either side of the question.

[6]See Page, xxv–vi.

[7]Cf. A. Lesky, *Die Griechische Tragödie*, 147–48, who also stresses that in the *Medea* Euripides almost lets us forget the witch in favour of the person, though he adds that witchcraft has its proper place in the treatment.

retains the theatrical excitement, the *Grand Guignol* effects suited to the original Medea, sustains as well something of the tragic struggle between good and evil.

Such developments would surely be unnecessary if Euripides, as Kitto suggests, were merely illustrating the destructive power of passion by displaying one of its most helpless victims. Thus we may expect a theme and characterization more individually tragic than the predetermined victim of Kitto's description will allow.

Dramatic Analysis

The intense centripetal focus of this tragedy begins in the prologue. Its three parts, monologue, dialogue and a frightened anapaestic series punctuated by Medea's off-stage cries, produce their complementary effects in an ascending scale of excitement. The first speaker is the Nurse, and so our earliest impression of Medea comes through an intimate and sympathetic witness. Her news, that Jason has deserted Medea for the daughter of King Creon, is enclosed by accounts of the past services of Medea to Jason and to the city which has sheltered him, and, hideous as these services have been, they are presented in the light of Medea's passionate devotion to her husband. The description of Medea's mood suggests a savage, wounded animal and in the Nurse's apprehension of some monstrous deed (perhaps against the children, whose sight Medea now abhors) we get our first warning, from the one who knows her best, of what Medea can become, when wronged.

Enter the Tutor, leading the children of Medea. As the bearer of fresh news—that Creon is about to exile Medea—and more particularly as the guardian of the children, he increases the sense of apprehension and makes it more specific. The Nurse redoubles her worried chatter:

> O keep the children from her . . . for even now I saw her glaring at them like an angry bull. . . . She'll not leave this fit, too well I know it, till she has charged at someone. May it be enemies, not friends, she chooses! (90–95)

Two savage cries, off-stage, provide the final impact of this prologue: Medea screams her wrongs and curses husband, children, "all the house." (111–14) The brief intensity of these cries, contrasted with the Nurse's long-winded moralizing, brings the prologue to a chilling climax. The series of emotions traversed—sympathy, apprehension, horror—anticipates in a few rapid strokes the responses which, in the same sequence, the coming action will evoke.

This sinister blend of effects is repeated, in choral terms, in the *parodos*, where the brief songs expressing sympathy and fear are harshly punctuated by Medea's off-stage cries. The direction of this tragedy requires that the Chorus should *begin* by feeling sympathy for Medea. Thus, singing as women rather than as Corinthians, they remind us (208–12) that it was Jason's vows, by which Medea now curses him, which first induced her to take her ill-starred voyage to Greece.

The contrast between the fury of Medea's initial cries and the controlled and calculated rhetoric of her opening address to the Corinthian women has already been compared with the presentation of Phaedra in the *Hippolytus*.[8] The same dramatic purpose is served in both cases: that of showing in striking contrast the most elemental and the most civilized or even sophisticated aspects of the same personality. What difference there is between the two contrasts is due to the difference between the two women. Even in hysteria, Phaedra seeks to cloak her naked passion (this impulse is, indeed, the *cause* of her hysteria); later, in her discourse on human frailty (her own included) one feels that she expresses her own character more truthfully than does Medea in *her* official bid for sympathy. Freudians, no doubt, could express these same distinctions more accurately in terms of the *ego*, the *super ego* and the *id*.

Medea's purpose in her opening speech (214–66) is, purely and simply, to win the Chorus of female citizens to her side. As a piece of rhetoric (this time needing no apology for dramatic relevance) the speech is one of the poet's finest passages.[9] It begins on a note of specious but ingratiating familiarity, moves on to the briefest possible indication ("I'm finished, good women, my husband has betrayed me!") of the speaker's plight, and then concentrates with a wealth of poignantly familiar detail on "woman's lot," a trouble which the Chorus shares. "We women are a timid lot . . . but wronged in marriage, there's none more murderous!" All Medea has asked is silent co-operation. By the end of her speech, the Chorus, to a woman (*δράσω τάδ'*! 267), regards her vengeance as its own.

The poet's purpose in this passage is, perhaps, more complex than Medea's, though it has much in common with it: we, too, like the Chorus, are destined to begin in pity then to move through fear to horrified revulsion. But to see the larger dramatic purpose of the speech we must consider it in relation to the whole presentation of Jason's barbarian wife.

Prior to this speech, Medea is known to us only as the terrifying witch

[8]See above, chapter 2, p. 35.

[9]On the influences of sophistic rhetoric on the speech, see P. Mazon, *Revue de Philologie*, 3me série, XXVII, 119–21.

whom the dramatist has received from the tradition; even if we have no direct knowledge of that tradition, both deeds and character of *that* Medea have been emphatically made known to us in the opening portions of the play. Now, for the first time, we are introduced to another Medea: a woman and a foreigner who can move the Greeks of the Chorus, and perhaps of the audience, with that disciplined compound of passion and reason which the Greeks called rhetoric. Despite her outlandish background, this Medea manages to strike a common chord in people who (as Jason so tactfully reminds her later) regarded their own society as a privilege which a barbarian must enjoy on sufferance. Thus it is that the dramatist begins, at least, to endow his folk-tale witch with something of the stature which a tragic heroine requires: here and in subsequent encounters with Creon, with Jason and with Aegeus, the many aspects of Medea's powerful personality—eloquent and cunning, wise and passionate by turns—are gradually revealed.

In facing Creon, Medea must play the fawning hypocrite to win at least a day's reprieve from exile. With nice irony, the dramatist endows her with the insight and skill to twist what should most tell against her—her reputation as "a wise one" and Creon's protective love for his own daughter—to serve her purpose. The exchange with Creon has other qualities as well. Medea's appeal "for her children's sake" to Creon's paternal instincts keeps the "children theme" before our minds, while the passage in which Medea allays Creon's fears about her special powers allows Euripides a sly, contemporary aside on the slander which clever people must suffer in society.

While something of Medea's power appears even in the scene with Creon, the full force of her personality is necessarily muted by the situation. This briefly *piano* effect is more than redressed by her next and most dramatic encounter. Here Medea's greatest advantage is achieved at the expense of, and in contrast to, the traditionally "epic" figure of Jason, for the hero of the good ship Argo cuts a very sorry figure in her presence. Generosity, absolute loyalties, action and feeling on the grand scale, are the hallmarks of the heroic character. Jason's quibbling rationalization of his actions Medea answers with the single word *ἀναίδεια* ("O utter shameless brazenness!" 472), as she launches into an impassioned account of all that she has done for him. Consistently, Jason plays the sophist to a heroic Medea: for past favours, he has really Cypris to thank, not her; besides, for a barbarian, life and fame among the Greeks is more than just requital of her service. Previously, horror may have been our main reaction to Medea's deeds for Jason. Now, confronted by Jason's niggling sums in settling the accounts of love, we are impressed by the wild generosity of passion which made them possible.[10]

The effect of the Aegeus scene on the "public image" of Medea seems often to have been missed by the critics, distracted, no doubt, by arguments concerning its allegedly "episodic" nature.[11] Surely we must be impressed by Aegeus' respect for Medea's advice and the readiness with which he confides in her. Nor does he speak in the tone which one reserves for one's witch-doctor: rather, they converse on terms of mutual regard—witness the warmth of their greetings (663–66) and the exchange of confidence and sympathy with one another's plight. It should be noted, too, that Medea's utterances acquire a sort of brisk professionalism, completely different in tone from other speeches in the play, as soon as Aegeus begins his consultation (see especially vv. 672–86); this is our only actual view in the play of Medea as a specialist, a professional "wise woman." And the readiness with which Aegeus accepts Medea's offer to put an end to his childlessness in return for future sanctuary at Athens shows a confidence in her powers at least equal to that which he feels in Apollo's oracle or in the wise and pious Pittheus of Trozen. In general, this treatment from the King of Athens does as much as anything to establish Medea in our minds as a "personage" not to be disposed of as a mere gypsy baggage from barbarian lands.

The Aegeus episode is, of course, important for other reasons as well; it heralds, as we shall see, a turning-point in Medea's career of vengeance and in the sympathy which the Chorus has hitherto afforded her.

[10]There are some who would argue that Jason is "justified" in his treatment of Medea (see, for example, R. B. Palmer, *CJ*, LIII, 49–55): so he may be, legally, and so the dramatist could have made him appear, morally, if he had wished to. But if Euripides wished us to sympathize with Jason in this play—or, indeed, to have any use for him at all—one wonders why he let him cut such a sorry figure in comparison with Medea in this scene, why he made him so insensitive and stupid concerning her throughout the play and, in particular, why he afflicted him with such revolting arguments at vv. 526–44.

[11]The scene might appear to offend against Aristotle's views on the need for a necessary or probable sequence of action in the plot of a tragedy (*Poetics* 1451b 33–35). See Kitto, 196–97, and Page, xxix–xxx, for two very different defences against this rather tedious criticism. My only reservation about Page's discussion of the scene is that I do not think it can be stated categorically that it is here that Medea gets the idea of taking vengeance on Jason by murdering the children. This *may* be true—and certainly Aegeus' plight turns *our* thoughts toward the special need of kings for sons. But Medea may have thought of harming her children, and through them Jason and his house, before this: see vv. 112–14.

In her encounters with Creon and Aegeus, Medea has assumed soft-spoken roles which circumstances have forced upon her. After both these encounters, the essential single-minded Medea reappears in impassioned outbursts alone with the Chorus. ("Do you think," she reassures the Chorus at 368–69, about her attitude to Creon, "that I'd have ever fawned on *that* one, if I'd not been weaving wiles to serve my ends?") There is, however, a terrible difference in the content of these two speeches, and this gulf is marked by the sharp contrast in tone between the earlier and later choral lyrics of the play. In the first of these speeches (364–409), Medea shows, it is true, a sinister delight in pondering the different routes—poison or the knife—by which her enemies may be despatched, but however much her oath "by Hecate, the sharer of my hearth" may chill us, it is still her enemies she speaks of killing.

In the lyric (almost "a song for feminists") which follows this speech, the Chorus is still full of sympathy for Medea. As often in Euripides, the first strophe and antistrophe generalize on the situation (here, "the injustice done to women") while the second strophic pair applies the theme directly to the tragic sufferer:

Now rivers flow upstream and the established course of justice is reversed—for now 'tis *men* who are unjust and laugh at oaths. . . . (410–14)
Through the ages, man-made songs show women faithless, but if we women had the gift of song, we'd sing a different tune. . . . (421–29, paraphrase)
So with you, Medea. Love brought you across the seas to Greece. But now, abandoned (for no longer do Greeks reverence marriage oaths) you have no refuge, no paternal home, as a royal rival destroys your marriage bed.
(431–45, paraphrase)

The chorus which follows the encounter with Jason is not, however, quite as single-minded in its championship of women and Medea. The first strophe, praising moderate love, decries that excessive passion which ruins judgment and virtue; the answering antistrophe, which praises self-control (*sôphrosynê*), decries the adulterous love which causes strife. Thus, in the generalizing part of this lyric, the Chorus glances at the faults of both Medea and Jason in turn. In the second half, however, nothing distracts attention from sympathy for the deserted and homeless foreigner.

The decisive change in the dramatic action and in the attitude of the Chorus occurs after the scene with Aegeus, for it is then that Medea announces the awful means by which she plans to take vengeance on her husband. The excellence of the play's structure is well illustrated by the placing of this crisis and by the kinds of effect which precede and follow it. The gradual revelation of Medea's personality has now been completed, save for one essential feature which is to give the *agôn* its tragic meaning. The "children theme," so essential to this meaning, has been kept constantly before our minds: in the frightened premonitions of the Nurse and in Medea's own off-stage curses (36–37, 89–95, 112–14); in Medea's exploitation of Creon's paternal instincts, and, ironically enough, in Jason's own claim that *he* is acting for his family's sake: "For what need have *you* of children?" he asks Medea (565; see also 488–91, 557–65 for other recurrences of the "children theme" in this episode). The Aegeus episode itself is, of course, vital both to this theme and to the mechanics of the plot. Aegeus' own royal trouble, childlessness, and the lengths to which he goes to cure it, is our most forcible reminder of a king's essential need of sons. Again, in promising the outcast sanctuary in Athens, Aegeus unwittingly removes the only barrier to Medea's plans and her last reticence in revealing them to the Chorus.

Medea's three addresses to the Chorus (214–66, 364–409, 764–810) follow an ascending scale in keeping with the gradually increasing impetus in plot and theme. In the first and most rhetorical of these, Medea's passion is rigorously subordinated to her immediate purpose of winning the Chorus to her side. The second speech with its curse by Hecate and its pondering of the various means of murder, is both more savage and more sinister, but it tells us little of Medea's actual intentions. Only after the scene with Aegeus does she shout for all to hear the full horror of the vengeance which she plans.

One of the most shocking effects of this speech comes from the lack of horror which Medea displays herself. The plan to send her children to the princess bearing poisoned robes is told with hideous matter-of-factness, and only an occasional word or phrase (ᾤμωξα, 791, ἔργον ἀνοσιώτατον, 796) suggests any hesitation at the awful plan of slaying her children for the sake of vengeance on their father. All this suggests that the hints given in the prologue told the truth, that Medea has from the start been determined on this course of action. The main emphasis of the speech is that laughter from one's enemies is not to be endured (see 797, 807 ff.), and the cry, "grievous to my enemies and kindly to my friends" (809) serves as a grim reminder of the accuracy of the Nurse's description (at v. 38) of Medea's spirit.

It is in the ode (824–65) immediately following these dreadful revelations that the Chorus begins to withdraw its allegiance from Medea. The first strophe and antistrophe deal, in highly poetic terms, with the purity and beauty of Athens. Euripides may well have enjoyed pleasing his fellow citizens and himself with such idealized pictures of his city, but here he does not do so at the expense of the dramatic situation. The point of the description appears in the second strophic pair: "How," asks the Chorus (at 846 ff.), "will such a city ever welcome you, Medea, a child-murderer polluting all you meet?" Now the respect and chivalrous treatment which Medea had won from the King of Athens has been one of the most impressive features of her earlier presentation; the immediate effect of that treatment, however, has been to confirm Medea in her secret and terrible decision. Thus to dwell as the Chorus does on the hideous uncongeniality between Medea the child-murderer and the pure and serene haven which she has chosen in an effective way of expressing the self-destruction which her plans involve. The terms in which Athens is described are admirably suited to this purpose: it is the physical serenity of the place which is stressed, for this is the aspect which is particularly vulnerable to the pollution with which Medea threatens it. Thus, Athens is "the sacred, unplündered land—where golden Harmonia produced the Muses nine"; the land whose children "ever culling illustrious wisdom, stride spendidly under skies of glorious brightness." (825–32) What sharper contrast to the black deeds of Medea could we find than all this bright serenity? Even Cypris, so dread a goddess in Medea's case, "breathes moderate, pleasure-wafting breezes on this land." (836 ff.)

The actual execution of Medea's plot against the Princess needs little comment. It provides, of course, one of the most exciting and theatrical of the playwright's intrigues and suggests, perhaps, at least one reason why the *Medea*, of all Greek drama, has survived most successfully as a play which is still presented on the stage. The gulling of the pompous Jason, unaware as ever of his wife's true nature; the contrast between the children's innocence and the glittering fatality of the gifts they bear; the suspense, heightened by the vivid anticipations of the Chorus (978–88), as to whether the Princess will yield to the "heavenly charm" of these adornments; the gruesome account, in the messenger's speech, of the switch from delight to anguish, then all the gory details of the deaths themselves: all this provides many opportunities (and none is missed) for melodrama and irony of the more obvious sort. Such effects are legitimate enough in themselves, particularly in view of the sort of creature which Medea is to become before the last scene is ended; nevertheless, a tendency to overplay this aspect of the drama, from the second scene with Jason to the murder of the children, has sometimes obscured certain more subtly tragic effects with which it is combined. Thus far the dramatist has presented a Medea who combines the elemental passion of the folk-tale witch with certain qualities of mind, emotion and personality which let her tower above the several royal and (conventionally) heroic characters who appear beside her on the stage. Now, in her last speech to the Chorus (764–810) this human and potentially tragic Medea vanishes: instead we hear an embodiment of the *alastôr* (the avenging spirit from Hades) coldly announcing child-murder as a necessary part of her revenge. If this is the Medea which we are to watch without relief to the play's end, then both the Chorus and ourselves have been the dupes, both of the "heroine" and of the dramatist, for yielding our sympathy and interest. Fortunately, however, it is the air of cold inflexibility which is false: a cloak of desperate resolution hiding the maternal anguish as well as a device by which the dramatist may, in the end, present that anguish more effectively.

The agony of Medea begins quietly and unexpectedly in the scene with Jason. The "reconciliation speech," the apology to Jason, Medea accomplishes with all her usual aplomb. The first onset of grief suddenly occurs at the entry of the children, summoned to heal the reconciliation, when Jason thus addresses them: "Only grow up! Your father and whatever gods are kindly will assure the rest! Soon may I see you glorying in the strength of youth. . . ." (918–21) In each instance, the effect of Medea's tears is so veiled by her ambiguous explanations, so muted by her resourceful ironies, that some critics have taken the tears themselves as a calculated device for securing Jason's sympathy. But Medea's dissimulation only shows us the measure of her will in masking, with characteristic ingenuity, the anguish which, for a moment, overcomes her. So viewed, this scene anticipates, in miniature, the major struggle to come.

The alternation of the human and the fiendish Medea in the following scenes corresponds to the curious interweaving of the tragic and the macabre elements in the double catastrophe. The chorus (976–1001) which follows the despatch of the children with the gifts heralds both deeds of violence: the first strophe and antistrophe anticipate, with sinister vividness, the temptation of the Princess and its fatal results, while the concluding strophic pair expresses grief for the woes of Jason and Medea, respectively, in the coming murder of the children. The report of what has happened at the palace is divided, most remarkably, into two parts. The Tutor's announcement that the children and their gifts have been accepted is, to his surprise, greeted with sullen gloom by Medea; on the other hand, the Messenger's announcement in the following episode, of the deaths which the gifts have caused is received with hideous joy. In between these two reports comes the most crucial passage (1019–80) in the play: that agonizing self-debate in which

Medea twice revokes and twice confirms her decision to slay her children.[12] After the Messenger Speech, lengthy (μὴ σπέρχου, 1133, Medea has ordered, in one of her most chilling moments) with all the harrowing details, we are brought with the speed of necessity to the final catastrophe for, Medea argues desperately, if their mother does not kill the children now, some hostile hand may do so. (1236–41) But δέδοκται at the beginning of the speech (1236) reminds us of the truth of the matter: the original decision to slay the children was a part, perhaps the major part, of the original plan, before the fatal gifts were sent. Medea utters her final determination with the grim conviction that for her a life of misery must now begin: "Steel your heart for one brief day—then mourn thereafter!" (1247–49)

A final brief and despairing lyric (1251–70) precedes the off-stage murder. It is significant that now the Chorus no longer addresses its pleas to Medea but to the "nature" deities, Earth and Sun (Medea's grandsire) to restrain this unnatural murderess, this embodiment of a vengeance-driven Erinys (1260), which Medea has become. For Medea herself they have only despairing questions and equally dismal prophecies.

Why are the two deeds of violence, in many ways so different, presented in this interwoven fashion? Partly, no doubt, for the practical reason that the poet does not wish to lose dramatic impetus by having to work up two separate crises. But there are, I think, reasons more significant than this.

From her folk-tale chrysalis, Medea has emerged, in this play, as a human heroine with the power to achieve her ends in a highly civilized social context (as Jason reminds her) against all odds. So far, however, save for a few hints in the second scene with Jason, her passion for vengeance has been tempered by no redeeming emotion: though human, she is not sympathetic (the Chorus sympathizes with her situation rather than with her): we cannot achieve any degree of identification with her. Again, so far there has been no essential conflict in this play. True, Medea, abandoned and alone in a hostile state, has had to bend two kings, a Chorus of Corinthian women and an ambitious husband to her will, but this achievement is only the measure of her greatness: in this play, Medea herself is really the only one capable of resisting Medea.

[12]Lesky (152) emphasizes the psychological uniqueness in Greek tragedy of this speech of Medea's, distinguishing it sharply from demonstrations of inflexible will, such as we find in Sophocles' *Ajax*, in that here we see an individual struggling with conflicting powers which seek for the possession of her soul. See also Pohlenz's sensitive account of Medea's *agôn*, 255–56.

Regarded as a tragic figure, the Medea of the earlier scenes corresponds to a hate-ridden Philoctetes as yet undisturbed by the friendship of Neoptolemus, or to a stubbornly resentful Achilles, untried by the loss of Patroclus.

Medea's first full statement of her plans (in the last of her three addresses to the Chorus) has shocked us by its coldness. More recently, in the second scene with Jason, we have seen signs that this frozen determination does not represent the whole Medea. Now, when the child-murder suddenly becomes imminent with the success of the first phase of the plan, Medea's resolution falters for the first time. Thus the great speech at 1019 ff. is essential to the characterization of Medea and to the meaning of the play.

If Medea's sudden flood of emotion, her passionate regrets for lost maternal joys, should strike us as commonplace, let us remember that that is just its purpose. We are meant, simply, to realize that Medea loves her children as deeply as any woman does. So, too, the sudden effects of the children's smiles, and of Medea's lightning switches from "I cannot do it" to "I must," and back again, far from being bathetic melodrama, are essential to the realistic presentation of the struggle in Medea's soul. Without this scene, what Medea eventually becomes would indeed smack of melodrama. That monstrous figure attains tragic significance only when we see it as the result of a conflict—of a victory, as Medea herself expresses it (1079–80)—of her all-consuming passion for vengeance over her better counsels. To grasp the nature of this struggle, we must see the good in Medea before we see her at her worst. The plot requires that something of her lethal savagery should appear before the ultimate horror of the child-murder, but had we already seen her gloating over the details of her palace butchery the sympathetic presentation of her own agony would have been impossible. So it is that the *first* news from the palace, that the children and their gifts have been accepted, is greeted sadly by Medea, and that the horrible sequence to this news is postponed till after the emotional climax at vv. 1019–80. By the time that the second bulletin, showing the first results of Medea's cruelty, arrives from the palace, Medea's self-debate concerning her children, and with it the dramatic need for our sympathy, is over; indeed, the wholehearted gloating over the Messenger's hideous account, contrasting so sharply with her despondent reception of the Tutor and his news, may be meant to illustrate the new Medea, now totally committed to evil, who emerges only after the completion of her interior struggle.

In the concluding passages of the play, after the murder of the children, the monstrous and inhuman aspects of Medea are played up in a variety of ways. The Chorus by its reference to Ino (1282 ff.), intimates that no human mother could bear to live after slaying her children and Jason echoes this thought when he cries, "Can you still look upon the sun and earth, after enduring such an impious deed?" (1327–28) And yet Medea lives and flourishes. More significant, perhaps, is Jason's bitter reference to the unnatural deeds of Medea—deeds from which *he* took the profit—against her own family in Colchis. During the very human action of this play, little has been made of these dark deeds, save as examples of Medea's devotion to the ingrate Jason, but now that "Medea the fiend" has triumphed over the human heroine this reminder of the barbarous, magic-working Medea of the folk tale is all too apposite. Jason complains that the *Alastôr* which should pursue Medea for these deeds is pursuing him instead, but we who have witnessed the moral destruction of Medea in the preceding episode are all too well aware that the *alastôr* has not missed its mark. As for the murderess herself, Medea the avenger, in the final scene with Jason, has quite defeated Medea, the tortured mother: ". . . Call me lioness or Scylla, as you will . . . as long as I have reached your vitals. . . ." (1358–60) "My grief is solaced if *you* cannot mock!" (1362)

The "improbable" and inorganic ending of the play—Medea's departure in the Sun-god's fiery chariot—is a feature of the play which appears to have irritated Aristotle. (*Poetics* 1454b 1–2) However, such macabre touches, such departures from the real world of tragedy, if they serve some purpose, are surely permissible when the tragic meaning has already been expressed. That, in this instance, the supernatural intervention is not meant to intrude on the real action of the play has already been shown by the fact that, earlier, the human and the tragic Medea has been concerned with such practical matters as the arrangement for asylum at Athens and the impossibility of escaping with her children from the vengeful Corinthians. (See, for example, lines 1236–41.) Thus the only point of interest in the *deus-ex-machina* ending lies in the symbolic purpose which this device fulfils. This has been variously expressed by critics in accordance with their different views of Euripides' "Medea theme." Kitto finds in the device the poet's answer to the Chorus's and Jason's idea that "Sun and Earth, the most elemental things in the Universe, have been outraged by these terrible crimes," while Lesky and M. P. Cunningham both regard the chariot scene as marking the fundamental, qualitative change which her awful deed has effected in Medea.[13] In terms of the present study, it seems fair to suggest that by this final macabre touch of symbolism, the poet is once again expressing the transformation of a human heroine back to the folk-tale fiend of magic powers.

[13]See Kitto 198–99; Lesky, 153; M. P. Cunningham, *CP*, XLIX, 151–60. An important distinction must, however, be made between Lesky's and Cunningham's interpretation of the theme and its *dénouement*: unlike Lesky (see above, note 12), Cunningham tends to dismiss the moral quality of Medea's struggle with herself and seems to regard her as basically the same ("a sort of witch," p. 153) throughout the play. Thus his view of the "transformation symbol," if we may call it that, suggests the sort of idea we get in Wilde's *Picture of Dorian Gray*, that of latent corruption finally made physically manifest (in Medea's case because of an act of ultimate evil) in a particularly shocking way.

11

THE *Electra*

Some Previous Views

Euripides' *Electra*, which is more unusual if not a better play than is sometimes realized, has suffered from a certain "categorizing" tendency in recent critics. Those interested in the more technical aspects of Euripidean dramaturgy discuss the *Electra* in connection with the *Ion*, *Helena* and *I.T.* Certainly the fact that all these plays contain a "recognition sequence" and an "intrigue," or *mêchanêma*, leading to revenge, escape, or both, by the principals concerned, does supply a good deal of common ground for formal criticism; several scholars, notably Professors Solmsen and Strohm,[1] have commented fruitfully on the various uses of these plot elements in the plays concerned. But this examination of shared technical features has, I feel, tended to exaggerate similarities in tone and dramatic purpose, and sometimes, even, to suggest a basic congeniality which does not in all cases exist. It is in this generalizing tendency that such criticism, however excellent in other respects, tends to come unstuck, for such generalizations seldom fit all the plays concerned with equal felicity. Thus when Solmsen suggests that the techniques and the rationalistic criticisms of these plays tend to replace more meaningful content, and again that the sensitive but passive and "*tychê*-ridden" characters in these plays contrast sharply with the strong and

[1]See F. Solmsen, *Hermes*, LXIX (1934), 390–419; Strohm, *Euripides*, 75 86. An earlier example of a similar approach is to be found in E. Howald, *Untersuchungen zur Technik der Euripideischen Tragödien*, chap. 5, "Intriguenstücke"; here some interesting contrasts with Solmsen's conclusions are to be found, particularly in the use of observations about plot technique in the various "recognition plays" as evidence for their respective dates. See chap. 15, pp. 268 ff., and notes 3, 21, 22. See also, in sharper contrast with Solmsen's views here, Zuntz's convincing arguments against grouping the *Electra* with the other plays of recognition and intrigue (Zuntz, *The Political Plays of Euripides*, 69, n. 1).

confident personalities which dominate the action of such plays as *Medea, Hippolytus* and *Hecuba,*[2] one wonders whether these statements apply as well to the *Electra* as, say, to the *Helena* and the *Ion*. Strohm, it is true, shows some awareness of this danger when he indicates some characteristic differences between "the tragi-mythical Electra" and plays like the *I.T.* and *Helena.*[3] Nevertheless, he too tends to stretch the similarity between the plots of the "recognition plays" by suggesting that they are all concerned with self-salvation and "opponent-injury" (the "τίσις-σωτηρία complex");[4] such descriptions, one feels, apply better to the *Electra* than to the *Helena*, and better to the *Ion* than to any of the other three. This example is perhaps of minor importance in itself, but considered with what has just been said, it helps to illustrate the tendency to lump together plays which, particularly in the case of the *Electra*, exhibit distinctive features of plot and tone, owing to the very different dramatic purposes involved. By its very nature, the *Electra* theme must, almost inevitably, involve a recognition scene and some kind of plan for vengeance. Since we know from other plays of Euripides that these were plot elements which he treated in an original and "virtuoso" manner, we may guess that he will do so here also, and that he may employ techniques similar to those found in corresponding scenes in other plays. But the points of comparison end here; as to the more obvious differences (such as the fact that in the *Electra, I.T.* and *Helena* the recognition sequence is completed before the *mêchanêma*, the vengeance-intrigue, begins, whereas in the *Ion* both plot elements are resolved together), these are due as much to differences of dramatic purpose and of the requirements of the plots as they are to differences in dramatic technique.[5]

A similar tendency toward categorization has led Professor Kitto to describe Euripides' *Electra* as a "melodrama" (in company with *Orestes, Phoenissae, I.A.*) and so first cousin, at least, to the other "recognition plays" which are described as tragicomedies.[6] Kitto's argument proceeds

[2]See Solmsen, 397–400.

[3]See Strohm, 82 ff., 90, 132.

[4]*Ibid.*, 75; cf. 80. Cf. also Zuntz's criticisms of this and similar points in his excellent review of Strohm's book in *Gnômon* 31 (1959), 404–11.

[5]Contrast Solmsen, *op. cit.*, 400 ff., and see my comments in chap. 15 (p. 268 and n. 3, p. 274 f. and n. 21) mentioned above.

[6]See Kitto, *G.T.*, 332, and chap. 12 in general; for the discussion of *Electra* in particular see pp. 332–44. Cf. chap. 11 for his discussion of the "tragicomedies." The fundamental point in common between melodrama and tragicomedy is, according to Kitto, that both aim at theatrical rather than tragic effect. The difference between the two "species" seems to be less clearly marked. In the case

by other paths than do the more technical studies just referred to, yet it too, in the last analysis, involves a comparable misunderstanding of the relation between the varied effects of the play and the total dramatic conception. Kitto begins with a skilful and, on the whole, acceptable demonstration that Euripides' Electra is not tragic in the way that Sophocles' Electra or even Euripides' own Medea is tragic. In the one case, she lacks the common, representative "human" qualities which impart a certain universality to Sophocles' Electra, however particular her circumstances; on the other hand, she lacks Medea's totally passionate nature which, wherever it be found, must cause catastrophe. However, Kitto's fundamental error, in my opinion, lies in his too ready acceptance of the view that because the characterization of Electra is not tragic (at least in this critic's sense of the term) therefore the play as a whole must be melodramatic. It is a fatally easy transition for a categorizing critic to make—particularly if the categories are already waiting for the play. Euripides' character of Electra is too extreme, too unpleasant, for us to accord her that modicum of common humanity with which we may identify ourselves; nor does she quite reach Medea's catastrophic class: therefore, she must have been created simply for the theatrical enjoyment which the audience may get from watching a weird character talking and acting in an extreme and unpleasant fashion. "She is Medea without the tragedy—but with all Medea's *Grand Guignol* effects; in other words, a hero of melodrama."[7]

Much of what Kitto says about Euripides' *Electra*, particularly with regard to its emphasis upon the hideous,[8] is true. It is also true that, as in many plays of Euripides, including some unmistakable tragedies, some of the rhetorical passages do contain ideas and effects introduced for the sake of the immediate interest and enjoyment, however macabre, which they provide. Nevertheless, if it can be shown that the whole characterization of Electra and, to some degree, even the rhetorical passages in the play, serve one overriding dramatic idea, then surely we are bound to take the play more seriously than Kitto's use of the term melodrama implies.

---

of *Electra* and *Orestes* it is that these plays "are grim and not gay, and are based on character drawing rather than on the excitements of an intricate plot." But this description is applied specifically only to the *Electra* and the *Orestes*, of the four plays designated as "melodramas"; moreover, "character-drawing" is not something which one immediately associates with "melodrama," while plot-excitement *is*.

[7]*Ibid.*, 336–37.

[8]*Ibid.*, 339.

The Euripidean Approach to the Myth

Aeschylus conceived the murder of Clytemnestra by Orestes as a part of a divinely ordained sequence of disasters from which good, in the form of an advance in human understanding in its struggle with evil and suffering, would eventually be achieved. With the degree of divine and human motivation and responsibility present at each stage in this sequence of disasters we are not here concerned. However, it will not be debated that in the *Choephori* neither Orestes nor his relatively minor partner Electra is represented as having, or expecting, much choice in their unquestioning fulfilment of Apollo's command; indeed, one might say that in this and the final play of the trilogy there is a gradual diminution, as compared with the *Agamemnon*, in the importance of the human element, and a corresponding increase in the emphasis on divine control and on the competing conceptions of justice represented by Apollo and the Furies.

Sophocles, concentrating on but a single phase in this sequence of disasters, reversed this Aeschylean emphasis by placing at the centre of dramatic interest a tragic Electra whose heroic fulfilment and personal destruction are achieved in her dedicated career of vengeance. It is not always recognized that Sophocles' Electra has long been busy at vengeance, every day doing what she can to bring public contumely on the murderers of her father, before Orestes arrives on the scene. It is this which has destroyed her, as we see first in her exchange with the Chorus ("I know I am horror-faced," she replies to their remonstrances, "but pity will not let me go!"), in the poignant contrast between her and the nubile Chrysothemis (all that a young girl should be—in other circumstances), and, most tellingly, in the debate with her mother, some of whose most sinister and steely characteristics are already mirrored in Electra herself.

Euripides' Electra is the negation of each of these two conceptions of "the avenger." (If one could be sure of the historical facts, one would be inclined to suggest that Euripides created her with these specific contrasts in mind.[9]) The command of Apollo is made to play the least

[9]To my mind, the literary (or philosophic?) declension just described is the clearest and most convincing indication that Euripides' *Electra* is the last of the three plays concerned. However, if fresh external evidence were suddenly to prove the priority of Euripides' play over Sophocles', this would not change the position of Euripides' play in the "ideal" sequence here suggested. More specific arguments urging the priority of Sophocles' over Euripides' *Electra* are to be found in Denniston's edition of Euripides' *Electra*, xxvi-vii, Steiger, *Philologus*, LVI, 569,

possible part in the action of the play, for the motivation of Electra, whose character dominates that action particularly as far as the matricide is concerned, is quite independent of it; the invocation of the dead Agamemnon and his fellow shades, that other supernatural dimension so powerfully employed in the Aeschylean version, Euripides reduces to but a few lines. (677–83) Sophocles' Electra also, it is true, has her own motives for vengeance, apart from any Apolline command, but whereas her motivation lies rather above the ordinary human level, that of Euripides' heroine lies considerably below it.

It is as if Euripides, looking first at the "facts" of the legend on the one hand, and then at the other possible treatments of it, had decided: "So much for the supernatural (or 'mythological') and the 'heroic' treatment of such events. *My* play will present the sort of Electra who, shored up by no divine commands or absolute ideals of loyalty, will, in certain circumstances, seek to slay her mother." Thus Euripides presents, in its required setting, a deft and damning portrait of a matricidal woman in action in which nearly every detail contributes to the required characterization and situation, or else to the "realistic" (and certainly "subheroic") atmosphere, both social and psychological, in which such a grim conception can be realized.

Dramatic Analysis

Once we have grasped this unifying focus of the play, its various detailed effects begin to fall into place and to fulfil their proper function. Most of these details have been so well described in several excellent commentaries on the play[10] that it remains only to indicate, in general

---

Parmentier, *Euripide*, IV, *Électre*, 176 ff. and Mazon, *Sophocle*, IV, *Electre*, 134. The reasons for placing Euripides' play later than Sophocles' are, however, stronger than the arguments used for dating Euripides' *Electra* precisely to 413 B.C. On this specific point, Zuntz's arguments (*Political Plays*, 64–71) are well founded and well supported by the metrical evidence adduced by Ceadel and Zielinski (whom he cites) and by that of Descroix (*Le Trimètre Iambique*, 58) and, more recently, of Matthiessen (*Elektra etc.* 169–70). Of these, only Matthiessen is willing (with Zuntz) to allow the metrical statistics completely to override the traditional considerations for dating the production of the play to 413.

[10]See in particular Grube's shrewd observation of various details in the characterization of Electra and of the peculiarly Euripidean treatment of the murders themselves. Grube does not, however, look for one overriding dramatic idea which will account for most of the peculiarly Euripidean innovations in the setting, plot and characterizations of the play. I am also much indebted to many of Kitto's observations on the play which, apart from the central thesis which he makes them serve, illustrate most acutely those new aspects of the avengers and their deeds which Euripides has shown us.

terms, how well they serve the common purpose which I have suggested.

We must first of all take note of the obvious. Euripides, like Sophocles and for similar reasons, must be sure that the greatest attention is centred on Electra alone. In a play where individual characterization and motive are paramount, only one of the two matricidal children can be of real importance; what we see or hear of the other must, in some way, contribute to our understanding of the central character. Obviously, in the case of both Sophocles' and Euripides' treatments of this theme, Electra must be chosen. She is the one who has been present to store up her vengeance throughout the régime of the usurpers; more important, she is the one who can be presented as choosing more freely (from heroic or from neurotic motives), since, by tradition, it is Orestes who receives the command of Apollo. Sophocles has treated Orestes (and the command of Apollo) in a way admirably suited to his dramatic purposes; Euripides' way, like every other aspect of his play, is quite properly different. As far as the influence of Apollo is concerned, Orestes, once the dread deed of matricide is being forced upon him, mentions the god's command only to call it in question (971, 973, 979, 981); it is Electra, herself quite independent of such influence,[11] who now grasps at it (972, 980) simply as an additional spur to her reluctant brother. For the rest, the obvious effect of the timid and tentative Orestes presented in this play is to emphasize the strong and vindictive character of his sister.[12]

The same focussing process is at work, though less obviously, in nearly every passage of the play. Not since *Medea* has Euripides concentrated so effectively on a single character and her situation (though *Hecuba*, when properly understood, may be thought to approach this degree of

[11]It is not clear when Electra first learns of Apollo's command (presumably she knows of it before the play begins) nor does it matter much. Throughout the play, her own murderous motivation is obviously quite independent of it. Even in her exchanges with Orestes on the subject (e.g., at 279 ff., before she knows who Orestes is, and at 967 ff., before Orestes himself introduces the "Apollo-motivation"), Electra depends on natural (or unnatural) rather than supernatural motives for her matricidal urge.

T. England (*CR*, XL [1926], 103) expresses much the same point about Electra's motives, though he tends, perhaps unjustly, to tar Orestes with the same brush.

[12]Cf. Grube's observations of the contrasts between Orestes and Electra at two crucial moments of the play, first at 280 ff. (when Orestes clearly postpones revealing himself to Electra just after she has shown her matricidal intent) and second at 647 ff., where Electra takes over the conversation from Orestes to arrange the murder of their mother. (See Grube, 302 and 306, respectively, and notes *ad loc.*)

concentration). In Electra's appearances with the Chorus, with her husband, with her brother, even with the poor, optimistic old tutor, Electra shows, in a wide variety of aspects and circumstances, the same characteristics of the bitter, self-pitying, sharp-tongued virago and the whole setting of the play at the peasant's hut, with Electra as the peasant's wife, provides an invaluable asset in this presentation.[13] In the prologue particularly the characterization shows remarkable consistency in a variety of contexts. In her opening passage (54–63) Electra strikes the dark, complaining note which she is to sustain throughout the play. Here, as in the two more formal laments which follow (the monody at 112–66, and Electra's share in the *kommatic parodos*), the harsh lot of Electra takes marked precedence over the sacrilegious slaughter of her father. The same emphasis is skilfully repeated in dramatic terms. Electra's complaint about carrying water (55 ff.) is immediately shown up by her gentle peasant-husband who says, first, that he has told her not to do it (64–66), and second, that it's a very slight labour in any case. (77–78) Electra's complaint of lack of raiment for the feast to which the Chorus bids her is immediately shown up by her refusal of the glorious clothes the Chorus offers. In both cases, it is the chance of self-martyrdom which Electra is seizing, and besides (as the Chorus observes of Electra's refusal) Electra would rather moan than pray (193–95); indeed, the cynical attitude which she expresses toward the gods (198–200) is in keeping with the human motivation of her actions throughout the play. In the first episode, Electra repeats each of these complaints and hypocrisies in her "message" to Orestes (300–38): to the specific repetitions about the water-carrying and the lack of raiment (304–9), she now adds the exaggeration, "Banned from the festal rites . . . !" (310) for which we have been well prepared, and she observes the same priority of outrage suffered (*her own*, 300–13, before her father's, 314–31) which we have noticed in the prologue and the *parodos*.

That these details provide not so much "realism" for its own sake (as Kitto would have it), as realistic aspects of a potential matricide, is clear enough. From them we may proceed to other less obvious elements in the central theme. The peasant-husband's hospitality calls forth a particularly shrewish outburst of self-pity from Electra, and even Orestes'

[13]It is a mistake to regard the various details of poverty, home management and domestic bickering *simply* as typical devices of the new Euripidean realism (though they are that) or of the sort of bourgeois parody of tragedy by which, as Parmentier (186–87, cf. 178–79) suggests, Euripides appealed to the declining taste of the Athenian audience. They are also essential accoutrements in the characterization of the sort of woman that *Euripides'* matricidal heroine must be.

reflections on the signs and causes of virtue among high-born and low-born, rich and poor alike, reflect obliquely on Electra as well as on her lowly but more worthy spouse.[14] Even the much-discussed recognition scene, though it includes some irrelevant (and irreverent) mockery of Aeschylus,[15] contributes more substantially than is often realized to the poet's central purpose. In the first place, the "recognition by the scar" is particularly well suited to the pragmatic (as opposed to the mythological and the ideal) issues of this play. In the second place, it has been well observed that Euripides seeks to reduce, as much as possible, the emotional potentialities of the recognition, presumably to prevent Electra from appearing in a sympathetic light;[16] this purpose is the more readily achieved by devoting a good deal of the dialogue to the refutation of the Old Man and his Aeschylean tokens by a scornful and very Euripidean Electra.

It is recognized that the ways in which Aegisthus and Clyemnestra are brought to their doom place these victims, at least for the moment, in a better light than the avengers. The latter point is neatly underlined by the poet when he has Electra assure her rather dubious accomplice, the Old Man, that the mere news that she has given birth will suffice to bring her mother running. Orestes relies on the piety of Aegisthus for the chance to play his profane and bloody part in Aegisthus' country sacrifice—and he is not disappointed. Electra counts on some remnant

14See for example, vv. 369–70 (the contrast between parents and children with regard to nobility) and 375–76 (the suggestion that poverty is a disease that teaches evil ways: it is Electra's poverty-bred *invidia,* quite as much as grief for her father, which, as we shall see in her scene with Clytemnestra, motivates her hatred for her mother.)

See also the interesting comments of John Jones, *On Aristotle and Greek Tragedy*, 239 ff., on Euripides' treatment of the farmer-husband of Electra, which he regards as typical of the poet's "ripping open of the status-defined surface of things" which had hitherto dominated Greek tragedy.

15I have no desire to enter into the long debate on Euripides' "refutation" of the Aeschylean "recognition clues." Suffice it to say that I am unimpressed by the various attempts to defend the Aeschylean tokens in terms of realism and probability—however unexceptionable they may be in the kind of drama which he was writing. (See Denniston's references to Wilamowitz, Tucker and Verrall on this point, as well as Denniston's thorough discussion of the whole problem in his note to Euripides' *El.* 520–84.)

16See, for example, Kitto, who says of the recognition itself: "No transports of joy are allowed to come between us and the grim story that Euripides is working out for us." (338) I would be inclined to put the matter more positively: the relatively joyless recognition, and the querulous argument which precedes it, are all part of the harsh character of Electra and of the atmosphere of contention which Euripides' theme requires.

of maternal duty and affection in Clytemnestra. It would be idle to pretend that Euripides introduced both the elaborate innovations here involved purely for the sake of his main dramatic theme. The murder of Aegisthus by the sacrificial cleaver, just as he bends to discover the sacrifice's augury, is (as Kitto regards it) an exciting theatrical effect, and one feels that both here and in the luring of Clytemnestra Euripides takes pleasure (and expects that his audience will, too) in the novelty, as well as in the greater interest and plausibility, of his murder plots. However, these intrigues, particularly the second of them, do accord well with the major theme of the play, and with the particular atmosphere which it requires. Electra's plan and its execution emphasizes the degree of *personal* loathing our matricidal "heroine" must have for her mother, and the contrast between Clytemnestra's rich attire and servants and the poverty of Electra's home and garb, illustrates, in suitably realistic terms, the basis of this hatred in the resentful envy of Electra.

In the same way, the main rhetorical passages in the play, which Kitto and others[17] regard purely as a diversion, also contribute to the central characterization and to the realistic and faintly sleazy social climate in which it must be expressed.

In Electra's vaunt over the severed head of Aegisthus, we hear not a furious indictment of her father's murderer (this occupies but two of some fifty lines) but a sarcastic tirade on the folly of those who marry their adulterous mistresses and on the plight of those who marry wives more illustrious than themselves. Once again, *part* of the reason for this somewhat surprising subject of Electra's vaunt must be that the themes of adultery and of dominant wives are well suited to Euripides' and his audience's enjoyment of such rhetoric; indeed the inappropriate but very Euripidean aphorisms at vv. 921–24 and 933–35 may tempt some to think that the passage has very little dramatic relevance at all.[18] Nevertheless, as elsewhere in the play, the main impetus to Electra's bitterness stems from her own outcast situation; the nobler motives which animate Sophocles' Electra come a poor second with *our* "heroine." Thus, as in the case of the "recognition scene," the poet once again refuses his

[17]See Kitto, 339–40; cf. Parmentier, 181, ". . . elle [Electra] débite des moralités bourgeoises où l'on reconnaît Euripide lui-même s'addressant à la partie la moins raffinée de son public."

[18]"Whoever must marry his adulterous mistress is a fool if he thinks she'll be a chastely faithful wife to *him*." (921–24) "Despised are those sons who are known by their mother's, not their father's, names." (933–35) Neither of these generalizations (here briefly and somewhat freely rendered) seems particularly applicable to the Clytemnestra-Aegisthus situation—at least as we know it in other versions of the legend.

Electra the opportunity of making a "sympathetic" impression on the audience, and makes her dwell instead on those features of the much envied life at the court which must reflect unfavourably on the usurpers.[19]

This point becomes still clearer in the following (and major) rhetorical passage in the play, the "debate" between Clytemnestra and Electra, where the themes of adultery and usurpation are developed further. Once again, both speakers, in realistic, almost sordid terms, replace the mythological and "heroic" motivations found in Aeschylus and Sophocles with the emotional and psychological motivations of jealousy and sexual passion. In Clytemnestra's defence of her husband-murder, the rescue of the wanton Helen (a poor exchange, in Clytemnestra's view, 1027 ff., for her daughter's life) and the outrage offered to herself by Cassandra's presence (1030–34), feature as prominently as the sacrifice of Iphigenia, the more "respectable" motive for her crime. By the same token, Electra's charges against Clytemnestra emphasize her mother's adulterous nature. In both these speeches (as in Electra's earlier vaunt), the particular and relevant instances of adultery tend to get forgotten in the flood of Euripidean aphorisms which such a subject almost inevitably brings on. Witness Clytemnestra's aside on the weakness of her sex, which must always repay infidelity in like coin (vv. 1036–38), and the crowd-catching pronouncements of Electra (vv. 1069–75) on the proper—and the improper—ways for army wives to conduct themselves when their husbands are off at war.

In all of this the actual murder of Agamemnon (which should, one would suppose, be the nub of the matter) almost gets lost entirely. When Electra does return to it, she does so in a way which reminds us, at last, of the true purpose of this rhetorical exchange. Why, Electra asks her mother, if you slew to avenge a daughter, did you then proceed to procure a husband at the expense of your other children? (1086 ff.) The selfish, embittered motive of Euripides' matricide appears again. In sharp contrast to Sophocles' heroine (who refuses, with jeers at the compliant Chrysothemis, the enemy's gifts), *this* heroine is vexed to the point of murder by the loss of her patrimony:

Why, when you'd slain your husband, did you not bestow our father's halls on us? Your son, and not your paramour is exiled; and I, your daughter slain by living death twice crueller than my sister's sacrifice.

(1088–93, slightly paraphrased)

[19]Grube, (309), suggests another "psychological" reason, similarly related to the characterization of Electra, for the subject-matter of the vaunt over Aegisthus' corpse: it is Clytemnestra, not Aegisthus, whom Electra hates; therefore, her jeers at him must be intimately connected with Clytemnestra.

The scene ends, as Clytemnestra is ushered into the hut and to her death, with some of Euripides' most sinister ironies. Electra comments on the slain Aegisthus: "Great pretensions has he, for he dwells in my house." (1120) And, to Clytemnestra as she enters, "Take care lest you befoul your raiment in our smoky hut!" (1139–40) Before we conclude that such chilling effects are signs of "melodrama," let us remember the similar ironies on the lips of Dionysus as he lures Pentheus to his doom in the *Bacchae*. (963–70)

The psychological treatment of the matricide is continued even after the murder of Clytemnestra in the emphasis on human remorse for what has been (at least for the main instigator, Electra) a passion-motivated crime. Electra makes clear her own responsibility for the deed at vv. 1182–84, 1224–25; her remorse and horror can be detected at 1183–84, 1198–1200, 1230; however, she never goes so far as to say she wishes the deed undone. Neither Electra nor the Chorus (which blends awareness of the justice of Clytemnestra's death with horror at its matricidal aspects) so much as mentions Apollo. Orestes' anguished emphasis on the physically maternal aspects of his mother as he murdered her (1206–9) are in keeping with the almost coarse naturalism which we have noted throughout the play. It is Orestes who makes the one obscurely phrased reference to Apollo in this passage, a rebuke which leads directly into the subject of the epilogue:

> O Phoebus, you have commanded an obscure justice in your oracles, but you have brought to pass woes which are all too clear. [Here the point appears to be that the propriety of Apollo's insistence that a son should kill his mother, however guilty, is uncertain, but that the horror which such a deed occasions is not.] You have brought it about that we murderers shall sleep far from our native land. [Literally: "You have bestowed murderous beds far from Greece."] (1190–93)[20]

It is significant that the Dioscuri, speaking as *dei ex machina*, echo first the human judgment of the matter which the Chorus has expressed and then the cautious criticism of Apollo which Orestes himself has ventured:

> She [Clytemnestra] has vengeance, but you [Orestes] did not act justly. [So much for the "human level."] But Phoebus, Phoebus—still, he is my lord; my lips are sealed. Yet, wise as he is, he did not give you wise answers at his oracle. (1244–46)

[20]Both text and interpretation are somewhat uncertain at vv. 1190–93; see Denniston's excellent note *ad loc.*

These and other lines (1266–67, 1296–97, 1302) make it quite clear that Apollo, in the view of the Dioscuri, is officially responsible for the matricide. (At v. 1302, Apollo is again rebuked for his advice and at vv. 1301, 1305–7, it is further suggested that "fate" and the ancestral doom, i.e., from Tantalus, Pelops and Atreus, share this responsibility with Apollo.)

These comments by the Dioscuri, together with their instructions and prophecies to Orestes regarding his trial[21] and exile, have little bearing on the action of the play itself. There, as we have seen, it is Electra whose role predominates, and her motivations and characterizations have had nothing to do with the instructions of Apollo. Indeed, the almost artificial independence of the "mythological" epilogue (reminiscent of the "mythological frame" which we have noted in other plays of Euripides), is here underlined by the emphasis on Orestes, rather than on Electra, when the human agents are considered at all. Electra, when she insists on being heard (1295 ff.), is included by the Dioscuri both in the moral exoneration which Apollo's responsibility bestows, and in the general ancestral doom which she shares with Orestes. This secondary, "family associate" role accords so poorly with the dominant and personally motivated role of Electra in the play, that it helps us to dissociate the "meanings" of the epilogue, that ironical, mythological "tidying-up" of which Euripides was so fond, from the real meaning provided by the dramatic action of the play.[22]

The Chorus

The tone of the Chorus in this play ranges from that of a group of Argive women closely concerned with the state of their friend Electra, to that of the detached singers of "*entr'acte*" diversions which seem, at times, to justify the term *embolima.*[23] Its relatively minor function is

[21]See vv. 1258 ff., where interesting differences from the Aeschylean version of the founding and the original purpose of the Areopagus are to be observed.

[22]For a very different view of the relevance of the *deus ex machina* to the theme and action in this play (and elsewhere, where it occurs, in Euripidean drama), cf. Andreas Spira, *Untersuchungen*, esp. pp. 101–12. (I have already ventured certain criticisms of this view, particularly as applied to Euripides' *Electra*, in my review of Spira's book, *Phoenix*, XVI [1962], 127–29; the final paragraph is the one most relevant to the present discussion.)

[23]What dramatic and thematic relevance there is in the odes at vv. 432–86, 699–746 will be considered later. The term *embolimon* in its full technical sense should, no doubt, be restricted to the choral songs of the successors of Sophocles and Euripides, since Aristotle so restricts it, when he tells us that Agathon first

indicated by the fact that the *parodos* is tacked onto Electra's monody, as the women seek unsuccessfully to persuade Electra to join them at the festival of Hera, as well as by the brevity of three of their subsequent odes.

It is in the *parodos* and in the lyric comments on each of the murders that the Chorus shows itself most involved with the theme and action of the play. As we have seen, its invitation to the festival and its offer of clothes to Electra give the lie to the social neglect and even rejection on which Electra tends to insist (304–13), and its gentle rebukes (190, 193–95) remind us of the godless nature of Electra's bitterness against her royal enemies.

In the final *stasimon* (1147–63), we hear the Chorus's most outspoken vindication of the murder of Clytemnestra which is about to take place. Denniston has aptly remarked the contrast between this initial judgment and the shocked outcries, still mingled with some pleas of "justification" which follow the matricide itself, as the Chorus hears the cries of the defenceless mother and sees the murderous children coming onstage covered with their mother's gore. "The 'prosperous wind' of 1147–48 is forgotten. It is now not the wind which has changed, but the spirit of Electra that bows to the wind of moral law."[24] This switch in the Chorus's emphasis from the justice to the unholiness (1201–05) of the deed neatly reflects the play's emphasis on the personal rather than the abstract aspects of the issue, though it must be admitted that the continued division in its utterances between "justification" and horror (see 1168–76 and 1185–89) keeps the two aspects of the issue before our mind. But, as the characterization of Electra has shown us, it is the personal element epitomized by the bitter *invidia* of the protagonist which dominates this play and relegates Orestes and the mythical "justification" of Apollo's commands to the background.

With some justice, Parmentier has described the two odes at vv. 432–86 and 699–746, the "Arms of Achilles Chorus" and the "Golden Lamb Chorus," as a series of lyrical pictures analogous to an artist's

began the practice (*Poetics* 1456a 29 ff.: for an interesting, if hypothetical, discussion of the precise technical sense of the term, see Roy Flickinger, *The Greek Theatre and Its Drama*, 144–46). Nevertheless, it should be noted that Aristotle begins his discussion of the practice in the sentence immediately following that in which he has criticized the dramatic relevance of the Euripidean chorus in general, in comparison with the Sophoclean chorus. Therefore, whatever technical difficulty justifies the emphasis on Agathon as the originator of *embolima*, it is hard to escape the conclusion that, in Aristotle's opinion, the seeds of this practice were already present in the Euripidean usage.

[24]Denniston, in his note to 1147–1232.

illustrations of the mythical background of the play.[25] In the first of these, only a gesture is made toward relating the tapestry directly to the dramatic business on hand: after four strophes devoted to Achilles, his majestic voyage to Troy and the glorious emblazonings on his armour, the Chorus turns on Clytemnestra: "The leader of men like this you have slain, O Tyndarid, by your adultery. By death will the gods requite you." (479–83) Even here, however, we should note the reminder of the adulterous aspect of Clytemnestra's crime which Euripides' version of the myth plays up.

In the other ode, a similarly slender relevance is provided for the account of Thyestes' adulterous treason and of Zeus' outraged reaction (he reverses the course of the sun) to his conduct: had Clytemnestra remembered such cautionary tales of divine wrath, she might never have dared to slay her husband. (See vv. 718–46.) It may not be fanciful, however, to find in the latter ode more specific applications to Euripides' treatment of the Electra theme: the mythological expression of horror at Thyestes' unnatural deed anticipates, perhaps, the horror of the coming matricide (an act more contrary to nature than either Thyestes' or Clytemnestra's deeds) and the explicit disbelief which the poet expresses (737 ff.) in the literal truth of the myth here cited may reflect a similar attitude to the supernatural interpretation (i.e., "the command of Apollo") of the present action.

[25]Parmentier, 188.

12

THE *Orestes*

A Preliminary View

To the casual reader (and to not a few critics) the *Orestes* gives the impression of involving several different kinds of action with no clear relation between them. Let us begin by setting these down as three phases, however loosely connected, in the post-matricidal career of Orestes in the hope that some thematic line may begin to appear in the play as a whole.

(*i*) 1–469. The first part of the play concentrates on the *pathos*, or suffering, of Orestes. Here it is the *affliction* of the crazed matricide which takes all our attention: in his sleep, as Electra gently tends him, telling us all his troubles and fiercely hushing the Chorus, which performs its sympathetic song-and-dance on tiptoe; at his awakening, as, after a few moment's peace, mad visions of the Furies threaten him again (255 ff.); finally, in his first interview with Menelaus (385 ff.), who inspects and quizzes him—"Now when did the madness begin?" (401); "And what do your visions *look* like?" (407)—in the manner of a visiting psychiatrist.

(*ii*) 470–1012. With the entry of Tyndareus, representative of Orestes' human prosecutors, the treatment undergoes violent change. Psychology gives place to rhetoric and introverted remorse to a series of debates in which, as the hero confronts Tyndareus and Menelaus and finally the Argive tribunal, the various traditional aspects of Orestes' deed appear. We are no longer concerned, as before, with the *absolute* situation; Orestes is now contending not with his conscience but with his fellow men, with the social "justification" of his deed and even, justice apart (646 ff.), with his desperate need of an ally (Menelaus) to help him save his life. Throughout these shifting arguments, the sophistries of debate and the interplay of spurious "rhetorical" emotions contrast sharply with the emotional intensity of the earlier passages of the play.

(*iii*) 1018–end. The condemnation of Orestes and Electra by the Argive tribunal ushers in the third, and violent, phase in the action. Plans for final defiant gestures of vengeance grow, as the taste for life returns, into increasingly wild and savage plans for escape at whatever cost in murder and destruction. It is the rapid and in places improbable sequence of action in this final panel of the play which has, perhaps, caused the *Orestes* to be classed with plays of intrigue and melodrama such as the *Ion*, the *Helena* and the *I.T.*[1] Admittedly, there are points in common between these plays and the *Orestes*, but to regard this part of the play simply as exciting action presented "for its own sake" tends to obscure certain thematic developments which, even in the final phase, accompany the melodramatic entertainment.

Despite the obvious looseness of structure, we can already discern a clear line of development with regard to the hero: Orestes evolves from "patient" to self-defender, to aggressor, his experience travelling the full cycle from overwhelming, grovelling remorse back to that active and vengeful violence which first caused his undoing.

Orestes' two companions seem to represent unresolved elements in the hero's own nature. Cold Pylades remains unchanging both in his fidelity to Orestes and in his murderous counsels. Unrepentant and unafraid, he is the catalyst in the second series of violent actions (against Helen and Hermione) as he was in the first. In Electra, on the other hand, we find that element of warmth, of passion even, completely lacking in Pylades and showing only intermittently in Orestes; it appears in her fiercely protective tendance of Orestes, in her extreme despair after the tribunal (Orestes is the more resigned of the two here, despite his comparative weakness earlier) and finally in her passionately unbalanced plan of violence against the innocent Hermione. Though only Orestes' sister, she must, in her devotion, replace the other women whom the grim circumstances of his life deny him: protective mother in the opening phase of the action and later, for a moment, sweetheart, in that

[1]So Kitto, who labels both the *Electra* and the *Orestes* "melodrama," and describes them as being "of the same kind of drama as the tragi-comedies" (i.e., *Ion*, *Helena*, *I.T.* and *Alcestis*, by his account), on the grounds that they are not "tragic" but "aim rather at being theatrically effective" (*G.T.*, 332, and chaps. 11–12, *passim*). But, apart from other points to be noted, we should remember that neither of these plays rests on that "impossibility" of situation which Kitto has, with some justice, taken as the essential feature separating the tragicomedies from "tragic, that is to say, universal reality." (*ibid.*, 315)

daring and yet deeply moving moment of the play when both face death together. (1045–55)

But though much of the talking and some action is left to these two acolytes, it is Orestes (even when asleep) and Orestes' fate which dominate the play.

Some Previous Views

Though many critics have stressed the contrasts in tone and subject matter which they find to exist between one or another of the parts of this play, few have attempted to find any dramatic sequence or any single theme which might mitigate or even account for these apparent disjunctures.[2] Such defences as have been attempted have led to excessively vague suggestions of sequence, e.g., "progressions," on the part of the poet, from the study of the individual conscience to that of social reactions to the matricide;[3] or progressions, on the part of the characters, "from folly to reckless criminality" (true enough, but what is the point in this progression?), "from delusion to mania," "from realism to nightmare."[4]

Frequently, analysis of the play as a whole has foundered on two related points: overconcentration on its interesting "Euripidean" features (e.g., the psychological and sociological treatment given to the divinely motivated material of the tradition),[5] and refusal to see that it is in the experiences of Orestes throughout the action, rather than in the rhetorical and traditional arguments woven into it at various appropriate points, that we must look for the thematic material of the play.

Pohlenz is one of the few critics to find in the social dimension which Euripides adds to the Orestes theme some explanation of the psychic

[2]Thus Masqueray (140) bluntly describes the first half of the play as a treatment in the Euripidean style of the material of Aeschylus' *Eumenides* and the second as simply a melodramatic mixture of various improbable excitements. Grube (390) describes this disjuncture more accurately as a break in the emotional continuity which comes at the moment when the prospect of vengeance dominates the minds of the conspirators. Neither critic, however, offers any explanation of this apparent fault.

[3]See F. Chapouthier, in his introduction to the play, *Euripide*, VI, 11. On the next page, we find a similarly limp attempt to describe the two successive subjects of the play: "Will Orestes win his trial?" and "Will he win vengeance and escape?" (*ibid.*, 12)

[4]Kitto, 349–50.

[5]See, for example, H. Weil, *Sept Tragédies d'Euripide*, 673–75, and H. Steiger, *Euripides* (Leipzig, 1912), 29 ff., who rightly but too exclusively, insist on these important points.

change which Orestes undergoes in the course of the dramatic action. While acknowledging Euripides' subtle depiction of the crippling power of guilty conscience in the first part of the play, Pohlenz describes the resurgence of Orestes' will to live in terms of what he regards as a commonplace in Greek popular philosophy, namely the view that pains and passions can be overcome by circumstances which take the full attention of the mind and will. Thus, in Pohlenz' view, it is the threat provided by the hatred of his fellow men which stimulates Orestes' urge for life and causes him to take his fate in hand.[6]

Like Pohlenz, Lesky finds the resurgence of Orestes' *Lebenswille* and its causes to be the significant link between the first and the later parts of the play. Orestes' new-found vigour he imputes first to the hope, then to the justifiable hatred which Menelaus inspires in him. Thus by a concrete application of a similar idea he is able to show more specifically than Pohlenz does how Orestes' ultimate participation in the "vengeance-and-escape" plot is part and parcel of that new will to live which the false Menelaus has unconsciously helped generate.[7]

Closely related to this problem of thematic and structural unity is the question raised by H. G. Mullens[8] concerning Orestes' own apparent inconsistency about his guilt. (Compare, for example, vv. 395–96 and 591–96.) This, we are warned, should be taken "as an indication of a division in Orestes' mind, not as inconsistency on the author's part." This sensible view characterizes Mullens' approach to the play as a whole: since the play is "dynamic," its action describing "a process of demoralization, interpretation too must be progressive." Thus another example of inconsistency in the morally declining Orestes is to be found, according to this critic, in the fact that Orestes ends by approving for himself and his sister that very quality of homicidal vengefulness which earlier in the play he had repudiated.[9] These points, particularly the contrasting attitudes which Orestes shows, early and late in the play, toward kin-slaughter, are valid and important, and Mullens is right to warn us against dismissing them as Euripidean carelessness. Whether or not they are to be explained simply by the theory of Orestes' demoralization throughout the action of the play is another matter. It may be

[6]See M. Pohlenz, 412–13.

[7]See A. Lesky, *Die Griechische Tragödie*, 206–11, for the most succinct statement of Lesky's view of the *Orestes*; cf. also his article in *Wiener Studien, Zeitschrift für kl. Philol.*, LIII (1935), 37–47. The summary given above is based on the first of the works here mentioned.

[8]H. G. Mullens, *CQ*, XXXIV (1940), 153–58. The quotations in the following two sentences are from p. 153.

[9]*Ibid.*, 155–56.

that these "inconsistencies" on Orestes' part are part of an unconscious process of self-revelation in which what Orestes turns out to be at the end is what, for all his remorseful self-shielding, he really was at the beginning, the monster (as Euripides saw him) who could murder his mother.

Dramatic Analysis

From our previous discussions, some reasonable sequence between the parts of the *Orestes* has already appeared: Orestes' initial despair relieved only by the apathy of sleep, yields in the second part of the play to the stimulus first of hope, at the appearance of Menelaus, and then of active human opposition from Tyndareus and the Argive tribunal; after the condemnation the strong tonic of anger and bitterness, particularly against his father's canny brother, converts this "victim," once powerless against his own devils of remorse, into a self-liberating fiend of vengeance against his human enemies. Can we now, developing hints already dropped, find answers (at least of the kind in which drama deals) to the unresolved question about Orestes' original responsibility which the first sombre passages of the play present? This play has usually been regarded, and rightly so, as a study of the effects of private guilt and of public persecution on Orestes. Can it also be a study, at an advanced stage in the hero's career, of the kind of person capable, in the first place, of so hideous a crime as matricide?

As the play proceeds through the three phases we have described, we experience a gradual withdrawal of sympathy for Orestes which coincides with a gradual increase in the aesthetic distance between ourselves and the dramatic action. In the end we see as an object of horror, a "specimen," what we had begun by regarding as a suffering subject with whom we could, to some degree, identify ourselves. In the first, or "pathological," phase we are drawn to Orestes by his helpless suffering and his inward-looking remorse; besides, his condition, due largely to the novelty of the dramatist's presentation, is fascinating in itself. It has been the fashion, in emphasizing the psychological subtlety of this presentation, to rationalize the Furies into nothing but the fevered projection of Orestes' own guilt-crazed mind. This they may be in the last analysis; certainly Electra's reassurance at vv. 258–59 has the true sound of rationalism about it. Nevertheless, an at least partial belief in the reality of "the mythological dimension" (acceptance of the Furies and of Apollo must go together) is, at this point in the play, necessary both for Orestes and for our own sympathy with him. This blend of horrors real and mythological, which is Orestes' conception of his plight, finds subtle expression in the first dialogue between the hero and Menelaus. Prompted by Menelaus' questions ("What precisely *are* you suffering? What's your *disease*?" 395), Orestes' description of his state moves from the psychological level, in which he speaks of awareness (σύνεσις) of guilt, and the pain it brings (396, 398), through the ethical (". . . madness, punishment for my mother-murder," 400), to the mythological level ("Three night-black hags I seemed to see . . . the Awful Ones . . . alas! that dread pursuit!" 408, 410, 412). Here it is a brilliant touch to insert Menelaus' comment on pain: "dread is that divinity, yet curable" (399)—thus marking the transition from the literal to the mythological by a quasi-metaphorical usage.[10] Immediately after Orestes has described the Furies (even the rationalist Menelaus dares not name them), he names their mythological "cure" (ἀναφορά, 414), "Apollo, since he bade me slay my mother." (416)

Thus, at this point in the play, both Apollo and the Furies are important to Orestes (and so to the dramatic development) for precisely the same reasons. It is quite wrong to suggest, as Norwood does, that "the religious sanction . . . has in Euripides' hands become . . . a small, rather shabby stage-property, hung upon the back-scene."[11] As long as Orestes and Electra *feel* guilty, they invoke the responsibility of Apollo (as they do some seven times in the first part of the play) and *blame* him.[12] If the Furies are simply a disguise for Orestes' own feelings of guilt, Apollo is also the disguise behind which Orestes and Electra hide, unconsciously no doubt, their awareness of their own responsibility, and their own motives for the matricide.

As the play moves into the "rhetorical" phase, we are to witness the gradual elimination of Apollo and the Furies, and a gradual increase in emphasis on human responsibility for the murder of Clytemnestra and its redress. The new secularism is introduced first by Tyndareus, father of Clytemnestra, who regards any murder, retributive or otherwise, as an affront to human law (*nomos*) and punishable by it (500–25); Orestes continues the debate on this level by giving, for the first time,

[10]On Euripides' intention in having Menelaus use θεός in this context, see Pohlenz, 413, who suggests that it is Euripides' way of showing that feelings not under one's control, such as Orestes has described, have as good a right to be called "gods" as feelings of guilt have to be called *Erinyes* (Furies).

[11]Norwood, *Greek Tragedy*, 275.

[12]See vv. 28–30, 162–65, 191–93, 260–61, 276, 285, 416–20; nearly all these references, by Electra or Orestes, to Apollo's responsibility for Orestes' deed carry a note of reproach or blame or bitterness.

his own motives for his deed, though the shame he feels before Tyndareus (462–69, 544–45) leads him to include the authority of Apollo as well in his defence.

Tyndareus' speech on *nomos* ushers in the whole social dimension which many regard as Euripides' most important contribution to the Orestes legend.[13] According to Tyndareus, legal action was open to Orestes in redressing the murder of his father: exile, following prosecution for bloodshed (*αἵματος δίκην*, 500) was the procedure to have followed in the case of Clytemnestra, in accordance with "the common law of all the Greeks" (495) and wise ancestral custom never to let blood-guilty ones appear before one's eyes. (512–13) If we are to take Tyndareus seriously, Orestes now becomes subject, in our eyes, to a whole new order of guilt: in addition to the personal horrors which traditionally afflict the matricide, he is now seen as one who has outraged the laws of the land. And surely we *are* expected to take Tyndareus seriously. It is departing from the Euripidean situation to argue, as Grube does, that this "championing of legal process is . . . futile," on the ground that it would hardly have been possible for Orestes to bring Clytemnestra and Aegisthus to justice.[14] Apparently the dramatist intends us to accept precisely this possibility: otherwise Orestes would surely have pointed out the absurdity when (570–71 ff.) he endeavours to refute this specific charge of Tyndareus by other arguments. Euripides chooses to ignore both historical *and* circumstantial difficulties for the sake of placing the matricide, or *anyone* who requites blood with blood, beyond the pale, even in heroic times. The climax of Tyndareus' speech as far as the larger theme of the play is concerned is to be found in his idealistic championship of *nomos* (so reminiscent of the ideal of Euripides' Theseus):[15]

[13]See for example N. Wedd, in the introduction to his edition, xxx–xxxi; Pohlenz, 414 and 417; Weil, 675; Steiger, 32–33. It is true that most comments concerning the social and judicial treatment which Euripides gives to the theme centre around the popular tribunal which Orestes faces; however, both Weil and Wedd point to Tyndareus' appeal to *nomos* (in connection with both Clytemnestra's and Orestes' crimes) as an example of Euripides' enlightened, contemporary treatment of the myth.

[14]Grube, 384.

[15]With Tyndareus' remarks on *nomos* here and at vv. 492–95, compare Euripides, *Suppl.* 526–27, 538 ff., 561 ff., 575, 669–72. In the passages cited from the *Suppliants*, of course, *nomos* is considered in an international context; all the sentiments there expressed represent Theseus' attitude or policy, or else (312–13) arguments which help him form that policy.

I shall defend the law to the limit of my powers, and put a stop to this blood-guilty beastliness, the constant ruin of the land and cities in it.
(523–25)

It is hard to imagine that so Euripidean a sentiment and its application to the present situation are not to be taken seriously.

Significantly, in view of Orestes' final actions in the play, it is the adulterous quite as much as the murderous quality in Clytemnestra which the matricide urges in his defence. Otherwise, the multiple and in places traditional nature of his arguments typifies that blurring of the stark realities which the rhetorical treatment of Orestes' situation inevitably introduces. However, it is the fact that Orestes now reveals motives of his own for his awful deed that is of greatest importance for the dramatic development of the play. Not until the end of the speech is Apollo mentioned ("... *him* I obeyed ... slay *him*!" 593, 595) and this is to be the last time that Orestes alludes to the god at all until the epiphany at the end of the play. In the various kinds of rhetorical exercise and "politicking" which inform the central portions of the play there is little concern for the personal remorse of Orestes, and so this divine shield from the devils that have plagued him earlier is no longer needed.

At the farthest remove from those early cries of tortured conscience is Orestes' plea (640 ff.) for Menelaus' support in his coming contest with the Argive citizens. Here *Peithô* (the patroness of that rhetoric whose end is persuasion at any price)[16] is the only guiding spirit. ἀδικῶ: "Grant I am wrong," Orestes begins his speech (646)—and proceeds to argue on this basis that Menelaus should help him. It is a perfect example of the sophistic *Adikos Logos* parodied by Aristophanes: it is right that Menelaus should now do wrong for Orestes' sake, since Agamemnon, Orestes' father, once did wrong for Menelaus' sake. (646–51) Skilfully "planted" in Orestes' plea are references to Hermione (658 ff.) and to Helen (669–72):[17] thus, with deft irony, the poet anticipates Orestes' later treatment of both ladies. Here Menelaus' women serve as part of Orestes' rhetorical appeal; later, he is to threaten to rid the world of their evil presence. In both cases, however, it is his own safety which is the real issue. Thus the present plea to Menelaus already goes some way in the gradual revelation of Orestes.

Orestes' trial before the people of Argos (reported at 866–956) provides the third and final opportunity for rhetorical display. The public

[16]Compare the second part of Hecuba's speech to Agamemnon at *Hec.* 813 ff.

[17]Here even Orestes, like Hecuba at a similar low point in the abuse of rhetoric, admits a qualm of shame. Cf. *Hec.* 736–51.

debate, with its contemporary political overtones, is, of course, a favourite scene from Euripides' repertoire of side-effects.[18] Several familiar figures are here: the time-serving herald, mixing fair arguments with foul, the impudent demagogue (this time an imported one),[19] the honest farmer, rough in appearance but shrewd of speech. In Orestes' defence, there is now no reference (as there was in his speech to Tyndareus) either to Apollo or to his father's *Erinyes*; in place of anguished personal necessity, the matricide pleads social, as much as familial, motivation of a deed which was to preserve the state from the onslaughts of reckless wives in general. So is rhetoric once again suited to its audience and its occasion.

The condemnation of Orestes and his deed by this tribunal has been hailed by more than one critic as an enlightened "democratic" victory over a barbarous mythical tradition.[20] Possibly—but I find it hard to believe that this was Euripides' chief purpose, at least in this particular passage. The play has already moved well away from "the mythological aspect" of Orestes' situation which, as we have seen, has been reserved for other purposes; besides, the poet seems to have presented rather a shabby public trial (with decidedly demagogic overtones: see 902–6, 944–45) to represent a great victory of enlightened popular judgment.

In the final phase of the action, following the condemnation of Orestes and Electra to die by their own hands, Orestes, at the suggestion of Pylades, decides to take vengeance on Menelaus, who has abandoned the house to which he was most indebted, by slaughtering Helen. Electra adds further savagery to the plan, by suggesting the kidnapping of Hermione, Menelaus' daughter, as a means of blackmailing Menelaus into securing the trio's liberation by the Argives. The execution of these plans is frustrated by the miraculous wafting of Helen into the heavens and by the *ex machina* appearance of Apollo who hastily assures the "proper ending" to the myth by packing Orestes off (after a year's exile) to his trial and acquittal at Athens, betrothing Electra to Pylades and Orestes to (of all people) Hermione, and retiring the ambitious Menelaus to Sparta to ensure Orestes' eventual reign over his reconciled Argive citizens.

Opinions differ concerning this lively finale in accordance with the

[18]Cf., for example, *Hec.* 105 ff., where the fate of Polyxena is tossed this way and that in public debate and is finally decided by the most effective and crowd-pleasing speaker.

[19]This is quite possibly a veiled reference to Cleophon, according to the Scholiast on this passage, and to the arguments of Chapouthier (p. 9) and others.

[20]See, for example, Weil, 675; cf. also above, nn. 5, 6, 13, for references to other critics with similar views.

various views which we have already noted about the play as a whole. Some would regard it as a sort of comic opera *cadenza* to round off the action, now that the serious psychological and sociological themes have been presented; others regard it in a more sombre light as the final and not improbable stage in the demoralization of Orestes; finally, those who have enjoyed the play as mere melodrama from the start continue so to enjoy it, finding in this frantic spate of action at the end merely an acceleration of pace rather than a change in the essential tone of the piece.

Admitting a decided element of melodrama in these concluding passages, can we find in them some development of the theme which we have been discussing, some further revelation of the essential Orestes, however exaggerated by the new desperation which now assails him?

A remarkable feature of the intrigue of our three conspirators, as we now may call them, is that while their violent plans are at first cloaked in some honourable trappings, all possible traces of justification are gradually stripped from them. We should bear in mind from the start that Orestes has only escaped public stoning by the promise that he and Electra will take their own lives forthwith. Now the plan of slaying Helen arises from the professed motives of dying gloriously avenged on ones' enemies and ridding the world of a wicked woman. (See vv. 1098–99, 1116–17, 1131–32, 1163–71, where both Pylades and Orestes insist on their willingness to die provided only that they are avenged on Menelaus and where, 1131–32, Pylades points out that the intended murder is saved from being dishonourable in that they plan to slay a woman who deserves such punishment.) The plan is further tinged with heroic honour in that its sponsor Pylades, in contrast to Menelaus, has freely chosen death rather than dishonour.

So emphatic are these professions that we can hardly miss the slightly hollow note when the hope of self-preservation *by this same means* begins to appear. As he warms to his theme, Pylades slips insensibly from thoughts of honour to those of civic gratitude, to (in the last two words of a lengthy speech) escape from death. (See 1131–52, and note the nicely balanced irony saved for the final emphatic sentence: ". . . gloriously dying—or else gloriously saved!") And precisely the same effect is echoed in the speech of Orestes which follows. After a splendid speech (1155 ff.) on the glories of dying avenged on his enemies, in a manner worthy of his father, Orestes, with a nice sense of anticlimax, finishes with the pious hope that perhaps they may not have to die after all! (1172–76)

Later, in the attempted execution of the plot against Helen, the poet gives, in a brief ironic flash, yet another light on Orestes' instincts. Granted that most of the scene in which the Phrygian eunuch and sometime "defender" of Helen appears has its effects outside the mainstream of the drama, one brief exchange between him and Orestes seems relevant to our discussion. The Phrygian has been presented as one who will do and say anything to save his skin. "Why," asks Orestes (1522), "should a *slave* fear to die, and thus be rid of ills?"

PHRYGIAN: All men, even slaves, delight in life.
ORESTES (*releasing him*): Well said; your wit has saved you. Go inside.
(1523–24)

Orestes has recognized a kindred spirit.

Worse is to come. Electra's suggestion (1181 ff., especially 1191–1203) concerning Hermione finishes at one stroke both the remnants of the idea of dying nobly and the saving notion of molesting only wicked women, for self-preservation by blackmail is its only end, and the new victim (we must not think of the *Andromache*, which presents a slightly older and more tarnished Hermione) possesses that very innocence which Pylades has warned against in choosing victims.

This gradual declension of honour in the deeds and, especially, the motives of Orestes and his companions must surely cast a shadow on that earlier picture of Orestes as the suffering innocent. Indeed, certain hints appear which suggest that the poet means us to remark a sinister resemblance between the two murderous fits and their ambiguous motivation. In earlier passages, both Electra and Orestes have expressed a horrified revulsion from their matricide for which they bitterly reproach Apollo. (See vv. 191–94 and vv. 285–93, respectively; note Orestes' term of loathing: ἔργον ἀνοσιώτατον, 286). Again, at the first mention of Helen which reaches Orestes' ears, Orestes has cried with prophetic horror to Electra, "Don't be like those wicked women" (he immediately links Helen with Clytemnestra), "for there's a danger that you may!" (251) Both passages have their sinister doublets (in sense) in the concluding scenes. In terms traditionally associated with Clytemnestra, Orestes in the end praises Electra for her fiendish plot against Hermione: "O man-souled woman, though in body feminine, how much worthier of life than death. . . ." (1204–6)[21] And in his last dialogue with Menelaus, Orestes glories in the past as in the present plans for slaying "evil women" (1588–90) and even regards his murder of Clytemnestra

[21]For the "man-minded" or "man-souled" quality associated with Clytemnestra as well, cf. Aeschylus, *Ag.* 11, and for Electra's similarity to her, cf. Sophocles, *El.* 608–9.

as one of his prime qualifications for the throne of Argos. In this sinister connection, in the mind of Orestes, between Electra and Clytemnestra, and between Clytemnestra, Helen and even Hermione, who is surely included in Orestes' expression "evil women" at v. 1590,[22] we see some explanation of the hero's Hamlet-like insistence on the adulterous character of his mother.

In all this we are reminded of Tyndareus' championing of "the common law of all the Greeks" (496), with its origins in ancestral wisdom bidding man not to requite blood with blood, not even, indeed, to let the blood-guilty come into one's sight, for fear of reprisal in like terms. (512–15) One bloody deed begets another, for they are like in kind. The only solution, the poet seems to be telling us, is the outlawing of all such violence (international as well as familial?) whatever justifications may be claimed for it.

The epilogue, by which Hermione's life is saved, and in which, for the rest, the poet seems engaged in repairing the torn fabric of the myth, need not, I think, seriously affect our view of the dramatic action. Orestes' cry to his divine mentor should, however, be noted:

> Hail, Prophet Loxias, to thine oracles!
> No lying prophet wert thou then, but true.
> And yet a fear crept o'er me, lest I heard,
> Seeming to hear *thy* voice, a Fury-fiend. (1666–69)[23]

---

[22]Wedd, misunderstanding the passage, finds the plural difficult to explain; see his note *ad loc.*

[23]The translation is A. S. Way's (in the Loeb edition) which, for once, seems singularly apt. (Italics are mine.)

PART FIVE

TRAGÉDIE MANQUÉE

13

THE *Phoenissae*

The Trilogy and the Adaptation of the Myth

The *Phoenissae* is in some ways the most original, in other ways the most traditional, and in all ways the most perplexing of Euripides' plays. Of the many problems which it presents, the more technical ones concerning the trilogy, the sources of the legend and the questioned authenticity of certain passages, particularly the *exodos*, have been studied elsewhere: where these problems arise in the present study, it must suffice simply to state tentative conclusions based on the evidence and scholarship available.[1]

[1]On the last-mentioned of these problems, see my article, "Themes in the Final Scene of Euripides' *Phoenissae, Phoenix,* XXI (1967), 92–101.

The possibility of the *Phoenissae's* trilogy relations arises first from the fragmentary statement in Aristophanes' *Hypothesis,* καὶ γὰρ ταῦτα ὁ Οἰνόμαος καὶ Χρύσιππος καὶ ... σῴζεται, and is further supported, in my opinion, by what we can guess of the subject matter of the *Oenomaus* and the *Chrysippus.* (For the legend of Oenomaus, see Apollodorus, *Epitome* 2. 4 ff. and other references in Roscher, III. 1. 764 ff.; for Chrysippus, see Apollodorus *Bibliotheca* 3. 5. 5, Schol. *Phoenissae,* 1760, the third *Hypothesis* to Sophocles, *O.T.* and other references in Roscher, I. 1. 902 ff.) Schwartz (*Scholia in Euripidem,* p. 244) and Pearson (xxxiii–xxxiv of his edition) take the mutilated sentence of the *Hypothesis* as referring not to a trilogy but simply to a connection between the legends of the plays concerned. Nauck (*Euripides* II³ [1880], xl), Weil (*Etudes sur le drame antique,* 163–64), and Schmid-Stählin (I. 3. 570) accept the trilogy *Oenomaus, Chrysippus* and *Phoenissae* on this evidence, though Weil argues against any significant connection between its members. Th. Zielinski (*Mnem., nov. ser.* LII [1924], 189–205) presents the most determined and, on the whole, convincing arguments for a connected trilogy consisting of these plays. See also Méridier (*Euripide* V, 132 and references there given), who also supports, though more moderately, the idea of a connected trilogy so constituted.

For studies of the traditional material involved in the *Phoenissae* itself, and of Euripides' adaptation of this material, the editions of Pearson and of Méridier and, on certain points, the article by Zielinski just referred to, are again most useful.

There is good evidence that the *Phoenissae* was the third play of a trilogy of which the preceding two plays were the *Oenomaus* and the *Chrysippus*. What we know of the legends on which these plays must have been based suggests at least two points of connection between them and the *Phoenissae*.

In the first place, each of the three plays seems to have involved a curse by a father either on his children or on a lover of his children: Oenomaus cursed Pelops, his daughter's suitor, as he (the father) died, overcome by the lynch-pin trick in the chariot race; Pelops cursed Laius for the latter's abduction of Pelops' son Chrysippus—a curse all too terribly fulfilled by Laius' son, Oedipus; Oedipus in turn cursed *his* sons and later (*Phoenissae*, 1610–11) accounted for this awful deed as the transmission, through him, of the curse on Laius. It is with the fulfilment of this curse from Oedipus that the present play is concerned.

Secondly, we note a certain affinity of evil between the three curses, or at least between the situations which occasioned them: the rivalry of Oenomaus and Pelops is occasioned by the former's incestuous love for his own daughter; Laius' guilty passion for Chrysippus ends in the rape and murder of the innocent son of Pelops; the fulfilment of the curse laid on Laius leads to further unnatural deeds, albeit unwitting ones, in the parricide and incest committed by Oedipus; and Oedipus' unnatural cursing of his sons (described by Jocasta, in the present play, as stemming from the illness [νοσῶν, 66] induced by his dreadful experiences) is brought to its fulfilment by the unnatural fratricide of Eteocles and Polyneices.

In all this, there is surely the potential material for a connected trilogy, and the approximate date of the *Phoenissae*, 409–7,[2] places it in the same general period as that other connected trilogy of Euripides, the "Trojan trilogy" (*Alexander*, *Palamedes*, *Troades*, 415 B.C.). In the *Troades*, as in the *Phoenissae*, there is little overt reference to the

[2]Most editors agree with these *termini* on the basis of Schol. Aristophanes, *Ranae* 53 and of Euripides' departure from Athens not long after production of the *Orestes* in 408 B.C. If one accepts the *Oenomaus*, the *Chrysippus* and the *Phoenissae* as a trilogy, then the year 408 is, of course, excluded. For detailed arguments about the date of the play, see the various editions and, in particular, W. Schmid, *PhW*, LVI. In sum, 409 seems the most likely date; cf. also Goossens, *Euripide et Athènes*, 628, n. 62. However, if this date be accepted, the archon "Nausicrates" mentioned in Aristophanes' hypothesis cannot (as Schmid argued) be explained as an ἐπιλαχών functioning at the time of the presentation, since we know from the argument of the *Philoctetes* that Glaucippus was archon at the time of the Dionysia of 409.

preceding plays, but there, as at *Phoenissae*, 1610–11 (Oedipus' reference to the curse on Laius transmitted, eventually, to his own sons), there seems to be at least one allusion to material contained in them.

In default of any certain information on the *Oenomaus* and the *Chrysippus*, we cannot push this argument much further but, in addition to the intrinsic interest of the possibility here sketched, one point of some relevance to the interpretation of the *Phoenissae* appears. In the successive *crimes passionnels* of the mythological material here reviewed, there seems to be a significant element of human fault and responsibility worked into these legends of fulfilled curses and inherited dooms—a human element, moreover, of a kind which held a peculiar fascination for Euripides. If, in the present play, we should find any indication, however ambiguous (Euripides, like Aeschylus to a greater degree, was not averse to "double motivation"), of personal responsibility on the part of the doomed brothers, we should suspect that such motivation probably had parallels in the earlier plays of the trilogy.

The particular choices and adaptations by Euripides of the various legends concerning the final agonies of the doomed house of Laius provide some hints as to the theme and dramatic purpose of the *Phoenissae*. The most striking Euripidean innovations in *tragic* treatments of this material and its background are as follows: Jocasta's survival of the discovery of Oedipus' identity; the presence of Oedipus in Thebes throughout the siege of the Seven; various details recounted of the earlier life of Oedipus and his defeat of the Sphinx; the sympathetic treatment of Polyneices; the oracular advice of Teiresias and the results, particularly the sacrifice of Menoeceus,[3] which arise from it; and the curious blending of the separate themes of Oedipus' exile and Antigone's defiance of Creon.

What do these adaptations of the traditional material tell us of Euripides' purpose in the *Phoenissae*? There are, I think, two or three preliminary indications. The continued presence of Oedipus and the repeated references to the effects of his miasma upon his family and the

[3]There is some difference of opinion concerning the originality of "the Menoeceus incident." Zielinski, *Mnem.*, n.s. LII (1924), 202, relates this self-sacrifice of Creon's son to the loss of Haemon which we hear of in Sophocles' *Antigone*: he suggests that both versions stem from an original legend in which Creon, the moderator of the State during the time of fratricidal strife, offers up his son, on Teiresias' advice, in order to win victory *and power for himself*. Zielinski's reconstructed original legend (which we need not consider in all its details) does suggest, albeit in a much more heinous form, something of the political opportunism discernible in Creon in the present play.

state, seem to emphasize the supernatural, the "fatalistic" aspects of the situation; the increased importance of Teiresias' prophecies and its influence on the later part of the action tend to increase this effect. On the other hand, the debate between the warring brothers, which the sympathetic treatment of Polyneices and the new role of Jocasta as arbiter make possible, leads to a decidedly humanistic treatment of the traditional material. This duality is surely no clumsy accident upon the poet's part, for, as we study the play, we find that Euripides tends to exaggerate rather than to reconcile the contrast between the religious and the profane attitudes to the situation. Finally, one is struck by the tremendous amount of legendary material which this play embraces: in addition to possible innovations, nearly everything in the tradition, from the first warning given to Laius to the exile of Oedipus and the burial issue over Polyneices' body, is included. This fullness has, as we shall see, proved the most troubling feature of the play for editors and critics, but attempts to alleviate it by removing one or another element as an "interpolation" run counter to the obvious desire of the poet to pack as much as possible of the tradition into it. Thus it is clear that in this play Euripides has no intention of concentrating with properly tragic intensity on any single theme.

Some Critical Defences of the *Phoenissae*

Complaints about the structure of the *Phoenissae* begin with the writer of the third Argument (who complains about its "overfulness" and about the dramatic pointlessness of several scenes)[4] and have continued ever since. Apologists for the play have tended to defend its unity by subordinating its varied elements to one central episode or to one overriding theme, or else to explain its "overstuffed and episodic nature" in terms which have little to do with dramatic composition.

The first of these approaches can be applied honestly to this play only when the underlying element chosen is so general or so "archetypal" that it lacks any real cohesive force. Thus Grube finds the unity of the play in the fate of Oedipus and in the working out of the curse which he laid upon his sons, "the last great calamity to befall Oedipus himself."[5] In a sense, this account is true, but it is too general to explain

[4] παραπληρωματικόν and, if Wecylein's emendation is correct, ἐπεισοδιῶδες are the terms used; this early critic of the play complains particularly of the dramatic pointlessness of Antigone's *teichoskopia* and of the episodes in which Polyneices and Oedipus respectively appear.

[5] Grube, 354 and 370.

the structure of this or any other play. It does not, for example, explain why Eteocles and Polyneices in *this* play have the sort of debate which they do have, whereas in Aeschylus' *Septem* the two brothers fulfil the curse without any debate at all. Nevertheless, Grube's recognition of the importance of Oedipus to the whole meaning of the play is a major contribution which helps to allay the ancient fantasy (begun by the writer of the third Argument) that the appearance of Oedipus at the end of the play is just one more irrelevant and pointless episode.

In contrast with Grube's relatively simple scheme are attempts, so dear to the heart of German critics, to assert some underlying philosophic or political thesis to be the unifying theme of the play. The ingenious analysis of W. Riemschneider[6] is typical of this approach. This critic argues that the action of the piece is played out between two poles: on the one hand, Oedipus, the (personally) innocent bearer of that miasma which, after ruining his family, now threatens the state; on the other hand, the city-defender Creon who, supported by Jocasta, seeks to keep Oedipus and those within Oedipus' "field of power" (i.e., Eteocles and Polyneices) from ruining the State. The first struggle between these polar opposites is the unsuccessful attempt of Jocasta to prevail over her sons' personal vendetta in the interests of the State; the final crisis takes place between Creon and Oedipus and here, at last, the source of the city's woes is finally expelled.

Conceptually, Riemschneider's plan is excellent: one can only wish that the play *did* express this powerful theme, in clear dramatic terms. However, if Euripides really intended this as the dominant theme of the *Phoenissae*, he has surely concentrated dramatic sympathy in the wrong persons and dramatic interest in the wrong places: Oedipus and his champion, Antigone, are far more sympathetically presented than is the politician, Creon, and the *agôn* shared by Jocasta, Eteocles and Polyneices is certainly the central scene of the play.[7] Perhaps the clearest instance of the sort of distortion to which Riemschneider's preconceptions lead him is his treatment of Menoeceus' self-sacrifice. This incident, which even the poet seems to forget once its limited purpose has been fulfilled, is exalted by Riemschneider as the climax to which the preceding thousand verses have been leading.[8] Unfortunately, its satisfies Riemschneider's design more successfully than it does Euripides'.

Thus, various attempts at "unifying" the *Phoenissae* tend to impose on

[6]W. Riemschneider, *Held und Staat in Euripides' Phönissen*; for the points discussed see especially pp. 9–12, 22–23, 33–34.

[7]Cf. J. Duchemin, *L'Agôn dans la tragédie grecque*, 80.

[8]Riemschneider, 33–34.

it a structure either so loose as to be meaningless, or so neat that the play itself will not support it.

More promising are the accounts which accept the apparently episodic nature of this play and seek to explain it in terms of the peculiar purpose of the poet. Thus Pearson, after trying with limited success to group the various incidents around a central focus, finally explains, rather than defends, the play's lack of structure as due to the fact that "the main outlook of Euripides upon his subject was that of realism pure and simple" and that the poet's purpose was "to depict the sorrows of the house of Oedipus in such manner as to portray men and women as they lived, their loves and their hatreds, their sufferings and their lamentations."[9] One cannot fail to be impressed by the honesty of Pearson's argument throughout, but his conclusion, if true, must lead us to despair of the *Phoenissae* as a play. If "realism" forces a dramatist to forsake dramatic structure (are there no well-constructed "realistic" plays?) then he has forgotten, for the time being, how to be a dramatist.

Less willing to admit the censure implicit in his description of the play, but leading the reader to the same despair of "Euripides the dramatist," is Kitto's defence of the *Phoenissae*. This critic cheerfully admits the play's "problems"—dramatic irrelevance, throw-away scenes, inconsistent characterization—in a series of rhetorical questions to which he provides a single "answer":

> To ask all these questions is to see the answer at once. Euripides is not developing a tragic theme, or he would need neither this amount nor this variety of material; not even a non-tragic but dramatic theme, or the material would have more cohesion. . . . Out of the Theban legend he is creating what we may call a dramatic pageant, presenting scene after scene for the sake of their immediate and cumulative effect, but not for the sake of an inner drama; therefore he needs a lot of material but need not be particular about its cohesion.[10]

But surely a play must be judged as a play, even if not as a tragedy. If the *Phoenissae*, as Kitto suggests, lacks all the dramatic virtues and has, moreover, no overriding tragic idea (by which, in the case of the properly tragic plays of Euripides, Kitto has explained peculiarities, or even absence, of structure),[11] then surely there is little left to justify this critic's insouciant defence of it.

[9]A. C. Pearson, *Euripides, the Phoenissae*, xxvii–xxx. In reaching this conclusion, Pearson comments on the unsuccessful attempts of Wecklein, Decharme and others to establish a coherent structural plan for the *Phoenissae*.

[10]Kitto, *G.T.*, 356.

[11]Cf. *ibid.*, 185 ff.

Theme and Structure

Everything about the *Phoenissae* informs us of Euripides' peculiar intention in this play, and of his peculiar attitude to the mythical material on which he draws. Thus far we may agree with Kitto; it is only when we are told that the dramatist has written a pageant, not a play, that we need be wary. The "overfulness" of the play, its inorganic, even incoherent structure, must, of course, be intentional: far from being embarrassed by an abundance of material, Euripides has gone out of his way to include everything possible, and has even added to the tradition. What, then, *is* the intention?

Three points have emerged from the preceding discussion: that Euripides is not, in this play, concentrating with tragic intention on a single theme; that the trilogy material contains a series of deterministic curse fulfilments which illustrate, paradoxically, the disastrous results of human passion; that of the new elements introduced into the legend, some are designed to fit the "mythological," some the humanistic or secular aspects of this paradox.

All this gives a strong preliminary indication that Euripides is planning, in this play, a series of paradoxical confrontations of the world of myth (in which the pattern of events is determined by some external and supernatural force) and the "real" world of Euripidean drama, where events are usually presented as the result of human passions and human folly. Since the treatment is to be non-tragic, the more of these ironic sequences, or rather, *non-sequiturs,* the greater the variety which a dramatic virtuoso can work into his paradoxes. We need not, for example, be restricted to the dualism of "myth *versus* reality"; reality itself, in one passage, is to dissolve into the artificial world of rhetoric, which thus becomes a third member of this series of contrasting contexts in which the final struggles of the house of Laius are treated.

It is some such game as this, I believe, that we must show to be at work in the *Phoenissae*. More important still, we must show that it is a game played by the manipulation of *dramatic* counters: by the alternation of "sacred" and secular passages, by the recurrence of ambiguous terminology employed now in one way, now in another, and by other devices which will allow the ideas belonging to one passage to be penetrated by those belonging to another. The major dualism, of course, concerns the causes of fratricide and this is skilfully sustained throughout the play, a "fatalistic" passage giving place to one in which the brothers insist on determining their own fate, and *vice versa.* Characteristically, each pole cannot resist giving hints of the existence of its opposite.

The execution of this plan begins with Jocasta's prologue. In one easy sweep of narration, the poet brings in every element of the past and future history of the house of Laius which will be significant in this play, though Jocasta, as she names her names (not only Oedipus and his children, but also father Cadmus, father Menoeceus and Creon, her "brother from the same mother"), is unaware of the bitter roles these names must soon sustain.

Since the point of Jocasta's prologue is to suggest, by review and by anticipation, the whole chain of woes upon the house, it is natural that it should stress the externally imposed necessity of an inherited doom, once Apollo's warning to Laius was ignored (17 ff.). Of similar effect is the repeated use of the word *tychê*, or some cognate term, throughout Jocasta's speech, for, as in many other passages in Euripides,[12] this term is to recur whenever supernatural motivation seems ascendent in the action of the play. The speech opens with an apostrophe to the Sun, "mounted on his chariot of inlaid gold" (2) and closes with a prayer to Zeus "who dwells in heaven's bright folds" (84); in both passages, the bright imagery is darkened only by the word δυστυχής used first of the woeful day of Thebes' founding (4) and finally (87) of the present unhappy sharers in the city's doom. So also, at each key point in Jocasta's narrative, *tychê*, in some form reappears: Oedipus "happens" (τυγχάνει), somehow, to have learned the Sphinx's riddle (49–50); Oedipus' sons shut away their father "so that his *tychê* might be forgotten" (64–65), and it is the illness caused by this same sad fate of his (τύχη, 66) which Jocasta alleges to be the cause of Oedipus' cursing of his sons.

But even in this prologue where divinely appointed *tychê* predominates, natural causes begin to appear as well, as we see human passion, folly and weakness, and the (misdirected) human search for knowledge, co-operating in the divine fulfilment of prophetic warnings and familial curses. Laius, δαιμόνων βίᾳ (18), begets a son in drunken passion (21); it is Oedipus' haughty temper (μέγα φρονῶν, 41) which leads him to slay the man who was his father; and even his cursing of his sons is to some degree rationalized as due to the illness induced by his unhappy fate. (66) Human, and so partial, knowledge, conspires with *tychê*, first to set Laius and Oedipus on the fatal track which leads to their meeting, and secondly to win for Oedipus (who "happened to know" the Sphinx's riddle) a wife-mother whom, in his ignorance (οὐκ εἰδὼς τάλας, 53), he

[12]On Euripides' use of the term *tychê* with the connotation of a divinely apportioned lot, see E. G. Berry, *The History and Development of the Concept of Theia Moira and Theia Tychê down to and including Plato*, 26 ff.

cannot recognize; knowledge again (μαθών, 59) loses King Oedipus his eyes, when, as in the case of Laius (μαστεύων μαθεῖν, 36) and the youthful Oedipus (ἐκμαθεῖν θέλων, 34), his human thirst for it brings ruin. In each of these details, Euripides strains both language and the mythical tradition to edge even the "necessitous background" to his present plot with human and naturalistic motivation.

Perhaps the most significant of these ironic rationalizations, in which the prologue abounds, lies in the incomplete parallel which the actions of Oedipus' sons provide to those of his father, Laius. Eteocles and Polyneices first seek to lay the ghost of Oedipus' evil *tychê* by keeping him under lock and key (64–65); then, when he curses them, it is their *fear* of the curse which, as in the case of Laius' fear of the prophetic warning, leads to the fatal evasive action (69–74; cf. 23–26, 35–37). But with Eteocles and Polyneices, no long arm of coincidence—or of fate—but merely each one's nature as we are to see it in this play, is needed to bring the matter to fulfilment. As Euripides reaches that part of the myth which has aroused his dramatic interest, we find that, in fact, no supernatural explanations of the coming fratricide are indispensable.

The *teichoscopia* shared by Antigone and the Paedagogus (88–201),[13] adds little to our theme. We should, however, note the favourable impression of Polyneices provided by Antigone's strong sympathy for him—an impression which is underlined by a grim piece of anticipatory irony: "How splendid in his golden armour shining like the bright rays of the rising sun!" (168–69) The image recalls the flashes of light at the beginning and the end of Jocasta's dark prologue.

The main fare of the long first episode (we will consider later the relation between the choral lyrics and the dramatic action) is the set debate between the warring brothers, with Jocasta acting as adjudicator. An effective passage between Jocasta and the rebelling exile Polyneices provides a skilful transition between the sombre god-ridden determinism of Jocasta's prologue and the purely secular and human interest of this central *agôn*. Jocasta, her tone a blend of love and gentle remonstrance, changes from a Cassandra-like prophet of gloom to a very human mother as she greets her long absent son. (310 ff.) Polyneices, too, cuts a very human figure—and one far removed from that strife-loving embodiment of the family curse which we may imagine (from Aeschylus' "off-stage" presentation of him, among other impressions)

[13]Doubts (for the most part ill-founded) concerning the authenticity of the *teichoscopia* are based in part on the doubts about the *exodos*, where Antigone appears again. (See above, note 1.)

to be the traditional picture of the rebel brother. His timid entry, as he jumps at every sound and shadow (263–71), his nostalgic delight at the familiar sights of home (357 ff.), his concern for his mother's grief (371–75) and his affectionate familial inquiries in which even Oedipus is included—all this belies such a conception and almost allays our fears that he could wish the city or his family any harm.

Thoughts of the curse, of the doom from the gods hanging over the city, are kept for the most part in the background. Jocasta mentions the matter twice, once (350–53) in the lyric passage with which she greets Polyneices, once (379–82) in her conversation with him, and the first of these references is coupled with a possible human explanation ("love of strife") for Polyneices' present situation. Indeed much of the conversation between mother and son remains on the extremely mundane level of generalizations, based on Polyneices' experience, about the life of exile. But perhaps the most significant point in this transition from the mythical world of the prologue to the contemporary world of sophistic debate in which the coming *agôn logôn* is to be conducted is to be observed in the *style* of Polyneices' utterances. These abound in paradoxes (357, 431), antitheses (such as that between *ergon* and *logos*, at 389), antithetical jingles (433–34) and other similar tropes, such as the resounding Euripidean aphorisms contrasting wealth and power with impoverished nobility, with which Polyneices ends his speech. (439–42)

The sophistic overtones of this preamble are well fulfilled in the three-cornered debate which now ensues between Jocasta and her warring sons. Few plays exhibit as well as the *Phoenissae* the contention of Hans Strohm about the "unproductive" nature of the Euripidean *agôn*: that these verbal battles simply review the fixed positions, or oppositions, from which the trouble has arisen, but are never in danger of leading to some fresh line of action.[14] There are, however, other ways in which this *agôn* is important, for here the most original aspects of Euripides' treatment of his traditional theme appear most clearly. Here, it is true, the poet expresses the inevitability of this fraticidal strife in strictly human terms, but in the sophistic hot-house in which he performs this operation, the heroic and tragic elements of his theme perish as surely as do the mythological.

Jocasta, as "chairman" of the debate, pacifies the hostile contestants, introduces the themes of "justice" (452) and "wisdom" (460) and con-

[14]See H. Strohm, chap. 1, pp. 3–49 *passim*, especially 37–38; cf. also Duchemin, 117–23, whose view of Euripides' use of the *agôn*, though it differs in several respects from that of Strohm, also finds better support in the *Phoenissae* (and, perhaps, in the *Hecuba*) than in many other Euripidean plays.

cludes her preamble with a neat aphorism on "conciliation" (461–64) which sets the seal of artificial formalism on the whole proceeding.

In content, Polyneices' speech is a plain statement of his obvious rights. The sophistic aspect of the debate is, however, maintained in Polyneices' phraseology. Picking up the key words of Jocasta's exhortation, he exploits them to good effect throughout his speech. *Dikê* occurs three times at the climax of his appeal (490 and 492), while the rhetorical flourishes with which he frames his argument first reject and then accept the alliance of justice and τὸ σοφόν:

Just pleas need no contrivances . . . but the unjust argument (ὁ δ'ἄδικος λόγος), being ill itself, needs the cure of cleverness (φαρμάκων . . . σοφῶν). (470–72) These points I have made not prettily decked out but just in the eyes of the wise as of the ignorant (καὶ σοφοῖς/καὶ τοῖσι φαύλοις). (494–96)

The fear of the clever speaker who may give a specious appearance of justice to the basest argument seems to have been a common reaction in the days when sophistic influence on debate was strong, as the opening lines of Socrates' defence in Plato's *Apology* (17 a–c) and the *agôn* of Aristophanes' *Clouds* (889 ff.) make clear. Polyneices' protestations prepare us well for the eruption of Euripides' own version of "The Unjust Argument" in the mouth of Eteocles.

Eteocles' speech (499–525) provides the climax to the "sophistic-rhetorical" treatment of our theme. True to the popular conception of the wicked sophist, he "justifies" his position by all manner of tricks and philosophic clichés strung together in no logical sequence. Subjected to the familiar "*onoma-ergon*" argument, Jocasta's "wisdom" and Polyneices' "equal rights" become but empty names; since all such arguments are relative, strife (ἔρις) must decide them. (499–502) Slipping out of this Protagorean role, Eteocles next plays "Callicles" or "Thrasymachus," or whatever contemporary model of the "will-to-power" school the poet had in mind. Once absolute power (τυραννίς, 506) is declared the highest good, "right" and "wrong" are redefined in terms of its attainment; thus Eteocles' peroration echoes in some respects the sentiments of Sophocles' most sophistic character,[15] and provides a fitting target for Socratic argument:

If to do wrong is ever right (εἴπερ γὰρ ἀδικεῖν χρή), then 'twere best to do wrong (κάλλιστον ἀδικεῖν) for the sake of tyranny—and, for the rest, to live a pious life! (524–25)

---

[15]With the "sophistic" clausula (*Phoenissae* 524–25) of Eteocles' speech, compare the peroration of Odysseus' crafty attempt to assuage Neoptolemus' moral scruples in Sophocles' *Philoctetes*, 81–85.

The tone of this speech, so academic in its opening gambits, so rhetorical at its close, heightens that sense of the artificial which this whole scene imparts. If, in its central *agôn*, the play has moved far from its mythological context, it has moved just as far from the ultimate realities of life with which true tragedy is concerned. After this exchange, it becomes impossible to picture either Polyneices or Eteocles as poised on the brink of tragic catastrophe.

Jocasta, abandoning with her sons the tragic level, penetrates still further into the sophistic *elenchus* to confound their arguments. (The principle of equal rights, for example, is easily re-established by illustrations from the spheres of politics and nature.) Time and again this formidable mother defeats both sons at their own game of words. (Note especially vv. 543–45, 553, 569—answering Polyneices, *charis* for *charis*, at v. 431.) But when it is over, each brother remains in exactly the same position and each illustrates in the ensuing quarrel precisely the faults (*pleonexia*, 601–3, on Eteocles' part; treason and betrayal, 616 ff., on Polyneices'), for which his mother has upbraided him. The climax, each brother declaring his readiness for fratricide to gain his ends (621–22), seems to demonstrate the old Euripidean theme, the defeat of reason by the passions, and to underline the immediate and *human* causes of the coming catastrophe. Yet with Jocasta's cry, "Flee your father's *Erinys*!" and Eteocles' answer, "Let the whole house perish!" (624), we are suddenly brought back to Necessity: both to the curse of Oedipus upon these two and (cf. vv. 19–20) to the fate ordained for the whole of Laius' house.

So far, indeed, there has been nothing but the *appearances* of things, and the understandable fears of Jocasta based upon them, to make us believe that the crisis now looming up is the work of some supernatural power. True, Oedipus' curse upon his sons does seem to be nearing fulfilment and in a way which *suggests* (witness Eteocles' cry, "Let the whole house perish!") that that curse itself is but an extension, a passing on, of the original fate which Laius' propagation of Oedipus was destined, according to Apollo, to bring upon all his family. Yet the curse itself and the processes of its fulfilment can readily be understood in human terms. The poet is at pains to stress the fact that it was Oedipus' sick temper (νόσος) induced by his cruel lot and by the incarceration inflicted on him by his sons, that caused the old man to utter the curse (63–68; cf. 872–77). And it was the sons' *fear* of the curse, not the curse itself, which induced their dangerous evasive action: that decision to rule alternately which, given the characteristics of the brothers observed in the *agôn*, must lead to strife between them.

This sort of critical rationalization, βίᾳ Τειρεσίου, would not, of course, be justified if we were discussing a play such as Aeschylus' *Septem* or Sophocles' *Oedipus Tyrannus*, where the tragic heroes are presented as bringing their fate upon themselves unawares, or at least coincidentally, while they are pursuing some higher mission which they regard as separate from or transcending their personal destiny. This distinction becomes clearer in that episode of the *Phoenissae* which follows the verbal *agôn* between the brothers.

The most significant point about the curious debate on strategy which now takes place between Creon and Eteocles is that it is Creon who advocates, contrary to Eteocles' battle-plan, the idea of meeting the seven attacking chieftains with seven chosen Theban leaders and picked bands at the seven gates. In Aeschylus' *Septem*, Eteocles' reasoned choices of each Theban captain who will meet each attacking chieftain, announced by the Messenger, provide the great central passage in the play and are basic to the tragic idea expressed in it. Aeschylus characterizes Eteocles as, first and foremost, a general, a city-defender: it is his generalship, not personal *philotimia* or fratricidal anger, which determines his decisions. Each choice of an appropriate Theban captain is the free choice of a wise general, yet with each choice we see the chances as to who will man the seventh gate narrowing. Thus, when Polyneices is named as the attacker of the seventh gate, Eteocles' choice of himself as the defender appears both as the culmination of a series of free and dispassionately appropriate choices (for who else but Eteocles can "balance" Polyneices?) and as the beginning of that terrible fulfilment of the curse which we have seen moving inexorably closer with each "free" choice of Eteocles . . . and both these aspects are clearly recognized by Eteocles in his horrified acceptance of the role which "duty" and the curse seem to coincide in laying upon him.[16]

How different is the procedure in Euripides' play! Here, not only is Creon, not Eteocles, the one to suggest the "Seven-*versus*-Seven strategy," but also the actual arranging of these seven contests is purposely sidetracked. Instead, our attention is directed again (754–56) on Eteocles' conscious and personal desire to meet and slay his brother in battle and, as we shall see from the messenger speeches which follow, the manner in which the brothers do meet in battle is kept quite separate from any strategic "luck-of-the-draw" in which the sinister operation of a divinely appointed *tychê* might seem to have a hand. Thus the essential difference between the two presentations is that, while the *generalship* of Aeschylus' Eteocles (comparable, in this respect, to that other city-defender,

[16]See Aeschylus, *Septem*, esp. vv. 653–55, 673–75.

Oedipus) involves him, with what looks like predetermined "accident," in the slaughter of his brother, both brothers, in Euripides' play, clearly chose to kill each other in the pursuit of their personal rights and ambitions.

In addition to making this fundamental point, the scene between Creon and Eteocles suggests other themes to be developed later. Thus, Eteocles' instructions to Creon include the ratification of Haemon's and Antigone's betrothal, the consultation of Teiresias (an important and productive *motif*) and the anticipatory denial of burial rights to Polyneices couched in terms (note such expressions as *κἄν φίλων τις ᾖ*) which seem designed to frustrate the more extreme of scholarly tamperings with this play's *exodos*.

From Teiresias (summoned, it will be noted, *after* the temporal adviser Creon), we expect and get (865 ff.) "the supernatural view." Even here, certain surprisingly humanistic terms creep into the prophet's explanations of divine wrath at the neglect of repeated warnings from the gods: e.g., the reference (871) to the *sophisma* of the gods, the same very rationalistic term which has been used of the plottings of Oedipus' sons to hide their father's *tychê* (64–65); the decidedly human motivation, anger and illness (876–77) by which Oedipus' cursing of his sons is explained. But Teiresias' main function in the ambiguous motivation of this play is his divine message (899–90, 911–14) that only by the sacrifice of Creon's son Menoeceus can Thebes still be saved.

Once again, in Teiresias' explanation of this oracle, we are reminded of Jocasta's prologue. The trouble with Thebes, we now learn (930 ff.), goes back to Cadmus who angered Ares by the slaughter of his dragon (hence the expiatory sacrifice of a descendant of the *Spartoi*): Jocasta, too, has suggested, albeit obscurely (4 ff.), that Theban woes go back to Cadmus' day. With this introduction of a divine *μῆνις* for ancient deeds beyond recall, we seem plunged into a mythological morass hopelessly at odds both with the passionate realities of the present situation (Oedipus' sickness, and his sons' lusts for "justice" and for power) and with the sophistries in which rhetoric has cloaked them. Not surprisingly, the word *tychê*, the sign, already observed, of the irrational, mythological aspect of our theme, begins to reappear in connection with Menoeceus' (and his family's) fate, twice (892–97) in Teiresias' speeches on the subject, but more significantly when Menoeceus himself appears.

Needless to say, Creon, the pragmatist, the strategist (it was he who, 712 ff., checked Eteocles' gallant but dangerous impulse to engage the enemy outside Thebes) uses his information from Teiresias to save, rather than to sacrifice, his son's life before the city hears of it. Menoeceus, however, is a more worthy Euripidean minor character. (It is only minor characters in Euripides who sacrifice themselves.) After feigning acquiescence in his father's plans for his safety, he gladly embraces his fate in terms which shed a new light on Euripidean views, at any rate, of *tychê*, *anankê*, and human freedom:

> . . . how well I've lulled my father's fears to reach the fate I wish (ὥσθ' ἃ βούλομαι τυχεῖν); *he* would save me and, while robbing the city of its fair fortune (πόλιν ἀποστερῶν τύχης), give me the coward's part to play.
>
> (991–94)

A moment later, he describes such a situation as his as a "divinely imposed necessity" (ἀνάγκην δαιμόνων, 1000), yet makes it quite clear that he could, if he wished, play the dishonourable role of rejecting that necessity. Finally, the concluding lines (1015–18) emphasize the view suggested in the first quotation (993, above) that a city's *tychê* is determined by the patriotic devotion of its citizens.

These lines clearly show us that the *anankê* of the gods is not the absolute and immutable necessity which it is sometimes thought to be.[17] Of more immediate importance, perhaps, is the light which the passage throws on the central situation of the drama. Even in the mythological context of the present episode, it seems clear that the accursed brothers, too, must have the power to embrace or reject the "divine necessity" which hovers over them, and to determine their own and so their city's *tychê*.

It would be a mistake, however, to exaggerate the importance which "the Meneoceus episode" has for the mythological interpretation of the play. As far as one can judge from the text, Menoeceus' self-sacrifice has no discernible effect on the fortunes of the city: the sacrifice itself is given only the most passing reference (1090–92) in the first messenger speech; Eteocles completely ignores it when he offers to let the victory

[17]It is tempting to use this passage (*Phoen.* 999–1005; cf. also *I.A.* 443, 511) to refute Page's contention that, because of the celebrated "yoke"—or, as Page would have it, "yoke-strap"—of Necessity passage (ἐπεὶ δ' ἀνάγκας ἔδυ λέπαδνον, Aeschylus, *Ag.*, 218), we must believe that the Aeschylean Agamemnon had no choice but to sacrifice Iphigenia. (See Denniston and Page's edition of Aeschylus, *Agamemnon* [Oxford, 1957], xxxvi–xxxviii and note to v. 218). Now Menoeceus appears to use the expression ἀνάγκη δαιμόνων (*Phoen.* 1000) in much the same way that Aeschylus speaks of ἀνάγκη in connection with Agamemnon's dilemma; yet it is quite clear that Menoeceus considers himself as having a choice here, for he declares how base and cowardly it would be to choose the alternative of fleeing from this necessity.

depend on single combat between himself and Polyneices, and finally (and most tellingly) the dramatist slyly inserts a military as opposed to a supernatural explanation for the final routing of the Argives after both sides had watched the reciprocal slaughter of the brothers.

Thus the total effect of the "Menoeceus episode" is to disparage, rather than otherwise, the mythological interpretation of the play. The words of Menoeceus which stay with us are the final ones—that it is up to the *citizens* to provide a good *tychê* for their city—and the judgment on the warring brothers which this implies on any level of interpretation is all too clear.[18] Even Jocasta, that other spokesman for the myth and the curse, has, in one of her less fatalistic moments, placed responsibility for what is happening in the same place: "Twin follies, when they meet, bring woe most hateful." (584–85)

Any lingering belief that the *Phoenissae* could have aroused—or could have been meant to arouse—the tragic emotions of pity and fear, must surely be dispelled by the four great messenger speeches (1090 ff., 1217 ff., 1356 ff., 1427 ff.) on which the *dénouement* of the play depends. In content and technique, these two pairs of speeches, each with its style suited to its particular effect, each with its subject nicely apportioned so that both climax and diminuendo receive their proper emphasis in the final pair, comprise all those elements in which a professional rhapsode might well have delighted. No attempt is made to inject that tragic element which we have found missing in the verbal encounter between the brothers. Nowhere in this final clash do we find that essential blend of inevitability and of accident (or, at least, of "unawareness") or that mitigation of heinous deed by some higher dedication. Here, as in the scene in which Eteocles plans his strategy under Creon's direction, the poet expressly rejects the opportunities of making either brother tragic in the way in which Aeschylus' Eteocles is tragic. Polyneices is mentioned (1123 ff.) in the middle of the Messenger's account of the Seven Chieftains against the Seven Gates, and no ranging of chief against chief is included to give that "Russian roulette" impression which is so striking a part of the *Septem*'s tragic effect; here the challenge and the acceptance of single combat (1223–37) emphasize the express choice of each to slay the other, for no other reason than that each stands in the other's way. No action could be less enhanced by tragic ambiguity, or less touched by any sense of the inscrutable will of the gods, for all men's strivings. Jocasta has already underlined for us the simple and sordid

[18]Cf. Grube, 364, who emphasizes the point that these final words of Menoeceus "put his conduct in the strongest contrast with that of the others" (i.e., of Creon, as well as of Eteocles and Polyneices).

motivation of both the brothers. It is a nice touch of irony on the poet's part, that, at the conclusion of this personal vendetta, the crowd should mutter about *tychê* (1370), thus reminding us of that other, *mythological* picture, two pawns in the grip of a divinely appointed fate, which has been sketched for us from time to time throughout the play.[19]

The authenticity of the *exodos* of the *Phoenissae*, or at least of large portions of it, has long been the subject of debate. The present discussion is based on the acceptance of at least the main themes suggested in our text: the joint lamentations of Oedipus and Antigone; the edicts of Creon exiling Oedipus and forbidding the burial of Polyneices; Antigones' *initial* rejection of the burial edict; her subsequent decision to guide her father into exile.[20] With which aspect of Euripides' ambiguous attitude to the mythological tradition does his treatment of these new themes agree?

> O Polyneices, so rightly named "a man of strife," alas, O Thebes! And yet your strife was no strife in reality; rather, murder brought to accomplishment by murder ruined the house of Oedipus with dreadful bloodshed. . . .
> (1493–97)

"Your strife was no strife . . ." with these words and others like them we are brought back to the world of mythology, with its human puppets and divine monsters, this time to the *Erinys* arising from Oedipus' slaughter of the Sphinx whose sport (χάρματ' Ἐρινύος, 1503), according to Antigone, the hapless corpses of both her mother and her brothers are. (See vv. 1502–7, by which vv. 1495–97, above, may be explained.) To the ancient Oedipus as well, Antigone sounds the same note of exoneration: the *alastôr* and godsent bane on the house are to blame for all. (See vv. 1555–58; 1579–81.)

With the entry of Creon, who now arranges matters to suit the gods' will and his own, the "theological view" again begins to look a little suspect. By a belated interpretation of Teiresias' advice (compare 1590–94 with 867 ff.) and a vague reference to the will of god, Creon proceeds to exile Oedipus and to follow Eteocles' instructions forbidding burial to Polyneices. When one considers both this dubious interpretation of the divine will and Creon's own rejection of Teiresias' much more explicit advice when it threatened his own family, one begins to see in

[19]"And many, exchanging looks with one another, wept at [the brothers'] misfortune (τύχης), that it was so great." (1370–71) There is irony of a different kind in the fact that several editors have suppressed these lines as unworthy of the poet: so Valckenaer, Porson, Dindorf, Paley and Murray, who bracket 1369–71 (Nauck brackets only 1370–71); see Paley's note *ad loc.*

[20]See my article referred to above, note 1.

Creon nothing but a political opportunist supporting his own interests by suitably selected oracles.[21]

Similar inconsistencies attach to the "supernatural view" of both Oedipus and Antigone. Oedipus answers Creon's order of expulsion with a fine, pathetic speech (1595–1624) listing all his deeds and sufferings to the account of fate (ὦ μοῖρ', ἀπ' ἀρχῆς ὥς μ' ἔφυσας ἄθλιον, 1595); even his self-blinding and his cursing of his sons, he attributes to the curse on Laius (ἀρὰς . . . Λαΐου, 1611) transmitted, by some god's will, to himself and to his sons. (1610–14) Antigone, too, stresses both the personal innocence of Oedipus and the harm which, as one accursed, he has brought upon them all. (1494–96, 1504–7, 1555–58) Yet both Oedipus and Antigone cry out bitterly against Creon's order for Oedipus' exile and seem to see no reason for it. (See vv. 1620–21, 1644.)

More striking than this inconsistency is the ambiguous treatment accorded Oedipus' intelligence. Far from being suppressed, as one might expect in a passage purporting to treat Oedipus and his family as puppets of fate, this celebrated feature of the "self-made King" becomes the subject of a series of paradoxical word-plays in which we may suspect another hint of irony at the expense of the mythology on which the *exodos* is based. At 1505–6, Antigone praises her father's intelligence in reading the Sphinx's riddle, so hard to understand (δυσξύνετον ξυνετὸς μέλος ἔγνω). At 1612–14, Oedipus claims as proof that he is but the unwitting instrument of Laius' curse, the fact that he is not so witless (ἀσύνετος) as to have plotted against his own eyes and the lives of his sons. Finally, at 1726–27, the hitherto sympathetic Antigone seems to contradict herself in her remark to Oedipus: "What have you to complain of? Doesn't Justice normally see human wickedness (literally "wicked men") and requite men's folly?"[22]

[21]With this sinister impression of Creon, compare the still more unpleasant picture of him in Zielinski's reconstruction of the original myth (above, n. 3).

[22]τί τλάς; τί τλάς; (1726): " 'Endure'? What do you mean '*endure*'?" Antigone is sarcastically echoing her father's self-pitying δεινὰ δεῖν' ἐγὼ τλάς of the preceding line. Paley astutely cites *Alc.* 807, where we may find precisely the same form of question indignantly taking up a word used by the preceding speaker. (Antigone's words have here, I think, been seriously misunderstood by some editors, mainly because they have attempted to make them consistent with Antigone's previously indulgent attitude toward Oedipus' deeds.) This interpretation is also supported by the critical attitude expressed in the next sentence, which I find hard to take as a statement, as some editors do, rather than as a rhetorical question. If "the gods" were the subject, it could be a statement, but it would surely be too perverse to speak of "Justice" not requiting human wrong-doing and folly.

The various inconsistencies and ambiguities just observed are not, of course, the main effects of the *exodos*; rather, they are the hints by which Euripides usually conveys his own ironic doubt whenever, for one purpose or another, he chooses to deal with myth in a literal fashion, as opposed to his usual symbolic manner. In focussing the greatest attention on the suffering Oedipus, the aged and accursed father who has destroyed his sons by handing on the curse that blights him, the dramatist has clearly chosen to end the play as he began it, that is, by presenting the fratricide of Eteocles and Polyneices as the grisly finale of a necessitous and pre-ordained sequence of suffering. From a theatrical point of view, it is true, the closing scene in which Antigone guides Oedipus' hand in his last farewells to his slaughtered family, and then leads him off-stage to share his exile, provides a suitably sombre close to this tale of violence and horror. But the main point of the *exodos* is that it returns to the tone and the perspective of Jocasta's prologue, the two together providing a mythological framework for the central action of the play whose rhetorical and rhapsodic overtones have, as we have seen, little to do with either myth or tragedy. Thus the whole piece may be regarded as a series of ironic variations on a theme, a *tour de force* in which both the supernatural world of myth and the real world of Euripidean tragedy are each in turn exploited with a cynical virtuosity hardly equalled elsewhere in Euripides.

The Function of the Chorus

One aspect of the *Phoenissae* has been, as we have observed, the presentation of the whole sequence of Theban woes, from the time of Cadmus onwards, as one supernaturally related doom. On this, the mythological level of the play, the Chorus plays a detached yet fairly vital role; detached because it has not itself any direct concern in Theban affairs; vital because of the peculiar ability of dramatic-lyric style to roam through time and, as in the choral odes of the *Agamemnon*, to make lightning connections between the immediate and the impending action, and various crucial moments of the past. Here, too, the identity of the Chorus is particularly well suited to its role: as the Phoenician kin of Cadmus, the maidens reinforce, from their first utterances, the chilling reminder which Jocasta (4–6) has given in the prologue of that unhappy (δυστυχῆ) day when Cadmus left Phoenician shores to come to Greece. Such suggestions of familial doom may be made consciously or unconsciously by the Chorus; sometimes, for example, we hear it making innocent observations in terms or in sequences which we find sinister, and sometimes we find the poet using his Chorus for occasional shafts of prophetic irony.

The very words in which the Chorus first recounts its approach to the distant Theban kin (κλεινῶν 'Αγηνοριδᾶν/ὁμογενεῖς ἐπὶ Λαΐου/πεμφθεῖσ' ἐνθάδε πύργους, 217–19) carry an unconscious reminder both of Laius' kin-assailant and of the approach of another member of the family which is, at this moment, going on outside the walls. The ironic parallels become stronger as the Chorus speaks of its kin-sympathy with the suffering city in terms which again remind us of more sinister relationships, and of an imminent and grimmer kin-sharing of mutual woes:

Common are the griefs of kin. . . . (243)
Common our blood and kindred our children through Io, the horn-bearing maid. (247–48

In the first stasimon (638–89), the Chorus continues its function of developing the mythological pageantry of Thebes, with tales of the city's founding and of the origin of its Dionysian cults, and with invocations to those divine beings most intimately related to its past. In the midst of this peaceful, familiar tapestry comes a sudden, chilling apparition:

. . . and there, by the green flowing streams (of Dirce) was the dragon of Ares, savage guardian, glaring about him with far-ranging glances. . . . (657–61)

There follows, in rapid sequence, the whole story of Cadmus' slaying of the dragon, and of the sowing of the dragon's teeth, and of the bloody despatch of the first *Spartoi*. Here, then, we have the first clear anticipation of the grim sequel to these events which is soon to be developed in the Menoeceus theme. But the first hint of the dragon theme has already appeared in the mesode of the *parados*; there, the Chorus's casual reference (232–33), amid the sights of Delphi, to the cave of the (Pythian) dragon which Apollo slew must surely be meant to anticipate that more relevant dragon slain by Cadmus, in the present passage.

As the action of the play progresses toward the long-anticipated catastrophe, the Chorus, though still turning at times to happier *motives* in Theban mythology, dwells with ever-increasing insistence on the themes of Ares and his dragon, of the Sphinx and of the train of human suffering which sprang from the slaughter of these monstrous divinities. True to the manner of tragic-lyrics, these themes occur and recur in response to dramatic rather than to chronological necessity, but at whatever point we may enter this sequence of woes, we are inevitably involved in the whole mythological complex before we are released. Thus the third stasimon (784–833) opens, as Eteocles leaves to defend the city, with a rebuke to Ares and an oblique reference, in the expression "race of the Dragon's seed" (795), to the ancient cause of Ares' wrath. In the antistrophe (801–17), two other malevolent influences on Thebes are regretted: Cithaeron, which saved Oedipus, and the Sphinx. Then, without pause, we are rushed on to the present stain upon the house and the city: the sons of Oedipus' incestuous bed. In the epode, we return (818 ff.) to the primal affliction, the dragon of Ares, and that "glorious reproach upon the Thebans" (821), the race of the dragon's teeth.

The third *stasimon*, then, throws the various mythical elements at us with little regard for the connections between them. However, the next *stasimon* (1019–66), which follows Menoeceus' departure to his voluntary death, organizes these elements in a particularly sinister pattern. The strophe deals with the Sphinx and her depredations; the antistrophe, in its opening lines (1043 ff.), with the short-lived triumph of Oedipus ("We rejoiced, then grieved again," 1046) before worse woes, in the form of Oedipus' incest and son-cursing, followed from his disposal of the Sphinx. Only now does the Chorus turn to the theme of Menoeceus' self-sacrifice, for now its place in the curse-ridden sequence can be clearly expounded, and its ultimate failure to end that sequence can be clearly implied.

He has our praises, that man who goes to his death for his native land, . . . who ensures victory for the city's bastions at the seven gates. May we too, O Pallas Athena, be mothers of sons like this—Pallas, you who inspired that stone-throw which drew the Dragon's blood, urging Cadmus to the deed, whence some scourge (ἄτα) from the gods fell with savage depredations (ἁρπαγαῖσι) on this land. (1054–66)

Thus the most recent bloodshed in the royal house (the sacrifice of Menoeceus) is related directly (as Teiresias has already indicated) to the slaughter of Ares' dragon, and indirectly to the grim levy exacted by the Sphinx, for this too, as the language of vv. 1065–66 makes clear, was the result of Ares' anger. Clear too is the prophecy which this dire song implies: Cadmus' defeat of the dragon and Oedipus' triumph over the Sphinx delivered the city to worse woes, and so Menoeceus' propitiation of Ares may save the city but will bring no end to the woes in store for it.

The final chorus (1284–1306), which follows Jocasta's hopeless sally to part the duelling brothers, is little more than a lamentation in advance for the coming fratricidal slaughter. Even here, however, there are evocations of the mythological background of this catastrophe: in the cry to Zeus and Earth (1290), the progenitors of this ill-starred race, in the "Oedipodal language" (ὁμογενῆ δέραν, ὁμογενῆ ψυχάν, 1291) occurring in certain descriptive details referring to the kin-slaughter, and in the likening of the two brothers to two murderous beasts (δίδυμοι θῆρες,/φόνιαι ψυχαί, 1297), which cannot fail to recall those other monsters, the Sphinx and the dragon of Ares, ever lurking in the background. Finally, the whole catastrophe is summed up as the work of those spirits of vengeance which have been aroused by each successive slaughter in the past: πότμος ἄποτμος ὁ φόνος ἕνεκ' Ἐρινύων. (1306)

14

THE *Iphigenia at Aulis*

A Preliminary View

The *Iphigenia at Aulis*,[1] for all its weaknesses, has one dominant aspect which gives it point. To demonstrate this it will be necessary to begin with a brief analysis of its somewhat diffuse action.

Agamemnon, faced with the dilemma of Calchas' prophecy at Aulis, has summoned Iphigenia to Aulis on the false pretext of marriage to Achilles. The first part of the action develops the well-known dilemma of the King over his daughter's sacrifice: first, his despatch, after much agonizing, of a second letter cancelling his first instructions about Iphigenia; second, his two debates with Menelaus who first upbraids Agamemnon's paternal hesitation and then (moved somewhat improbably by Agamemnon's grief) argues *against* the need of sacrificing Iphigenia, despite the pressure from the Greeks which Agamemnon himself now urges. That this is false agonizing and that Agamemnon, unlike his daughter later in the play, is merely playing with his emotions to deceive his conscience, is clear enough: once the arrival of Iphigenia

[1]Considerable doubt prevails concerning large areas of our text of the *I.A.* The problem of the double prologue (vv. 1–163) is, perhaps, soluble (see below, note 11), and the complaint about the opening of the second episode is, I think, exaggerated (the neglect of Clytemnestra at this point could well be due to Agamemnon's and Iphigenia's poignant interest in one another, and the dramatist's interest in both). With regard to the *exodos*, however, particularly the messenger speech reporting Iphigenia's miraculous rescue by Artemis, we must agree with the majority of scholars who, on the basis of stylistic and textual difficulties, dramatic inconsistency and conflicting external evidence (cf. Aelian, *N.A.* vii. 39), have rejected the passage as comprised of a congeries of late interpolations. It seems probable, nevertheless, that the original ending, like the spurious one, did include, in one form or another, the saving of Iphigenia by Artemis. On the manifold problems concerning the text of the *Phoenissae*, see, among others, Parmentier, "L'*Iphigénie* d'Euripide"; Page, *Actors' Interpolations in Greek Tragedy*, Part II; and the Introduction and Notes to England's edition of the *I.A.*

and her mother is announced, he accepts with something like relief the "necessity" (as he calls it, 443, 511) of persevering in his original dread resolve.

The second movement of the play revolves around the grim enlightenment (by a family servant) of Clytemnestra as to the true purpose of her daughter's presence. Here the ironic contrast between the playful affection (before the revelation) of Iphigenia with her father and her subsequent reproachful pleas and lamentations is supplemented by the reactions of Iphigenia's two "defenders," Clytemnestra and Achilles, both of whom, for all their protestations, show themselves to be motivated by concerns as selfish as that of Agamemnon himself.

The third movement triumphantly displays Iphigenia's choice of martyrdom: her sudden and surprising decision to sacrifice herself willingly for her countrymen. (The new *motif* is not presented until Iphigenia's declaration at 1368 ff., but it takes its cue, perhaps, from Agamemnon's equally surprising speech at the end of the preceding movement.) The whole preceding action of the play is now seen to have taken place for the sake of this somewhat romantic transformation scene, for the characterizations of the variously corrupt or counterfeit heroes contribute by their contrast (whatever their own intrinsic interest) to the greater glorification of the maiden heroine.

With the pathetic effects and final happy ending of the messenger speech (which describes the sacrifice and the last-minute substitution of a hind by Artemis) we will not be much concerned. The play (though not, I think, a tragicomedy or melodrama) is clearly not a tragedy: there is no meaningful relation between the character of the heroine and the fate externally imposed upon her, and no real significance, beyond the "edification" of martyrdom, in the sacrifice itself. Since, in the end, the play becomes simply a spectacle of youthful heroism—a Menoeceus scene or a Macaria scene given top billing, as it were—there is no reason why we and the heroine should not be rewarded for our agonies by the "happy" version of the legendary sacrifice.

The Myth and Its Adaptation

The origins and the primary significance of the Iphigenia myth have been the subject of several fascinating studies,[2] but we must restrict ourselves here to the version which Euripides treats, with a few preliminary

[2]In addition to the standard accounts to be found in dictionaries of Greek mythology, see, for example, the interesting and, on the whole, convincing arguments of S. Reinach, *REG*, XXVIII (1915), 1–15.

indications of new features or new emphases which the dramatist himself has introduced. The epic account (as far as we may judge it from Proclus' summary of the *Cypria*) appears to have formed the basis of Euripides' version. In it, Iphigenia is lured to Aulis for the same reasons, and by the same bethrothal ruse, as in Euripides' play, and is eventually saved by Artemis, who snatches her away to the land of the Taurians and sets a hind in her place on the altar at Aulis.[3] To Proclus' account of the epic tradition, we may, perhaps, add the further details appearing in Apollodorus and Hyginus, that Odysseus was sent to negotiate with Clytemnestra with the plea that Iphigenia was to be given to Achilles as pay for his military services.[4] Aeschylus and Sophocles also wrote tragedies, now lost, on the subject of Iphigenia; thus the humanization of this primitive myth as a vehicle for portraying domestic and political intrigue had, no doubt, already made some progress by the time that Euripides took it up. Of Aeschylus' play we know practically nothing; Sophocles' play seems to have dealt with much the same basic material as Euripides', though the general view is that it adhered more closely to the Cyprian account.[5] Whether the roles of Clytemnestra (whose presence in Sophocles' play seems assured) and of Odysseus began in the epic or in the tragic tradition we cannot be certain; nor, for our purposes, does it matter very much. It has been suggested that the major changes which Euripides introduced in the legend may have been the substitution of Menelaus for Odysseus as a leading proponent of the

[3]*EGF*, 19; cf. also Schol. *Il.* 1. 108. For a full list of ancient references on the Iphigenia myth, see Roscher, *Lexicon* II. 1. 298–305; further discussion of the various points raised in the present summary of the tradition on the Iphigenia myth will be found in the preface to H. Weil's edition of the *I.A.* in *Sept Tragédies d'Euripide.*

[4]Apollodorus, *epit.* 17. 8; Hygin., *fab.* 98. (In Apollodorus' account, Odysseus is accompanied by Talthybius; in Hyginus', by Diomedes.)

[5]For the fragments concerned, see *TGF*, pp. 31, 197–98, and Pearson, *The Fragments of Sophocles*, 218–23. Nauck suggests that Hyginus' account may reflect the contents of Sophocles' play. Note especially frg. 284 (Pearson 305) in which, according to its authorities, Odysseus appears to be congratulating Clytemnestra on her illustrious "marriage-kin" (Achilles). The complicity of Odysseus in the intrigue tallies with the accounts of Apollodorus and Hyginus, and, since these are both similar in other respects to what Proclus tells us of the *Cypria*, Pearson argues that Sophocles probably followed the *Cypria* more closely than did Euripides; cf. also Roscher, 298, and Welcker, I. 107. With regard to Clytemnestra, however, H. Weil (303–4) argues that it was not until the Iphigenia myth was treated in tragedy that Clytemnestra was brought to Aulis, and that the references to the sacrifice at Euripides' *I.T.* 6–33, according to which Clytemnestra did not come to Aulis, preserve the original, more barbarous version.

sacrificial intrigue; the development of the role of Agamemnon, particularly in his early attempt to save his daughter, and the emphasis on the ultimate willingness of Iphigenia (the spiritual kin, as we have observed, of other Euripidean martyrs) to be sacrificed for her country's sake.[6] It seems probable, too, that Euripides has considerably developed the role of Achilles, characterized, as we shall see, in the dramatist's best melodramatic manner; in the starker versions of the myth he need function but passively, as bait for Iphigenia, though it has been argued by one scholar that here Euripides is developing in his own way an ancient version of the myth in which Achilles, as Iphigenia's real suitor, was involved in a "substitute sacrifice" theme.[7]

When these various modifications of the myth have been studied in their proper contexts, we may see in the end that they are all part of a single intention of the dramatist in his original approach to a well known subject. The possibility seems worth examining, since there has been a tendency in recent discussion of the *Iphigenia at Aulis* either to dismiss it as merely "theatrical" ("this West-end half-tragedy," Kitto has called it)[8] or to emphasize its pathos and its purple passages at the expense of its design and its real dramatic point.[9]

Professor Kitto's view of the play is somewhat difficult to evaluate because the conclusions which he draws about the total effect of the play do not seem to be entirely justified by his valid insights into individual aspects of it. He includes the *Iphigenia at Aulis* among the "non-tragic" plays of Euripides in which "theatrical reality takes the place of tragic, that is to say universal, reality" and in which, since little attempt is made to make the artificial plots appear credible, our serious interests and emotions are not engaged. With Kitto's description of the *Iphigenia at Aulis* as non-tragic, we may certainly agree: as he shows us, no attempt is made to present either Agamemnon's dilemma or Iphigenia's plight as "credible." Moreover, both the divine and the

[6]See L. Parmentier, " 'L'Iphigénie à Aulis' d'Euripide," 266–67, and Weil, 305–6.

[7]P. Roussel, *REG*, XXVIII (1915) 234–50.

[8]Kitto, G. T., 366. For Kitto's full discussion of the *I.A.* see *ibid.*, 366–73; for his general description, discussed below, of the "theatrical" nature of the so-called tragicomedies and melodramas alike, see *ibid.*, chaps. 11 and 12, esp. pp. 315–17, 332; for alleged examples of this theatricality in the *I.A.*, see *ibid.*, 371–72.

[9]See, for example, A. Rivier, 79, 81, 84, and André Bonnard, *Mus. Helvet.*, II, 87–107. Bonnard, it is true, does attempt (90–95) to find the structure and tragic point of the play in the ironic lack of cohesion between the various human attempts to save Iphigenia. He attempts, too, to give this theme a certain universal application: "Ce tragique du désordre du monde . . . etc." (96)

human causes of Iphigenia's situation are quite external to herself. When she does eventually become involved in the action, it is to transform, in a manner more spectacular than "probable," the fate imposed upon her into a personal victory. Thus Iphigenia's is not a tragic characterization, and certainly the Agamemnon of this play, on the grounds of stature alone, could never be confused with a tragic hero.

However, the idea that for the reasons just suggested the *I.A.* must be regarded merely as episodic and theatrical is not, I think, quite justified. Here, perhaps, the critic is to some degree the slave of his own categories. As we shall see later, all Euripidean plays which, for one reason or another, cannot be said to deal with universal tragic themes, are then rigorously limited, in Kitto's account of them, to the relative frivolity of tragicomedy and melodrama. Must Agamemnon (or, for that matter, Iphigenia herself; or Ion or Creusa in the *Ion*), fall all the way from being "not tragic" to being "undeserving of our serious interest?"[10] Even Iphigenia's situation, though too artificial for real tragic involvement on our part, does provide more serious interest than Kitto allows it. The *idea* of her sacrifice, if not its precise circumstances, is possible and even moving. Once we grant this, we may find more than incidental and individual nuggets of entertainment in various parts of the play. Thus it may be argued that the treatment of Agamemnon and of even the lesser personages in the play has some bearing on its emotional climax, and that the transformation of Iphigenia, far from being included as one more theatrical thrill, gives the play whatever meaning it has. If our analysis supports these suggestions, then we may conclude that the *Iphigenia at Aulis*, though not a full-scale tragedy, is something more than a series of diverting incidents, dextrously organized into a merely formal unity.

Dramatic Analysis

Authentic or not, the opening dialogue[11] between Agamemnon and his old servant etches in highly dramatic fashion the mood of the King—

[10]Kitto, 368.

[11]The unusual anapaestic prologue (omitted in Murray's text; see his note to 49 ff.) shared by Agamemnon and the old servant is interrupted at vv. 49–114 by a monologue from Agamemnon which states the whole situation in conventional form and which is somewhat clumsily worked into the context of the anapaestic dialogue. Most editors agree that we have here two originally distinct prologues. I agree with the view of Parmentier ("L'*Iphigénie* d'Euripide," 267 ff.) and Pohlenz (I, 460–61) that both are Euripidean but that since Euripides left the play in an unfinished state he never reduced the prologue to a dramatic unity.

his sense of urgency coupled with his desperate indecision. Here, too, Agamemnon expresses more pithily than ever again the root of all his troubles, the sweet bite of ambition (22–23), tainted now by hypocrisy ("I envy the unknown and unrenowned. . . ." 17 ff.), and now by fear of opposition from men and gods alike. (24–27) The servant himself scores his master's plaints as unkingly (28) and vividly describes (34–42) the frantic indecision "bordering on madness" of Agamemnon's repeated scribbling and erasing, sealing and unsealing, of the mysterious letter he would send. Our awareness of the King's fatal vacillation increases when, in the more conventional part of the prologue, he tells us that he has already, under pressure from Menelaus, reversed his original decision to spare his daughter's life.

This focus of attention, so clearly set in the prologue, is maintained as long as Agamemnon's decision—and his indecision—determine the action; then our interest in Agamemnon is gradually reduced as our interest in Iphigenia increases, until we come to see his ultimate role, like that of all others in the play, as subsidiary to her final domination both of the action and of the meaning of the play. For the present, however, we need to know all we can of Agamemnon and his motives, and no more dramatic way of doing this could be found than the violent altercation which now ensues between the King and his brother Menelaus, who knows him best. Here, too, in addition to the obvious theatrical values of such a confrontation, we find the whole projected war, and so the threat to Iphigenia's life, appearing as a shabby affair, the result of personal ambition on the one hand and of lust, or, at best, a misplaced uxoriousness, on the other.[12]

The encounter between the royal brothers is deftly handled: it is the kind of thing which the dramatist particularly enjoys. Here he follows a well established pattern: a crisp exchange of insults, then two sustained rhetorical indictments, in which each antagonist impugns the motives and the character of the other, finally a second brief passage of *stichomythia* to conclude the quarrel. The natural and spontaneous vigour of the incident is in no way sacrificed to its larger purposes: rather, the necessary characterization of Agamemnon and the motives of both brothers in this war appear quite naturally in the course of their exchanges. The cool insolence of the "junior," Menelaus, followed by

[12]Parmentier (266) has suggested that Euripides here gives to Menelaus what was the traditional role of Odysseus in the myth of Iphigenia's sacrifice for the opportunity which this change provides of an *agôn logôn* between the two famous brothers.

his deft thrusts at Agamemnon's weakest points, tell us much about the stature of the King:

AGAMEMNON (*who has just discovered Menelaus' interception of his messenger*): Have you no shame? What rights have you in my affairs?
MENELAUS: My will's my right. I was not born your slave.
AGAMEMNON: Outrageous! Am I not to be allowed to manage my own household?
MENELAUS: No, for you're too shifty-minded. You are now, you were before, and you will be again. (329–32)

This treacherous "double-mindedness" of Agamemnon is scored at length in Menelaus' formal indictment of his brother. Allowing for a certain vindictive exaggeration (as well as for certain contemporary overtones in this typically "political" Euripidean *rhesis*)[13] we see emerging a very different figure from the self-effacing individual, "drafted" for high office, which Agamemnon has sketched of himself in the prologue. (84–86) To the description of Agamemnon as a typical political climber (fawning in his candidature, cool and unapproachable after his appointment as general), Menelaus adds the more relevant news that, when first the dilemma arose at Aulis, Agamemnon was eager of his own accord to sacrifice his daughter to his overmastering ambition.

It is significant that in his reply (378–401), Agamemnon does not attempt to repudiate these charges. Rather, he scores Menelaus' own passionate motive in this war; soon Menelaus' sworn allies ("those misguided, marriage-craving suitors" pictured, 391 ff., as driven mad by Hope) and, indeed, all Greece ("Hellas, like you, some god has driven mad!" 411) is included in the King's sweeping indictment of this senseless war.

This same emphasis on passion and "madness" appears in a variety of contexts throughout the play, whenever the causes of the war are mentioned. In Agamemnon's prologue, Menelaus, raising an army against Troy, is described as "racing in frenzy throughout Greece" (77); later, Achilles speaks of the "strange longing for this expedition" (which), "not without the gods, has fallen upon Greece" (808–809); finally Agamemnon, even as he defends the war to his daughter, again speaks of "a certain passion" (1264) maddening the Hellenic host. This is the theme to be developed later, when the sacrificial maid herself

[13]Note particularly the generalized descriptions applicable to fifth-century political types and situations at vv. 339–48 and 366–69. H. Grégoire, in "Euripide, Ulysse et Alcibiade," 102–4, makes out an ingenious case for the application of this indictment to Alcibiades, before and after his successful candidacy of 408 B.C.

arrives. For the present, in sharp contrast to the selfless nobility of Iphigenia, the brothers' quarrel serves only to emphasize their own self-gratifying motives in the war.

The picture which the dramatist has gradually been revealing of the weak but complex character of the King is further developed in the next two episodes. When the Messenger announces the arrival of Clytemnestra and Iphigenia, Agamemnon gives up any attempt to save them as suddenly and as arbitrarily as he has made all his previous decisions. From this point on, he appears to accept the sacrifice as something fated and necessitous (see vv. 441, 443, 511–12).

And yet why does Agamemnon give up so easily? It is interesting that, until pressed by Menelaus, he gives no practical reason for this new change of mind. Agamemnon is, as one critic has described him, "a man not sure of himself or his motives."[14] His natural desire is to save his daughter, but his half-suppressed ambition to lead the Greeks to Troy is still more of a spur than he himself realizes. His acceptance of the sacrifice of Iphigenia at this crucial point in his dilemma shows an easy fatalism not unfamiliar in such mentalities when the burden of decisive action becomes too great for them to bear.

These characteristics—vacillation, a weak fatalism and, paradoxically, personal ambition—are laid bare (with brilliant irony on the poet's part) in the King's second debate (471–542—*after* the announcement of Iphigenia's arrival at Aulis) with his brother. Menelaus, when he was *opposing* Agamemnon's attempt to save his child, has already shown us something of the unpleasant side of Agamemnon's inconsistent character. Now, by changing sides himself and urging the rescue of Iphigenia, Menelaus (whose only dramatic function is the revelation of Agamemnon) effectively shifts full responsibility for the sacrifice of Iphigenia on to Agamemnon himself. The irony is particularly effective when Menelaus refutes each fresh "pressure" ("Necessity," 511–12; "the army," 514, "Calchas," 518 ff.; "Odysseus," 522 ff.) which the King alleges to be forcing him to the sacrifice. While we may not, perhaps, dismiss Agamemnon's fears as completely ridiculous, they are certainly exaggerated (the fear of Odysseus, with which Agamemnon finally shouts his brother down, is surely developed to an almost hysterical degree) and they change too rapidly for us to have much confidence in any one of them. Not only is the King a man of mixed and uncertain motives: he fails to see what motive really dominates him. Even as he is expressing the motive of fear, the dramatist reminds us

[14]Grube, 426. For other views of the Agamemnon of this play, see below, notes 15 and 21.

of his stronger motive of ambition by the deft insertion, in the King's own castigation of Calchas and Odysseus, of the words *philotimon* (520) and *philotimia.* (527) As both Menelaus and the audience know, the charge of overweening ambition applies first of all to Agamemnon; indeed, in the prologue (21–23), the King himself has named honour as both a delight and a danger of the royal condition.[15]

We are now at a crucial moment in the play. The grip of Necessity (real or imagined) seems finally to have asserted itself, and Agamemnon has changed his mind for the last time. After the entry of Iphigenia and Clytemnestra in the next episode, Iphigenia gradually assumes the dominant role and we begin to see the portrayal of Agamemnon, his character and his motives, in its proper perspective.

A most effective choral lyric (543 ff.) signals this new direction in the play.[16] At first vaguely, finally by specific allusions to the destructive love of Paris and Helen, it looks back beyond the war motives of Agamemnon and Menelaus to their original causes. Within this frame, we find a brief but brilliant anticipation of the role which the virgin Iphigenia will play in the resolution of these passionate conflicts:

> Training well-instilled leads on to virtue; for wisdom is the sense of reverence and to discern the right by proper judgment brings with it an all-transforming grace; therein lies the source of ageless fame for mortal life. It is a great thing to track down virtue: for women, it is in accord with Love, and is private, whereas in men, an inborn sense of order (*their* virtue) has many facets and helps make their city greater.[17] (561–72)

Perhaps it is not too fanciful to see in this passage an ironic contrast between Agamemnon and Iphigenia as they finally appear in the action of the play: a certain order (or *kosmos*) within is precisely what Agamemnon has been observed as lacking, whereas Iphigenia's virtue is to go far beyond the private and domestic sphere (in effect she gives up Cypris to amend the ravages of Cypris; see vv. 1378–86) to include those city-saving qualities here associated with a *man's* virtue.

Between the dilemma of Agamemnon, with which the first part of

[15]For interesting "political" interpretations of the Agamemnon of this play, see Pohlenz, I, 460, and F. M. Wassermann, *TAPA*, 80 (1949), 174–86. Both these critics regard this characterization of Agamemnon as Euripides' picture of the typical Athenian office holder in the latter part of the fifth century!

[16]For the most part, the choruses of the *I.A.*, while not irrelevant or merely decorative, suggest only an accompaniment, a sort of lyric expansion, of certain moments in the action. However, both the present ode and that preceding the fourth episode make significant contributions to the theme of the play.

[17]On the difficult passage at vv. 569–72, I have followed England's text and general interpretation; see his notes *ad loc.* For a contrary view, see Paley *ad loc.*

this play is concerned, and the ultimate self-dedication of Iphigenia, comes a long and occasionally tedious series of encounters. In four lengthy episodes, the principal male and female characters (Menelaus, never more than a dramatic convenience in the play, has now dropped out entirely) are allowed to meet in constantly changing "arrangements" and circumstances which provide a great variety of dramatic dialogues, ironic misunderstandings, and set rhetorical declamations. Successful as these scenes are in themselves, do they provide anything more than that transient excitement, that "picturesque and diverse ornament" which, according to Kitto,[18] here replaces tragic meaning? Even amid the alternating effects of pathos, comedy and sheer melodrama, it seems possible to detect some organic relation, some meaning more comprehensive than that which purely episodic drama can provide.

The two encounters between Agamemnon and Iphigenia exemplify the double aspect of these scenes. In the first, the dramatist exploits to the full the pathetic ironies of the situation in which this joyful, lively girl, half-bride, half-daughter in her emotions, greets the sorrowing father who knows that he is soon to have her slain. Here, the particular piquancy of the exchange lies, perhaps, in the fact that its ironic effects are never extraneous to the human emotions of the scene but rather appear quite naturally in their expression. In this, Euripidean irony is very different from the brilliant verbal irony of Sophocles: there is, for example, nothing in the work of the younger dramatist to match the word-plays, the ingenious images, which anticipate the tragic discovery of Oedipus. Euripides, who uses irony more sparingly, uses it also more pathetically, with, perhaps, a deeper concern for the individual feelings of his characters. Thus, the most telling of Iphigenia's unconscious ironies arise in the sort of expressions one expects from this affectionate and carefree child. Vainly she tries to tease her father from his royal frowns: "Think now of me and turn aside from care." (646) "Stay home now, father, with your children!" (656) "How long you've been away at Aulis' gulfs!" (660) How vague and distant is the war to Iphigenia: "Oh *bother* spears and Menelaus' silly woes!" . . . "Is Troy far away? . . . Can I come, too?" (658, 662–64, 666, in sense at least).

There is no doubting the effect of all this on Agamemnon. He cannot bear it:

> Now depart within for none but maids to see. First one sad kiss and your right hand . . . (678–79)
>
> Oh breast, oh cheeks, oh golden hair, what burden Phrygia's town has laid on you . . . (681–82)

[18]See Kitto, 368–71 and chap. 11, *passim*.

The somewhat theatrical effect of this scene depends in large part on the vivid characterization of Iphigenia, whose youthful vitality and girlish trust in her father contrast so sharply with the grim realities of her situation. Nevertheless, this initial characterization has point beyond its immediate piquancy. When Iphigenia discovers the truth, much of her reproachful supplication suggests of her past relationship with her father just that jocund quality which we have witnessed in this initial scene, and the bursting vitality of her first appearance is echoed in grimmer circumstances with that poignant praise of life which, in a heroine of Greek tragedy, sounds ominous indeed:

For man, to see the light of day is sweetest joy. Below, there's nothing: he's mad who prays to die. Even base living profits more than noble death. (1250–52)

This same love of life is to achieve still fuller significance in the *dénouement* of the dramatic action.

The initial presentation of Clytemnestra and Achilles cannot, perhaps, be quite so fully justified in terms of the drama as a whole. It would be dishonest not to admit a certain immediate enjoyment of this scene before seeking to give it a broader significance. Clytemnestra is presented as an amusing mixture of *grande dame* and *femme de ménage* who is more concerned with the wrong (compounding earlier wrongs!) done to *herself* by Agamemnon's deception than with the imminent loss of her daughter's life. But it is the presentation of Achilles, now as a dashing Homeric warrior, now as a self-conscious product of sophistic training, which provides the more striking parody. The comic note is sounded from the start, when we see the gauche young soldier, terrified and brusque in a sudden encounter with a grand lady whom he does not know and whose familiarity he cannot understand. Achilles' punctiliously aloof treatment of Agamemnon's spouse suggests, perhaps, a mischievous reversal of a celebrated situation in the *Iliad*: "What's this? My hand in yours? I'd be ashamed before your lord to touch what is not mine." (833–34)

Achilles' speech when he learns the truth—that he has been Agamemnon's dupe and that Iphigenia has been lured to her death by a pretended betrothal to him—is a burlesque of both the heroic and sophistic styles, for by a bold stroke the dramatist makes the Centaur-trained young warrior a champion of the rationalistic school of ethics:

My lofty-minded spirit stirs me to action! Yet it has learned to relax amid troubles and to rejoice moderately also, amid triumphs. We rationalists are the kind of men who live their lives properly, with proper judgment. Yet there are times when it is pleasant not to think too much, just as there are other times when it is useful to have judgment. (919–925)

By such ponderous deliberations, Achilles reaches the conclusion that, since Agamemnon's plot is immoral, and since his own name, if not his will, has been party to the plot, he must clear both by resisting it. Once this point has been decided in a rational manner, he works himself up into a properly furious heroic mood ("No . . . by Nereus, sire of Thetis . . . lord Agamemnon shall not lay a finger on your child!" 948–50), remembers (at 959–60) to echo *Iliad* IX. 388–97 to the effect that he needs not Agamemnon's daughter—countless other maidens are pursuing him—and even strains at the end (albeit apologetically) for some semblance of the real godlike Achilles: "Keep calm! Like some mighty god have I appeared to you, although I'm *not* one. But such I will become." (973–74)

However, Achilles' eloquent outburst (928–43) against the immorality of Agamemnon's plot against his daughter reaches a sad anticlimax in the hero's later admission that (as in the Briseis affair in the *Iliad*) it is only his own wounded pride that concerns *him* in this matter.[19] ("Agamemnon ought to have *asked* me for my name to trap his daughter! . . . this much I'd have granted to my country . . . and to the voyage to Troy. . . ." (962–63, 965–66) With similar bathos, the fire-breathing of the heroic Achilles of vv. 948 ff. and 973–74 expires on the true sophistic note:

But let us *persuade* her father . . . (1011)
. . . and if persuasion wins, I need not budge. . . . The army would not blame me, if by reason rather than by strength I should prevail. (1017–21, in part)

Neither Clytemnestra nor Achilles can be said to affect the action of the play substantially; both characterizations are, as Kitto has argued, sketched more for their immediate value as entertainment than for any larger purposes. Nevertheless, all these characterizations, those of Clytemnestra and of Achilles as of Agamemnon and Menelaus, may be said to contribute something to the ultimate impact of Iphigenia and of the emotional climax of the play. The authentic vitality and heroism of Iphigenia show up the more sharply in contrast with the parody of these qualities where we would expect to find them—in Achilles; and

[19]Contrast Roussel, *REG*, XXVIII, 234–50, who considers in great detail (and with great solemnity) the whole question of Achilles' sense of responsibility as *kurios* of Iphigenia. Cf. also Pohlenz, 463–65; Grube, 436; Roussel, 234–50, all of whom take the Achilles of this play rather more seriously than I have taken him, and present his moral perceptions in a somewhat kinder light.

the ultimate generosity of Iphigenia is deployed to advantage against the ignoble motives of Agamemnon and Menelaus and the basic self-interest even of her "allies," Clytemnestra and Achilles.

To the pleas of his wife and daughter, Agamemnon replies with a surprisingly impressive speech.

I know what must be pitied, what must not. I love my children; I were a madman otherwise. It is terrible for me to dare these things, yet terrible also not so to dare: for do the deed I must. (1255–58)

It is a strong opening; both in style and decision, the King (unlike his former self) sounds like a man who has grasped the awful dilemma and decided what is right. He points to the serried ranks of ships and "all the lords of Greece in brazen arms" (1260), who cannot voyage to Troy save by his daughter's sacrifice; now, for the first time, he speaks of the issue in terms of national, rather than personal, honour and safety:

It is not Menelaus, child, that has me in his thrall . . . but Greece. It is for Greece, whether I wish it or not, that I must sacrifice you. This it is that overcomes us, for she must be free, as far as it is in our power, both yours and mine, to make her so, that Grecian homes should not be robbed by barbarous hands. (1269–75)

How much should we allow this speech to affect our earlier impressions of Agamemnon? Some critics feel that it does much to restore his credit; Grube, for example, remarks, "Here the King, whose motives are mixed, . . . nevertheless achieves a certain dignity . . . his ambition is here more closely linked with the greatness of Greece. . . ."[20] There is no denying that this is the most (if not the only) impressive speech which Agamemnon has uttered so far. Has he suddenly realized that this war is worthwhile after all, that he was wrong in hesitating to sacrifice his daughter? Or is he merely making a virtue of what he now feels to be necessity, and adding a respectable reason to those less reputable ones which have urged him to the sacrifice? Opinion is divided.[21] It is significant that never, before this speech, has Agamemnon expressed, even to himself, any patriotic justification of this war. If Euripides had wished us to regard him as a tragic figure, torn, as in

[20]Grube, 435. For other views on this speech of Agamemnon's, see the following note.

[21]Contrast Wassermann, "This Panhellenic anticipation of Alexander . . ." (185) with Bonnard (91–92) and Pohlenz (464) neither of whom believes Agamemnon's new motives but both of whom believe that Iphigenia's heroism lies in her self-sacrificing acceptance of Agamemnon's account of the matter. Cf. the similar view of Rivier, 82.

Aeschylus' *Agamemnon*, or like Pelasgus in Aeschylus' *Suppliants*, on the horns of a terrible dilemma, surely he would not have emphasized so exclusively his personal fears and ambitions, shabbier motives than those which now appear.

On the other hand, despite the mixed motives allowed the King (see 1264 ff. and 1271 ff.) the dramatist gives no clue, in the present speech, that we are to regard Agamemnon as playing a hypocrite's part; indeed, had he done so, he would have weakened the effect of the speech not only on Iphigenia but also on us, the audience. In this thought, surely, lies the answer to our problem. Iphigenia must be supplied with a worthy motive for her own heroic decision later on. If it should be made too clear that she has been, in any sense, duped into accepting her sacrifice heroically, we would respect her and her decision the less, and that would be fatal to the finale of the play. As for Agamemnon, we have made up our minds about him before this scene begins: as a character, he has already served his purpose in the play. Thus Euripides calmly changes his perspective, even though, from a dramatic point of view, this may not be a good thing to do. Agamemnon is now to be considered simply as the voice of authority informing Iphigenia of a noble cause in which she is called upon to join her fellow Greeks:

A certain passion maddens the Hellenic host to sail with all speed against the barbarians' land, and put an end to rape of Grecian wives. (1264–66)

The propriety, both dramatic and psychological, of Iphigenia's celebrated change of heart at the end of the play has been hotly debated since Aristotle first objected to this alleged inconsistency in her characterization.[22] As the Greek soldiers are hurrying to drag her off by force, and as Achilles is bracing himself to protect her, Iphigenia suddenly announces (1368 ff.) her readiness to die for her fellow Greeks. Her motives have been variously explained but surely we are expected to take at face value her own avowal:

Listen, mother, to what has occurred to me as I pondered these matters. I have decided to die: this is what I want to do, to act in a manner worthy of renown, putting aside all ignobility. Now, look at the matter with me mother, see how well I argue it: the whole country, mightiest Greece, now looks to me . . . (1374–78)
[Here Iphigenia enumerates all the good that she believes her sacrifice will make possible: victory and vengeance for the Greeks and the future happiness of Greek homes, freed from barbarian outrage; and it is here and in

[22]Aristotle, *Poetics* XV. 1454a 31 ff. Since nearly all the critics have joined battle on this issue, it seems pointless to attempt a survey of divergent views.

the following lines that the anticipatory irony noted at vv. 568–72, on man's and woman's virtue, finds its clearest fulfilment.] Sacrifice me, sack Troy. This will be my memorial throughout the ages, this, my children, my marriage, and my enduring glory. (1398–99)

We must grant, of course, that Iphigenia undergoes a major change of attitude with remarkable speed: indeed the poet obviously intended this effect, for he does not even allow Iphigenia to leave the stage between her bitter monody (1279 ff.) lamenting her fate, and her present heroic acceptance of it. Nevertheless, the most striking feature of Iphigenia's martyrdom is that in it she exhibits precisely the same characteristics, generous affection and abounding vitality (extending even to a ban on mourning, 1438 ff., and on self-pity, 1447) as she has shown us earlier in her unheroic appearances. It is this, perhaps, which saves Iphigenia's scenes from being merely episodic, and her characterization from complete inconsistency. For in her most attractive qualities, Iphigenia runs true to form: never was there a more vibrant, cheerful and affectionate martyr! It is only the heroic mould which, owing to circumstances and, one must admit, the dramatist's requirements, she acquires with such surprising speed.

Is it just, then, to say as Kitto does[23] that there is no significance, beyond the thrill of a purely theatrical reversal, in Iphigenia's decision? To Clytemnestra, Iphigenia says:

It is not right that I be too much in love with life: for you bore me as a gift for all the Greeks, not for yourself alone. (1385–86)

". . . and not for *myself* alone," she might have added, for this has been her earlier view of her life. What had happened to Iphigenia, as she ponders her father's descriptions of the noble purpose of this war, is a new awareness that her life may have some meaning and value beyond her own immediate enjoyment of it.

If Euripides were here concerned with a properly "tragic" heroine, one whose fatal decision we should expect to arise from some fatal seam already observed in her character, then we might justly complain that the new "heroic" Iphigenia contrasts too sharply with the lovable child, at first thoughtless and carefree, and then aghast at her unexpected danger, whom we have seen before. However, what we have here is not "tragic characterization" but a somewhat theatrical presentation of generous,

[23]Kitto, 369–70; cf. his similar comment on Iphigenia's fate in the play: "What happened to Pelasgus [in Aeschylus *Suppliants*] is filled with significance; what happened to Iphigeneia remains what happened to Iphigeneia. We are no wiser . . ." (368)

almost naïve, heroism contrasted with the various types of adult selfishness with which the rest of the play abounds.

But what of the cause for which all this heroism is expended? If, as we have earlier been led to believe, this war is ignoble, or futile, or both, does this fact detract from Iphigenia's glory? Critics who raise this question usually argue that Iphigenia's motives and decision are to be praised for themselves, whether or not they spring from a true evaluation of the war.[24] This seems to be what Euripides would have us accept; the relation of virtue to knowledge is, perhaps, a matter for philosophers rather than for martyrs. Nevertheless, this is one of the least satisfactory features of the play, for, as we have seen, its treatment involves a certain inconsistency at least in dramatic perspective. The "selfish" characterization of Agamemnon, itself one of the necessary effects of the play, requires that the war be viewed as a sordid affair of personal ambition and personal desire; now the "noble" characterization of Iphigenia requires that this earlier picture should be, if not erased, at least withdrawn, so as not to spoil the effect of Iphigenia's sacrifice. Withdrawn and, perhaps, replaced: in presenting Iphigenia with a noble motive, the dramatist leaves us with the uncomfortable impression that we, too, are now to believe in this war, which now conforms to the type of all "just" wars. Thus Euripides acquires, at the same time, a stirring trumpet-call for his finale. "Defence of freedom . . . of the home . . . of the Greek way of life . . ." so eloquently do Agamemnon and Iphigenia plead this theme, so enthusiastically does the Chorus develop it, that the spectators too, once more aware in their own day of the threat from barbarians across the sea,[25] must surely have responded to it.

[24]See references to Bonnard, Pohlenz and Rivier above, n. 21.

[25]The *I.A.* was produced posthumously, at the court of Archelaus of Macedon in 406 or 405 (together with the *Bacchae* and *Alcmaeon at Corinth*). Pohlenz (466–67) argues that, since the emphasis at the end of the *I.A.* on the security and freedom of Greece can hardly be explained by the Trojan War situation, its true significance is to be found in the contemporary situation where, in the declining years of Euripides' life, there was a real danger that the Persians were again beginning to play a decisive role in Greek affairs. (Cf. also Grégoire, 100–6.) It was, Pohlenz thinks, particularly relevant that the panhellenic feeling should be expressed in the court of Archelaus, the Macedonian King, who "wanted to be Greek."

PART SIX

ROMANTIC TRAGEDY

15

THE *Ion*

Technical Virtuosity

The varied aesthetic delights of the *Ion* distract attention (as they are meant to do) from certain teasing puzzles in its interpretation.[1] When we come to examine the latter, we must never lose sight of the dominant characteristics of the piece: the structural virtuosity of the sustained recognition theme and the various reversals, each packed with theatrical excitement, which contribute to it; the deft and pathetic (though never tragic) characterizations of its leading figures, Ion and Creusa; and above all the pervasive irony which plays over the whole. It is such effects as these which determine the tone of the play and which should also determine our attitude toward it. If we forget them in too solemn a discussion of its meaning, we may ourselves become victims of that irony which, at one time or another, makes sport of so many of its characters and, perhaps, of that prophetic god whom we might suppose, from the prologue, to be in charge of their erratic destinies.

Whatever problems the *Ion* may provide, the problem of structure is not one of them. As Kitto has well observed of Euripides in connection with the plots, character drawing and dramatic relevance of his tragicomedies, ". . . the dramatist who has been accused of utter helplessness suddenly becomes a model of virtuosity."[2] In this play we have not merely a reversal in conjunction with a recognition scene, but a whole

[1]Of the various works consulted in this connection, the following have been found most useful or, in some cases, most provocative: Murray, *Euripides and his Age*, 118–24; Norwood, *Greek Tragedy*, 236–43; Grube, chap. 9; Kitto, chap. 11; Rivier, *Essai*, 123–29; Delebecque, *Euripide*, chap. 10; Solmsen, "Euripides' *Ion* im Vergleich mit anderen Tragödien," *Hermes*, LXIX, 390–419; Wassermann, "Divine Violence and Providence in Euripides' *Ion*," *TAPA*, LXXI, 587–604; the editions of the *Ion* by Wilamowitz, Verrall, Owen, Parmentier and Grégoire, all of which are listed in the bibliography.

[2]Kitto, 312–13.

series of reversals, both real and ironic, to accompany a variety of "recognitions" unconscious, illusory and, ultimately, real. In the first half of the play, both the external and the psychological "facts" of Ion's encounter with Creusa are reversed in his encounter with Xuthus. Between Ion and Creusa there is a natural sympathy, a kind of unconscious recognition of their real but unknown relationship; between Ion and Xuthus there is constraint on the one hand and clumsiness on the other in the false recognition which the oracle has thrust upon them. In the second half of the play the situation in which Creusa attempts to slay Ion, not knowing he is her son, is immediately reversed by the situation in which Ion attempts to slay Creusa, not knowing she is his mother. Nor are these two sets of reversals kept in their separate compartments: nowhere in Euripides are both the causal and the ironic relations more tightly drawn between the dramatic expectations set up in the first half of the play and their fulfilment in the second half. Creusa's all-important decisions to reveal her secret and to take vengeance upon Xuthus and Apollo by murdering Ion are the direct result of the first "revelation" (by the oracle) and of Xuthus' false recognition of Ion; furthermore, the second encounter between Ion and Creusa (itself the reversal of Creusa's prior attempt on Ion's life) provides an exact contrast in tone and language to the unconscious affinity so clearly expressed in their earlier exchanges. Finally, all of these misconceptions, plots and counterplots are resolved in the single recognition scene which is the climax of the play.[3]

The peculiar structure of the *Ion* is admirably suited to the full exploitation of its ironic possibilities, for it enables the same ironic situation to be played up in a variety of different ways. Indeed, so fundamental to the theme and plot is this ironic play between the real and imagined situations that, in this drama, the irony becomes almost an end in itself and not (as in more serious drama) a means to an end,

[3]On this aspect of the resolution of the *Ion*, cf. Solmsen's comparison of it with other Euripidean plays in which the recognition theme plays a part (Solmsen, 390–406). In all four of these "recognition" plays (*Electra, I.T., Helen, Ion*) Solmsen describes two plot complexes, *anagnôrisis* and *mêchanêma* (a crafty intrigue, usually designed for some personal end, such as escape or vengeance), as the major constituent elements. In the other three plays the two elements are kept in separate parts, the recognition theme being worked out before the *mêchanêma* begins; in the *Ion*, on the other hand, the *mêchanêma* is a stage on the way to the eventual recognition and is subordinated to it. This is undoubtedly one of the features which contribute to the satisfying unity of the *Ion*. (Solmsen's inferences from this and similar comparisons concerning the date of the *Ion* will be considered later.)

a way of heightening the tragic climax which gives final expression to its meaning.

Is this technical brilliance in plot structure and the use of irony all that we should look for in the *Ion*? Before drawing our own conclusions about its tone and purpose, other more "serious" interpretations of its meaning must be considered. And as soon as we begin to look for anything more than theatrical meaning in the *Ion*,[4] certain puzzling contradictions begin to appear.

The Paradox of the *Ion*

The chief paradox of the *Ion* lies in the contrasting effect of its "national-dynastic" theme and of its treatment of Apollo, the deity supposedly presiding over its fulfilment. On the one hand, if we consider the parentage and destiny of Ion, born of Apollo's union with the Athenian princess Creusa and destined to become the eponymous ancestor of all the Ionian race, we have a tale which reflects great glory on the Athenians. This, taken in conjunction with the constant references, mythological and topographical, to things Athenian, and with the (on the whole) sympathetic treatment of Creusa, championed by an Athenian chorus, has led several critics to regard the play as having a predominantly propagandist appeal glorifying the position of Athens as the natural leader of the Greeks. On the other hand, if we consider the divine source of much of this Athenian glory, we find a most inadequate god: shifty, devious and bungling, the Apollo of this play lacks even the foresight (a conspicuous lack in the god of prophecy) required to plan successfully his own solution of the Ion problem. Indeed, it is only through the unforeseen human element that the divine parentage of Ion (and with it all the *kudos* which it brings to the Athenians) becomes common knowledge at all, and Apollo (who had meant to keep his paternity a secret) is forced, in order to prevent matricidal bloodshed, to let the truth appear. The propagandist fanfare of Athena's further dynastic prophecies does much to mitigate this effect, but even here we are reminded of the shabbier aspect of Apollo who (as Athena tells us) ". . . has thought it best not to appear before you, lest any blame for what has passed should be made manifest." (1557–58)[5]

[4]Cf. Kitto, 318, "The plays [those previously described as tragicomedies] are a constant appeal to our intellect, but in order that we may appreciate the intrigue, the wit, the irony, not in order that we may grasp a thesis."

[5]As Owen notes, *ad loc.*, Athena "is adroit in letting it be ambiguous where the blame falls." (The Loeb translation of line 1558 is surely wrong: "Else must he chide you for things overpast." 1558 OCT is 1557 Loeb ed.)

This simplification of the paradox of the *Ion* contains perhaps some bold statements about the play as a whole, and none of these would pass unchallenged by one or another of its commentators. Indeed, the two aspects of this paradox (which has not generally been recognized as such) have tended to divide the play's critics into two more or less opposed camps, so that one aspect has frequently been stressed to the detriment, and sometimes to the exclusion, of the other.

The Myth and Its Adaptation

Critics emphasizing the political and propagandist aspects of the *Ion* find considerable support in the background of the myth itself and in the particular adaptation of it which Euripides has chosen to develop. As Grégoire has remarked, Ion and Xuthus were strangers to the ancient Ionian tradition; they were "created" for specific political purposes by the genealogizing epic of the seventh century, Xuthus being inserted into the Hesiodic catalogue to mark the affinity between Ionians and Achaeans, while the function of Ion was chiefly to associate the Ionian patronym with the state of Athens.[6]

The first reference to Xuthus occurs in Hesiod[7] where he is described, along with Dorus and Aeolus, as a son of Hellen. In Herodotus the Ionians are twice said to have taken their name from "Ion, son of Xuthus," and in the second of these passages the reason is added that Ion had served as *stratarchos* for the Athenians.[8] In another Herodotean passage there is a reference to the tradition that the four Athenian tribes took their names from the sons of Ion.[9]

A full account of the relations of Ion and Xuthus with Athens is given by Pausanias.[10] According to this account Xuthus, when driven out of Thessaly by his brothers Aeolus and Dorus, fled to Athens where

[6]See Grégoire, 155–56. In addition to the ancient sources cited, the present summary discussion of the Ion myth makes considerable use of the introductory material in Grégoire, 155–65, in Wilamowitz, 1–11, and in Owen, ix–xvii.

[7]Hesiod, frg. 7 (Rzach). Lines 3–5 of the same fragment name the sons of Aeolus, and it is thought (e.g., Grégoire 155, Owen x) that the sons of Xuthus, including Ion, were probably also given in the missing part of the passage.

[8]Herodotus 7. 95. 1, 8. 44. 2. Owen (x) in citing these passages also notes that the word Ξουθίδαι is explained by Hesychius as *οἱ Ἴωνες. Ἴων γὰρ Ξούθου* (cf. Herondas, *ἐνύπνιον*, 79), and that in Aristotle (*Resp. Ath.* 3) Ion is named as the first *πολέμαρχος*, "summoned to the help of Athens because of the unwarlike quality of her kings."

[9]Herodotus 5. 66. 2.

[10]Pausanias 7. 1. 2–5.

he married a daughter of Erechtheus and by her begat two sons, Ion and Achaeus. Xuthus was later driven out of Attica and settled in Aegialos on the north coast of the Peloponnese. Later Ion (who had in the meantime become king of the "Aegialian Ionians") was called on for help by the Athenians, who made him their leader in a struggle against the Eleusinians.

There is no definite evidence that Apollo rather than Xuthus was regarded as the father of Ion before Euripides wrote his play; however, there are several considerations which render it unlikely that the divine parentage of Ion was a Euripidean invention. So fundamental an innovation was not typical among the tragic adaptors of myth, not even of those of Euripides (perhaps the boldest of his brethren in these matters);[11] moreover, it seems probable that Sophocles' (lost) *Creusa*, also referred to in ancient times as the *Ion*, treated the story of Ion's supernatural birth.[12] Finally, the cult of Apollo *patrôlos* appears to have been established at Athens long before this time (originally, perhaps, as Jacoby thinks, by Solon) and, in this connection, the Apolline parentage of Ion is referred to as an established tradition by the Platonic Socrates; Wilamowitz and Grégoire are doubtless right in believing the cult to be of pre-tragic origin.[13]

[11]The more typical Euripidean adaptations of myth usually involved changes in emphasis to suit his theme or the interweaving of different mythical traditions (as in the *Andromache*) or the development of little known local legends by attaching them (as in the *Hecuba*) to myths already well established in the literary tradition.

[12]So most commentators; see, for example, Welcker, I, 391 ff., Pearson, *Sophocles, Fragments*, II, 23–24. Georges Dalmeyda, (*REG*, XXVII, 43–50) has suggested that the scene of Sophocles' play may have been Athens; but the indications which he finds in Euripides' *Ion* that the Delphic setting is an innovation in it are by no means convincing. (See also, in rebuttal to Dalmeyda's argument, Th. Colardeau, *REG*, XXIX, 430–34.)

The identification of Sophocles' *Ion* with his *Creusa* is generally accepted (see, for example, Pearson, *op. cit.* 23 and frgs. 319, 320), though there has been some disagreement (see, for example, Wilamowitz, *Ion*, 11). Apart from the fact that (as Grégoire has pointed out, 163) it would be difficult to imagine the plot of this play without the Apollo motif, some of the fragments themselves could well fit a tale of secret birth. Most suggestive in this connection is fragment 352, which refers to circumstances in which deception is pardonable, and fragment 357, ἄπελθ', ἄπελθε, παῖ· τάδ' οὐκ ἀκουστά σοι. The latter fragment might be referred to Xuthus' contemplated revelation of his ancient escapade (Welcker) or "equally well" (Pearson) to Creusa's distress when forced to reveal her story. However, these are matters of conjecture, as indeed are Welcker's interpretations of several other fragments by analogy with Euripides' *Ion*.

[13]See Plato, *Euthydemus* 302D; Socrates, accused of not being a true Athenian because he has denied that Zeus is his πατρῷος replies that not Zeus but Apollo

The appearance of Apollo as father of Ion fits naturally enough into the Athenian development of the myth, and with its purpose of strengthening Athens' claims to Hellenic leadership. Athens had her own myth of autochthonous origins; how much more satisfactory then if the two myths could be conveniently reconciled, if by one stroke the foreign part of Ion's parentage and the human adulteration of the autochthonous Athenian stock could both be excised from the mythical tradition.

It seems likely, then, that in writing a play which brought the father of the Ionians so exclusively within the Athenian orbit, Euripides was developing in more definite form a legend which was already current in Attica. Wilamowitz has well expressed the probabilities of the matter:

Thus Euripides has taken over no definite myth but rather something which was related and believed not only because it served the imperial tendency to make Athens the mother state of the other cities of the empire, but also because it fitted in with the [existence of] the oldest shrine of Apollo in a grotto of the northern rocks of the city.[14]

Apart from various details of plot and characterization, this critic rightly regards the emphasis on the new life, through Ion, for the seed of Erechtheus (see especially *Ion* 1463–67), as Euripides' most important contribution to the myth. In Athena's prophecies (1581 ff.) concerning the sons of Ion's sons, themselves to be founders of the four Athenian tribes, we find a patriotic extension of the tradition already cited from Herodotus:

And the sons of Ion's sons shall, in the fulness of the allotted time, found island cities in the Cyclades and mainland towns along the coast, to be a strength unto my land. The plains along the straits as well, on Asia's as on Europe's side, they are to colonize. And for this boy's name, Ionians they shall be called and win renown. (1581–88)

The other major Euripidean innovation concerns the genealogy of Xuthus: Athena in the epilogue (1589 ff.) prophesies that two sons Dorus and Achaeus will be born to Xuthus and Creusa, while according to the Hesiodic genealogy Dorus and Xuthus (as well as Aeolus) are brothers, all sons of Hellen.[15] The obvious propagandist advantage of

---

is πατρῷος for the Athenians διὰ τὴν τοῦ Ἴωνος γένεσιν. See also Wilamowitz 2 ff., Grégoire 160. For discussion of the origins of the Apollo *patrôios* cult, see F. Jacoby, *Atthis*, 40, 272 (n. 226), 393 (n. 20) and *CQ*, XXXVIII, 65–75; cf. also John P. Barron, *JHS*, LXXXIV, 35–48.

[14]Wilamowitz, *Ion*, 9 (my translation).

[15]Hesiod, frg. 7 (Rzach).

this is that the founders of the Dorian and Achaean races now appear as Athenian born and sharing, through Creusa, in the autochthonous Athenian stock. Xuthus himself is described in the *Ion* (63–64) as "the son of Aeolus, son of Zeus." This change is presumably made in anticipation of the other more important one; for if Hellen were given as Xuthus' father, Euripides' audience might also remember that Xuthus should be Dorus' brother, and not his father by Creusa, as the dramatist's propagandist change requires.[16]

Considerations for Dating

This at least potentially propagandist material in the *Ion* makes its date a matter of greater interest in the play's interpretation than is often the case in Euripidean drama. Scholars looking for a suitable international context for the play tend to place it between the Peace of Nicias (421) and the Sicilian expedition (415); for Athens, during the earlier part of this period particularly, was in a relatively optimistic mood concerning her imperial position and was ready to pursue a fairly vigorous policy in order to maintain and, if possible, improve it. A peculiar description of Achaea as "the coastal land near Rhium" has led several critics to settle specifically on the year 418 as the probable date of the play's production, for they believe this emphasis on Rhium to have been prompted by Alcibiades' activities in that area in the preceding year.[17]

While political and historical considerations tend to place the *Ion* in the "middle period" of Euripidean drama, or at least in the latter part of it, certain arguments based on form, style, and *genre* tend to favour a somewhat later date.[18] Owen has successfully rebutted the formal and

[16]Euripides himself describes Aeolus as son of Hellen in frg. 14 (*Aeolus*) and (possibly) in the *Melanippe sapiens*. See Nauck, *Euripidis Tragoediae* III², 4 and 129.

[17]See Grégoire 167–68, Owen xxxix–xli, and Thucydides 5. 52. Delebecque (chap. 10) agrees with Grégoire's account and seeks to reinforce it by other historical parallels to the action and details of the play. His chief additional arguments concern the building of the Erechtheum (227–28), which he believes to have been begun at about this time, and the renewed opportunity after the Peace of Nicias for the Athenians to visit Delphi. (237–38)

A good bibliographical summary of various arguments for the date of the *Ion* is to be found in Solmsen, 390, note 1.

[18]Wilamowitz' changes of mind about the date of the *Ion* underline this double aspect of the problem. Originally (*Analecta Euripidea*, 173, 178–79) he placed the *Ion* between 420 and 416. While admitting that in its external form it is like the later plays, he nevertheless grouped it with the "Attic" and historical tragedies in which, he maintained, Euripides, like Aeschylus, used myth to counsel and

stylistic arguments advanced for a late date (such as 412 or 411) for the *Ion* and concludes that on these grounds, as well as on political grounds, the play may be regarded as "coming somewhere midway among Euripides' extant plays."[19] Arguments for the date of the play which are based on *genre* and "tone" and on the type of plot material and plot construction used in it are, though interesting in themselves, more difficult to evaluate. Judged in these terms, the *Ion* appears to have a good deal in common with the later kind of Euripidean play variously described as "romantic," "melodramatic" and "tragicomic."[20] Here we must turn again for a moment to Solmsen's comparison of the *Ion* with the *Electra*, the *Iphigenia Taurica* and the *Helen*. There we found that the plot structure of all of these plays had much in common in their concentration on the devices of *anagnôrisis* and *mêchanêma*, but that the *Ion* was the most successful dramatically, mainly because the "recognition-complex" and the various psychological subtleties which form a part of it were allowed to predominate.[21] This observation leads Solmsen to the further inference that the *Ion* exhibits a more mature, and so a later, technique than that of the other plays concerned. This is, however, by no means a certain inference, since (apart from the fallacy of "the later, the better") matters of plot structure must surely be largely determined by the kind of dramatic point with which the dramatist is concerned in any given play. It is clear that in the *Ion* the ultimate identification of the boy must be the point to which the whole dramatic action will lead. This obviously cannot be the case in the *Electra* where (on Solmsen's own demonstration) the recognition is itself a part of the means to the main end of revenge. Similarly it seems wrong to argue that the *Helen* is earlier than the other recognition plays because it lacks the varied and subtle ironies connected with the suspense

advise the Athenians on current affairs. Again, in "Die beiden *Elektren*," *Hermes*, 18 (1883), 242, note 1, Wilamowitz argued (partly on the basis of its alleged hasty construction) that the play might be a few years earlier than Sophocles' *Electra*. Later, influenced by the arguments of W. Kranz, *De forma stasimi* (diss. Berlin 1904) 43. 1, Wilamowitz placed the play between 415 and 412. (*Ion, Einleitung*, 24). He agrees with Enthoven's arguments (L. Enthoven, *De Ione Euripideo* [diss. Bonn 1880]) against every date before 415 but does not agree with him that the play should be placed with the *Helen* in 412.

[19] Owen, xxxvi–xxxix.

[20] We will return later to purely literary-critical discussions of the *Ion* as tragicomedy; here we are concerned only with this feature insofar as it may be used in arguments concerning the date of the play.

[21] Cf. *supra*, note 3, and Solmsen (390–406, especially 400–6. For Solmsen's inferences, now to be considered, about the comparative dates of the plays concerned, see *ibid.*, 406 ff.

of postponed recognition as well as the careful attention to probability in the recognition itself.[22] These ingredients, admirable as they are in the plays to which they belong, are not needed for the kind of dramatic point which the *Helen* seeks to make. Indeed they would be out of place there because a high degree of improbability is needed for its light-hearted and witty parody of myth.

Thus, while the plot structure and *genre* of the *Ion* do make us think of the later Euripidean plays such as the *Helen* (412) and the *Iphigenia Taurica* (411–409?) (recognition themes aside, the *Ion* is really not a bit like the *Electra*), there is really no reason that it should not have been written at least a few years before them. The political or propagandist aspect of the play, whether serious or ironical, would certainly best suit the years following the Peace of Nicias; and while this aspect may not be the most important one, it at least makes it difficult to consider a production date as late as 413 (the Sicilian disaster) or 412 (the Ionian revolt) when the idea of the Hellenic leadership of Athens could be little more than a tasteless mockery.[23] Finally, considerations of *genre* (a matter of which we are much more conscious than were the Greeks) can never serve as more than a general indication (if that) as to a play's date. If such considerations are pressed too closely in arguments for a late date for the *Ion*, one can always counter that this play has, as a tragicomedy, more in common with a play as early as the *Alcestis* than with a play as late as the *Bacchae*.

The Paradox Resolved

The aim [of the play] is not to prove anything at all, but to dramatize.[24]

. . . The first purpose of the dramatist in writing these plays [the *Ion* and the *Iphigenia in Tauris*] was to create an effective stage-piece; to exploit the resources of his art for its own sake, not for the sake of something bigger.[25]

. . . L'intérêt patriotique ne saurait motiver la composition du drame qui cherche à peindre des sentiments humains.[26]

---

[22]Cf. *ibid.*, 392–94.

[23]Cf. again the arguments of Grégoire, Owen, and Delebecque, referred to above, note 17, and Wilamowitz, *Hermes* 18 (1883), 242, n. 1. The events of 418 (battle of Mantinea) and, with more point, 413 (Spartan occupation of Decelea) are also referred to by Grégoire and Owen respectively as ones which could hardly have taken place when the *Ion* was produced.

[24]Grube, 279.

[25]Kitto, 315.

[26]Rivier, 124, note 3.

Any reader who has enjoyed the *Ion* must feel instinctively that these critics are right, at least in principle, in their appraisal of what is most important in the play.[27] Nevertheless, such appraisals tend to ignore, or at least to play down, certain paradoxical effects and certain contrasting elements in the plot material which are, for better or worse, all "part of the play." After our examination of the background material of the Ion myth, of Euripides' particular adaptation of it and of the historical circumstances in which, in all probability, it seems to have been produced, we must admit that there is at least one aspect of the play which is political and even nationalistic. In examining the political elements, we must decide not only whether they are subordinate to the dramatic ones, but also whether they combine or conflict with them, and particularly whether they can be reconciled with the incidental theological satire which most of the more literary critics find to be one of the play's comic effects.

Critics who favour a political approach to the interpretation of Euripides treat the *Ion* mainly as a piece of nationalistic propaganda. Thus Grégoire, who dwells at length on the various "pro-Athenian" passages of the kind which we have mentioned, extends this preoccupation to features of the plot as well. Creusa's scheming against the life of Ion, and indeed the whole intrigue concerning the false and true identification of his parents, are all explained in political rather than in dramatic terms: the necessity of insisting on, and defending *à l'outrance*, the autochthonous seed of Erechtheus against a (supposed) threat of foreign contamination.[28] In a similar vein, Delebecque (whose chapter on the *Ion* reinforces and exaggerates the political emphasis of Grégoire's study) describes the poet of the *Ion* as "l'interprête d'une véritable doctrine du racisme ionien" and the purpose of the play, like that of building the Erechtheum, as the consecration of successful imperialistic policy.[29] Thus to an even greater degree Delebecque emphasizes those

27". . . in principle," i.e., in their insistence on dramatic as opposed to political and propagandist interests. "Dramatic" interests may be said to include such matters as plot structure, characterization and treatment of *individual* feelings and fortunes; within this broad area there is still room for different emphases. Thus one finds that Rivier emphasizes the theme of mother-love, Kitto the virtuosity of plot technique, almost to the exclusion of other elements in the play.

28See Grégoire 170–74, esp. 172–73. The political bias of Grégoire's approach reappears later in his analysis, *ibid.*, 176: ". . . le sentiment patriotique est la principale excuse d'une péripetie qu'Euripide n'aurait pas osée dans une pure tragi-comédie d'intrigue."

29See Delebecque 231 and 228 respectively and the general tenor of his comments throughout chap. 10.

features of the plot which seem to him to have political significance, and in so doing he distracts attention from various dramatic and structural excellences of the piece.

Questions concerning the ultimate purpose of any given play are always difficult to answer since identical passages interpreted in accordance with the *parti pris* of the individual critic are often used to "prove" opposite conclusions.[30] Once we admit the political aspect of the *Ion*, its interpretation largely revolves around the question of the relative importance of this aspect. Now we have already suggested that there is one element in the play—the treatment of Apollo—which gives the impression of conflicting with, or even detracting from, the allegedly propagandist element. If this suggestion is found to be sound and if, moreover, the treatment of Apollo should be found congenial with the purely dramatic aspects of the play, then we will have at least an indication of the relative importance of the propagandist element. In this connection it is interesting to note that the "political" critics strenuously resist any idea of a satirical or unflattering picture of Apollo in the *Ion*. In Grégoire's study all thought of possible criticism of Apollo or of Delphi is swept aside because of the play's satisfactory conclusion from the point of view of patriotic Athenian feeling.[31] Likewise Delebecque, after summarizing various passages both "for" and "against" Apollo and Delphi, concludes that Apollo, despite a certain initial irresponsibility, is finally absolved since he has repaired his faults.[32]

At the other extreme from this approach are the views of the "rationalists" such as Verrall, Murray and Norwood, who regard the play as a satire on such myths of divine descent and on the kind of gods which such mythology can countenance.[33] The thorough-going rationalism of Verrall's view has already been refuted at various points by different scholars;[34] the most convincing argument against it is that it

[30]Contrast, for example, Grégoire's view of the political motivation of the peripety (above, note 28) with that of Rivier (124), who strenuously denies the political motivation of Creusa's attempt on Ion's life.

[31]Grégoire 178: "Jamais la critique des dieux n'a été moins dangereuse que dans cette pièce . . . les dieux mènent à bien, fort habilement [!] une affaire dont la complication dépasse l'intelligence humaine . . ."

[32]See Delebecque, 234–36.

[33]See Verrall, *Ion*, xi–xlv (cf. also Verrall, *Euripides the Rationalist*, 129–65, esp. 138 ff.); Murray 118–24; Norwood, *G.T.*, 238–40. Contrast Murray's comment, "The *Ion* is, of all the extant plays, the most definitely blasphemous against the traditional gods," with the view already quoted from Grégoire (above, note 31).

[34]See, for example, Wilamowitz, *Ion*, 18–19; Grube 278, note 3; Owen xxxii–xxxvi and notes to verses 1424–36.

spoils almost every dramatic effect in the play. If (to take one of Owen's best examples) Ion is not the son of Apollo and Creusa but, as Verrall argues, the product of some premarital amour of Xuthus, then all the ironic play on the mother-son relationship throughout the piece is ruined. Similarly the whole point of Apollo's plan miscarrying is lost if there is no plan of Apollo. As Grube has remarked, Verrall creates rather than disposes of difficulties by seeking to dispense with the divine element in the *Ion.* The less extreme view of Murray, who regards the play as an attack on the gods of traditional mythology without finding it necessary to expel them from the action, provides a more reasonable corrective to the defences of Apollo found among the political commentators on the play. Norwood, too, though he approves of Verrall's rationalistic account of the birth of Ion, at least shows more awareness of the spiritual quality of Ion's belief and disillusionment:

> The god who gives oracles to Greece is a trickster, and no celestial consolations or Athenian throne can compensate the youth Ion for the loss of what has filled his heart only this morning.[35]

Several other views of the meaning of the *Ion* fall between these two extremes while still revolving around the "nationalistic" and the "anti-Apollo" themes which we have already indicated. A few critics give clear statements of both themes while ignoring or minimizing the element of contradiction involved in their combination. Thus Wilamowitz regards the whole of this version of the Ion legend, including Euripides' original contribution to it, as having a distinctly imperialistic tendency and purpose; on the other hand he is equally emphatic that the play has a polemic purpose against Apollo and his oracle.[36] Owen, too, finds both Athenian propaganda and some criticism of Apollo in this play; the latter, however, he plays down as quite secondary to the play's main object as he describes it: ". . . to give reasons for the Athenian empire to hold together . . ."[37] However, Owen's attempts to mitigate the anti-

[35]Norwood, 238.

[36]See Wilamowitz, *Ion*, 1–9 (particularly 3 and 9) and 13–14 respectively. Wilamowitz' view of the attack on Apollo differs radically from the rationalistic approach of Verrall. He stresses particularly the faults of Apollo, and among these it is the god's inability to carry through his original plan that he rightly regards as being the most injurious to his reputation.

[37]Owen, xxi–xxii; cf. also xi–xii, where Owen dwells on the patriotic Athenian purpose behind this version of the myth, and xxxiii–xxxiv, where he suggests that the view of the play held by Verrall and H. B. L. (who emphasize the mythological satire) "underlines the rationalism of Euripides at the expense of his patriotism and his ability as a playwright."

Apollo impression conveyed by certain passages in the play are not entirely satisfactory.[38]

Of the various "political" critics of the *Ion*, Wassermann has perhaps posed the "Apollo problem" most bluntly. Describing recognition of Apollo as Ion's father as the main political purpose of the play, he asks:

Would it not be a strange procedure if Euripides had represented this divine father as a doubtful character, descent from whom would be much more of a disgrace than descent from a brave human hero?[39]

Wassermann's attempt at "a more positive evaluation" depends mainly on the arguments that Apollo is not actually guilty of the worst crimes of which he is suspected, and that the glorious political end to which his activities are directed justifies whatever may, when judged by human standards, appear harsh and violent in the process:

The god, representing the permanent forces of a far-sighted providence, while not concerned with temporary human sufferings and doubts (cf. 1615), has only his final objective in mind, the future political mission of Ion and his race.[40]

These arguments, which cannot be disproved, provide the most obvious line of the defence of Apollo; it is in effect the "official defence" which Athena gives in the epilogue, for Euripides knew that his tragi-comedy, particularly in view of the patriotic motif just discussed, could not be brought to a successful conclusion without it. Of course the Apollo of this play is "defended," and the most critical attacks on the god (such as Creusa's, for the abandonment of herself and her child) are ultimately answered. Nevertheless, shadowing the golden Apollo of Creusa's glorious "mythological" picture and the (politically) all-provident one of Athena's epilogue is the background impression of a rather furtive, shabby and inefficient god, which leaves its mark even when the official defence has rested.

It was Apollo's wish (so Hermes tells us in the prologue) that Creusa suffer her birth-travail in secret from her father (ἀγνὼς δὲ πατρί—τῷ θεῷ

[38]There is, for example, little point in saying that Euripides "is less bitter against Delphi here than in the *Electra*" (*ibid.*, xxxiv), or that the oracle has "come off better (here) than either in the *Electra* . . . or in the *Iphigenia* [*Taurica*]" (*ibid.*, xxi) when the plot material of the plays concerned is so different.

[39]Wassermann, 588; for the rest of the argument here summarized, see *ibid.*, 587–604.

[40]*Ibid.*, 590. Cf. Grube 277, whose arguments on this point closely parallel those of Wassermann save that, just as Grube has not overemphasized the patriotic theme of the *Ion*, so his defence of the Apollo of this play (277, cf. 264–65) does not need to be so heavy-handed and unqualified.

γὰρ ἦν φίλον, 14); so, too, the devious method of Ion's return to Athens is planned so that Apollo's mating may still be kept hidden. (72–73) Apollo's secrecy is, of course, necessary for the plot, but since there are no really valid "political" reasons for it, it gives the impression of his having something discreditable to hide—an impression which is sustained to the end by Athena's ambiguous excuse for his non-appearance in the epilogue (*μὴ τῶν πάροιθε μέμψις ἐς μέσον μόλῃ*, 1558). This furtive quality in Apollo accords ill with the dashing "Homeric" deity of Wassermann's description, who gives no thought to the conventions of human behaviour, whether those of heroic or of classical times. The pious Ion, too, with his half-incredulous astonishment that a god could act as Apollo has done,[41] unconsciously abets this insidious process of divine denigration. Finally, there is of course that most disastrous shaft against the god of prophecy's repute: the discrepancy between his own plans for Ion and the actual course of events. No amount of insistence by the critics on the "far-sighted providence" of the god or by Athena on the glorious future he has planned for Ion and his descendants[42] can ever quite erase the irony of this effect. Once again it is the poet's interest in the *plot* which, at the expense of the "patriotic theme," makes this satire possible and even necessary; for had Apollo's plan gone smoothly, the dramatic thrill of the *Ion*'s "close calls," ironies and theatrical reversals would have been lost.

This reconsideration of the position (and sometimes the plight) of Apollo in the *Ion* helps us, then, to put the political or propagandist

[41]In this connection Ion's comments (in which shocked disbelief vies with reproach against the god) concern not only Apollo's supposed abandonment of Creusa and her child but also the adulterous rape itself (339, 341, 437 ff., 1523–27) and finally the question of the god's veracity. (1537–38) Wassermann (590) excuses Apollo's violence thus: "A Greek god of this period has no ascetic inhibitions. A strong virility is just one aspect of his epiphany. Like all divine characters in Euripidean tragedy he combines primitive and advanced elements." True enough, but it was just this anthropomorphic aspect of the Homeric gods to which Euripides most violently objected (see, for example, *Hipp.* 120, *Bacch.* 1348, *I.T.* 389–91, *Heracl.* 1341–46); and in order to attack it he presents his gods in much cruder forms than do Aeschylus and Sophocles. In this case Ion's rather than Wassermann's reactions strike us as a sound indication of Euripides' views as to what the gods should be like.

[42]See Wassermann, 590, 601, and Athena's speech at *Ion* 1560–1605. The curious discrepancy between Hermes' statement (72–73) that Apollo intends to keep his paternity a secret even after Ion's return to Athens and Athena's statement (1566–67) that he had intended eventually to publish it, must be regarded as just one more of those ambiguous touches with which Euripides surrounds the Apollo of this play.

theme in its true perspective. This theme, which may have been only a sort of political trimming to the play, requires for its happy conclusion a relatively respectable Apollo as father of the Athenian father of the Ionians. This much the playwright grants it; as we have seen, the formal defence which critics have urged in Apollo's favour is (as far as it goes) impregnable. However, the fact that in the interests of plot (as well as for the sake of incidental satire) the dramatist was willing to weaken his "respectable" Apollo in the ways which we have mentioned surely indicates that the *Ion* is not, as the political critics would have it, primarily a nationalistic, propagandist play.

At the other extreme to taking the *Ion* too seriously we find Kitto's discussion of the play within his general description of Euripidean tragicomedy.[43] We must review a few salient features of this description in order to assess its application to the play. Kitto begins by distinguishing the conventions proper to tragicomedy: "One important difference is that the plot of a tragedy must appear real, but the plot of a tragi-comedy may be, and normally is, entirely artificial."[44] It is this essential difference which, according to Kitto, changes the form, tone, and effect of the tragicomedies. Once the serious basis of Greek tragedy, its contact with "real life," has been cut away, the primary purpose of the dramatist becomes simply to create an effective stage piece: "theatrical reality takes the place of universal reality." Formally this results in plays of deft and elegant construction; but since the doings and sufferings of the characters in them are fundamentally "unreal," a part of an impossible situation, they never seriously engage our emotions. The "thought-content" or meaning of the play (Aristotle's *dianoia*) is similarly affected: Kitto says of the *Ion*, for example, "Intellectual profundity is as alien to this tragi-comedy as is moral profundity."[45]

The principal results of this general "typing" of the *Ion* for Kitto's interpretation of its meaning should now be clear. We are to look for little serious meaning beyond our pleasure in its ironies and in the intricacies of its lively and adventurous plot. Consider the effect of this view on our attitude to Creusa's attempted murder of Ion: since events are no longer to be used to reveal tragic character, this event, like all the others, is to be treated purely from the point of view of its interest and theatrical excitement. Similarly, since the *Ion* by Kitto's definition of the tragicomedies can sustain no serious theme, the treatment of Apollo is dismissed as incidental satire ("an intellectual stiffening in a play

[43]Kitto, chap. 11, 312–31.
[44]*Ibid.*, 314.
[45]*Ibid.*, 317.

which is essentially one of incident and romantic colour"[46]) and the "patriotic" theme is almost completely ignored.

Kitto's general description of the ethos of tragicomedy accords well with the tone of the *Ion* and on the whole provides an excellent direction for the frame of mind in which we should approach the play. This description is, however, too consistently worked out for the material which it concerns: one feels that Kitto understands the tragicomic *genre* more thoroughly than Euripides does, a fact which is not surprising when one considers the matter historically. Thus while we find that much of the *Ion* conforms with Kitto's general description, there are moments in this play (as in others) when we find Euripides breaking Kitto's rules.

Kitto's treatment of Creusa's murder plot exemplifies both the merits and the shortcomings of his approach. His dismissal, as irrelevant, of any moral justification of the deed comes as rather a relief after certain heavy-handed discussions along these lines by other critics.[47] Such considerations are obviously uncalled for, since the dramatist himself wastes little time on them but (in accordance with Kitto's general description of his procedure) concentrates all his energies and our own on the exciting details of the plot itself. Nevertheless, the critics' worries about Creusa's moral attitudes are not entirely without justification. From what we have seen of her so far, sensitive and tactful in her dealings with Ion, full of *aidôs* in her reticence and needing the most extreme provocation (as she tells us so feelingly herself) to discard it,[48] we would *expect* Creusa to indulge in considerable self-debate before she commits herself to murder. That, instead, she is allowed simply to get on with it clearly shows us that the dramatist at this point has chosen melodrama, though he makes some attempt to disguise the change in the characterization of Creusa by means of the Chorus and of Creusa's old tutor. It is the latter who first suggests to Creusa the idea of murdering Ion; indeed, both the Old Man and the Chorus, with their theme of "Athens for the Erechthids!" show us for the first time the full force of the numerous earlier allusions to the legend of autochthonous Athenian origins. Nevertheless, as far as murderous efficiency is concerned, the roles of tutor

[46]*Ibid.*, 319.

[47]*Ibid.*, 325. Contrast with Kitto's treatment here Grégoire's (allegedly Euripidean) justification (171, cf. *ibid.*, 176) of Creusa's deed as "un acte de légitime défense patriotique" and Rivier's explanation (124) of it in terms of outraged and frustrated mother-love.

[48]Creusa's *aidôs* with regard to her encounter with Apollo is one of the means whereby the recognition scene is postponed in the most natural way. Cf. Solmsen's comment (397–98) on this and other examples of Euripides' psychological subtlety in the deployment of his recognition themes.

and pupil are soon reversed, and the Old Man finds himself, his own clumsy murder plan rejected, accepting the instructions of a far more deadly minister of vengeance. From now on, the Queen's actions, and the ironic situations in which they place her, will be all that interest us in Creusa—a far cry from the pathetic and, despite the improbable plot, potentially tragic characterization hitherto presented.[49]

There seems, then, to be a point in the non-tragic plays of Euripides when the dramatic treatment gives the impression, at least, of ambivalence. In the *Alcestis*, as we shall see, the tragic potentialities are still more prominent. Despite the basis of an "impossible" situation which doubtless indicates the *ultimate* direction of the play, the near-tragic theme attaching to Admetus' belated discoveries[50] is quite thoroughly developed in the latter portions of the play until Heracles' miraculous restoration of Alcestis finally destroys it. Kitto's description of the tone of the *Ion* provides a valuable corrective to those who have overworked its political or else its theological implications: clearly a play such as he has described exists more for the sake of its own dramatic (Kitto would say theatrical) effects than for the sake of such larger themes. Nevertheless, here again one wonders whether Kitto does not apply his own definitions too rigorously, whether in this instance the dramatist was being quite as relentlessly funny as this critic requires him to be. Of the whole mythological apparatus (which, Kitto rightly tells us, must be accepted, not "rationalized," for the sake of the play) we read:

> . . . the wit of the whole piece lies in the conspiracy which Euripides makes with the audience; the conviction that these things are false was held so widely in Athens that there is no point in pretending that they are false but great amusement in pretending that they are true.[51]

This view would reduce Euripides' purpose in treating the Ion myth to the level of a "superior" joke, rather in the spirit of those frightfully clever modern resurrections of Victorian melodrama where "the wit of the whole piece" lies in pretending to hiss the villain and to weep with the innocent heroine. Furthermore, if the wit of the whole piece depends

[49]Owen (xxvii) has compared the "unbalanced" Creusa of the second half of the play with Medea; however, there is no change such as we have noted in the case of Creusa in the *manner* in which Medea is characterized. Moreover, as both Solmsen (397–98) and Rivier (126) have indicated in their different ways, there is such a world of difference between the dramatic stature and the tragic potentialities of the two characters that any comparisons between them must be of a rather superficial kind.

[50]Cf. A. M. Dale, *Alcestis*, xxii, to be discussed later.

[51]Kitto, 320.

on this large conspiracy, then the pronouncements of Athena at the end of the play must be received with at least inward laughter. Now much as Euripides enjoyed satirizing the more pompous claims and the more ludicrous beliefs of his fellow-citizens, would he at any stage in the war have subjected to the cruelest ridicule the Athenian claim, here appearing in mythological terms, to leadership of the Ionians? Surely, rather, Euripides has selected and developed the Ion myth for the peculiar advantages which it provides for the ironies, the excitements and the reversals of a tragicomic plot, and also for whatever incidental capital he can make out of theological satire on the one hand and out of national propaganda on the other. Kitto regards the allusions to Delphic and Attic legends alike as all a part of the same sly humor; if this were really his chief intention in such allusions, then in his numerous references to the autochthonous legend alone Euripides would indeed have been running his joke into the ground. On the contrary, however, the constant references to things Athenian are most ingeniously worked into the fabric of the story; and the legend of the earth-born Erichthonius has, as we have seen, an important bearing on the xenophobic attitude of the Athenians (of Creusa and, more particularly, of the Old Man and the Chorus) which is so essential to the action of the play.[52] Both in his treatment of these matters and in his own development of the patriotic Athenian version of Ion's story, Euripides' adaptation of his mythological material has been too calculated for us to dismiss it as simply a humorous side-effect. It would be difficult without some such mythological celebration as this to do honour to contemporary Athens within the convention of fifth-century tragedy, though sometimes, it may be admitted, Euripides seems to be caught between two fires in his appreciation of the symbolic uses of myth and his satirical crusade against its literal acceptance. Thus, just as in one passage in the *Hercules Furens* Heracles is made to doubt the whole mythological convention on which his story in the play is based, so too in one passage in the *Ion* the dramatist pokes fun at the legend of autochthonous Athenian stock.[53]

If to his tragicomedy Euripides has chosen to add this political superstructure, there is surely no need for us either to reject it or to let it

[52]The *Ion* provides one of the few instances in later Greek tragedy where the Chorus, by revealing the situation to Creusa, is allowed to affect the action drastically.

[53]Cf. *H.F.* 1341–46 and *Ion* 542. The *Ion* passage concerned is not one of those ostensibly connected with the myth of Erichthonius: Ion, exasperated at his "father's" inability to tell him who his mother was, finally remarks sarcastically, "No doubt I was born of Mother Earth!" and Xuthus (not thinking) replies, "Land bears not children."

affect our enjoyment of the play. Possibly the minor propagandist strain is a little more than the stuff of the play can bear; but usually when it conflicts with the dramatist's own sense of satire or with his concern for plot and theatrical effect, it is not the play which suffers. Provided that we do not read the *Ion* too solemnly with the political critics or too "aesthetically" with the formal purists, these minor inconsistencies in tone and (rarely) in substance need not greatly bother us. The Greeks mingled serious issues with their lighter entertainments more casually than we do. Should we not, then, regard this play in the way that perhaps the Athenians did, as a brilliantly constructed *jeu d'esprit*, alternately moving and amusing and rendered no less pleasing by a mildly ironic measure of Athenian self-flattery?

16

THE *Helena*

The Myth and Its Adaptation

The presentation of Euripides' *Helena* must indeed have struck the Athenian audience as a revolutionary one. Versions of the myth which tell of Helen spending the period of the Trojan War in Egypt do not appear to have been widely circulated at the time Euripides' play appeared, and the dramatist seems to have shown his usual "magpie genius" in composing elements from diverse sources, including his own imagination, into a new whole.

The chief pre-Euripidean sources for (differing) accounts of an innocent Helen are Stesichorus and Herodotus. Of Stesichorus,[1] we learn from Plato (*Phaedrus* 243 A-B; cf. *Ep*. III. 319 E) that he wrote a palinode criticizing Homer's account of Helen, denying that she ever went to Troy and (*Rep*. 586 C) declaring that, in ignorance of the truth, a wraith of Helen was fought for by those at Troy. A recently published papyrus containing part of a commentary on Stesichorus mentions two such palinodes of Stesichorus and adds the information that according to Stesichorus, Helen herself remained with Proteus (of Egypt) during the Trojan War. This last point, however, seems contradicted by Plato's remark of Helen of the palinode that Helen "never embarked in the well-benched ships" (*Phaedrus* 243 A), unless we are to imagine (with Bowra) that Stesichorus, like Euripides later, had Helen miraculously transported to Egypt. (The transference of Helen wrapped in *aither* is to my mind, a very *Euripidean* ruse and one particularly suited to the *Helena* in which *aither* appears in several contexts.)

[1]All the material relevant to Stesichorus cited in this paragraph is to be found in Denys Page, *Poetae Melici Graeci*, pp. 104–6, nos. 192, 193. See also C. M. Bowra, "The Two Palinodes of Stesichorus," *CR*, n.s. XIII (1963), 245–52. I have, however, ventured to differ from Bowra's interpretation of the evidence on a few points, particularly with regard to the presence of the Helen-of-the-palinode in Egypt—and how she got there!

Moreover, a passage in Dio Chrysostom (*Or.* II, 182) appears to contrast Stesichorus' "palinode" account of Helen both with the version that she was abducted by Paris *and* with the version that she went to Egypt. Thus (in my opinion) all that we can safely conclude of the Helen of Stesichorus' palinode(s) is what we have cited from Plato in the first place. On the other hand, that Stesichorus was the first to introduce the wraith of Helen seems highly probable. The legendary circumstances of the palinode's composition, (see *Phaedrus* 243 A-B), Plato's repeated association of this version with Stesichorus alone, and the statement, made in this connection, in the papyrus account that Stesichorus blamed both Homer and Hesiod, all suggest Stesichorus' originality on this point; at any rate, this evidence casts considerable doubt on the tradition (based on a scholiastic paraphrase of Lycophron = Hesiod 266, Rzach) that Hesiod first introduced the *eidôlon* of Helen.

Herodotus (II. 112–20) presents a rationalized version of Helen's Egyptian sojourn: that, when she and Paris were shipwrecked off Egypt, King Proteus kept her but sent Paris on his way to Troy; that Menelaus, though receiving his wife and possessions back safely after the Trojan Wars, was subsequently pursued by the Egyptians for sacrificing two Egyptian children (πρᾶγμα οὐχ ὅσιον, as the account not unreasonably observes) to obtain favourable winds. Herodotus adds his view that Homer knew the Egyptian version but suppressed it.[2]

The Homeric passages relevant either to Herodotus' allegation or to Euripides' version may readily be summarized: *Il.* VI, 289–92: Paris and Helen are said to have been in Phoenicia. *Od.* iv. 351 ff.: Menelaus tells of being detained in Egypt by gods wrathful that he had not made sacrifice. Eidothea, daughter of Proteus, tells Odysseus how he may overpower Proteus and wrest from him the secret of the gods' displeasure. In none of these passages is Helen actually mentioned as being with Menelaus. However, Helen's presence in Egypt is mentioned or implied in two other passages: *Od.* iv. 227–30 and 125 ff., where she and Menelaus are said to have received gifts from Polybus and his wife, of Egyptian Thebes.

[2]Herodotus' own reason (II. 120) for accepting the "Egyptian version" is interestingly rational: he cannot conceive of the more substantial Trojan leaders, such as Priam and Hector, sacrificing Trojan blood and soil so that Paris might have a wife. This is precisely the view of "Hector," though not of "Priam," in Giraudoux's contemporary adaptation, *La Guerre de Troie n'aura pas lieu* (Paris, 1936); however, Giraudoux, with cynical wisdom, dramatizes the further melancholy belief that reason can accomplish little, once the gods of war are roused. Cf. also Euripides' comments on the matter in a splendid and sombre lyrical passage, *Hel.* 1151–64.

Finally, in this account of relevant pre-Euripidean material we may mention the causes of the Trojan War as they appear in the *Cypria*:[3] Zeus and Themis arrange the divine beauty contest, in which Helen is used as a bribe by Aphrodite, in order to lighten Earth's burden of men by the war between Trojans and Greeks which will ensue.

Homer, cyclic epic, Stesichorus and Herodotus: however different their versions, Euripides appears to have adapted elements from each (or from other sources now lost to us which agreed with them) and in the end to have produced a version of the Helen myth quite different from any which had gone before. For the causes of the Trojan War, he goes back (or has Helen go back; see vv. 36–40) beyond the ethical explanations of Herodotus (II. 113–15) and Aeschylus (*Ag.* 355–66) to the more primitive formulation of the legend as it appears in the *Cypria.* The wraith of Helen, and the war fought in error for it, is presumably based on Stesichorus, while some aspects of the Egyptian sojourn (Helen's entrustment to the virtuous Proteus, v. 47, for example) are reminiscent of the virtuous Egyptians of Herodotus' account. On the other hand, Menelaus' shipwreck in Egypt with the *phantom* Helen, his escape with the real one, the assistance of Theonoe, daughter of the late King Proteus, and the pursuit of the Egyptians seem to be very Euripidean adaptations of several strands of legend which we have seen in Homer and Herodotus. Theonoe, indeed, combines qualities not only of Homer's Eidothea and of the god-fearing King Proteus of Herodotus' Egyptian tale but also those of a decidedly fifth-century mystic (see, for example, 865–67 and 1013–16). Finally, in the actual transference of Helen (44) wrapped in *aither* to Egypt, while the phantom Helen (also composed of *aither*, 584, which occurs again, in quasi-mystical contexts, at vv. 866 and 1016) goes to Troy, one would like to think (though the point cannot be proved) that Euripides is combining Stesichorus' "supernatural" explanation of Helen's innocence with the natural or "possible" tale of the Egyptian sojourn which was told by Herodotus and (perhaps) suppressed by Homer.

Detention in Egypt, escape and pursuit all occur in one form or another in the earlier tales, but with what different motivation do they occur in Euripides. The idea of a love-smitten, jealous Egyptian King (Proteus' son) who wants Helen for himself is, as far as we can tell, Euripides' invention, and one well suited to those elements of romance and lively action so typical of Euripides' non-tragic plays. Even the business of Helen's wraith, though borrowed from Stesichorus, must have been developed by Euripides, for the particular kind of ironic effect

[3]*EGF*, I, 17 ff. (Proclus' summary) and 20–21, 24 (nn. 1 and 6).

in the scenes involving the real and the phantom Helen can only be imagined in dramatic terms—and in Euripidean dramatic terms at that.

But perhaps the major innovation of the play lies in the characterization of Helen, which contrasts strongly with what we know of traditional attitudes toward her, including those developed by Euripides himself. Granted that this tradition was twofold, with suggestions on the one hand that she was but the pawn of the gods (sometimes even a Zeus-sent *Erinys*)[4] and on the other that she was a shameless wanton, yet these frequently shade into one another with precisely that degree of ambiguity with which the Greeks, particularly in earlier times, tended to surround all ideas of moral responsibility. It is unlikely that the fully drawn Euripidean picture of Helen the faithful, pining wife (rivalling Penelope herself as an ingenious deceiver of would-be rivals) was equalled even in Stesichorus' palinodes. Since it is in Euripides himself, particularly at *Troades* 766–73, that we find the most bitter treatment of Helen, it is not surprising that the present play was called ἡ καινὴ 'Ελένη, "the new Helen" (Aristophanes, *Thesm.* 850). The poignant grass-widow now presented must have struck Euripides' audience as startling and even incredible, and must have contributed in no small part to that air of fantasy on which the whole feeling of this play depends.[5]

In the light of this novel characterization of Helen and of the more obviously fantastic elements which we have already noted in the plot of the play, we should have little difficulty in including the *Helena* within that group of plays which Professor Kitto has characterized as tragicomedies.[6] But when the structure of the *Helena* has been examined, we may find that the poet has woven, as warp to the woof of his fantasy, certain underlying suggestions of truth into his ironic treatment of contemporary views of it. It may be that in this play, as in others of his tragicomedies, the poet indulges in a form of *spoudaiogeloion*, a peculiarly Greek blend of the grave and the gay, which Kitto seems, on the whole, to deny him.

Dramatic Analysis

One finds in the *Helena* such a variety of good things that there has been a tendency to impute its success simply to the sum total of these

[4]So, *pace* Denniston and Page *ad loc.*, I would interpret Aeschylus, *Ag.*, 737–49.

[5]Cf. Zuntz's lively account, based on the parody of Euripides' *Helena* in Aristophanes' *Thesmophoriazusae*, of the probable effect of the play's novelty on an Athenian audience. (G. Zuntz, "On Euripides' *Helena*: Theology and Irony," *Euripide, Entretiens sur l'antiquité classique*, VI, 202–3.)

[6]See Kitto, *G.T.*, 312 and chap. 11, *passim.*

varied effects. However, no discerning critic should regard a play simply as a series of vaudeville stunts. The more varied the effects, the greater is the need for some unifying theme which may be seen recurring in a variety of forms. The structure of the *Helena* depends on the numerous and skilfully interwoven variations on the "appearance and reality" dichotomy, which appears now as one, now as another, of those "paired opposites" in which the sophistic mind delighted, and the various progressions in the plot—the alternation between the hope and despair of the waiting wife in the first half, and between failure and success of the escape plot in the second—are effected by ingenious manipulations of this theme.[7]

The plot of the first half of the play centres on Helen's hopes for reunion with her long-lost husband, and the main obstacle to their fulfilment is the sense-deluding appearance of the *eidôlon*, the wraith of Helen. But the note of illusion, of deceptive appearance, is introduced long before the comic scene in which Menelaus refuses to accept the lovely evidence before his eyes. The delusions of the present action are anticipated by Helen's account in the prologue of Zeus' deception of Leda when, *appearing* as a swan, "he by guile his pleasure wrought." And the aside which Helen adds ". . . if this account be really true" (21)

[7]Many critics have, of course, noted in various terms the constant interplay between appearance and reality in the *Helena*, though none, perhaps, has considered in detail the effects of this theme on the structure of the play. I mention here a few of the studies which I have found particularly useful on this general subject; the degree of my indebtedness to one or another of them will become clear as the chapter progresses.

F. Solmsen, "*Onoma* and *Pragma* in Euripides' *Helen*," CR XLVIII (1934), 119–121. Solmsen's study is particularly useful in its precise indications of sophistic influences on this play and on recognition themes in Euripides generally. John Griffith, "Some Thoughts on the *Helena*," *JHS*, LXXIII (1953) 36–41. This is a development of Solmsen's study, but useful for observations of philosophic and rhetorical influences on certain specific passages of the *Helena*. Zuntz, "On Euripides' *Helena*" (above, note 5): "This interplay of narrower and wider spheres of understanding which reveals error to be truth and truth . . . to be error; this irony gives the play its lightness and verve as well as its profundity." (223) Anne N. Pippin, "Euripides' *Helen*: A Comedy of Ideas," *CP*, 55 (1960), 151–53. Miss Pippin's study of the *Helena* is, perhaps, the one to which the present chapter is most indebted, as the following quotation will indicate: "The language, the plot, and the very form of the *Helen* all have been made to express this tension between what is and what only seems to be." (152) In this connection, Miss Pippin's observation of the parallel between the deception of Paris and the deception of Theoclymenus has proved particularly suggestive. However, Miss Pippin's study, like the last two referred to above, does tend at times to emphasize the philosophic aspects of the *Helena* to the detriment of its other aspects.

hints that even this tale of deception may itself be a deception—a warning, perhaps, that may be applied to the *mythos* now to be unfolded. A moment later, Helen refers in the same tone, even in the same syntactical form, to the illusory quality of her own beauty, τοὐμὸν δὲ κάλλος, εἰ καλὸν τὸ δυστυχές, "My beauty, if indeed misfortune *can* be fair . . . (27)

The same paradox, that an apparent good can actually be an evil, and *vice versa*, is repeated later, after the scene with Teucer, when Helen expounds her sad lot to the Chorus in more philosophic terms. Here, after an incredulous aside on her mythological origins ("Who ever heard of a woman being born from an egg!" 257–58) and a rational explanation of her troubles to accompany the mythological one ("due in part to Hera, in part to my own beauty," 261), she pines for a *baser* appearance (αἴσχιον εἶδος, 263) which would have brought her *fairer* fortune than the *apparent* good of beauty. The contrast between appearance and reality becomes more explicit as Helen bewails her undeserved reputation for adultery among the Greeks:

For in the first place, though I am not corrupt, I have an ill repute, and this is a greater evil than actually being evil, namely, to possess the *reputation* for non-existent evils. (270–72)

The contrast between actuality, *being*, and the unfortunate reputation which Helen bears, is emphasized by Helen's pathetic insistence on such words as οὐκ οὖσ' ἄδικος (270) for her actual state, τὰ μὴ προσόντα . . . κακά (272) for her undeserved reputation, and τῆς ἀληθείας (271) for the reality of evil which she would rather possess than the false reputation for it!

These gambits are but the overtones anticipating and accompanying that play on appearance and reality which affects the plot. The main deception of the senses which is to frustrate Helen's hopes in the first part of the play is described in the Prologue as a false δόκησις.

And Hera . . . turned to air (ἐξηνέμωσε, a lovely word) my Paris mating . . . fashioning a breathing likeness from the heavens . . . and Paris thinks he has *me*— a false "seeming" (κενὴν δόκησιν, 36), for he has me not. (31–36)

To these insistences on *dokêsis* are added, a moment later, a reminder of the familiar *onoma-ergon* (the nominal *versus* the actual) antithesis: "My name alone, not I, was set as valour's prize. . . ." (43)

In the opening monologue Helen, though, not unreasonably, depressed by ten years of grass-widowhood, has remained optimistic about her eventual reunion with Menelaus. Not until Teucer's announcements that

Menelaus has dragged Helen from Troy and then that Menelaus has himself perished at sea, does Helen's hope turn to despair.

The little scene in the prologue between Teucer and Helen serves as a dramatic prelude to the more important encounter between Helen and Menelaus.[8] As such, it is full of dramatic anticipations and minor ironies in which realities are consistently rejected for illusions. This is true of Teucer's belief and Helen's in Menelaus' death at sea (itself an anticipation of the deception of Theoclymenus in the second half of the play), of Teucer's and Menelaus' acceptance of the phantom Helen as the real one and of Teucer's consequent rejection of the real Helen (to whom he apologizes [80] for being angered by her mere likeness to the real Helen). The game is played back again by Helen a moment later when she warns him (119), futilely of course, against *dokêsis*, appearance in its deceptive aspect.

By the end of the scene between Helen and Teucer, the first movement of the play's recurrent rhythm has been completed. Hope has yielded to despair at the false news of Menelaus' death at sea and this despair is rehearsed first in lyrical then in rhetorical terms in the *kommos* at 179 ff. and in Helen's speech at 255 ff. Formally plaintive and appealing, this pretty lyric shared by Helen and the Chorus touches us for a moment with a pleasing melancholy. However, since we have never been convinced (nor are we meant to be) by the reality of Helen's situation, we are not moved by this lament. Just as we have not taken seriously the whole business of the wraith, and of Helen transported by *aither*, so we are prepared to expect her deliverance by some equally impossible device.

It is the Chorus that swings the pendulum toward hope again with the appropriate suggestion that Helen test this mere rumour of Menelaus' death by consulting the prophetess Theonoe "who knows everything." Hope now restored, its embodiment Menelaus promptly appears himself, missing Helen by a few seconds. Thus begins a slapstick prelude to the recognition scene with Menelaus, king and hero of the Trojan Wars, dressed in rags and quailing ("O where is my glorious army now?" 453) before a fierce old Portress. The irony continues on a wittier

[8]H. Grégoire, *Euripide*, V, 17 ff., imposes rather a heavy political interpretation on this scene between Teucer and Helen on the grounds that its presence is *dramatically* unnecessary and even superfluous. However, among the many possible defences of the scene in dramatic terms, one might point out that without it the important scene between Helen and Menelaus (which depends on Helen's previous awareness of Menelaus' deception by the *eidôlon*) could not have been composed as it is. For a more extensive defence of the dramatic values of this scene, and for some interesting contrasts which it presents with Euripides' other "recognition plays," see Strohm, *Euripides*, 77.

level as Menelaus ponders the news that "Zeus' daughter Helen" (470) is being jealously guarded against any possible Greek visitors within the King's palace. With the ponderous logic of Strepsiades, Menelaus proceeds to enumerate the stultifying coincidences between this situation and the situation as *he* knows it: that both here in the palace and back in his seashore cave where he has left her, there lies a woman with the same name, parentage and native land. "One Zeus there is in Heaven" declares Menelaus. (491) Sound theology seems to be leading him in the right direction, namely that the coincidence is too great to be possible, when sophistic cleverness gets the better of him: he cunningly applies the *onoma-pragma* antithesis and decides that the oneness, the apparent identity, of the two Helens consists only in the identity of the names concerned. "Many men and cities and women over the world have the same name," Menelaus consoles himself (497–99), only to refute his own conclusion a moment later by his self-assurance that no one will spurn *him* from the door once his famous name is heard. (502)

The recognition scene provides us with an excellent example of the tragicomic uses of irony. It reverses in one way situations such as the great Oedipus-Jocasta scene in the third episode of Sophocles' *O.T.*, for in the *Helena* the hidden relationship, if revealed, would be a cause of great joy, not horror; it reverses in another way the recognition (in any of its versions) between Electra and Orestes, for though in both the ultimate recognition brings joy, not sorrow, it leads in the present instance toward a happy escape of the reunited ones, in the other toward a partnership in the tragic catastrophe of matricide. (This is one of several reasons why it seems wrong to place, as some critics do, the *Helena*, the *I.T.* and sometimes the *Ion* in the same category as the *Electra*, simply because all have a recognition scene and an intrigue or *mêchanêma*.[9])

The comic play on appearances begins with Helen's refusal (541–54) to believe in the identity of Menelaus (for whom she has just been pining) because he *looks like* a ruffian, and with Menelaus' refusal to accept the evidence of his senses because of his experiences, his labours at Troy (593) which won him the other Helen. The philosophic parody

[9]See, for example, Solmsen, *Hermes*, LXIX, 390–406, discussed in chap. 14 on *Ion*, n. 3, and Strohm, 75 ff. Strohm, it is true, distinguishes carefully between "intrigues" which involve vengeance or, at least, injury to the enemy, those which involve escape and those which, like the *Helena*, as Strohm thinks, involve both. He is led to consider the so-called *Wiedererkennungsdramen* together because of his interest in the dramatic techniques involved in the transition from recognition to *mêchanêma*. (Cf. 78 ff.)

involved shines through such antitheses as "eye *versus* mind" (575), "physical appearance *versus* mental awareness" (577) and "name (*onoma*) *versus* body (*sôma*)" (588), a variation of Menelaus' own argument in the preceding scene, by which Helen now attempts, fruitlessly, to persuade Menelaus of her identity. The messenger speech which concludes the recognition—and with it Helen's ludicrous embarrassment—reports the departure of the wraith-in-the-cave for the heavens, explaining the false opinions (based on mere appearances) which have caused both the war fought for a wraith and the undeserved infamy of the virtuous Helen.

We now expect the action of the play to quicken, as the plot (after the happy fulfillment—ἀδόκητον, beyond expectation, 657—of Helen's hopes) takes an entirely new direction. Structurally speaking, we think of this plot as a "recognition sequence" followed by a successful intrigue leading to the escape-and-happy-ending typical of tragicomedy. In this conception, the episode with Theonoe has its place, for the Egyptian seer, on whose complicity any successful intrigue must to some degree depend, is an obstacle to be overcome. It must be admitted, however, that Theonoe refuses to remain simply a passive obstacle to be circumvented. Both she and her suppliant Helen have important things to say, even if the saying of it provides a slight structural embarrassment: indeed, the *reason* why the prophetess decides to aid Helen and Menelaus proves to be, if anything, more important than the simple plot convenience that she does.

Theonoe, who knows all, goes straight to the heart of the matter: Hera and Aphrodite are both at this very moment debating the fate of the fugitives before Zeus; the former would aid, the latter frustrate, that safe restoration of Helen on which the vindication of Helen's good name, and the shaming of Aphrodite, depend. Then come the crucial lines:

> Finally, it depends on *me* whether, as Aphrodite wishes, I ruin you by telling my brother of your presence, or whether, siding with Hera, I save your life by keeping the secret from the King. . . . (887–90)

There has been much controversy on the theological and philosophical implications both of this passage and of the debate which now ensues between Theonoe and her suppliants. Kitto and Zuntz represent the two extremes in this controversy, with Kitto somewhat perversely regarding the whole business as all part of the fun and games of tragicomedy, and Zuntz, who considers the passage the most significant one in the whole play, making, perhaps, too solemn an effort to render a completely consistent account of it.[10] To my mind, the most fascinating part of the debate lies in the sharp contrast between the lofty ethical level on which Helen and Theonoe (who in this passage talk in the same terms) discuss the issue, and the passionately selfish level on which, as we have just seen, the gods of mythology are prepared to decide it. The contrast is all the more striking and paradoxical in that Helen and Theonoe still speak of their ethic as divinely based. Thus Helen adjures Theonoe not to sacrifice her own piety (εὐσέβειαν, 901) for her wicked brother's sake, for "god abhors violence." (903) She bids Theonoe rather to examine "the will of god (τὰ τοῦ θεοῦ) and of her dead father" (Proteus) in the matter. (914) Finally, in the most impressive appeal of all, Helen declares:

> *If*, seeing that you are a prophet and hold with divine matters (τὰ θεῖ' ἡγουμένη), you now destroy your father's just policy and gratify instead your unjust brother, then surely 'twere a base thing that you should know all divine matters, . . . and *not* know the things which are just (τὰ . . . δίκαια).
> (919–23, omitting one phrase where the text is uncertain)

In reaching her decision to help the fugitives, Theonoe, like Helen, also draws her inspiration on ethical matters from a source quite different from the gods of mythology, including Zeus. The source of her inspiration (if that is the right word) is first hinted at in Theonoe's opening lines as she proceeds onstage with the ritual pomp of the prophetess:

> Conduct me with the bright glow of torches, and fumigate with sulphur according to the solemn rite the furthermost recesses of the *aither* [upper air or airy fire], so that we may receive the pure breath of the heavens (οὐρανοῦ). (865–67)

[10]See Kitto, 326, and Zuntz, "On Euripides' *Helena*," 204 ff. Explicit criticisms are made of Kitto's view by Zuntz, 209–10, and are, indeed, implied throughout the chapter. Though I have found many points in Zuntz's subtle discussion of Theonoe most useful, I cannot agree with his rejection of the view that Theonoe regards herself as in any sense an arbiter between Hera and Aphrodite. Verses 887–90, quoted above, seem to me to express this idea clearly. ". . . how [in this case]," asks Zuntz (206), "could she thereafter so earnestly have advised her protégés (vv. 1024 ff.) to pray for the goodwill of those very deities?" Very easily, for this is part of Euripides' mocking of traditional piety by devotees better than the gods whom they worship; indeed Theonoe herself, in her piety, even asks Aphrodite's pardon (1006–7) for deciding the issue against her! Zuntz's insistence (205), to save the priestess' theological position, that "the mythological scene ends with v. 886 . . ." and that "τέλος δ' ἐφ' ἡμῖν (887) looks forward not backward" is arbitrary in the extreme. Pohlenz's translation and interpretation ". . . but the decision rests with me" (here cited by Zuntz) is surely the right one.

It must be admitted that there is some obscurity in this passage both with regard to the text of v. 866 and to the ritual referred to therein;[11] however, what is important here is the reference to *aither* and to "the pure breath of the heavens" in connection with the priestess Theonoe's activities. Later in answering the pleas of the fugitives, Theonoe speaks of that piety which she inherits from her father Proteus in terms not of service to the conventional gods but of "a great temple of justice" which is, by nature, within her (1002–3). Finally, Theonoe gives us this interesting reason for honouring her dead father's obligation to defend and rescue Helen:

> For there is a recompense (*τίσις*) for these matters among the dead as among the living. The mind (*νοῦς*) of the dead continues not to live its individual life (*ζῇ*); nevertheless [after death] it keeps a certain consciousness forever (*γνώμην . . . ἀθάνατον*), as it falls in with the immortal *aither*. (1013–16)[12]

Thus the inner and the outer references of the piety which Theonoe and her father share are, respectively, to that "temple of Justice within," and to the mysterious *aither* from which Theonoe first sought aid, and which seems to be Theonoe's translation of those divine matters (*τὰ τοῦ θεοῦ*) to which Helen has referred her at v. 914. The prophetess does, it is true, refer to the mythological gods when she prays for gentle treatment from Aphrodite, though, as a professed virgin, she has little to do with her. But the selfish motives of these divine ladies have had nothing to do with her decision, which is made on a higher level altogether, and there must surely be a touch of irony, on the part of the poet if not of the prophetess, when she reminds the fugitives (1024 ff.) to pray to both goddesses for a safe return.

It is the gods of popular mythology whose chaotic, arbitrary and often cruel decisions have caused the confused and "impossible" situation on

[11]In v. 866 I have followed Paley's translation as emended at two points by Pflugk and Hermann, respectively, to read: *θεῖου δὲ σεμνὸν θεσμὸν αἰθέρος μυχόν*. See Paley's note *ad loc.*

[12]It is the *γνώμη*, or consciousness, which *νοῦς* keeps after it has ceased to live in the full (individual) sense, which, apparently, makes possible a sense of satisfaction or of suffering for duties done or not done. On some of the difficulties and possible implications of this interesting passage, see the brief discussion between Zuntz and Lesky (Zuntz, 234–35, on which my own interpretation to some degree depends) and Grégoire's comments in his note on this passage. Grégoire reminds us that according to Herod. II. 123—a passage not far removed from the "Helen story" in Herodotus—the Egyptians first proclaimed the immortality of the human soul, and suggests that Euripides sought "to Hellenize and modernize" the old belief by expressing it in terms of Anaxagoras' philosophy. On this last point, cf. also Griffith (above, note 7).

which this whole fantasy depends. But here, for a moment, Euripides has drawn aside the mythological veil, and shown us what *he* conceives to be the true springs of justice and order: the integrity and the ethical sense of personages like Theonoe, responding to a somewhat vague inspiration from that *aither* which is the soul of the universe.

We may seem to have wandered far from our theme with this account of Theonoe; however, the passage seems to serve as a reminder (among others in this play) that in the midst of tragicomedy Euripides can turn a fantastic theme to the service of a serious, though not necessarily tragic, idea. Besides, it may not be fanciful to see in this contrast between divine matters as discussed in this passage and the shabby beliefs of popular mythlogy another kind of contrast between reality and the counterfeit coin which often passed for it. Be that as it may, we surely have in this debate one more example of the philosophic overtones, satirical or otherwise, in which this *jeu d'esprit* abounds.

Perhaps in response to the serious theme of the "Theonoe episode" (and the hint of mythological criticism implied in it) comes the profound and moving passage (1137–64) in the second part of the next stasimon. The first of the two strophes concerned repeats, this time in theological terms, the paradoxes, the contradictory appearances, which we have already found in the world of the senses and the passions: here the unexpected and contradictory course of *divinely* appointed fortunes is pictured as leading to the disgrace of a daughter of Zeus himself. Helen, for all her innocence, is named unjust—and godless. (The heaviest irony—and significance—must surely lie on the last of the alleged epithets of Helen: a human heroine, unjustly accused, by divine plan, of betrayal and perfidy, is called "godless"!)[13]

The last strophe of this chorus (1151–64) looks directly, for the first time in this play, at the chaos of the war-torn and still threatened world in which Euripides himself was living. Here the constantly shifting delusion which provides both the substance and the "dynamics" of the play is to be seen in that *ignis fatuus* (in this case Helen, or her wraith) which leads so unnecessarily—and yet, it would seem, so inevitably—to war. The dramatic context in which these thoughts occur reminds us once again that, even in Euripidean tragicomedy, we may find sombre

[13]This use of ἄθεος (1148) as practically synonymous with ἄδικος in the same line helps to refute the view that there is no implicit criticism in Euripides' almost exaggerated emphasis on the immoral qualities of the gods of traditional mythology. (On the attitude to the gods in this strophe—as well as in the play as a whole—and on the related text problem of the final verse, 1150, see Zuntz, 217–20).

observations occasioned by situations which, as they are presented in the play, are impossible and fantastic. There can surely be little doubt, here, of the solemn, even emotional tone of the old poet as he writes, in the bitter years of 413–12, of the mindless cruelty of settling differences by war.

In this comment on war, with its contemporary overtones, Euripides is perhaps giving a political turn to his theme of the illusions of appearance on which men feed to their sorrow. Grégoire, who often tends to see Euripides' plays in too exclusively political terms, has surely commented wisely on at least one aspect of the poet of the *Helena*:

> . . . il a vu dans l'histoire de εἴδωλον une sorte de symbole. Pour lui, à ce moment précis, toutes les guerres sont, comme la plus fameuse, des erreurs sanglantes, des folies.[14]

In the second half of the *Helena*, the action is more rapid but the irony and wit keep pace with it. This action concerns the escape plan of Helen and Menelaus: that of outwitting King Theoclymenus by a mock burial at sea for the (allegedly) drowned Menelaus. From the tragicomic point of view, the scheme is properly ingenious, improbable and productive of a lively sense of adventure. Moreover, like the long-frustrated recognition sequence, it is based on a confusion of identity, of delusive appearances, almost as fantastic as that which concerned Helen and her phantom. But whereas in the earlier sequence the ultimate reunion of Helen and Menelaus depended on *dispelling* the illusion of Helen's wraith (of "laying the ghost of Helen," as it were), the new sequence of action depends for its success on *preserving* the false appearances of the mock funeral by which the amorous King Theoclymenus (delighted by Menelaus' reported "death") is hoodwinked. That Euripides was quite conscious of the parallel between the false appearances in the first and second parts of the play seems clear from the almost identical descriptions of the delusion of Paris with the wraith and the delusion of Theoclymenus with the reward promised for the funeral: each of them only *thinks* (δοκεῖ) that fair Helen is within his grasp (compare vv. 35–36 and 1385–86).

A similar reversal of an earlier motif occurs, at least as far as appearances are concerned, in an ethical context. Here it is the concept of *charis* which is involved. Earlier in the play, Helen has warned Theonoe of the injustice of gratifying Theoclymenus by betraying Menelaus and herself to him. In that passage (see especially 900–04, 919–23) Helen has defined *base charis* in both its aspects: the baseness of the

[14]Grégoire, 23

favour itself and the baseness of the gratitude (*charis*) received.[15] Now, however, we find Helen asking Theoclymenus for "base" *charis* (gratitude for an ignoble deed) and (again apparently) fulfilling her side of the *quid pro quo* which she offers the Egyptian King. Theoclymenus' own sense of unworthiness saves Helen from having to put this proposal too crassly. Rightly mistrusting his own charms, he instinctively asks, when the "widowed" Helen offers to marry him at last, "On what terms? For one favour deserves another." (χάρις γὰρ ἀντὶ χάριτος ἐλθέτω, 1234.)

Similar, though minor, ironies on the same theme are played out between Menelaus and Theoclymenus: Menelaus, acting as one of his own sailors, speaks of the King's favour (*charis*) to Menelaus in giving him a good send-off (1273) and the King in turn (1281) promises to reward the disguised Menelaus for his help (*charis*) to Helen, in conducting her late husband's funeral. Finally, Menelaus promises to reward Helen herself with a fair report in Greece, if now she proves the sort of wife she ought!

The play on *charis* is further exploited in the final complication of the plot. Theoclymenus' embarrassing concern for Helen's safety introduces a new obstacle:

> Helen, don't embark! Distraught by your late husband's charms [*charis* in an erotic connotation, as not infrequently in Euripides], you may plunge into the sea! (1393–97, in part)

Charis in a new sense has aroused the King's fears, but the original *charis*, properly administered by Helen, soon restores the *status quo*: "New husband," she cries (already suggesting the base fulfilment she has promised) "what favour (*charis*) to the dead to die with them?" There follows a brilliantly ambiguous description of the rewards in store for Theoclymenus, as, once more, deceitful Helen acquiesces in the two base forms of *charis*—shameful gratitude for shameful favours (see vv. 1420 and 1411, respectively)—which *honest* Helen had repudiated in the scene with Theonoe. Once more, fond Theoclymenus, threatening to ruin all with his excessive concern for Helen, is kept at bay—and the

[15]*Charis* is, as we have seen, a favourite word of Euripides', no doubt because of its multiple aspects. In the passages with which we are here concerned, it occurs three times in the first scene with Theoclymenus (1232, 1273, 1281) and seven times in the second (1373, 1378, 1397, 1402, 1411, 1420, 1449). Of the various other passages in which Euripides exploits different shades of meaning in this term, see particularly the passages shared by Hecuba and Odysseus, and by Hecuba and Agamemnon, at *Hec.* 238–331 and 824–35, respectively, and the Nurse's speech in the *Hippolytus*, 507–15 (cf. 526–27), and my references to these usages in the chapters on these plays.

escape intrigue sweeps on to the swashbuckling success so brilliantly described in the messenger speech.

This ironic sequence—but one of several word plays so skilfully worked into the action of the escape plan—illustrates well the kind of parody of sophistic debate which I believe Euripides was intending in the latter part of the play. The "epistemological" satire which, in the first part of the play, the play on false appearances produced has now been replaced by the ironic treatment of ethical concepts.

One other passage in the later portions of the play needs, perhaps, a word of comment before we turn to the *deus-ex-machina* ending with which a Euripidean *jeu d'esprit* such as *Helena* must inevitably end. In the midst of the *mêchanêma*, in between the two scenes concerned with the gulling of Theoclymenus, comes the celebrated "Demeter Ode" (1301–68) which recent scholarship has been at such pains to defend from traditional charges of irrelevance.[16]

The first three strophes of this ode provide a vivid and picturesque version of the well known *hieros logos* concerning the frantic search, the earth-blighting despair and the eventual consolation of Demeter, after the abduction of Persephone. The apparent confusion, or identification, of Demeter with both Cybele and the Cretan Rhea, at one point or another of this ode, has occasioned considerable concern among the critics, though similar examples of "syncretism" are to be found elsewhere in Euripides—at *Bacchae* 120–34, for example.

Various "historical" and "mythographical" explanations of this passage (such as the view that Euripides was alluding to the recent introduction of Cybele-worship at Athens, or that a Minoan Helen, before she was secularized by the Greeks, was the original vegetation goddess to be carried off by an underworld power[17]) fail, even if they contain some elements of truth, to establish much dramatic relevance for the introduction of this myth. More promising is the interpretation of Miss Pippin. Pointing to the analogy of Persephone's situation, imprisoned in the house of Hades, and Helen's situation, imprisoned in Egypt, she suggests that "the Demeter-Persephone motif offers a promise at the outset that Helen will not be held captive forever."[18]

The final strophe (1353–68) of this ode must always remain something of an enigma. Here the Chorus appears to blame Helen's troubles

[16]See the list of such criticisms in the preamble to a recent defence of this chorus, C. P. Golann, *TAPA*, LXXVI (1945), 31 ff.

[17]See Golann, 34 ff., who rejects the first of these suggestions (originally Musgrave's) and defends the second.

[18]Pippin, 156.

on the wrath of the Magna Mater and then to suggest that she (like Demeter in the preceding strophe) may find rehabilitating power in Bacchic ritual and its accoutrements. "For," chides the Chorus, "you trusted in your beauty alone." In this passage, it seems hard to ignore the reminder, however harsh and inappropriate in the dramatic context, of Alcibiades' alleged profanation of the mysteries, which (as Grégoire remarks) was perhaps the greatest single cause of Athenian reverses in Sicily. But the question why Demeter, rather than Aphrodite, should suddenly appear as the cause of Helen's troubles, must continue to resist all dramatic if not "political" explanations.[19]

The allegorical and symbolic interpretations of this ode may, perhaps, be made a shade more specific, without doing violence to the delicate fabric of the play.[20] It is Demeter, not her daughter, who receives the consoling distraction of the Muses. Now Helen's mother has died of grief, but the restoration of an *innocent* Helen will restore sanity to her mother country which will then realize (as Aphrodite fears) the illusory basis of the war which they have fought. Is Euripides, then, playing the Muse to Athens' Demeter, offering the enchantment of his fantasy, and beneath the enchantment a lesson, to fellow citizens still suffering from war delusions as great as those at Troy?

What are we to make of the role of the gods in the ultimate restoration of Helen to her husband and her home? And how are we to regard the intervention and explanations of the Dioscuri in the *deus-ex-machina* finale of the play?

In one sense, of course, the Dioscuri provide assurance that all has happened in accordance with the will of the gods. (1648–49, 1660–61) In this sense the epilogue provides a fitting fulfilment of the prologue, in which Helen herself has told us of Zeus' plans for her ultimate safety with Menelaus. But as in the case of other divine or mythological frames to the action of Euripidean plays (those of *Hippolytus* and of *Ion* come particularly to mind), we are left with a certain sense of ambiguity between human and divine motivation. For all "the divine plan," who

[19]Grégoire, 13 ff., while admitting the difficulty, finds the contemporary political climate, "cette psychose du sacrilège," sufficient explanation not only for the final strophe but also for the whole treatment of the *hieros logos* of Demeter-Rhea. (The textual uncertainty of 1353–54 renders the precise nature of Helen's alleged offence against Demeter's rites still more obscure.)

[20]Miss Pippin (155) considers the play intended to divert the suffering Athenians, as Demeter was diverted by Aphrodite and the Muses. So too Zuntz (227) regards the symbolism of the Great Mother myth in this ode as a clue to the meaning of the *Helena*: "The play stands out as a παίγνιον as light as it is profound; an ethereal dance above the abyss."

indeed is actually responsible for securing Helen's safety? "The gods," the Dioscuri keep saying (1648, 1653, 1661)—but who exactly are these gods? Hera and Aphrodite cancel one another out (it is interesting, by the way, that we are never told the result of their debate before Zeus, 878 ff.), and their selfish motives have nothing to do with the choice of Theonoe. The latter, as we have seen, is the most decisive element in the actual action of the play. Though it conforms with Zeus' initial plan (see Helen's reminder to Theonoe at 909–16), we will recall that the repeated emphasis, both in Helen's appeal and in Theonoe's "deciding" speech, has been upon certain ethical and mystical aspects of Theonoe's responsibility, which take little account of traditional mythology. (Note, for example, vv. 919–23, 1002–3, 1009–16. It is interesting that Theonoe never directly mentions Zeus' plans for Helen.)

Finally, even in the "mythological" frame itself there are (as in *Hippolytus* and *Ion*) some slight cracks in the image of the divine master plan and its execution. First, there is the fact that the primary reason for the creation of the wraith of Helen is the spiteful jealousy of Hera (31–37); to this Zeus' utilization of the wraith for his Trojan War purposes is allowed to take second place (38–43). Then again there is the timing of the *deus-ex-machina* intrusion, as well as the terms in which the divine explanations are expressed. The Dioscuri arrive just too late to be of any real help to the fugitives, a fact which serves to emphasize the human agencies at work in the escape. Like Theonoe herself, they make no direct reference to the master plan of Zeus concerning Helen; instead, the phrase τὰ τῶν θεῶν, which they use for the divine will, reminds us of the lofty context, quite distinct from the strife of the goddesses before the throne of Zeus, in which Helen and Theonoe have discussed the matter.

It is in this sense, namely, that Helen has been restored in accordance with divine justice, that one is inclined to accept the Dioscuri's explanations. In terms of mythological drama (and Euripidean epilogues must always speak, at least formally, within this context), "divine justice" must mean "the will of Zeus," and so the Dioscuri *do* speak of Helen's ultimate fate in one isolated passage toward the end. (1666–69) Apart from this vague governance, Helen and Menelaus appear to have made their escape purely by a combination of Theonoe's noble and self-sacrificing decision and their own bold ingenuity—with no help at all from those mythological gods who first caused all the trouble.

17

THE *Iphigenia among the Taurians*

The Myth and Its Adaptation

The complex background, of myth and of cult, to Euripides' melodramatic account of Orestes' rescue of Iphigenia and the statue of Artemis from the savage land of the Taurians, has been much discussed in modern editions of the *I.T.*, as well as in other studies.[1] It should suffice as an introduction to this play to discuss a few much debated points in this material which are particularly relevant to deciding the poet's purpose and, perhaps, originality.

The multiple identity of Iphigenia herself, including her cult as a goddess both at Brauron in Attica (Strabo 9. 1. 22) and among the Taurians, where she was confused with "the Maiden," the goddess to whom the Taurians sacrificed sailors (Herodotus 4. 103), although mythologically interesting, does not in fact add much to our understanding of the play. The general situation in which the human Iphigenia of our play finds herself goes back, as far as extant record is concerned, to the *Cypria*, in which Iphigenia as daughter of Agamemnon and Clytemnestra was sacrificed, owing to the anger of Artemis, by Agamemnon, only to be saved at the last minute by Artemis and sent to Tauris, there to be made immortal.[2] It seems unlikely that it was Euripides who changed the immortal Iphigenia of the Taurians into the priestess of Artemis and made Artemis herself the recipient of human sacrifice; probably Grégoire is right in his guess that it was the text of the *Cypria* which suggested to certain Crimean settlers the identification of "the

[1]See especially the editions of Platnauer (vii–xiii) and of Grégoire (85 ff.). (The present summary is particularly indebted to Platnauer's treatment.) On more ritualistic and less literary aspects of the subject, see also S. Reinach, "Observations sur le mythe d'Iphigénie," *REG*, 28 (1915), 1–15, and A. Baschmakoff, "Origine tauridienne du mythe d'Iphigénie," *Bull. de l'Assoc. Guillaume Budé* (Paris 1939), no. 64, pp. 3–21.

[2]See Kinkel, *EGF*, 19, for Proclus' summary of the *Cypria* on these points.

Maiden" with Iphigenia, but that, generally speaking, this goddess, to whom human sacrifice was allegedly made, was assimilated to Artemis.[3]

Of more interest to us is the question whether Euripides invented the restoration of the Tauric Iphigenia and the Tauric Artemis by means of Orestes and Pylades. The following considerations suggest that this is at least probable: (*a*) there is no trace of this legend in earlier sources; (*b*) there is evidence of a temple of Artemis Tauropoulos at Halae, and of a cult of Iphigenia at Brauron (the two places named at the end of Euripides' play for the establishment of Artemis and Iphigenia in Attica), and of wooden images of Artemis (in one case specifically from Tauris) at both places;[4] at least part of this evidence refers to a time prior to Euripides, and we know from other plays of Euripides that it was a favourite device of the dramatist's to provide explanations, some of which were original, of perplexing cults and cult objects; (*c*) the particular *kind* of explanation of "the restoration" of Iphigenia and Artemis has that blend of mythological improbability and poetic appropriateness suggestive of Euripidean virtuosity: thus, while the pacification of the Furies (Orestes' interest in the matter, *I.T.*, 970–86) seems to have little to do with the statue of Artemis for which Orestes is sent by Apollo, there is, nonetheless, a certain artificial neatness in employing the guilt-laden Orestes, the end product of the violent deeds involving Agamemnon's immediate family, for the rescue of Iphigenia, from whose initial suffering the subsequent violence all stemmed.

The question of originality is perhaps of greater interest in the case of the *I.T.* than in that of most aetiological myths in Euripides. Usually, such aetiologies appear (as in the *Hippolytus*, for example), as "bonuses" appended more or less gratuitously to the end of the play. Here, however, though the aetiological point is not actually expressed until (as usual) the epilogue by the *deus ex machina*, the transporting of Artemis' statue is (as Spira has well observed)[5] an important feature of the whole action.

[3]Grégoire, 95–96; see also Baschmakoff (10 ff.), who thinks there is archaeological evidence from certain Scythian necropoleis that a part of ancient royal funeral rites may have included human sacrifice. He also argues for the ethnological identity of the Taurians on the one hand and the Cimmerians and the Circassians on the other and suggests (3 ff.) that the whole legend of Iphigenia was received from a "pre-Aryan" source at a time when the Greek people had not yet finished their preparatory period of racial formation.

[4]See Platnauer, vii–viii, and references there given.

[5]See Spira, 113–121, who argues further that the particular validity of the "Götterepilog" in this case serves to emphasize the play's essentially cultist character. (This may be going too far; there is, as we shall see, a good deal else in the play as well.)

It might be objected that the lost *Chryses* of Sophocles *may* have dealt with Orestes' and Iphigenia's escape from the Taurians and its sequel, but so little is known of this play that this possibility can do no more than cast a faint shadow over the reasonable belief, itself incapable of proof, that Euripides invented Orestes' rescue and establishment in Attica of Artemis' statue and its priestess.[6]

Dramatic Analysis

The *I.T.* is another of Euripides' romantic tragicomedies, based like the *Helena* on the ironic interplay of illusion and reality. It is, however, neither as witty nor as subtle as the *Helena*, with which it is frequently compared, and though its tone is more sombre, it hides less serious meaning behind its ironies and its exciting action. As in the *Helena*, the two halves of its plot depend on two successive delusions, but here neither the two halves nor the episodes within them are as skilfully related to one another as in the other play. Again, no single theme is served by these various episodes and ironies; indeed, apart from one aspect which we will consider later, it is a play of very little depth. Its chief dramatic qualities are on the surface and we may perhaps best judge them from a rapid survey of its lively plot.

In the prologue, Iphigenia and Orestes (the one alone, the other accompanied by his friend Pylades) provide us with all, or nearly all, the play's ingredients. Their assignments and their illusions, as here presented, are neatly complementary, and suggest, at the very beginning, the pattern which the plot will take. Iphigenia is the victim (in appearance at least) of Agamemnon's sacrifice at Aulis, while Orestes, as Agamemnon's avenger, is the matricide seeking to expiate his deed: Iphigenia is the priestess-guardian of Artemis' statue, while Orestes has been sent by Apollo to steal it and bring it home to Greece. Again, each is the victim of a similar delusion: each (Iphigenia owing to a deceptive dream; Orestes owing to the general misapprehension of Aulis) believes the other dead. Thus we are alerted for a recognition scene, and the savage rite of human sacrifice over which the innocent Iphigenia must preside is clearly to be the grim occasion of that meeting.

Between the two speeches which reveal all this, the stealthy entry and

[6]Cf. Wilamowitz, *Hermes*, XVIII, 257, who also believes in the originality of Euripides' theme. Cf. also Pearson, *The Fragments of Sophocles*, II, 327–28, and his references *ad loc.* (The fragments themselves are of little help in deciding the matter.)

tense dialogue of Orestes and Pylades (e.g., "Look! Watch out!" . . . "Is this the altar where they slaughter Greeks? . . .") provide, like a Treasure Island pantomime, just the right touch of melodrama, and the fact that the two youths remain standing before bloodstained slabs and what appear to be the severed heads of former victims (73–74) adds a further piquancy to the situation.

The kommatic *parodos*, in which Iphigenia explains her dream to the Chorus, has as its ostensible purpose the mourning of Orestes; in fact, however, by a skilful blending of past and present woes (dating from the ancestral strife over the golden ram), the poet succeeds in linking the beginning of his legend to its end and so prepares for the (Euripidean?) fusion of Iphigenia's and Orestes' destiny. Blending the misconception about her own death with her own misconception about Orestes, she gives unconscious emphasis to the fact that, appearances to the contrary, she and Orestes now share the same situation. As she prepares to make symbolic libation for the "dead" Orestes, Iphigenia laments:

> Never on your tomb will I shed tears or place a lock of my bright hair. For I am banished far from your native land and mine where (as it seemed) I died, poor wretch, in bloody sacrifice. (172–77)

It would be tedious to point out the many terms such as καινὰ . . . φάσματα (42 or δοκήμασι (176), by which the poet constantly keeps the theme of illusion before our minds. We should, however, note at this point an interesting sequence of words and ideas connected with ritual cleansing in several passages throughout the play. Iphigenia has first thought Orestes dead because in her dream (53–54) she has sprinkled with water the pillar which she now interprets to be Orestes—and this is the rite which she performs for the victims of Artemis. In the *parodos*, she pours libation (the word ὑδραίνειν is used again, v. 161, as at v. 54) in ritual burial rites for the brother she thinks already dead. In the end, however, it is to Artemis, not Orestes, that the cleansing by water is to be applied, at least in pretence, as part of the escape plan (1163 ff.), though by that escape with Artemis Orestes himself is finally to be cleansed of his matricide. The "escape ruse," the cleansing of Artemis from supposed pollution at Orestes' hands, is itself anticipated by Iphigenia's scornful remarks in the kommatic *parodos* about a goddess who is too fastidious to allow polluted people near her altars and yet enjoys human sacrifice herself. In this and in other ways, the whole "purification motif" running through the play is surely too marked to be incidental, especially since it is related to the final purpose of Orestes' mission with respect both to himself and to the rite of Artemis.

The first episode moves from melodramatic irony to a subtle indication of the Euripidean theme underlying the "purification of Artemis" with which the plot will later be concerned. The Herdsman's exciting account of the capture of Orestes and Pylades (the gallant fight against impossible odds, the miraculous sparing, unscathed, of the two strangers destined to be the goddess's victims) leads to the only cruel utterance of which Iphigenia is to be guilty in the play. Her heart, she tells us (344 ff.), once full of pity for her victims, has now been hardened by her dream about Orestes: a nice piece of irony in that it is her very grief for his imagined death which now seems likely to undo him in earnest. The speech ends with a most significant aside: Artemis' inconsistency in barring defiled worshippers from altars themselves defiled by human sacrifice leads Iphigenia to question whether such folly and such savagery can really be attributed to the goddess at all. (380–91)

The first and second *stasima* of this play, surrounding as they do the recognition scene and the hopeful plans for escape, provide a moving lyric development of the themes of exile and return. The first of these odes speculates prettily, with the appropriate mythological accompaniment, on the identity, the voyages and the hopes of the new exiles, Orestes and his friend; not until the last strophe is the emotional point of the song revealed: the singers' nostalgic wish for a Greek sailor to deliver them and bring them back to their paternal home. The theme of the delusive hopes of the voyager (413 ff.) and the bitter contrast between bloody altars and the holy streams of Dirce (398–406) is developed further in the second of these odes. Here (1089 ff.) the Chorus imitating the mournful song of the halcyon, sea bird bewailing its lost mate, picks up the strains of the earlier ode with its seascapes and its note of far-from-home; but now that the homeward journey of their mistress has been planned, the images of Greece come faster and more vividly and the contrast between the harsh realities of Tauris and the dreams of home lends a more bitter urgency to the preparations. (Among the many brilliant figures of these two sea odes, the bird imagery is particularly effective: starting casually with a passing reference to a sea-promontory white with birds [436], it develops in the evocative descriptions of the halcyon [1090 ff.] to culminate in the wishful conceit of a feathered chorus winging its way home to Greece. [1138 ff.])

It is in the haunting nostalgia of these two odes that one gathers, more than elsewhere in the *I.T.*, something of that melancholy beneath the fantasy, that murmur of the poet, perhaps, that in real life there is no happy ending, which I believe to be one of the meanings of these tragicomedies.

The recognition sequence falls into three parts: in the first, the preparation for the recognition takes the form of Iphigenia's strange plan to send one of the captives home with a message to Greece; in the second, Pylades, embarrassed by his comparative good fortune as the victim-turned-messenger, debates the problem of honour involved; in the third, the recognition itself takes place as a result of Iphigenia's "natural" revelations to Pylades.

Iphigenia's plan to send a message home grows, without her being fully aware of this, from her encounter with Orestes: from the desire, first, to save the victim who so strangely awakens her interest, and second, to exonerate herself from her compatriots' blame for killing fellow Greeks. Orestes' noble frustration of her first intention (he names Pylades instead of himself as the beneficiary of Iphigenia's plan) only deepens Iphigenia's regard for him. It now expresses itself in a series of unconscious and rather grim "kin ironies" in which she promises, though she must designate Orestes for human sacrifice, to fulfil the office of his absent sister in performing his obsequies. (628–35)

Pylades' good fortune sets him a-moralizing (Euripides, mischievously postponing the recognition scene, indulges, perhaps, in a little parody of contemporary ethical debate); struggling like a Socratic disciple, a Crito born before his time, with the problem of *doxa*, he confuses what *is* shameful with what the many think to be so:

I will seem to the many, for the many are base-hearted, to have got myself safe home by betraying you. . . . For such repute I feel both fear and shame. . . . (678–79, 683)[7]

But apart from the possible element of parody, the high-minded debate between the self-sacrificing friends itself provides one of those facile emotional effects which melodrama tends to exploit.[8]

Sophistic antithesis, the main technique for expressing the ironic contrasts of this play, becomes prominent again in the recognition scene itself. Something of the old *ergon-logos*, *sôma-onoma* antithesis underlies Iphigenia's duplication of written and verbal messages, and her insistence that if Pylades should lose the one, with the rest of his physical effects, he should deliver the other: "Saving your body, then you will save my words." (765) So, too, the somewhat jaded antitheses between

[7]Cf. Plato, *Crito* 45e ff. The coincidence in conception and terminology (the fear and shame felt before the opinion of "the many") between the Euripidean passage and Plato's account of Crito's debate with Socrates on a similar point, is quite remarkable.

[8]Cf. Cicero's approving comment (*De Amicitia* vii. 24) on the emotional effect of Pacuvius' treatment of this scene.

seeming and reality, living and not living, word and deed, high birth and low fortune, all recur in the "recognition dialogue" between brother and sister and in their comments on their past experiences (see vv. 773, 831, 855, 837–40, 850–51). Finally, *kairos* and *tychê* (the right moment" combined with good fortune) make their inevitable appearance (907–8), reminding us that the next phase of the action, the escape ruse, is at hand, and the familiar *tychê-technê* antithesis, first expressed by Orestes at v. 89, is again reflected in his warning that god helps those who help themselves. (910–11)

The last two scenes of the *I.T.* are concerned, predictably, with the escape plan itself, a messenger speech describing its execution (or, in this case, attempted execution) and a proclamation by the *deus ex machina* by which the god sees to it that divine plans, including the "happy ending" for the hero, are no longer frustrated. The escape plan which Iphigenia proposes ensures lively action for the subsequent messenger speech, and provides as well that ironic twist which one expects from such devices in Euripides. King Thoas is made to think that, in allowing Iphigenia to bring the statue to the sea, he is purifying the goddess from the taint of matricide; actually, of course, he is assisting in the ultimate purification rites of Artemis and of the matricide himself. (See particularly vv. 1221 and 1230–33 for expressions making this irony explicit.) Nor is the scene lacking in minor ironies, such as the King's comment on the Greek matricide ("By Apollo!" he swears, more aptly than he knows, "No barbarian would have dared a deed so terrible!"), and the very Euripidean rationalism which he is made to utter ("Perhaps an earthquake did it?" 1166) about the "miraculous" movement of Artemis' statue. On the whole, however, the "escape sequence" (the *mêchanêma*) is less skilfully handled than in some of the *I.T.*'s companion pieces, and the last-minute frustration of the escape seems introduced only to bring on Athena, *ex machina*, whose main function, as we shall see, lies somewhat outside the dramatic action of the play.

Few plays appear to illustrate better than the *I.T.* Professor Kitto's description of Euripidean tragicomedy as entertainment divorced from tragic reality and serious themes. It begins with a miracle, the survival of Iphigenia (whom tragedy has given up as dead); it provides, in a neatly evolving plot, a plenitude of excitements, bloodstains, "heroics," close calls and thrilling escapes; and it seems, at least at first glance, more innocent than, say, the *Ion* or the *Helena* of serious undertones and potentially tragic situations.

It is, perhaps, due to this lack of a theme closely related to the action that the structure of the play is, for all its skill, somehow less satisfying, less cohesive than that of either the *Ion* or the *Helena*. (Here we must disagree with Kitto's view that it is when the dramatist "is free to attend entirely to his 'form'" that he writes his best-constructed plays.[9]) The effect of the *Ion* resides in the poignancy of its highly complex situation and in the neatness and economy of its resolution: the unconscious *rapprochement* of mother and son and their dreadful intentions toward one another are, respectively, fulfilled and thwarted in the single moment of recognition at the end. In the *Helena*, the dialectic between illusion and reality is present in every fibre of the play; it is responsible for the essential unity of the plot which consists, to a high degree, in the ironic relation, and so *cohesion*, between its parts. Indeed, so consistently is this dichotomy presented that, for all our enjoyment of the play's fantastic wit, we finish with an awareness of the tragic aspects, in *real* life, of this gap between man's conception of his circumstances and circumstances as they really are. Compared with both these plays, the *I.T.* seems almost episodic, and this is due, I think, to the lack of relation which a linking theme would provide between the two main parts of the play.

As in the *Helena*, the dramatic development of the *I.T.* depends originally on the ironic interplay of the illusions of its central characters: Iphigenia, deluded by a dream, believes that Orestes is dead, and tries in her bitterness to set her heart against the Greeks confronting her; Orestes, deluded by the sacrifice at Aulis, believes Iphigenia dead, and regards the grim priestess before him as his mortal enemy. But whereas in the *Helena* the second half of the play repeats, in a different form, the "appearance-*versus*-reality" motif of the first half (the mock funeral of Menelaus deluding Theoclymenus as the wraith of Helen had deluded Menelaus), the escape ruse in the *I.T.* is unrelated to anything which has gone before. What irony does reside in this new motif (viz., the contrast between the real and the pretended senses in which Artemis is to be purified) is related to the *dénouement* of the play, and this *dénouement* is concerned with its mythological and ritualistic meanings rather than with its actual human action.

The Myth and the Play

What are we to make of the attitude to the gods, to mythology and cult, in the *I.T.*? It has already been remarked that the aetiological element (the "explanation," which Athena's instructions at the end of

[9]Kitto, 315; cf. 312.

the play [1446–69] provide, of certain cults of Artemis and Iphigenia in Attica), unlike many Euripidean aetiologies, directly involves an important part of the action. In recognizing this point, we need not go as far as Spira who imagines the explanation of the cult to account, to a considerable degree, for the purpose of the play.[10] This is to let the tail wag the dog. In terms of the drama as a whole, it is doubtful whether Euripides was more (or less) interested in the cults at Brauron and Halae *in themselves* than he was in any other ritual (such as the ritualistic mourning of virgins at *Hippolytus*, 425–30) for which an "explanation" is given at the end of a Euripidean play. What is important in the larger context of the play is the contrast to which this cult and its aetiology draws attention: the contrast between the savage Taurian version of the goddess Artemis and the civilized benevolent goddess which Euripides would have his fellow citizens regard as the image worthy of her and of themselves.

Whether, in the play itself, we are to regard Artemis as sharing from the first the more civilized view is, intentionally, left in doubt. It will be necessary here to review a few passages already mentioned. Iphigenia herself is ambiguous on this point. She speaks first of Artemis (or, possibly, of her rite)[11] as "fair in name only" and of the goddess as enjoying that sacrifice of live Greeks which Iphigenia as her priestess is forced to initiate. (35–39) Later (380 ff.), as she scores the nice distinctions (σοφίσματα) of a goddess who spurns the defiled from her altars and yet enjoys human sacrifice, Iphigenia comes to reflect that no god could be guilty of such folly: these and other tales of divine cannibalism are the result of men's projection of their own ferocity upon the gods. (To these passages we should, perhaps, add Iphigenia's quotation, at vv. 585–87, of one of her former captives who exonerates Iphigenia but speaks of the goddess as regarding these sacrifices as just.)

So far, then, we have one or two hesitant criticisms by Iphigenia of the Tauric Artemis, and one more downright (and perhaps more purely "Euripidean") passage in which criticism breaks into frank disbelief that a god could ever be as Artemis is here presented as being. Iphigenia's own uncertainty about where the goddess stands in this matter is repeated in the automatic fear (despite the views just aired) that Artemis will frustrate their attempt at escape with the statue (995), and the poet's own desire to keep both ideas before us is shown in the immediate

[10]See above, note 5.

[11]ἧς in v. 36 is generally thought to refer to ἑορτῆς rather than to θεά in the preceding line. Possibly the ambiguity is intentional—a sort of euphemism on the part of the speaker and the poet.

"correction" which Orestes offers (1012–14) to the effect that Artemis would surely welcome her transfer to Athens.

Running parallel with this ambiguous criticism of the savage rite of the Tauric Artemis is the presentation of Iphigenia's own attitude toward the Greeks. Artemis' ill will against Agamemnon and his followers stems (vv. 20–21) from the King's neglect of a promise of the best fruits of the year to Artemis. Iphigenia's cause for bitterness (doubtless the reason for her choice as sacrificial priestess) is considerably greater. However, the poet takes some pains to show that, for the most part, Iphigenia rises above her bitterness. Normally, she is gentle-hearted and sympathetic toward her victims (344–47) and, as the passages already cited show, filled with revulsion at her fell office; only after her dream of (as she thinks) Orestes' death, does she turn savage and prepare to vent her bitterness on these latest Greek captives, "whosoe'er they be" (348–50); in the same speech, she longs, with more justice, that Helen might reach the land of the Taurians, so that she might take sacrificial vengeance on her for the sacrifice at Aulis. (354–58) Yet once she has talked to Orestes, she starts trying to find ways to save him, even before she knows him, and after the recognition she declares (989–95) her constant longing for Argos and her wish, *holding no grudge against the one who slew her* (992–93), to re-establish with Orestes her father's house.

Thus, in a device not uncommon in Euripides' treatment of the gods of myth, the nobility of a human heroine shows up the barbarity of the goddess—at least as she is presented in the savage Tauric rite. Indeed, the correction of this conception of Artemis' worship (as it is implied by Iphigenia's attitude, by the "saving" of Artemis' statue and by the change which Athena announces in the rite connected with it) is surely analogous to Euripides' own criticisms of the traditional gods of Greek mythology in plays such as the *Hippolytus*, the *Bacchae* and the *Heracles*. In the first two of these plays, the gods are reminded that they should be "wiser" (*Hippolytus*, 120) and less passionate in their anger (*Bacchae*, 1348) than men. In the *Heracles*, old Amphitryon contrasts his sense of duty to his foster-son, Heracles, with the carelessness of the mythological father, Zeus (339–47), while Heracles himself, like Iphigenia in the present play, is made to express the view (somewhat inconsistent with the mythological account of his own labours) that it is man who has invented unworthy stories of the gods. (1341–46)

It is perhaps for this reason that the poet keeps ambiguous the Greek belief (represented mainly by Iphigenia) in the Tauric version of Artemis, as if to show that not only the Taurians but also Greeks who accept such views of Artemis are guilty (in this as in other cases) of a misconception of the nature of the gods. However, not until the end of the play, in Athena's description (1456–61) of the new form which Artemis' worship is to take, do we realize that Athens is to provide a more "civilized" version of the goddess and her cult. There the non-fatal human "sacrifice" to Artemis makes explicit the whole purifying action of the play, as far as its religious content is concerned. Artemis has truly been saved from the bloody defilement which Iphigenia has accused the Taurians of inflicting on her (380–91), but it is surely the conception of the goddess herself, rather than the cult which represents that conception, which is of prime importance to the poet.

The ritual drop of human blood, symbolic reminder of that grim rite from which Orestes nearly perished, is also a reminder (as Athena tells us, 1459) of that other close call, the "sacrifice" of Iphigenia at Aulis. Thus we may see a new appropriateness in that "myth-stitching" with which we have earlier credited Euripides. Orestes, in obedience to Apollo, has saved Artemis and his sister from the savage rites of the Taurians, and in making possible the new and gentler rites of Artemis, he expiates his own matricide, the last consequence of that original sacrifice.

PART SEVEN

SATYRIC (AND PRO-SATYRIC?) DRAMA

18

THE Satyr-Play

The *Cyclops*

In discussing Euripides' adaptation of the tale of Odysseus' adventure with the Cyclops, one must bear in mind another of the *Odyssey's* cautionary tales: one must sail between Scylla and Charybdis in refusing either to dismiss the play (with one critic) as "a competent piece of fooling" with "no subtlety, tragic or comic," or to regard it (with another) as a fifth-century parable "about a struggle for justice between two men who either distort justice or deny its existence. . . ."[1]

The comic elements in the *Cyclops* are closer to the strong mixtures of Aristophanes than to the slick plot complexities and ironies of Euripidean romance and of New Comedy. Thus we find slapstick blended with verbal wit, comic incongruities in the placing of serious subjects in absurd contexts, and various ingenious adaptations of Homeric material to satyric situations. (The first—and major—difficulty, that of getting Silenus and the satyrs into the situation in the first place, has been easily managed in the prologue, where Silenus has told us a tale of shipwreck and capture by Polyphemus similar to that awaiting Odysseus and his men, save that the satyrs are wanted not as food but as slaves—their traditional role, as we shall see, in the satyr-play.) An excellent example of a specifically "satyric" adaptation is to be found in the absurdly Bacchic flavour which Silenus and the Chorus, dry as they are, manage to give to their pastoral duties. The approach of the satyrs with their flocks of sheep and goats reminds Silenus of the sound of feet dancing the Sicinnis (κρότος σικιννίδων, 37 ff.) "up at Althaea's house, with Bacchus, in the old days. . . ." Presumably the satyrs come on dancing the Sicinnis as they hail their charges with a pretty "herding" song

[1]For the two quotations see, respectively, Grube, 448, and William Arrowsmith, in the introduction to his translation of Euripides' *Cyclops*, 230 (cf. also 227).

faintly reminiscent, in its assumptions of sheepish sensibility, of the Homeric Cyclops' address to his favourite ram (*Odyssey* 9. 447 ff.). The song ends on a note of mock-tragic pathos (63–81) as the Chorus sadly laments (like the deprived Maenads of the *Bacchae*) the loss of Dionysus and his accoutrements of dancing, love and wine.

Especially wine: enter Odysseus with an inexhaustible flagon of the stuff. (Here we have another skilful adaptation: inexhaustibility—implied in verse 147, as well as in the subsequent action—is, theatrically speaking, a more useful kind of magic than the special strength and flavour of the Homeric potion.) The wine-bibbing is, of course, a particularly apt device for a satyr-play and Euripides extends it, beyond Homer's use of it to get the Cyclops drunk, to include full exploitation of the tippling Silenus. This provides him, first with a comic bargaining scene (which has the practical advantage of keeping Odysseus and his men outside the cave, and so on-stage, while Silenus gets the viands from within), and later with a mildly slapstick "drink-cadging" scene, in which the crafty Silenus constantly gets the better of his drunken master Polyphemus.

Other minor but amusing parodies of tragic themes are achieved by further expansions and adaptations of the traditional tale. In Silenus' absence, the Chorus quizzes Odysseus on his exploits at Troy, but all it really wants to discuss are lascivious details about the wanton Helen. This leads in turn to a parody of the potentially tragic theme of misogynism: "Would that the race of women had ne'er been born!" cry the indignant satyrs, but, unlike Hippolytus some years later, they add the satyric qualification, ". . . except for my use alone!" (186–87)

Odysseus' boast of his Trojan exploits brings from the Cyclops the unexpected rejoinder: "A disgraceful affair—for one woman's sake to sail against the land of Troy!" (283–84)—a charge which has already been raised, in a more sombre context, by the Chorus in Aeschylus' *Agamemnon* (e.g., at 225–26, 447–48, 799–801), and which Odysseus now dismisses with truly Euripidean cynicism: "Don't blame us *men*! It was the god's affair." (θεοῦ τὸ πρᾶγμα, 285)

In the same vein, a new twist is given to another traditional feature of the episode. As in Homer, Odysseus counts heavily, in his dealings with Polyphemus, on *Zeus Xenios*, Zeus, the protector of the suppliant stranger. (Compare *Cyclops* 353–55 with *Odyssey* ix. 269–71.) Now, however, Odysseus qualifies his prayers with typically Euripidean blasphemy:

> Zeus, god of strangers, look on this! . . for if you don't, then vainly (we'll conclude) we call you Zeus, who are no god at all! (354–55)

—a remark which anticipates Amphitryon's harsh words to a much more neglectful Zeus, at *Heracles* 339–47.[2]

So much has been said so far about adaptations and "Euripidean touches" that it should perhaps be pointed out that in its main lines, as well as in a good many details, the *Cyclops* follows the Homeric version of the adventure with remarkable fidelity. In both, Odysseus emphasizes his heroic "Trojan" renown and (as we have seen) his rights as a suppliant in the eyes of Zeus; in both, Polyphemus is equally lawless and scornful of such claims; in both, Polyphemus devours some of Odysseus' men; in both, Odysseus devises and carries out the same plan for blinding the Cyclops and escaping with his surviving comrades. Even the (to us) rather desperate "no man" joke of the *Odyssey* is faithfully preserved—though with rather less point in the necessarily changed dramatic circumstances of the Cyclops' outwitting. Indeed, it is because of, rather than in spite of, the play's faithfulness to the main lines of the Homeric account, that the Euripidean touches are so striking. Thus, in turning to the most important of these, we must bear in mind Kassel's observation that it all turns out "according to Homer" in the end.[3]

The most original and diverting passages in the play undoubtedly occur in the first (or pre-prandial) interview between Polyphemus and Odysseus. We have, of course, been prepared for the grimmest aspect of Polyphemus by Silenus' answer to Odysseus' query about the local attitude to strangers ("They do say they are the sweetest-*tasting* men!" 125–26). However, it is truly marvellous to find a Cyclops who is so completely the amoral cannibal and at the same time so bland, so articulate, so well up in things. It is the essential aspect of the Cyclops

[2]Rudolf Kassel has also commented on Odysseus of the *Cyclops* as an "authentic bearer of Euripidean tragic motives" (Träger echt euripideischer Tragödien-motive); he cites, with the passage just considered (*Cyclops* 353–55), the other "argumentative prayer" (*räsonnierendes Gebet*) of Odysseus at 599–607 which ends with the similar threat that unheard prayers will lead one to think that Chance (*Tyche*), not Olympus, is the real ruler. See R. Kassel, "Bemerkungen zum Kyklops des Euripides," *Rh. Mus.*, n.f. 98 (1955), esp. pp. 284–85. Kassel's treatment of the *Cyclops* is rather different from the one attempted in the present chapter (for one thing, Kassel tends to neglect the humorous aspects of the play) but, in addition to the observation just quoted concerning the attitude to the gods, he does note the ironic and iconoclastic attitude toward the Trojan War and its heroes as typical of the "skeptical distance" between Euripides and his dramatic characters. And yet in the end the hero, and so the world of illusion, triumphs, "just as in Homer." This retention of the Homeric outcome, without further ironic comment, should be borne in mind in considering such rationalistic and sophisticated studies as that of William Arrowsmith, now to be discussed.

[3]See above, note 2.

which appears first (we will return to the Cyclops as sophist later)—in response to Silenus' barefaced false witness against Odysseus:

So! Then sharpen up the knives and light the fire . . . (241–43)
I've had my fill of lions and stags . . . it's time I ate a man again! (248–49)
[ODYSSEUS]: Now, Cyclops, listen in turn to what we strangers also have to say. It was like this. . . . (253 ff.)

The beauty of this, as of most of Odysseus' statements and arguments to the Cyclops, is the rhetorical tone of one "civilized" man (or state, even) to another. This tone is particularly marked in Odysseus' first and rather extraordinary plea for mercy (290–98) on the grounds that the Greeks have preserved the shrines of Poseidon and even the Sicilian home of the Cyclops from thieving Trojans. William Arrowsmith, suspecting an allusion to the political claims of contemporary Athens, comments cleverly:

> What Odysseus is urging here is nothing more or less than the argument which Athens had used to acquire her empire: Athens had saved Hellas and should have the rewards of her deed.[4]

However, Arrowsmith appears to me to carry his argument too far. By cunning quotations from Thucydides' speeches, he shows the ultimate cynicism of such Athenian arguments and so concludes of Odysseus' claims: "the irony lies in the fact that an argument normally used to deny mercy to others is here being used to obtain it." Even apart from the anachronism, in the context of the critic's argument, of the Thucydidean passages which he quotes,[5] this is surely loading Odysseus' speech with far more devious subtlety (on the poet's part) than it will bear, especially since it is this dubious part of Arrowsmith's interpretation which colours his whole view of Odysseus as an allegorical example of fifth century political depravity. Thus, Arrowsmith regards Odysseus' next plea, in the name of *nomos*, as "pure sophistry," "a mere convention of the weak to elude the strong," and Odysseus' ultimate recourse to brutal vengeance as a contradiction of that *nomos* which he has just invoked.[6] But both the "rights-of-the-suppliant" argument *and* the ultimate vengeance of Odysseus are in accordance with the Homeric version

[4]Arrowsmith, 228.

[5]The date of the *Cyclops* is not known, but it is generally regarded on metrical and stylistic grounds as an early play of Euripides, perhaps before 438. Even if the play is as late as 425 B.C., as Arrowsmith suggests (see his ingenious argument [p. 224, n. 1] connecting the *Cyclops* with the *Hecuba*), it still seems a bit unfair to descend as far as the Melian Dialogue, referring to 416 B.C., to exemplify the kind of moral climate which Euripides is allegedly parodying.

[6]Arrowsmith, 228–30.

which, in turn, is in accordance with Homeric ethics;[7] in neither case are we meant to be shocked or outraged by this "epic" (or, possibly, "folk-tale") style of vengeance, though, like Homer's audience, we may be aware that the *lex talionis*, through the powerful agency of the Cyclops' father, Poseidon, may overtake Odysseus in the end.

The same excellences and exaggerations seem to me characterize Arrowsmith's treatment of Polyphemus himself. He rightly berates the traditional view that Euripides is simply dramatizing "Homer's parable of the civilized man and the savage," and suggests that Polyphemus is "less Caliban than Callicles, an outright exponent of philosophical egoism and the immoralist equation of might and right."[8] This is a fair enough description of the Polyphemus of the speech at verses 316–46, which is full of splendidly expressed sophistries defending the hedonism of the belly ("*That's* the wise man's Zeus!" 337) and Cyclopeian self-sufficiency, while sneering at law and order (τοὺς νόμους, 338) as man-made embellishments. But because of such a speech to take Polyphemus so seriously as to talk, as Arrowsmith does at the end of his essay, of "a struggle for justice between two men [*sic*] who either distort justice or deny its existence . . ." is surely a distortion of Euripides' fun. At least half the time, Polyphemus is more monster than man and so is outside these solemn arguments. He is no more "all-Callicles" than he is "all-Caliban." (Can one, for example, imagine the fifth-century sophist, like a good honest cannibal, salivating and gulping, before and after taking his awful meal?) The point—and the humour—lies in the incongruity of the tone and sentiments imposed on the savage at certain moments, and this point is missed if such witty moments are prolonged and distorted to produce conclusions worthy of tragedy.[9] It is in the

7The argument is based on *nomos* in Euripides, on *themis* in Homer; compare *Cyclops* 299 ff. and *Od.* 266–71.

8See Arrowsmith, 227 ff., for this discussion of Polyphemus. Examples of the "traditional" attitude to Euripides' *Cyclops* will be found in Norwood, *Greek Tragedy*, 289–91 and, more recently in E. della Valle, "Saggio critico sul Ciclope di Euripide," *Atti della Accademia di Napoli* 13. 2. (1933–34), 3–32 (summarized in Marouzeau, *L'Année Philologique*, 1936).

9Arrowsmith does, it is true, remark the changes in *persona* which Polyphemus appears to go through. "Homeric cannibal," "Euripidean Callicles," "decadent, rather likable buffoon"; he regards this (wrongly, I think) as effecting a shift in sympathy in the Cyclops' favour, which will make Odyesseus appear all the more contemptible for his hideous revenge. Cf. also P. Masqueray, "Le Cyclope d'Euripide et celui d'Homère," *REA*, IV (1902), 184–87, and L. Méridier in his introduction (*Euripide*, I, 12); both these critics liken Euripides' Polyphemus to a more brutalized and less philosophic fifth-century immoralist. Masqueray (p. 186–87) adds the original suggestion that the contemporary Athenian audience would

speeches, not in the action, that the difference between the Homeric and the Euripidean treatment lies; hence it is a rhetorical, in places even a whimsical, difference. In terms of the action (and, if we *must* take this *tour de force* seriously, it is to the action, or plot, that we must look), Euripides' Odysseus is as guilty or as innocent as the Homeric Odysseus, since he suffers and performs precisely the same things in the same circumstances.

Some General Characteristics

Is it possible, from our knowledge of the *Cyclops* and from our fragmentary knowledge of the plot material of some seven other satyr-plays of Euripides,[10] to set down certain recurrent features of this *genre*, at least as it was employed by Euripides? Such a synthesis, however tentative, might prove useful in discussing other extant plays of Euripides which, for one reason or another, one may be tempted to regard as "pro-satyric" in some meaningful sense of the term.[11] To enlarge this description to include guesses about the satyr-plays of Aeschylus and Sophocles would be too lengthy and unrewarding a process in this context; however, a few comparative references to Sophocles' *Ichneutae*, the only other satyr-play besides the *Cyclops* of which a substantial amount has survived, may help us to verify certain typical characteristics of the *genre* in the latter half of the fifth century.[12] In the following list,

rather enjoy hearing Odysseus' irritatingly clever arguments squashed—even by brutality.

[10]The lost satyr-plays of Euripides were, as far as our knowledge of them goes, the *Autolycus*, the *Busiris*, the *Eurystheus*, the *Sciron*, the *Syleus*, the *Theristae*, and the *Sisyphus*. Except as otherwise noted, inferences about the plot material, plot *motives* and the like are here based on the fragments and other material in Nauck, *Euripidis Tragoediae*, III[2] (*Fragmenta*). Occasionally, the material in Nauck has been supplemented by reference to the fragments of a collection of Euripidean *Hypotheses* recently published in *The Oxyrhynchus Papyri*, vol. 27 (London 1962), no. 2455, pp. 32–69.

[11]Information surviving from the *didascaliae* is meagre, only three complete tetralogies being cited by name in the ancient evidence which has come down to us. Here the *Theristae* and the *Sisyphus* are listed as satyr-plays and the *Alcestis* is listed, but not as a satyr-play, as fourth in its tetralogy. Since from ancient sources we know of only six other Euripidean satyr-plays, including the *Cyclops*, it seems not improbable that Euripides allowed more than one non-satyric (or "pro-satyric") play to stand fourth in its tetralogy.

[12]Over three hundred more or less consecutive lines, some of them incomplete, of Sophocles' *Ichneutae* have been recovered. See A. C. Pearson, *The Fragments of Sophocles*, I, 224–70, and D. L. Page, *Greek Literary Papyri*, 26–53. The date of the *Ichneutae* is not known, but on purely formal grounds it is clearly earlier than Euripides' *Cyclops* (see Pearson, 231).

it will be noted that one characteristic tends to slide into another, for in any such synthetic formulation the divisions are bound to be somewhat arbitrary.

(*i*) Brevity. The *Cyclops* has only 709 lines and so is the shortest Euripidean play by a considerable margin. The next two, excluding the mutilated *Heracleidae*, are the *Rhesus* (the authenticity of which is still in question) with 996 lines, and the *Alcestis*, with 1163 lines. The *Cyclops* is several hundred lines shorter than the average length of a Euripidean play, which is close to 1400 lines. To this purely formal feature of the satyr-play, we should, perhaps, add another, the relatively simple lyric rhythms; however, this, like other aspects of the satyric chorus, probably belongs with the purely conventional features of form related to the origin of satyric drama. Such features will not necessarily be relevant to possible "pro-satyric" developments.

(*ii*) The element of slapstick, ribaldry of language and action and, if it suits the context, drunkenness. These characteristics, so obviously suited to the satyrs themselves, are particularly prominent in the *Cyclops* and in the plot situations of several other Euripidean satyr-plays (such as the *Syleus*, where Heracles as the rebellious slave probably indulged in a good deal of property-smashing). We should, perhaps, extend this category to include *an emphasis on physical action and adventure* in general. What we know of such mythological ruffians as Sciron, Syleus and Sisyphus itself guarantees an element of violence in the plays bearing their names, and the *Busiris* probably involved one of the more monstrous of Heracles' labours as well as the on-stage terrorizing of Eurystheus. The physical element, with a touch of buffoonery in language and action, is present also in Sophocles' *Ichneutae*. At vv. 85–90 ff., the satyrs sniff along the scent of the lost cattle of Apollo on all fours, like hounds. It is pleasant, too, to find Sophocles capable of such undressed language as "⌊Chorus⌋ Hoo! Hoo! Hoo! Hoo! [Silenus]: What're you 'hoo-ing' about?" and such almost Euripidean levity as "God! God! God! God!" to represent sheer mad excitement (v. 94, where see Pearson's reference to Wilamowitz's comparison with Euripides, *Helena* 560; it is doubtful, however, whether Wilamowitz regarded either of the passages as funny). On the grounds of coarse and "outrageous" elements in language or plot situation, one is tempted to include both Sophocles' *Banqueters* (Σύνδειπνοι), which some scholars *do* regard as a satyr-play,[13] and Euripides' *Aeolus*, in which the situation, at least, is as outrageous

[13]See Pearson's discussion and references, *Fragments*, I, xxi and II, 200–201; cf. also Norwood, *Greek Tragedy*, 174. (Frg. 565 certainly has a satyric smell to it!)

as anything in Aristophanes.[14] But in both these cases, we are, perhaps, closer to the "pro-satyric" than to the satyric play proper.

(*iii*) The enslavement and ultimate freeing of the satyrs. While it is often unsafe to generalize on these matters from our knowledge of the *Cyclops*, it is very tempting to regard the servitude and freeing of the satyrs as a conventional motif of the satyr-play. In the *Cyclops*, the mutual sympathy and alliance of Odysseus and the satyrs against the one-eyed ogre seems almost taken for granted (see, for example, 270 ff., 361 ff., 435–36), as if the audience expected it, and the many other lawless "villains" who people Euripides' satyr-plays (Autolycus, Sisyphus, Sciron, Syleus, even perhaps Eurystheus, viewed in some lights) can easily be imagined as playing the same slavemaster and jailer role *vis-à-vis* the satyrs as Polyphemus does in the *Cyclops*. (In the *Ichneutae*, however, while the freeing of the satyrs was again, apparently [see v. 57], a dramatic motif, their master, whether Apollo or Dionysus,[15] was not in this case an ogre or a villainous bully.) Generally speaking, satyrs, though lascivious, selfish and cowardly, are "sympathetic" creatures, and it is to be expected that they would be in alliance with the "hero" against the oppressor: enslavement with the prospect of freedom is one of the probable bases for such an alliance. But all this implies another more fundamental feature of the satyr-play, which we may consider next.

(*iv*) "Turning the tables"; discomfiture of the bully; progression of the "hero's" fortunes from bad to good. The *Cyclops*, of course, gives us a clear example of this and one in which the significant features may well be characteristic of the employment of this motif generally. There is a precise (and, in this case, hideous) poetic justice about Odysseus' vengeance on Polyphemus. The monster has offended horribly against the laws of hospitality and it is by Odysseus' "hospitable" treatment of him ("dearest of guests," the drinking Cyclops calls him, v. 418) that he is undone; the great single eye is the most monstrous feature of the ogre, and it is in the eye that Odysseus "does him." Now, in the case of the *Busiris*, the *Syleus* and the *Sciron*, a fairly precise reversal of the positions and fortunes of the oppressor and the hero seems likely to have taken place, a reversal, moreover, which, like that of the *Cyclops*,

[14]The plot of the *Aeolus* involved an unsuccessful plan for mass incest on the part of Macareus, one of Aeolus' sons who had seduced one of his sisters. See Nauck, III^2, *Fragmenta*, pp. 3 ff. (The fragment of Antiphanes' *Aeolus* which Nauck quotes has a distinct ring of tragic parody.)

[15]The vexed question of the master's identity in this play need not concern us further here; for the relevant arguments, see Pearson, I, 231–33, 253 (note to v. 218 ff.) and (against Pearson on this matter) Page, *GLP*, 29.

may have involved a certain irony, a suggestion of the villain being "hoist on his own petard." In the *Autolycus*, the master-thief of that name is foiled by an even greater master-thief, Sisyphus. In the *Eurystheus*, the labour imposed on Heracles, apparently that of stealing Cerberus from Hades, probably results in the terrorizing of Eurystheus himself by Cerberus.[16] One would like to think that the *Sciron*, in conformity with this theme of table-turning, followed the well known myth in which the Megarian robber, whose favourite pastime was kicking his victims into the sea, was himself hurled into the sea by Theseus. However, the surviving fragments of the play itself give us no real information, and a recently discovered fragment of a hypothesis of this play tells us only that Hermes, his identity unknown to his master, was kept as a trusted servant by Sciron.[17] Finally, it is clear that the *dénouement* of the *Syleus* concerned the discomfiture of Syleus at the hands of his rebellious slave Heracles, who (with much aid from the satyrs, no doubt) tore up his vines, feasted on his beef and his wines and (whether with murderous or merely lecherous intent it is uncertain) pursued his daughter through his vineyard.[18] We may conclude, then, that "turning the tables," the more or less violent discomfiture of the oppresser by the (originally) oppressed, was a recurrent feature of Euripidean satyr-plays. (The reversal of the *Ichneutae* we may guess to have resided in the conciliation of Apollo, Hermes' gift of the lyre more than compensating him for the loss of the stolen cattle.)

(*v*) Theft. The names and plot situations of several plays already mentioned (e.g., *Autolycus*, *Eurystheus*, *Sciron*) suggest that robbery and in some cases detection and reprisals were a stock ingredient of satyr-plays and, perhaps, of Euripidean satyr-plays in particular. In the *Cyclops*, as in the *Autolycus*, pilfering (by Silenus) is only a minor motif; in Sophocles' *Ichneutae*, the detection of and (perhaps) compensation for the theft appear to have provided the main plot interest of the play.

There are two or three other features of Euripidean satyr-plays which are related to those just described but which cannot be set down quite so categorically. One of these is the air of burlesque, sometimes even of parody, at the expense of traditional myths and legends. This impression derives partly from the fact that it was mainly the more "outrageous"

[16]See *Eurystheus*, fig. 372 (N) for the despatch of Heracles to Hades; see also W. N. Bates, *Euripides*, 248, and references and illustration there cited.

[17]*Ox. Pap.*, no. 2455, frg. 6.

[18]For the first part of this tale, see Nauck, III², *Fragmenta*, p. 185 and the references there given; the last detail is provided in *Ox. Pap.*, no. 2455, frg. 8.

legends which were suited to the buffoonery of satyr-plays, but also, perhaps, from a slightly "off-centre" treatment of a given legend, such as we have seen in Euripides' introduction of fifth-century sophistication and subtlety at certain points of the *Cyclops*. This point, it is true, can in the circumstances be illustrated only from the *Cyclops*, among Euripidean satyr-plays, though one feels that it might have been true of such plays as the *Eurystheus* as well, in view of the curiously realistic and tragic treatment which Euripides was able to give to another of Heracles' experiences. In Sophocles' *Ichneutae*, too, considerable liberties seem to have been taken with a traditional myth (as we find it, for example, in *Homeric Hymn IV, to Hermes*) to adapt it to the excitement and buffoonery of the satyr-play.

Finally, we may note a feature of the Euripidean satyr-play which is related both to this element of burlesque at the expense of myth and to the conventional *dénouement* of "the bully-boy bested" or "the spoiler spoiled." That feature is, of course, the intrusion of either a god, a demigod, or occasionally, a hero with some exceptional power, aided perhaps by some magical gift. Heracles is by far the most frequent of such extraordinary agencies by which the ogre is overwhelmed, but occasionally Hermes (as, apparently, in the *Sciron* and in Sophocles' *Inachus*) may be used. Even apart from the "overthrow of the bully," the gods and demigods, divine monsters and nymphs and the like seem to wander into the middle of things more readily in satyr-plays than in tragedy proper. And even Sophocles, in his tragedies more restrained than Euripides in the matter of divine epiphanies, presents Apollo, the nymph Cyllene and, perhaps (in the lost *dénouement* of the play), the youthful Hermes, all within one satyr-play.

19

THE *Alcestis*

The Myth and Its Adaptation

In an attempt to judge the nature and purpose of Euripides' treatment of the myths of Admetus and Alcestis, let us set down the bare events as Euripides gives them, together with what we know of this material from other sources.

Apollo tells us in the prologue of the *Alcestis* that he had enabled King Admetus to postpone his impending death by persuading the Fates to let Admetus off if he could find someone willing to die in his place; this sacrifice Alcestis, wife of Admetus, has accepted after both his parents had refused it, and now the appointed day for Alcestis' death is at hand. Apollo explains as follows his own involvement with Admetus: furious at the death of his son Asclepius, slain by Zeus' thunderbolt, Apollo had in turn slain the Cyclopes (makers of thunderbolts) and for punishment had been enslaved for a period to the mortal Admetus; it was during this sojourn that the threat to Admetus' life occurred and Apollo intervened, in gratitude for his human master's piety toward him.

After this monologue, Thanatos (Death), appears, to begin his fell office. After further unsuccessful attempts to dissuade him, Apollo prophesies that Heracles (identified by description rather than by name) will wrest Alcestis by force from Thanatos. In the course of the play, Alcestis dies, but not before her husband has promised her, in gratitude, a life of celibacy for himself and of cheerless mourning for himself and his house. During the funeral arrangements, Heracles visits Admetus' palace and, unaware of the situation, is hospitably entertained by Admetus; when he learns of his host's hospitable dissimulation, he rewards it by overcoming Thanatos in an off-stage wrestling match and restoring Alcestis to Admetus.

Even at first glance, a certain cleavage, a certain basic lack of congeniality, appears between different elements in this myth. On the one hand, we have an Olympian, Apollo, and his relations with a human hero, King Admetus; on the other hand, we have Thanatos, a creature of folk-tale, carrying off the King's wife who is, in turn, rescued by a sort of superman, Heracles. The only connection which Apollo has with the action of the play itself is that he first arranges the "privilege" of the substitute death; after a brief attempt to put off Thanatos, Apollo leaves the scene for good, and the final overcoming of death is effected in a manner quite alien to the mythical world which Apollo inhabits.

This initial impression of cleavage increases greatly when we look at the mythological tradition relevant to the play. There is evidence of early accounts of Apollo's bondage to Admetus (e.g., a passing reference in Homer, signs of a fuller account in the Hesiodic catalogue)[1] but no actual mention, before tragedy, of Alcestis' self-sacrifice. This does not, of course, mean that the Alcestis legend did not exist before then, but it may indicate that it was not always attached to the Apollo-Admetus story and that, consequently, it was not always a part of the main mythical tradition. The only known treatment of the Alcestis theme itself before Euripides is that of Phrynichus' *Alcestis*[2] of which we have only one actual quotation:

σῶμα δ' ἀθαμβὲς† γυοδόνιστον† τείρει
He constrains the fearless, limb-driven [?] (limb-mastered [?]) body.
(frg. 2)

This fragment is usually taken, though with no certainty, to refer to the wrestling match between Heracles and Thanatos. It is possible that Aeschylus' reference (*Eumenides*, 723–28) to Apollo's persuasion of the Moirai, by drink, to spare men's lives, and the Euripidean Apollo's casual reference to his tricking of the Fates (*Alcestis*, 12), may be allusions to Phrynichus' treatment of the theme. (If so, one is tempted to think Phrynichus' *Alcestis* must have been a satyr-play.) Apart from this, all we know of the lost play is that Thanatos appeared in it carrying a sword for the ritual cutting of Alcestis' hair. (frg. 3)

The "Hesiodic" account seems to have been concerned entirely with the background of Apollo's bondage to Admetus: Apollo's jealous

[1]There seems to be an oblique reference to Apollo's bondage to Admetus, son of Pheres, at *Il.* 2. 763–66; Homer's only reference to Alcestis with Admetus occurs in his naming of the parents of Eumelus at *Il.* 2. 713–15. For the Hesiodic references, see Hesiod, fragments 122–27 (Rzach) from the *Ehoiai*, or *Catalogue of Famous Women.* A scholium to Euripides, *Alc.* 1 (Hes. frg. 127) assures us that in the parts of the myth concerning Apollo's enslavement to Admetus, Euripides is following the common tale as told by Hesiod and Asclepiades. (The scholiast also adds several other ancient sources, including writers as early as Stesichorus and Pherecydes, for this part of the myth.)

[2]See Nauck, *TGF*, p. 720.

vengeance, with Artemis' help, on his beloved and unfaithful Coronis; his saving of Asclepius, his son by Coronis, Zeus' blasting of Asclepius for raising men from the dead; Apollo's reprisals against the Cyclopes (the makers of Zeus' thunderbolts) and his subsequent enslavement to Admetus in punishment. Only the last of these details is factually relevant to Euripides' plot, though there is a certain thematic overlap in the roles of Asclepius and Heracles.

Among the post-Classical accounts of the Apollo-Admetus-Alcestis myths, that of Apollodorus is of the greatest interest. Here it is worth noting that the myth ending with Apollo's enslavement to Admetus is told separately from the Admetus-Alcestis legend.[3] The former follows very closely the main lines of the early ("Hesiodic") version, while the Admetus-Alcestis legend differs in several respects from Euripides' version. The latter account runs as follows:

When Admetus reigned over Pherae, Apollo served him as his thrall, while Admetus wooed Alcestis, daughter of Pelias. Now Pelias had promised to give his daughter to him who should yoke a lion and a boar to a car, and Apollo yoked them and gave them to Admetus, who brought them to Pelias and so obtained Alcestis. But in offering a sacrifice at his marriage, he forgot to sacrifice to Artemis; therefore when he opened the marriage chamber, he found it full of coiled snakes. Apollo bade him appease the goddess and obtained as a favour of the Fates that, when Admetus should be about to die, he might be released from death if someone should choose voluntarily to die for him. And when the day of his death came neither his father nor his mother would die for him, but Alcestis died in his stead. But the Maiden [Persephone] sent her up again, or, as some say, Hercules fought with Hades [and brought her up to him]. [The last clause is omitted in the MSS.]

Here the most interesting differences from the Euripidean version are: the role of Artemis and the alternative explanations of the restoration of Alcestis. The anger of Artemis perhaps explains the unexplained "imminent death" mentioned as threatening Admetus in Euripides' version (*Alc.* 13), though there seems to be an interesting hint of a *non sequitur* in Apollodorus between the "appeasing of Artemis" and the favour obtained from the Fates. The peaceful version of Alcestis' return to life is, of course, the one more favourable to the gods of mythology (one should note, by the way, that Hades has been substituted for Thanatos even in the other version) and it is this version too which Plato follows (*Symposium* 179b 5 ff.), when he tells us that the gods returned Alcestis of their own accord in admiration of her

[3]See Apollodorus, *Bibl.* 3. 10. 3–4 and 1. 9. 15 respectively. The translation of the latter passage, quoted below, is that of Sir James Frazer.

deed. Robert suggests that Plato himself may have invented this milder version; however this may be, we may accept his view that the more violent version is the older one.[4]

It seems clear from all that has been said that the myth leading to the enslavement of Apollo to Admetus and the myth involving Alcestis' "substitute" death for Admetus were originally of quite separate and indeed fundamentally different origins. The former belongs to the anthropomorphic and essentially literary tradition of Olympian mythology; the latter, with its bargains and struggles with the monster Thanatos, that pathetically simple incarnation of human fears, suggests the primitive, superstitious and infinitely more urgent preoccupations of folk tale—until, of course, it becomes softened by late and artificial mythologizing. Indeed it is not until Hyginus (*Fab.* 49 and 51), in the second century A.D., and Zenobius (1. 18) that we find a continuous narrative starting from the myths of Apollo and Asclepius and ending with the death and restoration of Alcestis. Despite all contrary indications, Wilamowitz, followed by Ebeling, Séchan, Méridier and others, argues that this *consecutive* treatment found in the late writers goes back to the "canonical" formulation of the Hesiodic catalogue, which he also claims to be the source of the two accounts in Apollodorus; this view has been rightly rejected by Professor A. Lesky and Miss A. M. Dale.[5]

In default of evidence establishing the literary ancestry of the Alcestis theme prior to Greek tragedy, let us turn to the "arguments from probability" by which Robert, Lesky and others assert that the core of our story belongs to popular folk tale rather than to literary tradition. The most ambitious attempt to establish the actual folk-tale kernel of the Alcestis myth has been made by Lesky who, after discussing the relation of popular to literary mythology in general, outlines three European folk tales, preserved in German, Greek and Armenian folk songs, which contain elements of the basic situation in the *Alcestis*.[6] Stripping these songs of their individual developments and variations,

[4]C. Robert, *Thanatos* (Berlin 1879), 29–30.

[5]See U. von Wilamowitz, *Philol. Untersuchungen*, IX, 68 ff. and (on the alleged origins and significance of such popular religious poetry attributed to Hesiod), *Griechische Tragoedien*, III, 7 ff., in Wilamowitz's introduction to *Alkestis*. Cf. also Méridier, in his introduction to *Alcestis*, in *Euripide*, I, 46–47 and (in contrast) A. M. Dale, *Euripides, Alcestis*, ix. (Detailed references to the other critics mentioned will be made later in this chapter.)

[6]A. Lesky, *Alkestis*: *Der Mythus und das Drama*. The German, Greek and Armenian folk songs are outlined and discussed at pp. 20 ff., 27 ff., and 30 ff., respectively. Cf. also Christ-Schmid, I, 355–56, n. 1, where the folk-tale aspects of Euripides *Alcestis* are also stressed.

Lesky reduces the story to what he considers to be its simplest and oldest form: On the wedding day of a King, Death comes for the bridegroom; Death is willing to accept a substitute, but both the King's parents refuse the sacrifice; finally, the young bride intervenes and follows Death to save the life of her beloved.[7]

Lesky lists several variations and developments: husband dies for doomed bride (manly German version as opposed to eastern expressions of female inferiority!); a physical struggle with Death as well as (originally instead of?) a substitute death, and so on. *Whenever the physical struggle with Death is introduced, the husband himself is the challenger, and when, for one reason or another, he fails, his life is saved only by the self-sacrifice of his bride.*

It is interesting to contrast the way in which this duplication of methods for dealing with Death is handled in Euripides' play. Here, one device is used to save the husband, the other, his self-sacrificing wife. Moreover, in our *Alcestis,* the dramatist further separates the two devices (and so uses them to better effect) by attaching one of them to the mythical, "divine" prologue (where Apollo tells of persuading the Fates to accept Alcestis as a substitute), while reserving the other for the "folk-tale" *dénouement,* where a hero struggles with the primitive figure of Thanatos. Finally, in Euripides' version, the hero who struggles with Death is an outside agent, not, as in the folk songs, the husband himself. Thus, while both ways of foiling Death are presented, the husband engages in neither while gaining from both. Already we catch a glimpse of a whole new dimension, full of psychological and ethical possibilities, in Euripides' adaptation.

How did such a folk tale come to be attached to the end of a myth dealing with the enslavement of Apollo? Nobody knows, of course, but there have been some interesting guesses. Carl Robert points to Euripides' own words at *Alcestis* 445 ff. (where the Chorus prophesies that the Queen's fame will be celebrated in song at Sparta at the time of the Carnean festival, as well as at Athens) and suggests that it was at the Carnea, which honoured Apollo, and at similar popular celebrations of Apollo at Athens, that the simple folk song got its poetic development.[8] However, this still does not explain why it became attached to the Apollo myth in the first place. Thessaly, a region much given to chthonian cults, was surely a congenial place for such a folk tale to be developed, and Admetus, to whom Apollo was enslaved, was a Thessalian king. Other scholars go rather further in this matter and point to

[7]This is a paraphrase of the summary in Lesky, 41–42; cf. *ibid.*, 36–41.
[8]Robert, 29.

connections between Admetus and *Hades adamastos* ("the unconquerable") and between "Admetus the hospitable" and *Hades poludegmon, Hades poluxenos*![9] There are other possible links between the Apollo myth and the Alcestis story: Asclepius, Apollo's son, is the hero who, foreshadowing Heracles' role in our play, raised men from the dead, and Apollo himself is, of course, the Olympian opponent *par excellence* of the chthonic powers. In this connection, Aeschylus' reference (*Eumenides*, 723 ff.) to Apollo's cheating of the Fates in Admetus' interest is most suggestive, for it is in the *Eumenides* that we have the greatest literary expression of this aspect of Apollo.

In Euripides' *Alcestis*, we have two interventions from "outside," one by Apollo before the action of the play begins, and one by Heracles at its conclusion. Obviously, no one like Heracles was needed in the original folk tale: as we have seen, any Death-wrestling that was to be done was done by the husband himself. Nor does Heracles have any part in the Apollo myth. When did he come into the picture?

The possibility that Euripides himself first introduced the role of Heracles into the Alcestis myth has been raised by one or two scholars, most notably Ebeling, though his approach is very different from the one which we have been following.[10] It is true that this suggestion contradicts the view (rather uncertainly based on Phrynichus, fr. 1) that Euripides followed Phrynichus' *Alcestis* in this matter. Ebeling's argument that Phrynichus' play could hardly have extended from Apollo's outwitting of the Fates (see Aeschylus, *Eumenides* 723–28) to the rescue of Alcestis by Heracles, seems weak. Euripides himself "covers" this much, if we include what Apollo tells us in the prologue—and not much more than this would be needed to explain the (quite hypothetical) reference to Phrynichus' play in Aeschylus' *Eumenides*. It seems preferable to point out that no opinion concerning the content of Phrynichus' *Alcestis* can really be based on a tiny fragment in which text, meaning, reference and context are all uncertain.[11]

Ebeling's suggestion that the role of Heracles is Euripides' invention fits well with what he, in common with several recent critics, feels to be an important aspect of Euripides' treatment: the new kind of emphasis

[9]For a sympathetic summary of such views, see L. Séchan, "Le Dévouement d'Alceste," I, 490–514, esp. 493–98, and references to Wilamowitz and Bloch there given.

[10]See Herman L. Ebeling, *TAPA*, XXIX, 65–85, esp. 74–77. Cf. also Th. Bergk, *Griechische Literaturgeschichte*, III, 498, who believes that in Phrynichus' *Alcestis*, Alcestis' return was the gift of the gods of the Underworld.

[11]On this fragment of Phrynichus, cf. also Dale, xiii–xiv, and references there given.

on the role of Admetus.[12] It has not, perhaps, been generally recognized that this emphasis depends in large part on Heracles, for without the intrusion of that hero it would not have been easy to present the "restoration" of Alcestis as in some way related to the character and actions of Admetus. Indeed, without Heracles, very little in the way of decisive action would have been left for Admetus at all.

In the folk tale, no one ever wins the wrestling match with Death; nor would the somewhat sentimental "moral" ending which Plato chose have suited the sinister figure of Death in Euripides' piece. To achieve a happy ending within the chosen ethos a typically Euripidean rescuer must be imported—and in a pro-satyric play, what figure could be more suitable than Heracles? Throughout Euripides' work, we find him the most inventive of the dramatists, and the more remote his material, the more daring his innovations. The present device, the appearance of an unexpected rescuer from outside the immediate context of the legendary situation or (sometimes) of the poet's own plot, occurs in one form or another in the *Medea*, the *Heracles* and the *Andromache*, and in at least two of these instances, the "intrusion" appears to have been a Euripidean innovation in the legend concerned.

Finally, the motivation of Heracles' role provides a nice, ironical balance to the mythological introduction to the theme, and one consistent with Euripides' derogatory treatment of the Olympians, particularly of Apollo. The god, in saving his hospitable host Admetus, has placed Alcestis in her present plight and has proved unable to extricate her; now the hero Heracles, also in gratitude for Admetus' hospitality, succeeds by his "folk-tale methods" in doing what Apollo has tried and failed to do.[13]

The Play and Its Problems

The *Alcestis* is the only non-satyric play which we actually know, from an ancient hypothesis, to have been produced as the fourth play

[12]See Ebeling, 65–66, 76–77.

[13]The suggestion that Euripides introduced Heracles into the Alcestis story must, of course, remain conjectural. It should be added, however, that there appears to be no evidence in painting or sculpture to contradict either this view or the view previously expressed concerning the relatively late entry of the theme of Alcestis' self-sacrifice into the main tradition of Greek mythology. According to J. A. Paton, *AJA*, IV, 150–51, "The myth was not popular in the earlier art and no unquestioned representations of it have survived." J. D. Beazley, *Etruscan Vase Paintings*, 134, refers to but one uncertain representation of Alcestis on an Attic neck amphora (Louvre F60). The fourth-century Etruscan representations of the Alcestis story do not include the figure of Heracles.

in its tetralogy. The lengthy arguments among scholars as to whether, while lacking a satyr-chorus, it still preserved some features of the satyr-play, go back to the writers of the same hypothesis, one of whom calls the "change of fortune" (καταστροφή) in the play "rather comic" in nature, the other of whom (possibly commenting on the preceding remark)[14] describes the play as "rather satyric, because, unlike tragedy, its change of fortune brings delight and pleasure." The point is not entirely academic, since, if some affinity (not necessarily of the kind suggested above) can be found between the *Alcestis* and satyr-plays, the elements which seem to set the *Alcestis* off from the serious tragedies of Euripides need not induce us to place it, as Kitto has placed it (not very happily, in my opinion), among his so-called tragicomedies and melodramas. Moreover, if the term "pro-satyric" can be used of the *Alcestis* in a fairly significant sense, then it seems possible that Euripides wrote more plays of this kind. We have the names of only three complete tetralogies of Euripides (including that to which the *Alcestis* belongs), and a total of only eight of his plays are described anywhere in ancient sources as "satyric." This is much less than a quarter of the total number of titles (probably seventy-five) which can be safely attributed to Euripides, and so it is a reasonable inference that several plays which stood fourth in their tetralogy must have been "pro-satyric" in one sense or another.[15]

Miss A. M. Dale, in her edition of the play, has given perhaps the fairest of recent assessments of the pro-satyric elements in the *Alcestis*.[16] She speaks of the happy ending combined with "a curiously tart, almost bitter flavour"—which is just right for the *Alcestis*; of the presentation

[14]Miss Dale's explanation (xl) of the authorship of the second paragraph of the second hypothesis is doubtless correct.

[15]In this connection, it is interesting to note that the *Sisyphus*, hitherto accepted on Aelian's testimony as the satyr-play to the *Alexander*, *Palamedes* and *Troades* is listed in a recently discovered fragment of a list of Euripides' plays without the description "satyr-play." It is just possible that the mistake might be in Aelian and not in the papyrus fragment, and, if so, it could be due to the fact that a non-satyric (or "pro-satyric") *Sisyphus* stood fourth in this tetralogy. See Nauck, *Eur. Trag.*, 3, *Fragmenta*, p. 10, and *Ox. Pap.* (1962), no. 2456, respectively, for the two references above. Gilbert Murray, in his edition of the *Rhesus*, ix, x, has sought to explain certain oddities in the *Rhesus* on the grounds that it is a Euripidean pro-satyric drama. Were the Euripidean authorship of this play not so much in doubt on other grounds (see Preface, and references there given), it would be tempting to develop these suggestions in connection with the general characteristics of Euripidean satyr-plays tentatively suggested in the preceding chapter.

[16]Dale, xviii–xxii.

of Heracles as "discreetly reminiscent of the traditional burlesque of Heracles, the coarse glutton and drunkard who rouses himself to perform feats of strength against the local monster or bully"; of "the discomfiture of Death . . . who is not the majestic king throned in the underworld but the ogreish creature of popular fancy." To these reminders of the satyr-play, we might add the barracking between Apollo and Thanatos, the darkly comic irony, touched with ribaldry, of the concluding scene between Heracles, Admetus and the veiled Alcestis, and the element of theft and restoration, of death and resurrection, in the untimely visit and ultimate defeat of Death. And yet, in the end, Miss Dale plays it all down: the episode with Death is "passed over very lightly"; "the theme is satyric but not its treatment here; this is the adaptation of a satyric theme to tragedy," and so on. Though she has herself given us most of the arguments for regarding the Alcestis as essentially pro-satyric (as opposed, say, to tragic and to romantic drama), she refuses us the conclusion. It is her insistence on taking the play seriously throughout its action which prevents Miss Dale from regarding it as essentially different from tragedy.

It is at this point that Professor Kitto's observation concerning the nature of the *Alcestis'* plot provides a salutary correction: because the *Alcestis* is based on an impossibility, its action as a whole is deprived of tragic, or universal, reality, and so of serious tragic meaning.[17] A healthy young woman is "taken" by Death (himself featured as an ogre, a primitive projection of folk-tale imagination), because she chooses to substitute herself for her husband, who is actually due to die: a play which begins with a miracle can also end with one (as this play in fact does); in any case we cannot feel involved, in the way that tragedy requires, with Admetus' and Alcestis' sufferings, for their experience, the very conditions under which they live, is not drawn from the stuff of life as we know it or can even imagine it to be.

However, agreement with Kitto concerning the essential artificiality of the *Alcestis* does not mean that we should include the play, as he does, with Euripides' tragicomedies, for it may share this ingredient with them and still differ in other important respects.[18] Following Kitto's own lead, we have found the other essential features of the tragicomedies to include: a highly complex plot usually involving an interrelated recognition sequence and "escape-and-vengeance" intrigue; irony of a non-tragic kind (i.e., in which real joy is obscured by some illusory

[17]Kitto, *G.T.*, 315; cf. *ibid.*, 316.

[18]Kitto (312) summarily rejects any comparison between *Alcestis* and the satyr-play, without, however, discussing any of the relevant points.

misfortune), depending on witty plays on appearance and reality; sudden reversals throughout the action, depending on the skilful juxtaposition of contrasting scenes; theatrical excitements induced by combining probable sequences with surprise intrusions and coincidences. Such virtuosity of plot and ironic effect is missing from the *Alcestis*; indeed it is alien to its stark and macabre atmosphere. How much more difficult it is to regard the *Alcestis* as the forerunner of New Comedy (as plays such as the *Helena* and the *Ion* surely were) than to regard it as a development of the satyr-play, one which had moved closer to tragedy in its perceptions but which still retained a note of parody of tragic solemnity.

The approach (it is no more than this) to tragedy which the *Alcestis* makes may be seen in what happens to Admetus after his wife's death; it is made easier in that, while the *manner* of Admetus' rescuing is impossible, the actual situation in which Admetus finds himself is not. Most critics have, rightly I think, seen the presentation of the situation, and of the experiences of a husband deeply bereaved by his own selfishness, as an essentially serious aspect of the play, but there is not the same agreement either on the nature of that experience or on the relation, if any, which that husband's whole performance has to the happy ending. Here the main issues are whether, after the death of Alcestis, there is a change in Admetus' emotional and moral attitudes or merely in his awareness, i.e., in his understanding that one cannot have one's cake and eat it; and whether the return of Alcestis is to be regarded, seriously or ironically, as a reward of virtue, or simply as providing a happy ending with no significant relation to the character and actions of Admetus. The two issues are, of course, closely entwined. With regard to the first, Miss Dale has taken the refreshingly novel line that the change in Admetus concerns not remorse or even deeper grief but simply realistic awareness of the bad bargain he has made: "the irony of human intentions measured against their outcome."[19] This neat if somewhat astringent formulation of Admetus' situation comes, at first, as something of a relief from the effusively moralistic views of the King as a reformed man who now no longer deserves or needs to suffer.[20] However, when Miss Dale speaks of the speeches of the bereaved Admetus as simply part of Euripides' "rhetoric of the situation," and of the

[19]Dale, xxv; see also the whole discussion of this aspect of the play, *ibid.*, xxii–xxix.

[20]See, for example, Wilamowitz, *Alkestis*, intro., 92–93. Other excessively moralistic views of the *Alcestis*, particularly of its ending, are to be found in Méridier (above, note 5), 53; Séchan, "Le Dévouement d'Alceste," 329–53, esp. 344–45; Ebeling, *TAPA*, XXIX, 65–66, 76–77, 81; D. M. Jones, *CR*, LXII, 50–55. We shall return shortly to the arguments concerned.

poet himself as "a kind of λογογράφος who promises to do the best for each of his clients in turn,"[21] one feels that this critic is going too far in her reductions of the serious meanings, both ethical and emotional, which may surely be discerned in this play.

The emotional corollary to Admetus' "too-late knowledge" must, I think, be admitted, and Grube's comment—"A great change has come upon [Admetus] . . . his lamentation has the simple and touching beauty of a great and genuine sorrow"[22]—still stands as a valid correction of over-formalistic views of this play.

O hateful threshold! loathed, empty rooms! Yet where can I go . . . ?
(861–63)

ὦ σχῆμα δόμων [an untranslatable phrase, evoking the effect of the physical shape of Admetus' home upon his memory] . . . How can I bear to enter here again? How can I live here when my life has suffered such a change?
(911–14)

It is hard to see why we should take the grief expressed in these and similar lines simply as "the rhetoric proper to the situation" particularly as Euripides has been at such pains to prepare for this emotional peripety: witness, for example, the Chorus's prophecy of "a loss worthy of suicide" (228) and the contrast, in retrospect, with the narcissistic anguish of the King's farewells to Alcestis. It is impossible, of course, for one to be very effective in taking leave of a wife whose sacrifice of life on one's behalf one has accepted. Somewhat desperately, Admetus had sought to insinuate himself under his wife's sacrificial mantle. Thus (of the sun which Alcestis laments seeing for the last time): "He sees both you *and me*, two creatures who have fared so ill. . . ." (246)

The difficulty on which serious interpretations of Admetus' experience often founders is the restoration of Alcestis. The idea of knowledge won too late, at too great cost, must (*pace* Miss Dale) carry with it some connotation of remorse and guilt, the feeling that Admetus' suffering is, in some sense, justified.[23] Various unsatisfactory attempts have been

[21]See Dale, xxvii and xxviii.

[22]Grube, 142.

[23]The question of the justification or otherwise of Admetus, in accepting Alcestis' sacrifice in the first place, usually arises in connection with any discussion of his change of heart or attitude during the course of the play. Views such as those of M. Croiset, *REG*, XXV, 1 ff., and J. L. Myres, *JHS*, XXXVII, 195 ff., to the effect that Admetus did not ask and did not wish Alcestis to die for him, have already been ably refuted by Séchan, "Le Dévouement d'Alceste," II, 339–40. Of the scholars to whom we have already referred in this chapter. Wilamowitz, Séchan and Grube all mention some version of the "grand seigneur argument" or of the "dynastic argument" in exoneration of Admetus or in mitigation of his

made to carry the ethical theme into the happy ending. Wilamowitz, for example, suggests that once the scales have fallen from the King's eyes, the gods, and presumably the poet, feel that he has suffered enough—surely an unusual reaction for the gods of Greek tragedy![24] Others have attempted to find serious ethical significance in the fact that Admetus' final good fortune comes about as a result of his hospitality to Heracles—as if egregious hospitality outweighed egregious selfishness and lack of self-knowledge![25] But apart from the adequacy or otherwise of Admetus' virtue, such arguments fail to realize that since return from the dead is, for the Greeks as for ourselves, outside human experience, this part of the plot can hardly be taken literally as serious comment on an ethical situation. Grube, with more honesty than the critics just cited, does not attempt to reconcile the tragic and non-tragic elements in this play: ". . . one feels," he says, "that Euripides has failed . . . to use the comic to enhance the tragic."[26] However, such an explanation is acceptable only if no significant relation between the two elements can be discerned. The alternative solution is implied in the title of a recent article by Mr. Wesley Smith: "The Ironic Structure in *Alcestis*."[27] Smith makes one fundamental distinction in the material of the *Alcestis*, the distinction between the melodramatic plot and the ironic plot. The melodramatic plot (according to this critic) includes Admetus' hospitality to Heracles and its *dénouement* in the happy ending (one could perhaps extend it further back to include the hospi-

---

guilt. In my view, two considerations seem to weaken this argument. One is that Euripides tends to judge such matters by his own lights rather than by that of the dramatic date of his play; the other is that, even in the play, Pheres taunts Admetus for his ignoble cowardice (694 ff., 720) and Admetus himself clearly fears the criticism of his neighbours; surely neither of these passages could have been included if Euripides regarded contemporary ideas concerning the guilt of Admetus as entirely irrelevant. Therefore, it seems idle to argue, as Séchan and others have done, that Admetus is justified because he acts in accordance with the usages of some remote heroic age.

[24]Wilamowitz, *Alkestis*, intro., 92–3; earlier (*ibid.*, 88), Wilamowitz has expressed the view that Euripides has presented his Admetus as a man so *lebenswürdig* as to deserve the return of his wife; cf. Méridier, 53, who expresses a similar view of the worthiness of the chastened Admetus.

[25]Both Séchan (II, 344–45) and Jones attempt to relate Admetus' hospitality to Heracles *and* his remorseful grief to the happy ending. Séchan, for example, makes the ingenious suggestion that in the eyes of Heracles Admetus deserves the return of Alcestis because of his hospitality, while in *our* eyes he deserves it because of his love and his grief!

[26]Grube, 131; cf. 145–46.

[27]Wesley D. Smith, *Phoenix*, XIV (1960), 127–45.

tality to Apollo and *its dénouement* in the sacrifice of Alcestis); the ironic plot is that in which Admetus, for all his promises and protestations to Alcestis, repeatedly betrays those promises in the fulfilment of his famous hospitality. "Concurrently, the ironic plot offers an analysis and criticism of the attitudes and beliefs implied by the melodramatic plot and by the myth itself."[28] Thus the major irony of the play is found to reside in the fact that Admetus is ultimately rewarded for failing the real test (of fidelity) which the final dialogue with Heracles implies, even as he passes, however reluctantly, the mock test (of hospitality) which that boisterous champion inflicts upon him.

My only qualms about this thesis (which I have paraphrased considerably for the sake of brevity) is that, like Miss Dale's demonstration of the ἄρτι μανθάνω theme, it is a little too cold, a little too exclusively intellectual, and that it pays too little heed to the real change which does take place in Admetus. There is, I think, a point in the play at which one feels, whatever the logic of the situation, that the play could go either way, toward tragedy or toward comedy—and then the poet reminds us with his unreal "solution" that Admetus' situation rests originally on an impossibility. And just before the happy ending, we are brought back from the verge of tragic feeling by the suave intrusion into Admetus' grief of references to crying children, dirty floors and narky neighbours, annoyances which are real enough but hardly the stuff of tragedy.

Thus we have, in the *Alcestis*, the uncanny effect of a near-tragedy suspended in, and finally dispelled by, a faintly mocking fairy tale. It is this equivocal appeal to wit and to emotion which gives the play its uniquely disquieting piquancy.

[28]*Ibid.*, 127.

20

Epilogue

The various kinds of Euripidean tragedy were described, at the beginning of this study, as a series of declensions of one kind or another from what might be called the classic structure of "mythological tragedy" developed by Aeschylus and, with increasing definition, by Sophocles. Now that an illustration of this critical approach has been provided in the intervening chapters, the difference (already suggested) between critical formulations and absolute, objective truth has, no doubt, been clearly demonstrated. The general features and tendencies described are, I think, discernible in Euripides' work; their precise formulation, however, must depend on the individual critical imagination as much as on the plays concerned. For this reason it is dangerous to insist too rigorously on one's own categories; they are more useful as critical scaffolding than as material for final statements about a poet's work. "The play's the thing," and each play is, in its creation and in its reception, a separate and discrete experience. Thus the most important part of one's account of a dramatist must appear in the discussion and analysis of his individual works.

These considerations are particularly relevant to Euripidean criticism, for Euripides, of all dramatists, concentrates most on the dramatic effects suited to each new theme and resists most strenuously the generalizations which have, nevertheless, been thrust upon him by the commentators. The greater part of our evaluation, therefore, of our "conclusions about Euripides" has already been accomplished. What follows is merely an epilogue: backward glances at certain features of the playwright's work which frustrate too rigorous attempts to classify it.

We have described the classic situation of Greek tragedy as one in which the tragic hero, sometimes because of some single, doom-laden act, sometimes because of some fatal quality reflected in his whole career, comes into catastrophic conflict with the will of the gods. We have found this situation to be changed in most Euripidean tragedies. In two of them, which we may still style "mythological tragedy" with no apology, the same conflict is still there; even here, though the fatal resistance in the hero's nature to the necessitous order of things is still the cause of the catastrophe, the reality of the supernatural world has faded slightly under the load of symbolism which the gods must bear. In other Euripidean tragedies, we have found a marked reduction of emphasis on the supernatural, "mythological" world, and a corresponding decrease in the importance of the tragic hero and of the catastrophe. This description best applies to the "political" and to the "war" tragedies, in which the sufferers are relatively passive victims in no way responsible for their sufferings, and the external necessity invading their lives comes not from the mythological world but from man's own inhumanity to his fellow men. To be distinguished from these are the psychologically realistic tragedies such as the *Medea* and the *Electra*. Here, as in the group just described, the gods are again for the most part irrelevant, but now the tragic hero or heroine dominates the action and brings about the tragic peripety. Finally, we have in "romantic tragedy" a kind of inversion of the classic situations of tragedy: the supernatural world of myth is literally accepted but serves now as a basis for fantasy; other features of serious tragedy are similarly stood on their heads, as in the recognition scenes of the *Helena* and the *Ion*, in which, comic replacing tragic irony, hidden relationships lead, on discovery, to joy rather than to sorrow, and in which happy endings occur in spite of, rather than because of, the obtrusive plans of the gods.

Let us now suggest a few of the many points at which our analysis of various individual plays has corrected and supplemented the general impression provided by this no doubt oversimplified scheme.

Consider first Euripides' so-called mythological plays. Here, particularly in the *Hippolytus*, Euripides is undoubtedly closer than he is elsewhere to the Sophoclean type of tragedy in that the catastrophe is related, on the one hand, to the "character-revealed-in-action" of the tragic hero and, on the other, to the "will of the gods," however symbolically this may be understood. Here, according to our antithesis between the classic type of Tragedy and the pathetic, unheroic and "demythologized" type, represented in its extreme form by the *Troades*, one might expect to find Euripides' most powerful and highly individualized tragic characterizations. They are simply not there. In the *Hippolytus*, the whole logic of theme and action alike is predicated on the idea of Hippolytus as tragic hero; yet who has "taught" the play on this premise without having to explain too insistently for comfort how the more interesting, more moving, but non-tragic characterization of Phaedra is really ancillary to the tragedy of Hippolytus? A similar embarrassment awaits us in the incomparable *Bacchae*—and once again we are reminded, by the impression of total perfection which this play imparts, of the inadequacies of critical generalizations. The action, carefully followed, reveals that it is the *agôn* of Pentheus, his testing, and failure in that testing at Dionysus' hands, which is central; yet however convincingly we argue that the catastrophe is caused by Pentheus' blindness to the reality (mythologically expressed) of Dionysus, the fact remains that it is the awful beauty and the awful horror of Dionysianism itself which remain the dominant impressions of the play. For all our expectations, in neither of these plays does the tragic hero quite live up to his role. It is not that one looks for realistic characterizations or detailed "psychology" in such plays; what we do expect is that the hero of this kind of tragedy should not only dominate the action but should (like the Sophoclean Ajax or Oedipus or the Aeschylean Prometheus or Eteocles) dwarf all other elements in the play.

Where, then, if not in his "classically" tragic plays, are Euripides' concentrated studies of individual tragic heroes to be found? Phaedra gives us a clue. If she were not constrained, formally, to be secondary in the *Hippolytus*, if she were not, for the sake of the Hippolytus theme, doomed to be a relatively innocent victim, "pegged," as it were, by Aphrodite, then she would certainly have emerged as a full-scale tragic figure. (Who knows?—perhaps she *was* in the other *Hippolytus*.) What stops her from being tragic in the full sense is that she cannot be allowed freely, if inevitably, to choose her own passion and her own destruction, and that she cannot be granted the centre of the stage to fulfil her own catastrophic career. Now the characters who *are* granted these opportunities are (in the plays which bear their names) Medea and Electra among the major characterizations, Orestes and, with some qualifications, Hecuba, among the minor ones. Of these, Medea is by far the most intense and thorough study but all the others share with her, to some degree, the quality of dominating the action: all of them are personages for the sake of whom the action, the other characters and the play as a whole exists.

Now what strikes us about all these characters is their quality of desperation, of psychological eccentricity. Granted the force of circumstance in engendering the tragic struggle, each of them becomes what he or she does become (child-slayer, mother-slayer, mad dog of vengeance), not in conflict with the gods but in response to an inner necessity which, when circumstances call it forth, imposes itself at, literally, total cost. (Only Hecuba fails quite to fit this mould; with her, circumstance is, perhaps, the more powerful element: she *deteriorates* to her desperate condition, while the others are potentially what they become from the beginning.) No one in Medea's play is strong enough to resist Medea and her enterprise—except Medea: it is her own internal conflict, *thumos* against *bouleumata*, which she loses. Orestes is mad at the beginning of *his* play because he cannot face himself, the slayer of his own mother; then drawn out of that self-circle by social pressures, he unconsciously dramatizes, in his desperate search for safety, the very nature which has brought his guilt upon him. And we have witnessed similar though less drastic self-revelations in our studies of Electra and Hecuba as well.

We are forced, then, to the conclusion that Euripides' most powerful characterizations—though not, indeed, his greatest plays—are concerned with pathological personalities. This is not, after all, inconsistent with the more significant fact (noted by both Dodds and Kitto, in their different ways) that Euripides regarded the emotions and the passions as the most powerful elements of destruction in human life—though it is not, of course, a necessary corollary of that fact. Nevertheless, in the case of his most intense and vivid characterizations, the pathological element, limiting their universality, inevitably reduces their tragic appeal.

Some qualifications should also be made, perhaps, in our generalized description of the political plays and the "war plays" in which tragic victims, rather than heroes in the more dominant sense, suffer from outrages externally inflicted on them. Hecuba, for example, in the play of that name, fits the mould in one sense but breaks it in another: she fights back, and in the self-destruction which her vengeance brings may be said to compound her already tragic situation. The *Troades* is, perhaps, the only "pure" tragedy of innocent victims in which, while innocence is maintained to the end, interest continues to centre on the victims and on their responses to the outrages inflicted on them. In the political plays, on the other hand, particularly in the *Suppliants*, a new and not, strictly speaking, tragic interest is developed in the *champion* of these victims, the defender of the good life, the mender of the torn fabric of international society. The terms I have used hint at the mildly chauvinistic tone of the *Suppliants* and the *Heracleidae*, for in both cases the champion is an Athenian King. In neither play, it is true, do the idealized political themes degenerate into propaganda or political puppetry, with characters and situations bearing a clear one-to-one relation with contemporary reality, and in both a somewhat sardonic twist at the end of the theme restrains the contemporary citizen audience from any too optimistic patriotism. Nevertheless, these idealized political themes—abstractions, perhaps, from the world of Euripides' own political observation—drastically interfere with the pathetic, and so the tragic, element in all the political plays.

I have suggested that it is only in the "romantic tragedies" (and in the pro-satyric *Alcestis*, which shares some of their qualities) that supernatural myth is treated with apparent literalness, and that here the consistent irony, bordering at times on parody, justifies the "naïve" acceptance of a world rejected (in such literal formulations, at any rate) in serious Euripidean tragedy. Once again, however, the detailed analyses of the plays themselves suggest certain qualifications of this view. Occasionally, supernatural myth is treated neither ironically nor symbolically but simply exploited for its convenience in the expression of certain themes—in the *Heracles*, for example, for the sake of dramatizing the contrast between human morality and the gods of mythology; in the *Iphigenia at Aulis*, as a vehicle for the contrast (moving in itself) between youthful heroism and adult ambition. The *Heracles* succeeds as a tragedy thanks to its human theme, which has a certain validity apart from the mythological intrusion. Iphigenia, on the other hand, is merely touching; the potentially tragic element in her self-sacrifice is never realized, partly because it is introduced only at the last moment, but mainly because the rhetoric, satire and realism (political and domestic) which precede its entry inhibit our taking seriously the mythological idea on which Iphigenia's plight is based. (Even in Aeschylus, the theme of "une fille pour du vent" succeeds only as a significant moment, lyrically treated by the Chorus, in Agamemnon's past.)

As for the "romantic tragedies" or "tragicomedies" themselves, they have, perhaps, been underestimated because of the very characteristics (subtly described by Professor Kitto) which distinguish them from serious tragedy. These diverting fantasies, whose hidden springs of tragicomic irony are eventually savoured in happy resolutions, have a disturbing way of hinting at a state of affairs more real but less palatable than the ones presented in the actions of the plays. Their truths are not, then, limited (as Professor Kitto suggests) to a few satirical or hard-headed observations inserted in the incidental rhetoric with which such plays are decorated. If the situations on which they are based are "impossible" fantasy, so too, one feels, must be the optimistic view of life which they present. If Apollo—or any other god—really is as he is featured in the *Ion* (not merely lecherous but deceitful and lacking in divine *pronoia*), then, happy ending or no, the fool's paradise in which Ion himself believed has been exposed. If the strumpet of the *Troades* turns out, in the "impossible" circumstances of the *Helena*, to be a very Penelope in wifely virtue, then one fears that the Helens of "real life" may turn out to be the ones who go to Troy. By the same token, one fears that real wars, fought for reasons no more substantial than a phantom (as the Chorus hints at one point in the play) may not have such happy endings as the hero of that play enjoys.

Does Euripides' demythologizing of Greek tragedy, the pragmatic or the rationalizing gleam which he lets invade its mystery, succeed in marring it? In a strictly aesthetic context, when one is thinking of structure and its emotional effect, the answer may well be, "Yes." With the exception of his "mythological tragedies," few of Euripides' plays provide that intuitive awareness that one has witnessed an essential moment of heroic suffering, *sub specie aeternitatis* (both dimensions seem necessary to the experience). Nevertheless, virtuoso Euripides, tuning his instrument to suit his varying mood, does give us many insights into *ta gignomena*, into life as it appears to man. Pondering this, one hesitates, in the end, to press the invidious comparison with "classical" tragedy, especially of the Sophoclean kind. In terms of truth and its enjoyment, it may be that Euripides, with his varied and subtle courses, provides as rich a banquet as either of his mighty rivals.

Bibliography

NOTE: This bibliography includes all books and articles referred to in this book, except for certain standard collections and works of reference.

I. Books

BATES, W. N. *Euripides*. New York, 1961.

BEAZLEY, J. D. *Etruscan Vase Paintings*. Oxford, 1947.

BERGK, T. *Griechische Literaturgeschichte*. Berlin, 1884.

BERLAGE, J. *Commentatio de Euripide Philosopho*. Lugduni Batavorum, 1888.

BERRY, EDMUND G. *The History and Development of the Concept of* Theia Moira *and* Theia Tychê *down to and including Plato*. Dissertation, University of Chicago, 1940.

BLAIKLOCK, E. M. *The Male Characters of Euripides*. Wellington, 1952.

BRUNN, H. *I Relievi delle Urne etrusche*. Rome, 1870.

CHRIST, WILHELM VON. *Geschichte der griechischen Literatur*, bearbeitet von Wilhelm Schmid. Munich, 1912.

DELEBECQUE, EDOUARD. *Euripide et la Guerre du Péloponnèse*. Paris, 1951.

DESCROIX, J. *Le Trimètre iambique des iambographes à la Comédie Nouvelle*. Macon, 1931.

DUCHEMIN, J. *L'Agôn dans la tragédie grecque*. Paris, 1945.

FEUGÈRE, G. *De Socraticae doctrinae vestigiis apud Euripidem*. Paris, 1874.

FLICKINGER, ROY. *The Greek Theatre and its Drama*. Chicago, 1918.

FRIEDRICH, WOLF H. *Euripides und Diphilos*. Zetemata 5. Munich, 1953.

FRYE, P. H. *Romance and Tragedy*. Boston, 1922.

GIRAUDOUX, JEAN. *La Guerre de Troie n'aura pas lieu*. Paris, 1936.

GOOSSENS, ROGER. *Euripide et Athènes*. Brussels, 1962.

GREENE, WILLIAM CHASE. *Moira: Fate, Good and Evil in Greek Thought*. Cambridge, Mass., 1944.

GREENWOOD, L. H. G. *Aspects of Euripidean Tragedy*. Cambridge, 1953.

GRUBE, G. M. A. *The Drama of Euripides*. London, 1941. Reprinted 1961.

HARTUNG, I. A. *Euripides Restitutus*, 2 vols. Hamburg, 1844.

HIGHET, GILBERT. See Jaeger.

HOWALD, E. *Untersuchungen zur Technik der Euripideischen Tragödien.* Leipzig, 1914.

JACOBY, F. *Atthis: The Local Chronicles of Ancient Athens.* Oxford, 1949.

JAEGER, WERNER. *Paideia,* translated by G. Highet. 3 vols. Oxford, 1945.

JONES, JOHN. *On Aristotle and Greek Tragedy.* London, 1962.

KIRKWOOD, G. M. *A Study of Sophoclean Drama.* Ithaca, 1958.

KITTO, H. D. F. *Form and Meaning in Drama.* London, 1956.

——— *Greek Tragedy.* Second edition. London, 1950. (Later editions are now available.)

KNOX, BERNARD. *Oedipus at Thebes.* New Haven, 1957.

KRANZ, W. *De forma stasimi.* Berlin, 1904.

LEES, J. T. *Dikanikos Logos in Euripides.* Dissertation, Johns Hopkins, Lincoln, Nebraska, 1891.

LESKY, ALBIN. *Alkestis, der Mythus und das Drama.* Wien, Leipzig, 1925.

——— *Die Griechische Tragödie.* Stuttgart, Leipzig, 1938.

——— *Die tragische Dichtung der Hellenen.* Göttingen, 1956.

LUCAS, D. W. *The Greek Tragic Poets.* Second edition. London, 1959.

LUGGE, G. *Quomodo Euripides in supplicibus tempora sua respexerit.* Dissertation, Westphalia, 1887.

MACURDY, G. H. *The Chronology of the Extant Plays of Euripides.* Dissertation, Columbia University, New York, 1905.

MASQUERAY, PAUL. *Euripide et ses idées.* Paris, 1908.

MATTHAEI, LOUISE E. *Studies in Greek Tragedy.* Cambridge, 1918.

MATTHIESEN, K. *Elektra, Taurische Iphigenia und Helena.* Göttingen, 1964.

MÉAUTIS, G. *Mythes inconnus de la Grèce antique.* Paris, 1944.

MÉRIDIER, LOUIS. *L'Hippolyte d'Euripide.* Paris, [n.d.].

MURRAY, GILBERT. *Aeschylus.* Oxford, 1940.

——— *Euripides and his Age.* New York and London, 1913.

NOACK, F. *Iliupersis.* Giessen, 1890.

NORWOOD, GILBERT. *Essays on Euripidean Drama.* Berkeley, Los Angeles, London, Toronto, 1954.

——— *Greek Comedy.* London, 1931.

——— *Greek Tragedy.* London, 1920.

PAGE, DENYS L. *Actors' Interpolations in Greek Tragedy.* Oxford, 1934.

——— "The Elegiacs in Euripides' *Andromache,*" in *Greek Poetry and Life.* Oxford, 1936.

PAULKE, MAX. *De tabula Iliaca quaestiones Stesichorae.* Dissertation, Koenigsberg, 1879.

POHLENZ, MAX. *Die Griechische Tragödie.* 2 vols. Göttingen, 1954.

POWELL, J. A., ed. *New Chapters in the History of Greek Literature.* Oxford, 1933.

REVERDIN, OLIVIER, ed. *Euripide, Entretiens sur l'antiquité classique* VI. Fondation Hardt, Vandoeuvres-Genève, 1960.

RIEMSCHNEIDER, W. *Held und Staat in Euripides' Phönissen.* Warburg, 1940.

RITCHIE, WILLIAM. *The Authenticity of the Rhesus.* Cambridge, 1964.
RIVIER, ANDRÉ. *Essai sur le Tragique d'Euripide.* Lausanne, 1944.
ROBERT, CARL. *Thanatos.* Berlin, 1879.
SARTRE, J.-P. "*Les Mouches,*" in *Théâtre.* Paris, 1947.
SCHMID, W. and O. STAHLIN. *Geschichte der griechischen Literatur,* part 1, vol. III. Munich, 1940.
SÉCHAN, L. *Etudes sur la tragédie grecque.* Paris, 1926.
SNELL, BRUNO. *Scenes from Greek Tragedy.* Berkeley, Los Angeles, 1964.
SPIRA, ANDREAS. *Untersuchungen zum Deus Ex Machina bei Sophocles und Euripides.* Kallmünz, 1960.
STAHLIN, O. See Schmid, W.
STROHM, HANS. *Euripides, Interpretationen zur dramatischen Form. Zetemata* 15. Munich, 1957.
THOMSON, D. *Euripides and the Attic Orators.* London, 1898.
THOMSON, GEORGE. *Aeschylus and Athens.* Second edition. London, 1946.
VERRALL, A. W. *Essays on Four Plays of Euripides.* Cambridge, 1905.
——— *Euripides the Rationalist.* Cambridge, 1895.
WEIL, H. *Etudes sur le drame antique.* Paris, 1897.
WELCKER, F. G. *Die griechischen Tragoedien,* vol. II. Bonn, 1839.
WHITMAN, CEDRIC H. *Sophocles: A Study in Heroic Humanism.* Cambridge, Mass., 1951.
WILAMOWITZ, U. VON. *Analecta Euripidea.* Berlin, 1875.
——— "Einleitung in die attische Tragödie," in *Herakles.* First edition. Berlin, 1889.
WINNINGTON-INGRAM, R. P. *Euripides and Dionysus.* Cambridge, 1948.
ZIELINSKI, TH. *Tragodumenon libri tres.* Cracow, 1925.
ZURCHER, W. *Die Darstellung des Menschen im Drama des Euripides.* Basel, 1947.

II. Editions and Translations of Classical Authors

ARROWSMITH, WILLIAM, ed. and trans. *Euripides, Cyclops*: see Grene and Lattimore, eds.
BARNES, JOSHUA, ed. *Euripides, Supplices.* Leipzig, 1778.
BARRETT, W. S., ed. *Euripides, Hippolytos.* Oxford, 1964.
BENARDETE, SETH G., trans. *Aeschylus, Persians*: see Grene and Lattimore, eds.
BUTCHER, S. H., ed. and trans. *Aristotle's Theory of Poetry and Fine Art.* Third edition. London, 1902.
CHAPOUTHIER, F., ed.: see Méridier, Louis.
DAIN, ALPHONSE: see Mazon, Paul.
DALE, A. M., ed. *Euripides, Alcestis.* Oxford, 1954.
DENNISTON, J. D., ed. *Euripides, Electra.* Oxford, 1939.

DENNISTON, J. W. and DENYS PAGE, eds. *Aeschylus, Agamemnon*. Oxford, 1957.

DODDS, E. R., ed. *Euripides, Bacchae*. Oxford, 1944. (A second edition is now available.)

ENGLAND, E. B., ed. *Euripides, The Iphigenia at Aulis*. London, 1891.

FRAZER, SIR JAMES, ed. and trans. *Apollodorus, The Library*. Loeb Edition. 2 vols., London, 1921.

GRÉGOIRE, HENRI, ed. and trans.: see Méridier, Louis.

GRENE, DAVID and RICHMOND LATTIMORE, trans. *The Complete Greek Tragedies*, 4 vols. Chicago, 1959–60.

HERMANN, G., ed. *Euripides, Andromache*. Leipzig, 1838.

——— *Euripides, Supplices*. Leipzig, 1811.

JEBB, R. C., ed. *Sophocles, Oedipus Coloneus*. Cambridge, 1885.

——— see Pearson.

JEFFREY, T. T., ed. *Euripides, Hecuba*. London, [n.d.].

KIRCHHOFF, A., ed. *Euripidis, Fabulae*, 3 vols. Berlin, 1867–68.

LATTIMORE, RICHMOND: see Grene.

MARKLAND, J., ed. *Euripides, Supplices mulieres*. London, 1763.

MATTHIAE, AUGUSTE, ed. and trans. *Euripidis Tragoediae*, 3 vols. Oxford, 1821 (vol. 3: *Interpretatio Latina*).

MAZON, PAUL and ALPHONSE DAIN, eds. *Sophocle* II (*Ajax, Oedipe Roi, Electre*). Second edition, Budé. Paris, 1958.

MÉRIDIER, LOUIS, with F. CHAPOUTHIER, H. GRÉGOIRE and L. PARMENTIER, eds. and trans. *Euripide*. Budé edition, 6 vols. Paris, 1947–61.

MURRAY, GILBERT, ed. *Euripidis, Fabulae*. 3 vols., Oxford Classical Texts. Oxford, 1902–13, reprinted 1950–54.

———, ed. *Euripides, Rhesus*. Oxford, 1913.

——— Preface to F. M. Stawell's translation of Euripides' *Iphigenia in Aulis*. London, 1929.

NAUCK, A., ed. *Euripidis Tragoediae*. 3 vols. Second edition, Leipzig, 1869, and third edition, Leipzig, 1880–81.

NICKLIN, T., ed. *Euripides, The Suppliant Women*. Oxford, 1936.

NORWOOD, G., ed. *Euripides, Andromache*. London, 1906.

OWEN, A. S., ed. *Euripides, Ion*. Oxford, 1939.

PAGE, DENYS L., ed. *Euripides, Medea*. Oxford, 1938.

——— ed. and trans. *Greek Literary Papyri*, I. Loeb Edition. London, 1942.

——— see Denniston.

PALEY, F. A., ed. *Euripides with an English Commentary*. 3 vols. Second edition. London, 1872–80.

PARMENTIER, LÉON, ed. and trans.: See Méridier, Louis.

PEARSON, A. C., ed. *Euripides, The Heracleidae*. Cambridge, 1907.

——— *Euripides, Phoenissae*. Cambridge, 1909.

PEARSON, A. C. and R. C. JEBB, eds. *The Fragments of Sophocles*. Cambridge, 1917.

PLATNAUER, M., ed. *Euripides, Iphigenia in Tauris*. Oxford, 1938.

POWELL, J. A., ed. *Euripides, Phoenissae.* London, 1911.
SCHWARTZ, E., ed. *Scholia in Euripidem.* 2 vols. Berlin, 1887–91.
SHEPPARD, J. T. (SIR JOHN), ed. *Euripides, Hecuba.* Oxford, 1924.
STAWELL, F. M.: see Murray, Gilbert.
VELLACOTT, PHILIP, trans. *Euripides, The Bacchae and Other Plays.* The Penguin Classics. Harmondsworth, Middlesex, 1954.
VERRALL, A. W., ed. *The Ion of Euripides.* Cambridge, 1890.
WARMINGTON, E. H. *Remains of Old Latin.* Loeb Edition, London, 1935.
WATLING, E. F., trans. *Ajax* in *Sophocles: Electra and Other Plays.* The Penguin Classics. Harmondsworth, Middlesex, 1953.
WAY, ARTHUR S., ed. and trans. *Euripides.* 4 vols. Loeb Edition, London and Cambridge, Mass., 1912, reprinted 1958.
WEDD, N., ed. *Euripides, Orestes.* Cambridge, 1942.
WEIL, HENRI. *Sept Tragédies d'Euripide.* Second edition. Paris, 1879.
WILAMOWITZ, U. VON, ed. *Euripides, Alkestis* in *Griechische Tragoedien* III. Berlin, 1906.
———, ed. *Euripides, Hippolytus.* Berlin, 1891.
———, ed. *Euripides, Ion.* Berlin, 1926.
———, trans. *Griechische Tragoedien,* 4 vols. Berlin, 1899–1923.

III. Articles and Reviews

ABRAHAMSON, E. L. "Euripides' Tragedy of *Hecuba,*" *TAPA,* LXXXIII (1952), 120–29.
ADAMS, S. M. Review of *Aeschylus, Agamemnon,* edited by J. D. Denniston and Denys Page, *Phoenix,* XII (1958), 75–78.
ADKINS, A. W. H. "Basic Values in Euripides' *Hecuba* and *Hercules Furens,*" *CQ,* n.s. XVI (1966), 193–219.
BARRON, John P. "Religious Propaganda of the Delian League," *JHS,* LXXXIV (1964), 35–48.
BASCHMAKOFF, A. "Origine tauridienne du mythe d'Iphigénie," *Bulletin de l'Association Guillaume Budé* (Paris, July 1939), no. 64, 3–21.
BATHER, A. G. "The Problem of Euripides' *Bacchae,*" *JHS,* XIV (1894), 244–63.
BELLINGER, A. R. "The *Bacchae* and the *Hippolytus,*" *Yale Classical Studies,* VI (1939), 17–27.
BONNARD, ANDRÉ. "*Iphigénie à Aulis,* Tragique et poésie," *Museum Helveticum* II (1945), 87–107.
BOWRA, C. M. "The Two Palinodes of Stesichorus," *CR,* n.s. XIII (1963), 245–52.
CEADEL, E. B. "Resolved Feet in the Trimeters of Euripides and the Chronology of the Plays," *CQ,* XXXV (1941), 66–89.
CHALK, H. O. O. "*Aretê* and *Bia* in the *Herakles,*" *JHS,* LXXXII (1962), 7–18.
COLARDEAU, T. "Ion à Delphes," *REG,* XXIX (1916), 430–34.
CONACHER, D. J. "Freedom and Necessity in Greek Tragedy," *Queen's Quarterly,* LXVII (1961), 514–29.

——— "A Problem in Euripides' *Hippolytus*," *TAPA*, XCII (1961), 37–44.

——— "Religious and Ethical Attitudes in Euripides' *Suppliants*," *TAPA*, LXXXVII (1956), 8–26.

——— "Themes in the *Exodus* of Euripides' *Phoenissae*," *Phoenix*, XXI (1967), 92–101.

CROISET, M. "Observations sur le Rôle d'Admète," *REG*, XXV (1912), 1–11.

CRÖNERT, W. "Griechische literarische Papyri aus Strassburg, Freiburg und Berlin," *Nachrichten der Gesellschaft der Wissenschaften zu Göttingen* (1922), 1–17.

CUNNINGHAM, M. P. "Medea *apo mêchanês*," *CP*, XLIX (1954), 151–60.

DALMEYDA, G. "Observations sur les Prologues d'*Ion* et des *Bacchantes*," *REG*, XXVIII (1915), 43–50.

DEICHGRÄBER, KARL. "Die Kadmos-Teiresiasszene in Euripides' *Bakchen*," *Hermes*, LXX (1935), 322–49.

DODDS, E. R. "Euripides the Irrationalist," *CR*, XLIII (1929), 97–104.

——— "The *Aidôs* of Phaedra and the Meaning of the *Hippolytus*," *CR*, XXXIX (1925), 102–4.

EBELING, HERMAN L. "The Admetus of Euripides Viewed in Relation to Admetus of the Tradition," *TAPA*, XXIX (1898), 65–85.

ENGLAND, T. "The *Electra* of Euripides," *CR*, XL (1926), 97–104.

FINLEY, JOHN H., JR. "Euripides and Thucydides," *Harvard Studies in Classical Philology*, XLIX (1938), 23–68.

FITTON, J. W. "The *Suppliant Women* and the *Heraclidae* of Euripides," *Hermes*, LXXXIX (1961), 430–61.

GILES, P. "Political Allusions in the *Supplices* of Euripides," *CR*, IV (1890), 95–98.

GOLANN, C. P. "The Third Stasimon of Euripides' *Helena*," *TAPA*, LXXVI (1945), 31–46.

GOOSSENS, R. "Périclès et Thésée," *Bulletin de l'Association Guillaume Budé* (April, 1932), 9–40.

GRÉGOIRE, H. "Euripide, Ulysse et Alcibiade," *Académie Royale de Belgique, Bulletins de la Classe des Lettres*, 5e Série, XIX (1933), 83–96.

GRENE, DAVID. "The Interpretation of the *Hippolytus* of Euripides," *CP*, XXXIV (1939), 45–58.

GRIFFITH, JOHN. "Some Thoughts on the *Helena*," *JHS*, LXXIII (1953), 36–41.

HAMMOND, N. G. L. "Personal Freedom and its Limitation in the *Oresteia*," *JHS*, LXXXV (1965), 42–55.

JACOBY, F. "*Genesia*, Festival of the Dead," *CQ*, XXXVIII (1944), 65–75.

JARDÉ, A. "Sur la date d'*Andromaque* d'Euripide," *REA*, XXV (1923), 209–14.

JONES, D. M. "Euripides' *Alcestis*," *CR*, LXII (1948), 50–55.

KASSEL, R. "Bemerkungen zum *Kyklops* des Euripides," *Rh.M.*, n.f. 98 (1955), 279–86.

KIRKWOOD, GORDON M. "Hecuba and *Nomos*," *TAPA*, LXXVIII (1947), 61–68.

KITTO, H. D. F. Review of *Aeschylus, Agamemnon*, edited by J. D. Denniston and Denys Page, *Gnômon*, XXX (1958), 163–68.

KNOX, BERNARD. "The *Hippolytus* of Euripides," *Yale Classical Studies*, XIII (1952), 3–31.

KOSTER, W. J. W. "De Euripidis *Supplicibus*," *Mnem.*, series 3, X (1942), 161–203.

KUIPER, C. "De Euripidis *Supplicibus*," trans. by J. J. Hartmann, *Mnem.*, n.s. LI (1923), 102–28.

——— "De *Alexandro* Euripideo," *Mnem.*, n.s. (1920), 207–21.

LESKY, ALBIN. "Zum *Orestes* des Euripides," *Wiener Studien, Zeitschrift für klassische Philologie*, LIII (1935), 37–47.

MASQUERAY, PAUL. "Le Cyclope d'Euripide et celui d'Homère," *REA* (1902), 164–90.

MAZON, P. "De Quelques Vers d'Euripide (*Médée* 214–29)," *Revue de Philologie*, série 3, XXVII (1953), 119–21.

MCLEAN, J. H. "The *Heraclidae* of Euripides," *AJP*, LV (1934), 197–224.

MULLENS, H. G. "The Meaning of Euripides' *Orestes*," *CQ*, XXXIV (1940), 153–58.

MURRAY, G. "The Trojan Trilogy of Euripides," *Mélanges Glotz*, II (Paris, 1932), 645–56.

MYERS, J. L. "The Plot of the *Alcestis*," *JHS*, XXXVII (1917), 195–218.

NIHARD, R. "Le Problème des *Bacchantes* d'Euripide," *Le Musée Belge*, XVI (1912), 91–120, 297–375.

PALMER, R. B. "An Apology for Jason: A Study of Euripides' *Medea*," *CJ*, LIII (1957), 49–55.

PARMENTIER, L. "L'*Iphigénie à Aulis* d'Euripide," *Académie royale de Belgique, Bulletins de la classe des lettres*, 5e série, XII (1926), 266–73.

PATON, J. A. "The Story of Alcestis in Ancient Literature and Art," *AJA*, IV (1900), 150–51.

PICKARD-CAMBRIDGE, A. W. "The *Alexandros* of Euripides," in *New Chapters in the History of Greek Literature*, ed. J. U. Powell. Third series Oxford, 1933).

PIPPIN, ANNE N. "Euripides' *Helen*: A Comedy of Ideas," *CP*, LV (1960), 151–63.

REINACH, S. "Observations sur le mythe d'Iphigénie," *REG*, XXVIII (1915), 1–15.

ROBERTSON, D. S. "Euripides and Tharyps," *CR*, XXXVII (1923), 58–60.

ROUSSEL, P. "Le Rôle d'Achille dans l'*Iphigénie à Aulis*," *REG*, XXVIII (1915), 234–50.

SARTRE, J.-P. "Forgers of Myth—The Young Playwrights of France," *Theatre Arts*, XXX (June, 1946), 324–27.

SÉCHAN, LOUIS. "La Légende d'Hippolyte dans l'Antiquité," *REG*, XXIV (1911), 105–51.

——— "Le Dévouement d'Alceste," *Revue des Cours et Conférences,* XXVIII, I (Feb. 1927), 490–514; II (May 1927), 329–53.

SHEPPARD, J. T. (SIR JOHN). "The Formal Beauty of the *Hercules Furens,*" *CQ,* X (1916), 72–79.

SMITH, WESLEY D. "The Ironic Structure in *Alcestis,*" *Phoenix,* XIV (1960), 127–45.

SNELL, BRUNO. "Euripides' *Alexandros* und andere Strassburger Papyri," *Hermes,* Einzelschriften V (1937), 1–68.

SOLMSEN, F. "Euripides' *Ion* im Vergleich mit anderen Tragödien," *Hermes,* LXIX (1934), 390–419.

——— "*Onoma* and *Pragma* in Euripides' *Helen,*" *CR,* XLVIII (1934), 119–21.

SOURY, G. "Euripide, rationaliste et mystique d'après *Hippolyte,*" *REG,* LVI (1943), 29–52.

SPRANGER, J. A. "The Political Element in the *Heracleidae* of Euripides," *CQ,* XIX (1925), 117–28.

——— "The Problem of the *Hecuba,*" *CQ,* XXI (1927), 155–58.

STANFORD, W. B. "The *Hippolytus* of Euripides," *Hermathena,* LXIII (1944), 11–17.

STEIGER, H. "Warum schrieb Euripides seine *Troerinnen?*" *Philologus,* LIX (n.f. XIII) (1900), 363–66.

THOMPSON, E. A. "Neophron and Euripides' *Medea,*" *CQ,* XXXVIII (1944), 10–14.

VANDAELE, H. "L'Unité d'*Hécube,*" *Xenia* (1912), 10–24.

WASSERMANN, F. M. "Agamemnon in the *Iphigenia at Aulis,*" *TAPA,* LXXX (1949), 174–86.

——— "Divine Violence and Providence in Euripides' *Ion,*" *TAPA,* LXXI (1940), 587–604.

WESTLAKE, H. D. "Euripides' *Troades* 205–99," *Mnem.,* series 4, VI (1953), 181–91.

WILAMOWITZ, U. VON. "Excurse zu Euripides' *Herakliden,*" *Hermes,* XVII, 337–64.

——— "Die beiden *Elektren,*" *Hermes,* XVIII (1883), 214–63.

——— "Isyllos von Epidauros," *Philologische Untersuchungen,* IX (Berlin, 1886), 68 ff.

WINNINGTON-INGRAM, R. P. "*Hippolytus*: A Study in Causation," in *Euripide, Entretiens sur l'antiquité classique,* VI (1960), ed. Olivier Reverdin. Fondation Hardt, Vandoeuvres-Genève.

ZIELINSKI, THOMAS. "De Euripidis Thebaide Posteriore," *Mnem.,* n.s. LII (1924), 189–205.

——— "L'Evolution Religieuse d'Euripide," *REG,* XXXVI (1923), 459–79.

ZUNTZ, GÜNTHER. "Is the *Heraclidae* Mutilated?" *CQ,* XLI (1947), 46–52.

——— "On Euripides' *Helena*: Theology and Irony," in *Euripide, Entretiens sur l'antiquité classique,* VI (1960), ed. Olivier Reverdin. Fondation Hardt, Vandoeuvres-Genève.

Select List of Abbreviations

AJA	*American Journal of Archaeology*
AJP	*American Journal of Philology*
CJ	*Classical Journal*
CP	*Classical Philology*
CQ	*Classical Quarterly*
CR	*Classical Review*
D-K	Diels-Kranz, *Die Fragmente der Vorsokratiker* (sixth edition)
EGP	*Epicorum Graecorum Fragmenta* (Kinkel)
G.T.	*Greek Tragedy* (Kitto, second edition)
Griech. Trag.	*Die Griechische Tragödie* (Pohlenz, second edition)
H.S.C.P.	*Harvard Studies in Classical Philology*
JHS	*Journal of Hellenic Studies*
LSJ	Liddell and Scott, *Greek English Lexicon*, revised by S. Jones and R. Mackenzie
Mnem.	*Mnemosynê*
OCT	Oxford Classical Texts
Ph.W.	*Philologische Wochenschrift*
PLG	*Poetae Lyrici Graeci* (Bergk, fourth edition)
RE	*Real-Encyclopädie der classischen Altertumswissenschaft* (Pauly-Wissowa)
REA	*Revue des études anciennes*
REG	*Revue des études grecques*
Rh.M.	*Rheinisches Museum für Philologie*
TAPA	*Transactions of the American Philological Association*
TGF	*Tragicorum Graecorum Fragmenta* (Nauck, second edition)

www.ingramcontent.com/pod-product-compliance
Lightning Source LLC
La Vergne TN
LVHW090803070826
844660LV00022B/1064